Grasping Truth and Reality

Grasping Truth and Reality

Lesslie Newbigin's Theology of Mission to the Western World

DONALD LE ROY STULTS

WIPF & STOCK · Eugene, Oregon

GRASPING TRUTH AND REALITY
Lesslie Newbigin's Theology of Mission to the Western World

Copyright © 2008 Donald Le Roy Stults. All rights reserved. Except for brief quotations in critical publications or reviews, no part of this book may be reproduced in any manner without prior written permission from the publisher. Write: Permissions, Wipf and Stock Publishers, 199 W. 8th Ave., Suite 3, Eugene, OR 97401.

Wipf & Stock
A Division of Wipf and Stock Publishers
199 W. 8th Ave., Suite 3
Eugene, OR 97401

www.wipfandstock.com

ISBN 13: 978-1-55635-723-7

Manufactured in the U.S.A.

Contents

Introduction vii

1 A Brief Sketch of Newbigin's Life and Work 1

2 Missionary Theologian 21

3 Grasping Truth and Reality 61

4 Humanity's Need for Salvation and the Call for Radical Conversion 97

5 Newbigin's Critique of Western Culture 124

6 Newbigin's Response to Western Culture's Crisis 155

7 Living in Truth and Reality 197

8 Putting Newbigin in Perspective 232

Bibliography 281

Introduction

When J. E. Lesslie Newbigin retired from missionary service and returned to Britain in 1974, he discovered that his homeland was as much of a mission field as India. While he had been in constant contact with Britain and the West throughout his missionary career, what he saw upon his return ignited his missionary spirit and caused him to set out in retirement to discover the cause of the problem and propose an answer. It was not that he would discover something new; in fact, he had the answer all along but had to articulate it anew for the new context. The writings of Lesslie Newbigin have been available for decades, yet his importance has never been as recognized as it is today. He says what many missiologists and theologians believe needs to be said at this time in history.

While the Christian church has met with much success in evangelizing and discipling many peoples of the world, it has failed, many believe, to keep the Christian witness alive and vital in Western culture. Missionaries who feel so competent in their work outside the West return home to a situation that may perplex them. While excellent theologies and insightful missiological treatises continually pour off presses in the West, the general feeling is that the battle for faith on Western turf is being lost.

Newbigin's conclusion was that the Western world needed to be confronted with the gospel in a new and different way. It needed to be a *missionary* confrontation. Instead of the traditional approach to missions, however, Newbigin realized that it needed to be confronted *theologically*.

His observation of Western culture led him to conclude that the problem is its adherence to Enlightenment thinking that has led to a narrow *scientism*[1] and an epistemological dilemma. Modern science and the scientific method, in the form of *scientism*, added to the problem, making

---

1. A distinction is being made between a general view of science and the narrow, positivistic view of science that limits reality to the natural world and explains all phenomena as the effects of causes solely within the natural realm.

Introduction

human reason the measure of truth and limiting facts to only that which can be verified through controlled experiment.

Newbigin's contention is that the West is suffering from a loss of purpose because at the time of the Enlightenment it rejected a belief system that gave it purpose and also made it uniquely different from the rest of the world, particularly Asia. The Enlightenment reintroduced humanism and dualism into Western culture as well as the consequent problems Newbigin believes are associated with these two systems of thought. The most obvious result of these two systems of thought is the loss of purpose and the rise of skepticism.

He then set out to formulate a theology of mission which would engage the new context, calling for a missionary confrontation with modern Western culture. Throughout his career, Newbigin developed certain theological convictions that were expressed in his numerous publications. In seeking to confront the Western world, Newbigin utilizes these theological convictions as a means of evaluating the belief system of Western culture and as an answer to Western culture's spiritual problem, which is, Newbigin believes, central to Western culture's current situation. To fully understand Newbigin's approach it is necessary to articulate Newbigin's theological convictions and show how they were used by him to critique the belief system of the West.

The question that must be asked and ultimately addressed is whether Newbigin's vision for the restoration of the Christian worldview as the preferred worldview in Western culture is reasonable and adequate considering the present context.

As one reads Newbigin, two things became apparent: first, his post-1974 writings should be understood and analyzed theologically as well as missiologically, since the content of his writing is more theological than missiological. His writing is not so much about missionary method as it is about his theological convictions in contrast to the beliefs of Western culture. Second, what he writes is best described as a theology of mission. He is articulating theologically the missionary approach to Western culture.

There are certain characteristics that need to be taken into account when assessing Newbigin as a theologian of mission. First, he remained evangelical[2] in his theology while serving wholeheartedly in the ecumenical movement, a movement which at times has been dominated by

---

2. This term will be defined subsequently in the section that defines his theology.

a radical and liberal agenda. Second, he writes as a theologian while fully involved as a missionary and ecumenical leader and not as an academic theologian. While never demeaning the role of the academic theologian, his theological insights are meant to complement academic theology. Third, while he never attempted a systematic theology, it is evident upon reading his work that he is a systematic thinker with certain core theological convictions that dominate his thinking.

It becomes apparent, after considering these preliminary observations, that what is needed is a critical exposition of Lesslie Newbigin's theology of mission to the Western world. There are two main poles around which Newbigin's theological writing in reference to the Western world turns: epistemology and the nature of reality. The epistemological question addresses how God is known, which, for Newbigin, also addresses the question of how one knows reality. Knowing God, Newbigin explains, is to be in contact with ultimate reality. Newbigin believes that the Christian understanding of reality is broader than what modern science would allow because the Christian view encompasses more than just the physical universe. When one truly knows God, the result will be a radical conversion of both mind and heart. Integral to Newbigin's theology of mission is the idea of radical conversion, where the person who recognizes that knowing God requires a change that can only be accomplished by God. This conversion must not only change the heart but also the worldview of the person converted.

Newbigin's theology of mission culminates in his ecclesiology. His strong emphasis upon the community of faith and the role it plays in understanding and witnessing to the truth of the gospel has some similarities to 'post-modernism' in that it recognizes the collapse of modernism and emphasizes the role of community as central to understanding and communication. Newbigin's contention is that the church, as a faith community, is the means by which the gospel is made known to the world, which includes the Western world. It is differentiated from post-modernism, however, in that the truth of the gospel has universal implications and ramifications. Newbigin's solution is to reintroduce the Christian belief system into Western culture which will restore purpose to humanity and put them into contact with true reality through Jesus Christ. This is to be accomplished as the church witnesses in the public arena to the superior rationality of the Christian belief system.

Introduction

While serving as a missionary to South Korea a few years ago, a Korean colleague of mine said he was praying for America. I was a little surprised. Since I was focusing on learning his language and culture, I had not thought much about my own homeland and certainly did think of it as a mission field. His very insightful statement stuck in my mind and opened up for me a whole new way of thinking about Western culture. Reading Newbigin confirmed in my mind that America, as well as the whole Western world, was in need of a missionary witness.

I have seen the evangelical church in action in many parts of the world and it is bold, vigorous, and courageous. But when I turn to look at my own culture, I see something that was once a center for Christian faith and missions quickly becoming a continent in need of the gospel in a fresh and compelling way. It appears to be regressing into a pre-Christian paganism. I believe we need to hear what Newbigin has to say.

There are many who lament the situation in the West and may even suggest a certain approach for correcting a particular and specific issue but there are few who call for such a radical conversion of the core beliefs of Western thought and life as Newbigin has. Newbigin's vision for the recovery, re-conversion, and regeneration of Western society is very compelling. Before we make any judgments about the feasibility of such a missionary confrontation, we must first hear what Newbigin has to say. It is the intention of this book to introduce the reader to Newbigin's vision for mission to the Western church with the hope that you will find his vision compelling as well.

1

A Brief Sketch of Newbigin's Life and Work

EACH GENERATION SINCE THE modern missionary movement began in the eighteenth century has produced a few great missionary statesmen, persons whose thought and work were a major influence on the global missionary enterprise during their particular era and who have influenced subsequent missionary thinking as well. At the end of the twentieth century this honor, it would seem, fell upon Lesslie Newbigin, long time missionary to India and global ecumenical leader.

Before we address his theological and missiological thinking, we need to take a brief look at his life in order to get a clear understanding of the context that produced his theology of mission to the Western world.

A PRELIMINARY ASSESSMENT OF NEWBIGIN'S CONTRIBUTION

The Church of England Newspaper, in a banner headline at the top of an article reporting the death of Newbigin, states that he was "one of the century's foremost Christian statesmen," an assessment shared by many.[1] While much of his missionary career was spent in India or somehow related to the ecumenical movement, the work for which he became best known began after he retired to Britain in 1974. Upon his return, he was confronted with a situation he had not fully anticipated, a church that seemed in retreat and a land, once thought to be Christian, which was in need of serious missionary work. With many decades of missionary experience behind him, Newbigin set out to approach ministry in the Western

---

1. *Church of England Newspaper*, "Lesslie Newbigin dies after a short illness," 6.

world with the same assumptions that he had in doing missionary work in Asia.

The same article states that "in any discussion of values in public life and faith and culture, Newbigin's influence will remain seminal for years to come."[2] David Jenkins, Moderator of the General Assembly of the United Reformed Church, is quoted as saying that Newbigin "will be remembered as an outstanding figure in the Church of the twentieth century. He has proclaimed unity with great courage, probed for truth in turbulent times and has led Christians deeper into faith."[3]

George Hunsberger, the North American coordinator of The Gospel and Our Culture movement and author of a significant book on Newbigin, remarked that Newbigin's "vision of modern Western culture was clear and incisive."[4] Newbigin's theological thinking did not begin after retirement but began very early in his ministry and remained fairly consistent throughout his life.[5] There is evidence of the development of certain themes that appear early but blossom later in the heat of the challenge of a missionary confrontation with Western culture. Additionally, some new themes appear in his response to Western culture that are not present in his earlier writings, primarily because they emerge as a result of the demands of the context.[6] Vinoth Ramachandra believes that Newbigin "has mounted one of the most vigorous theological critiques of modern secular culture."[7]

A FAMILY INHERITANCE

Newbigin was, as are all people, a product of his time but also a recipient of certain personal characteristics inherited from his parents. A description of his father's personality leads one to believe that Newbigin

---

2. *Church of England Newspaper*, "Lesslie Newbigin dies after a short illness," 6.

3. Ibid.

4. Hunsberger, *Bearing the Witness*, 1.

5. Wainwright, *Theological Life*, 283. Chapter 1 of Wainwright's book "A Man in Christ," is an excellent introduction to Newbigin's life.

6. For example, there is no need to discuss the influence of Descartes in the context of India where Newbigin spent so many years laboring. The most obvious change in Newbigin's writings after 1974 is his discussion of Western philosophy and its influence upon the church and Western culture.

7. Ramachandra, *Recovery of Mission*, 144. Ramachandra holds both the bachelor and doctoral degrees in nuclear engineering from the University of London.

inherited a great deal of his personal characteristics from his father. In his autobiography, *Unfinished Agenda*, Newbigin mentions his father's energetic public life, which he somehow managed in addition to his work as a businessman. His father was a broad reader and 'radical' in politics, but, Newbigin observes, this "remarkably vigorous and effective public life was not what I perceived as a child."[8] He may have not been aware of it as a child, but he apparently inherited this same knack for public life, because for much of Newbigin's life he served the church in public positions with enormous energy both in the West and in India.

Newbigin has been described as a "small, polite but insistent man, whom his colleague Martin Conway calls 'an indefatigable terrier' in pursuing his convictions."[9] This characteristic can be observed as one reads his many books and articles. His vision is bold and his thinking is focused. His views are clear and repeated often with great force and passion. He does not seem to have a tentative bone in his body nor in his theological thinking. Geoffrey Wainwright, who first met Newbigin in 1963 and had the opportunity of seeing him on various occasions until 1996, says: "the physical and mental impression he made on me was one of disciplined energy."[10] As Wainwright followed Newbigin's ministry over the years, he was impressed "by the strength and consistency of his vision and its practical enactment."[11] Wainwright's perspective of Newbigin reflects the enormous role that he has played and continues to play on the global missionary scene:

> Throughout his life, his analytical penetration, his conceptual power, and his mental agility ensured the intellectual quality of his practical wisdom; and his ideas remain to be drawn upon by all those who still engage as he did in the tasks of commending the Gospel and defending the Christian faith, of the spiritual formation of individuals and the edification of the believing community, of reforming the Church and restoring its unity.[12]

---

8. Newbigin, *Unfinished*, 3.
9. Stafford, "God's Missionary," 3.
10. Wainwright, *Theological Life*, 17.
11. Ibid., viii.
12. Ibid., vi.

FORMATION OF NEWBIGIN AS A CHRISTIAN

Newbigin was born in Newcastle-upon-Tyne on the eighth of December 1909, the son of Presbyterian parents. He went on to attend the Quaker boarding school in Leighton Park where he recalls that he abandoned the Christian assumptions of his upbringing and his childhood. There was a strong deterministic view of history that was being advocated at the school at that time and he recalls a chemistry teacher remarking that "life is a disease of matter."[13] In the midst of such teaching, Newbigin's faith seemed to disappear.

There were, however, some positive influences for Christian faith on him as well. A book entitled *The Living Past* by F. S. Marvin had a strong influence upon him during his last year of school. He was strongly influenced later by *The Will to Believe* by William James.[14] James made a remarkable case for belief even though, Newbigin remarks, he was not convinced at the time.[15] The seed was planted, however, and it would sprout many years later into a full blown, mature, and well-reasoned faith.

It was during this period when his eyes were opened to 'structured sin.' He came to realize the economic and social consequences of competition in the business world. If his father's firm succeeded, he observed, it would mean the demise of another firm, thus putting people out of work. It was this awareness that would lead him later into the socialist political camp, at least in theory.[16] In an actual social situation that Newbigin would later encounter, he saw the shortcomings of socialism, and this led him to reconsider faith as a radical answer to the social situations of the world. His predisposition to action required him to be interested and involved in the public arena.

It was during his Cambridge years (1928–31) that he re-entered the Christian stream, although he approached the whole thing with reluctance and some skepticism. There were two prominent student Christian groups at that time in Cambridge, the 'evangelicals' of Cambridge Inter-Collegiate Christian Union (CICCU) and the Student Christian Movement (SCM).[17]

---

13. Newbigin. *Unfinished*, 5–6.

14. William James, *The Will to Believe*. New York: Longmans, Green and Company, 1912.

15. Newbigin, *Unfinished*, 6.

16. Ibid., 7, 9.

17. The early histories of the Student Christian Movement (SCM) and the Cambridge Inter-Collegiate Christian Union (CICCU) are intermingled, but later they separate, one

Newbigin was not comfortable with the 'evangelicals' because they would try to 'get at him' to believe. He was more comfortable to join in with the SCM because of their openness to talk about difficult questions. Newbigin recalls: "They were committed to their faith and ready to talk about it, but also open to difficult questions and ready to take me as I was—interested but skeptical and basically uncommitted."[18]

His journey to faith, or at least the recapturing of faith, must not be lost at this point. He began to get up earlier in the morning to read the Bible and to pray, much like the 'morning watch' of the Student Volunteer Movement.[19] He had learned from reading William James that it was not irrational to believe, and this idea came to the fore at this particular time to reinforce his move back toward real faith. Newbigin recognized the influence of James upon his thinking: "and with William James to support me I knew that I was not being irrational seeking the help of one of whose existence there was no proof."[20]

Newbigin was influenced by Arthur Watkins, captain of the college rugby team, who exhibited an "extraordinary gift of friendship."[21] Prayer was the focus of Watkins' life, and Newbigin felt impelled to learn how to make prayer a dominating factor in his life. Referring to Watkins, Newbigin observes: "He was the most vivid example I know of the fact that the grace of God is so overwhelmingly absurd that one can only laugh and sing."[22] It is difficult to know if this was meant as a backhanded compliment or as a straightforward observation of how God had marvelously (beyond his ability to explain adequately) worked a miracle in Watkins' life. Nevertheless, it had an influence upon Newbigin's journey at that moment.

Subsequently Newbigin went to Rhondda Valley in South Wales, under the auspices of the Society of Friends, to work among the miners of that district. The difficult conditions of the miners caused Newbigin to rethink his view of a political solution. He began to see faith as the answer to the real needs and problems of the miners and felt strongly that the

---

eventually moving to liberalism, while the other remained conservative and evangelical.
18. Newbigin, *Unfinished*, 10.
19. Ibid.
20. Ibid.
21. Ibid.
22. Ibid.

Society of Friends were not dealing with the real issues because religion had been excluded from the work. They needed to approach the situation from the standpoint of the Christian faith, the same faith "that was beginning to draw me."[23]

After a foray among the miners, Newbigin felt defeated and was at a low point in his life. He had been reading a book by William Temple[24] at the time. The experience with the miners and the book by Temple seemed to be working on his mind and heart. One night he had a vision. Newbigin describes it as follows:

> It was a vision of the cross, but it was the cross spanning the space between heaven and earth, between ideals and present realities, and with arms that embraced the whole world.[25]

He saw the cross as the answer to the "sordid and hopeless of human history" and something that promised victory and real life. "I was sure that night," Newbigin recalls, "in a way I had never been before, that this was the clue that I must follow if I were to make sense out of the world."[26]

This experience changed his perspective and his life. He became involved in the Cambridge Evangelistic Campaign at Preston, which were open-air campaigns in towns in the Midlands and the North sponsored by SCM. On one occasion he visited a tenement house after the preaching services in Preston. The experience further convinced him of the futility of 'the new social order.' In one of these tenement buildings three families lived in one flat, one man dying of tuberculosis. This desperate situation led him to lose hope in a socialist solution: "When I struggled to find words for that situation I knew once and for all that a merely humanistic hope was not enough. At that point my talk about a new social order was

---

23. Newbigin, *Unfinished*, 10.

24. Newbigin does not mention what book he was reading but there were two that were published around this time. He was most likely reading *Christian Faith and Life*; the other possibility would be *The Universality of Christ*. William Temple was a philosopher, reformer, an early advocate of Christian unity, and an apologist for a reasonable faith. He was the Bishop of Manchester (1921–29) and later the Archbishop of Canterbury (1942–44). His influence upon the students of his generation is well known.

25. Newbigin. *Unfinished*, 11–12.

26. Ibid., 12.

A Brief Sketch of Newbigin's Life and Work

impertinent nonsense."[27] When he went back to Cambridge at the end of this vacation period, he went back a committed Christian.[28]

The influence of SCM grew steadily in Newbigin's life. People such as John R. Mott, Jack Winslow (of Poona Ashram), William Temple (in the pulpit at Great St. Mary's Church), and John Mackay of Lima and Princeton were just a few who came by Cambridge and left a powerful influence upon students of that time. Newbigin began to read the *International Review of Missions*, the missiological journal of his day. He would later become its editor.

CALL TO MINISTRY AND MISSION

Newbigin began to attend what was called the General Swanwick, the great SCM conference held for a week in the summer. He attended the conference in 1930 along with 600 other students and it was here that he experienced his call to ministry:

> There was a tent set aside for prayer. On one afternoon near the end of the week I went into it to pray. No one else was there. While I was praying something happened which I find it hard to describe. I suddenly knew that I had been told that I must offer for ordination. I had not been thinking about this. But I knew that I had been ordered and that it was settled and that I could not escape.[29]

A sense of certainty came over him. He knew that his life was in God's hands.[30]

Newbigin's involvement with SCM intensified and he was invited to join the staff. He was a member of the University SCM Committee and was eventually sent to Glasgow as an SCM staff person. He was at Glasgow from 1931 to 1933 as SCM Secretary with responsibility for Glasgow University, two technical colleges, and an agricultural training college. At that time he obtained the eight-volume report of the Jerusalem

---

27. Ibid.
28. Ibid., 13.
29. Newbigin, *Unfinished*, 15–16.
30. Ibid., 19. It must be noted that this statement at this stage of his life could reflect in many ways his approach to epistemology many years later. Knowing God (or in this case God's will) is not just a matter of reasoning, it is very much a "knowing" based on a relationship with God.

Conference[31] and read it with enthusiasm. This was, it appears, the beginning of his intense interest in global missions.

Newbigin mentions that he spent a lot of time with Archie Craig,[32] a chaplain at the University, and makes a remarkable statement about the influence of this man on his life: "I continued to visit Archie almost every day that I was in Glasgow and to receive from him a kind of theological training which was, I think, more significant than anything before or after."[33] Helen Henderson,[34] his wife to be, was a colleague of his at Glasgow and their interest turned to the India field, which is where, as it turns out, they spent much of their missionary career.

Newbigin attended the Edinburgh Quadrennial of 1933[35] and was influenced on a particular issue that would not come to the surface again until the 1970s. Unlike earlier quadrennials that were dominated by the needs of traditional mission fields, this particular one was dominated by the crisis within 'old Christendom.' According to Newbigin, J. H. Oldham[36] spoke of the Europe's radical departure from the faith in following Descartes and the Enlightenment.[37] Oldham introduced an idea that would become the passion of Newbigin's ministry after retirement. The 'Christian' world had become a mission field, Oldham asserted,

---

31. Jerusalem Meeting I. M. C. 1928. The Jerusalem Conference was the first major meeting of the International Missionary Council after its founding in 1921. See John A. Y. Briggs, "Jerusalem Conference (1928)," in *Evangelical Dictionary of World Missions*, 516.

32. Craig was later the Moderator of the General Assembly of the Church of Scotland and the first General Secretary of the British Council of Churches.

33. Newbigin, *Unfinished*, 20–21.

34. Helen Henderson (later Mrs. J. E. L. Newbigin) is listed as a Scottish secretary (1930–32) of SCM in McCaughey, *Christian Obedience*, 218.

35. The SVMU (later SCM) decided to hold its first 'Quadrennial' in Liverpool in 1896. It was followed by another in London in 1900, Edinburgh in 1904, Liverpool again in 1908, 1912, and 1929, Glasgow in 1921, Manchester in 1925, and then Edinburgh in 1933.

36. When John R. Mott began to promote his dream of a world Christian student union, he traveled to Europe in 1891. When he visited Oxford (1894), his guide was an undergraduate student named J. H. Oldham, see Hopkins. *John R. Mott*, 91. Oldham was converted in an evangelistic meeting conducted by Moody at Oxford in 1892, see Keith Clements. *Faith on the Frontier: A Life of J. H. Oldham*, 18. He was also the General Secretary of the SVMU (Student Volunteer Missionary Union) before there was an SCM, as well as the organizer of Edinburgh 1910, see McCaughey, *Christian Obedience*, 48.

37. "A philosophical movement of the 18th century, concerned with the critical examination of previously accepted doctrines and institutions from the point of view of rationalism." *The American Heritage Dictionary*, Second College Edition, s.v. "Enlightenment."

A Brief Sketch of Newbigin's Life and Work

and this thought would become Newbigin's focus some forty years later.[38] Newbigin comments on what had *not* happened in the intervening years since those words were spoken by Oldham and his retirement in Britain:

> From the perspective of nearly a half century later I would dare to say that missionary thinking in Europe and North America had not yet met the challenge which Edinburgh gave to develop a genuinely missionary encounter with post-Enlightenment European civilization.[39]

Newbigin moved to Edinburgh to serve Dundee, St. Andrews and Aberdeen for the SCM. His greatest joy was getting to know D. S. Cairns,[40] "that splendid, scraggy theologian whose own faith was a victorious battle against doubt" but who also was effective in preparing students for the "onslaught of a pseudo-scientific positivism."[41] Newbigin moved back to Cambridge to receive his ministerial training at Westminster College, a Presbyterian College for training for ministry, where John Oman (1860–1939)[42] was the principal and a friend of the family. Oman's lectures would make a contribution to Newbigin's thinking and development. Newbigin, however, was not entirely pleased with the theological education he received at Westminster College. Having been heavily involved in student ministry with SCM, which strongly emphasized spiritual life, and then studying at a theological college where this was not the case caused Newbigin to reflect on this weakness of the Reformed tradition of training ministers. The whole area of the interior life was, according to his observation, ignored.[43]

---

38. Newbigin, *Unfinished*, 26.

39. Newbigin, *Unfinished*, 26–27.

40. Cairns was very involved in the SCM, became a close friend of J. H. Oldham, was professor and chair of Dogmatics and Apologetics at United Free Church College in Aberdeen (later renamed Christ's College), and then became principal in 1925 (retired in 1937 at 75 years of age). For the story of Cairns' life and career, see Cairns, *Cairns: Autobiography* (London: SCM, 1950).

41. Newbigin, *Unfinished*, 27.

42. Oman translated (with critical commentary) Schleiermacher's *Addresses*. Stephen Bevans, in his book *John Oman and His Doctrine of God*, says of Oman: "Even among the members of his own tradition, the United Reformed Church in England and various branches of Presbyterianism in Scotland, Oman's work remains a relatively forgotten part of the British theological heritage." *John Oman*, Bevans (Cambridge, UK: Cambridge University Press, 1992), 1.

43. Newbigin, *Unfinished*, 32.

It did not, however, keep Newbigin from significant spiritual experiences. While reading a commentary on Paul's Letter to the Romans by James Denney, Newbigin experienced a shift in his theological orientation that would further determine the direction and tenor of his life and ministry. He writes:

> That was a turning point in my theological journey. I began study as a typical liberal. I ended it with the strong conviction about 'the finished work of Christ,' about the centrality and objectivity of the atonement accomplished on Calvary. The decisive agent in this shift was James Denney. His commentary on Romans carried the day as far as I was concerned.[44]

Newbigin was not happy with the interpretation of God's role in the redemption as espoused by Karl Barth in his commentary on Romans or with C. H. Dodd's *The Epistle of Paul to the Romans*. Dodd's approach was to downplay and explain away the wrath of God in order to dismiss the idea that Christ's sacrifice would somehow placate the wrath of an angry God. Newbigin felt that there needed to be a balanced view between God's wrath and God's love. Wainwright explains Newbigin's feelings at that time:

> Newbigin was more persuaded by the tougher route to affirming the love of God followed by James Denney, the professor of systematic and pastoral theology at the Free Church College in Glasgow, in his commentary on Romans in *The Expositor's Greek Testament*. According to Denney . . . the mercy of God does not discount the holiness of God that cannot abide sin, and the freely given gift of righteousness to the sinner comes at a price to God.[45]

Newbigin was very active in some form of ministry during these years in Cambridge. He served as the superintendent of the Sunday School at the York Street Mission of St. Columba's Presbyterian Church. He was asked to be the secretary of the Cambridge branch of the Student Volunteer Movement Union (SVMU) where he tried to rekindle some interest in foreign missions. He was asked to be the president of SCM for 1934–35. The Cambridge branch hosted many Christian leaders of that

---

44. Newbigin, *Unfinished*, 30.

45. Wainwright, *Theological Life*, 31. Denney was Professor of Systematic Theology at the Free Church College of Glasgow for three years (1897–1900) and then became Professor of New Testament Language, Literature and Theology from 1900 until his death in 1917.

era, among them were Hendrik Kraemer and J. H. Oldham, both of whom influenced Newbigin's thinking in regard to missions. He was camp manager for Swanwick in 1934 and was the speaker at the Scottish National Conference at Glenalmond in 1935.[46]

TO INDIA AND BACK

In December of 1935, Newbigin was accepted by the Foreign Missions Committee of the Church of Scotland and was assigned to the Madras Mission. He was commissioned at the General Assembly in May 1936 and in July of the same year he was ordained by the Presbytery of Edinburgh. He and his wife, Helen, left Liverpool for Madras on the 26 September 1936 on *The City of Cairo,* which he described as a slow, one-class boat.[47]

Newbigin aptly describes the next chapter in his life as "India: There and Back Again"[48] because of the events that were about to occur. After some Tamil language study and the passing of his first language exams, Newbigin was ready to for an assignment. His heart was given over to direct evangelism. He would be assigned to Kanchipuram where he would visit village congregations by camping out in the villages. Before going to Kanchipuram, however, he desired to pay a visit to Dharapuram, where there had been rapid church growth under J. J. Ellis, a Methodist missionary.[49] Soon after he boarded a bus to Dharapuram he was involved in an accident that smashed one of his legs. He had to undergo a series of operations in India and then finally surgery in Edinburgh.[50] As he was mending from his operations he became the Candidate Secretary for the Foreign Missions Committee of the Church of Scotland. While performing these duties he became troubled that the missionaries that he was recruiting were being sent out without any formal missionary training.

During this period he was in touch with J. H. Oldham who convened a discussion group called 'The Moot.' The purpose of the group was to "reflect upon the human situation from a Christian perspective."[51] He wrote a response to a paper prepared for a meeting of The Moot by

46. Newbigin, *Unfinished*, 30–38.
47. Ibid., 39.
48. Ibid.
49. Ibid., 45.
50. Ibid.
51. Ibid., 48; See also Wainwright, *Theological Life*, 240.

Middleton Murray, a response that did not please Oldham. There is no indication given by Newbigin as to the reason for Oldham's displeasure. This situation and many others that would occur in Newbigin's life reveal a character trait in which he is willing to state his convictions even though there may be strong opposition to his views. In his writings he refers to these occasions with an unusual objectivity and maturity that allowed him to continue to work with those he disagreed with.

FOCUS ON EVANGELISM

In 1939 Newbigin returned to India. He went to Kanchipuram, one of the seven most sacred cities of India. Newbigin had a high appreciation for the evangelistic work of J. H. Maclean. He had worked in and around Kanchipuram for forty years, not only tirelessly preaching the gospel in the streets but also supervising village churches and schools. Even though he was jeered at and occasionally attacked, he was held in high regard by most orthodox Hindus and was seen as a holy man.[52] It is significant that Newbigin would hold such a person in high regard because, in many ways, his own life was a clear reflection of the idea of doing administrative work alongside the very strenuous but very rewarding work of street preaching, which Newbigin loved so much. Street preaching, for Newbigin, was important not only because the gospel was preached but also because it would be a confirmation to the parents of his students of what he was all about.

During this time, Newbigin met weekly with a study group comprised of Hindu scholars and Christians that met at the Ramakrishna Mission in Kanchipuram, a place known as a center for trained Hindu learning.[53] While Newbigin enjoyed this immensely he became convinced that the point of contact with Indian people would not be in such a religious setting as a monastery, but rather in the secular experiences of ordinary life.[54] It was in his visitation to the villages that Newbigin acquired a deep respect for the poor untouchables (called *Harijans* by Gandhi) who were subject to systematic humiliation at every point.

Newbigin loved to spend time in the villages also because it provided an opportunity to temporarily escape the pressure of administrative work. While over the years his ability at administration would become

52. Newbigin, *Unfinished*, 52.
53. Ibid., 58.
54. Ibid.

evident in his work with the International Missionary Council and the World Council of Churches, he clearly indicates that his heart was in street preaching and not administration. In the chapter of his autobiography, *Unfinished Agenda*, "Kanchi: Beyond the Villages"[55] he laments that he was required to "move up" to administration and he also lamented the meaning that administration had taken in the church. To be in administration was held in high regard in the church, demeaning the work of preaching and service to the church.[56] Such an attitude, he felt, was unfortunate.

THE QUESTION OF INDEPENDENCE

Another issue that is on Newbigin's mind at this time is the question of the Church and mission, and the question of independence. While the focus of this book is on Newbigin's theology related to mission to the Western world, it should be noted that he was also thinking and struggling with missiological questions. This question relates to the problem of dependency, when Western churches provide resources that can thwart local initiative, and independence that implies self-support. Newbigin is aware that it is not always so black and white. There are occasions when local ministries do not have the resources to be independent and so to cut off help prematurely is certain defeat for the mission. Consequently, even though there may be a workable general principle concerning independence and dependence, independence can be defined too narrowly, excluding any outside help and thus crippling the church in that locale.[57]

THE BISHOP AND THE BROADER ECUMENICAL WORK

Newbigin's primary focus during the middle 1940s was, however, the attempt to create a unified church in South India. During the year 1946–47 he is at home in Britain where he is again the Candidate Secretary for the Foreign Missions Committee. An important opportunity to be the Secretary of the British Council of Churches comes his way, strongly recommended by Oldham and Archie Craig, a friend of Newbigin's from his university days who had become the first General Secretary of the British Council of Churches. He turns down this opportunity because of his strong love for India. It was also during this time that he had the

---

55. Newbigin, *Unfinished*, 70–83.
56. Ibid., 70.
57. Ibid., 71.

time to promote the 'South India scheme,' the coming together of various denominations and churches in south India to form the Church of South India. The union took place and Newbigin was appointed a Bishop in the Church of South India on April 1947 at the age of thirty-seven.[58] He would serve in Madurai.

While his work as Bishop would require an enormous amount of oversight of the churches, he would also be busy on the ecumenical scene as well. He received an invitation to be a 'consultant' for the inaugural assembly of the World Council of Churches that would meet in Amsterdam in 1948.[59] He would attend the Lambeth Conferences of the Anglican Church in 1948 and 1958 in an attempt to achieve full communion with them, but this was not achieved, much to his disappointment.[60] In preparation for the World Council of Churches Second Assembly in Evanston, Illinois (1954), Newbigin led a group of twenty-five theologians whose job it was to prepare the theme of the conference. It was a group of some of the most well-known theologians in the world, including Karl Barth, Emil Brunner, Reinhold Niebuhr, Paul van Dusen, and others.[61] The theme was "Christ, the Hope of the World." In the initial meeting of the group, led by Paul van Dusen, there was considerable discussion about that the theme actually meant. The divide seemed to fall between the Americans and the Europeans. Newbigin had prepared a paper on the Apostolate of the Church, but it was attacked from all sides. He would have been utterly defeated except Barth came to his rescue with, as Newbigin explains, "all guns firing,"[62] not so much because he agreed with Newbigin but because everyone was against him.

For nine months, beginning in May 1952, the Newbigin family made their home in Edinburgh. He had been a Bishop in Madurai for four years. Now had time to do some serious preparation for the Kerr Lectures, later published as *The Household of God*.[63] The book had a great influence in many quarters, being translated into French, German, Chinese, and Japanese. It also had an effect upon those who wrote the *Lumen Gentium*,

---

58. Wainwright, *Theological Life*, 7.
59. Newbigin, *Unfinished*, 111; Wainwright, *Theological Life*, 8.
60. Wainwright, *Theological Life*, 9.
61. Newbigin, *Unfinished*, 131.
62. Ibid., 132.
63. Newbigin, *The Household of God*. London: SCM, 1957.

a publication of the coming from the Second Vatican Council. However, when it came to the actual delivery of the lectures in Glasgow, they seemed to "fall completely flat." [64]

Newbigin's goal at the 1952 International Missionary Council conference at Willingen, which had the theme "The Missionary Obligation of the Church," was "to challenge what I saw at the paralysis of missions, the practical exhaustion of the resources of the older churches propping up relatively static churches in the old 'mission fields.'"[65]

Not to be forgotten was Newbigin's continuing passion to train village teachers by providing books that they could study and reference. It was the motivation for writing the book *Sin and Salvation*.[66] In writing the book it caused him to think about the faith in which he was raised. He explains it in this manner: "I saw that the kind of Protestantism in which I had been nourished belonged to a 'Christendom' context. In a missionary situation the Church had to have a different logical place."[67]

Following the Second Assembly at Evanston, there were further consultations at McCormick Seminary in Chicago and at Union Theological Seminary in New York. Newbigin decided that Union was in danger of succumbing to a sort of a-historical Gnosticism. His view aroused much opposition; he "had to face an onslaught of angry criticism" that, Newbigin recalls, he had rarely experienced.[68] It confirmed to his mind the importance of what the committee of twenty-five was all about.

CHAIRMAN OF THE INTERNATIONAL MISSIONARY COUNCIL

In 1958 he was elected Chairman of the International Missionary Council and the Church of South India seconded him for five years as a Bishop without diocesan charge so he could work for the International Missionary Council.[69] His primary work was to lead the International Missionary Council into union with the World Council of Churches. He was very reluctant recipient of such an honor. He did not want to leave the ministry

---

64. Newbigin, *Unfinished*, 137.
65. Ibid.
66. Newbigin, *Sin and Salvation*. London: SCM, 1956.
67. Newbigin, *Unfinished*, 146.
68. Ibid., 151.
69. Wainwright, *Theological Life*, 9.

of Bishop in India and expresses his dislike of becoming a bureaucrat—an "ecumenical office-wallah" as he called it.[70]

He also gave the Noble Lectures at Harvard University in 1958 where he attempted to state the case for the missionary calling of the church in the context of the call for the unity of all religions. These lectures were published as *A Faith for this One World?*[71]

He took part in founding Assembly of the East Asia Christian Conference that took place at Kuala Lumpur. At the first assembly, D. T. Niles, the "main architect and driving force" behind the conference, instituted the John R. Mott lectures. Niles, Newbigin, and two others gave the first set of lectures. Newbigin dealt with the dilemma of needing to pull back foreign missionaries so the church can develop maturity but also recognizing the vast amount of evangelistic work yet to be done that requires the help of missionaries from the sending churches. Newbigin's missiology becomes apparent when he writes: "We have adopted wrong missionary methods, methods modeled on the style of colonialism and not on the sovereignty of the Spirit as the true agent of mission."[72]

Newbigin confesses his feelings of inadequacy in leading the International Missionary Council. It was "a deep and perplexing situation." It was difficult to know what to do. He admitted that his ignorance was "vast and profound."[73] He laments: "There was immense faith in the validity of modern western technology as a tool for 'development,' but much less conviction about the validity of the Gospel as 'the power of God for salvation.' Mission has been absorbed into inter-church aid."[74]

In the summer of 1960 was the fiftieth anniversary of the Edinburgh World Missionary Conference. It was also the summer of the Conference at Strasbourg sponsored by the World's Student Christian Federation. Everyone went into the conference with high hopes for the new generation to be fired by the vision of the earlier generation for church unity and missions, fortified by a strong theology. There was, however, a lot of indifference to theological issues. Newbigin confesses that it was person-

---

70. Newbigin, *Unfinished*, 158.
71. Newbigin, *A Faith for this One World?* London: SCM, 1961.
72. Newbigin, *Unfinished*, 166.
73. Ibid., 170.
74. Ibid., 168.

INTEGRATION

The final act of integration of the International Missionary Council and the World Council of Churches occurred at the Third Assembly of the World Council of Churches in 1961 (New Delhi). After the integration Newbigin became the Director of the new Division of World Mission and Evangelism. He found the days in Geneva (where the WCC headquarters is located) difficult and perplexing. There needed to be a division within the World Council of Churches that would focus on evangelism. Newbigin had painful memories of planning sessions where there was a lack of enthusiasm for the unfinished task of evangelism.[76] He also worked as editor of the *International Review of Mission*.

His convictions regarding evangelism and social activism were outlined on a scrap of paper during a retreat. They give insight to just where he stood on the issue of evangelism. They are as follows:

1. That it matters supremely to bring more people to know Jesus as Saviour.
2. That our responsibility in the political order arises out of the love command.
3. That is does not arise out of the expectation of being able to anticipate the establishment of any particular social or political order.
4. That the New Testament teaches us (a) not to expect success in our cause; (b) to expect the sharpening of the issues and the coming of antichrist; (c) that there is no hope apart from Christ.
5. The 'Rapid Social Change' thinking had not developed any coherent theology and is in danger of identifying the movement of revolution with the work of redemption.
6. That in so far as it distinguishes these two things, it fails to show a clear understanding of the sense in which being in Christ is different from and transcends involvement in 'Rapid Social Change.'[77]

---

75. Newbigin, *Unfinished*, 174; Wainwright, *Theological Life*, 11.
76. Newbigin, *Unfinished*, 196.
77. Ibid., 197.

The most telling statement is found in number 5, where Newbigin articulates what in fact did become the prevailing ideology and accounts for the resistance to evangelism that Newbigin encountered. These six convictions, in fact, clearly identify the difference between the convictions of the early framers of the ecumenical movement and where it was going in the 1960s and beyond. Social activism, even to the point of social revolution, was taking the place of the primacy of spiritual redemption.

In 1962 the BBC sponsored the first inter-continental debate about religious matters. The sponsors, Newbigin remarks, thought that "Honest to God" (the theme and title of a book by Bishop John A. T Robinson) was a new revelation of ultimate truth. They were disappointed with Newbigin and he was challenged to re-examine his most basic belief.[78] Newbigin realized that what was needed was a fully Trinitarian doctrine as a basis for missions. This view was not supported by Visser 't Hooft nor his colleagues in the Division.[79] Ultimately Newbigin failed to achieve what he had hoped for in the integration. He had hoped to use the resources of a global organization in places where evangelism was the most promising.[80]

In 1965 Newbigin returned to India as Bishop of Madras. A sermon preached at his installation service from Ephesians 4:11–12 gave him the opportunity to articulate his emerging ecclesiology. The Church is for the nation, he exhorted, not for withdrawing; a theme that would remain a pivotal point in his theology for the rest of his life.[81] Interestingly such a belief was entirely the opposite of the Indian concept of religion. He made it clear that Christianity in India would not be formed in the mode of Indian religions.

Newbigin was a delegate to the Uppsala Assembly of the World Council of Churches in 1968 and it was for him a shattering experience. The focus was not on global evangelism but on social radicalism. Making matters worse, according to Newbigin, was Donald McGavran's "deafening barrage" to promote evangelism and mission that was counter-productive. It put evangelism in the position of be-

---

78. Newbigin, *Unfinished*, 198.
79. Ibid., 199.
80. Ibid., 205.
81. Ibid., 214.

ing aligned with high-pressure propaganda of the Church Growth Movement.[82]

After a memorable trip home at the time of his retirement (a leisurely trip overland from India to Europe), the Newbigin family spent the three summer months of 1974 in Edinburgh. Here Newbigin read Barth's *Dogmatics*. His response was summed-up in one word: "enthralling."[83] But his realization regarding the spiritual condition of Britain was less than enthralling; he found a lot of contempt for the gospel.[84] For the next five years he was on staff at Selly Oak Colleges. Among his teaching responsibilities was a course on the Theology of Mission. He found that most courses on Theology of Mission were actually courses on Third-World theologies. This inspired him to write his own Theology of Mission textbook, eventually published as *The Open Secret*.[85]

In 1977 Newbigin was elected, much to his surprise, moderator of the United Reformed Church for one year. In 1979, Newbigin, now seventy years old, accepted the position of part time pastor of an "old slum church across from the gloomy walls of Winston Green Prison," near Birmingham, in order to keep the church open. He pastured for eight years, with the help of a young Indian pastor named Hakkim Singh Rahi.[86]

At the beginning of the next decade, a committee of the British Council of Churches had difficulty trying to define what a conference that would deal with the relationship between Church and Society should focus upon. Newbigin offered to try to provide assistance and in ten days presented the first draft for *The Other Side of 1984—Questions for the Churches*.[87] It was a success and sold around the world. It was the beginning of a new era for Newbigin.[88] Timothy Yates describes this new era: "Newbigin has embarked on a whole fresh missionary project in relation to societies living in the shadow of the European Enlightenment of the eighteenth century."[89]

---

82. Wainwright, *Theological Life*, 12; Newbigin, *Unfinished*, 232.
83. Newbigin, *Unfinished*, 241.
84. Stafford, "God's Missionary to Us," 25; Shenk, "Lesslie Newbigin's Contribution," 62.
85. Grand Rapids: Eerdmans, 1978, Revised Edition, 1995.
86. Stafford, "God's Missionary," 26; Wainwright, *Theological Life*, 14.
87. Geneva: WCC, 1983.
88. Conway, "Profile: Lesslie Newbigin's Faith Pilgrimage," 29.
89. Yates, *Christian Mission*, 237.

It was the beginning of a new aspect of mission that, although he had been introduced to the idea in the 1930s, he couldn't have anticipated. It was a very productive era as Newbigin sought to answer the question, "Can the West be Converted?" Wilbert Shenk identifies the quality that makes Newbigin's writings so appealing: "I suggest that makes Newbigin consistently worth listening to is his keen sense of context and his capacity to identify with his audience. He had the ability to articulate what for others remained only subliminal until he expressed it for them."[90]

CONCLUSION

This chapter has sought to show the path that led Newbigin to his work as a missionary to Asia and the events that turned his focus toward the Western world as a place for serious mission. His post-retirement realization of the spiritual condition of Britain and the memory of J. H. Oldham's challenge regarding the need for a missionary engagement with the Western world provided the basis for Newbigin's new endeavor. His theological and missiological passions merge to help him develop his theology of mission to the Western world.

In the next chapter we will go into more detail regarding the events of Newbigin's life and how they shaped his theological and missiological thinking, especially in regard to Western Culture.

---

90. Shenk, "Lesslie Newbigin's Contribution," 60.

2

Missionary Theologian

BEGINNINGS OF THE MISSION TO THE WESTERN WORLD

J. H. OLDHAM, ONE of early twentieth century's greatest missionary statesmen, planted in Newbigin's mind the idea that the Western world is a potential place for mission. Oldham was present at the ecumenical conference held in Jerusalem in 1928 and he began to raise questions about the gospel and secular culture, but they were not perceived as central to the missionary concerns of the time. They reappeared at The Edinburgh Quadrennial of 1933. Newbigin recalls:

> J. H. Oldham, in a profound and prophetic address, spoke of the radical departure of Europe from the Christian faith when it followed Descartes and the pioneers of the Enlightenment. In other words—though it was not said so bluntly—the mission field was here in the 'Christian world.'[1]

J. H. Oldham was a missionary statesman who greatly influenced the global missionary movement in the first half of the twentieth century, even serving as the organizing secretary for the great World Missionary Conference that became known as 'Edinburgh 1910.'[2] He was converted in an evangelistic meeting conducted in Oxford by Dwight L. Moody and dedicated his life to mission as the result of hearing an 1884 address by Robert Speer[3] on the motto of the SVMU, "The Evangelization of the World

---

1. Newbigin, *Unfinished*, 26; also in "Mission in the 1990's: Two Views, Part II Lesslie Newbigin," 101.

2. Information on Oldham's life and career comes from Clements, *Faith on the Frontier*.

3. Robert Speer was, along with John R. Mott and Sherwood Eddy, an early leader in

in this Generation." Oldham had the opportunity for study at the University of Halle under the foremost professor of mission of that generation, Gustav Warneck.[4] Newbigin reflects on the life and career of Oldham:

> One of the very few missionary leaders of this century who recognized at an early date that the greatest contemporary challenge to the missionary movement is presented by "modern" Western society was J. H. Oldham. No one did more to shape the ecumenical movement in its early days and to direct the attention of churches to the need to challenge the assumptions of contemporary society.[5]

Newbigin picked up on the theme that the Western church must challenge the assumptions of Western culture. He understood that the West had largely been ignored as a focus of mission by the modern missionary movement,[6] but that it cannot be ignored in the future.[7] Newbigin observes:

> England is as much a foreign mission field as India was for me in 1936. I have come to feel there is an English parallel to the picture of Jesus in the Ramakrishna Mission Hall. I mean, of course, that it has increasingly seemed to me that instead of allowing the gospel to challenge the unexamined assumptions of our culture, we have co-opted Jesus into our culture by giving him a minor role in what we call the private sector.[8]

His assessment of Western culture, as we noted earlier, is that it is in a 'profound crisis' and is showing signs of disintegration.[9] It appears to be a civilization imploding.[10] This led Newbigin to question whether Western culture could, in fact, be converted:

---

the Student Volunteer Movement in the United States of America. These three dominated the student missionary cause for the first four decades of the twentieth century. Speer would become a Presbyterian missionary statesman. See Hopkins, *John R. Mott*, 71. He was president of the committee that planned the Edinburgh conference of 1910.

4. Professor Warneck was the editor of the leading German missionary periodical and the most distinguished figure in German missions at that time. He was professor at the University of Halle. See *John R. Mott*, Hopkins (Grand Rapids: Eerdmans, 1979), 252. He also wrote an early theology of mission.

5. Newbigin, *Gospel in a Pluralist Society*, 226.

6. Newbigin, *Foolishness*, 2.

7. Newbigin, *Open Secret*, 2.

8. Newbigin, *A Word*, 100.

9. Ibid.

10. Wainwright, *Theological Life*, 335.

> Can there be an effective missionary encounter with *this* culture—this so powerful, persuasive, and confident culture which (at least until very recently) simply regarded itself as "the coming world civilization." Can the West be converted?[11]

The Western church finds itself in a missionary situation because the radical secularization of Western society has changed 'old Christendom' into a mission field.[12]

Europe is not really as secular as one might imagine, Newbigin observes, because there is "a marked growth in religiosity in Europe."[13] In a sermon in the University Church of St. Mary the Virgin, Oxford in 1981, Newbigin said that "the most aggressively pagan of the continents today is Europe," which worships a variety of gods.[14] Western culture can be more accurately defined as a pagan society that, in reality, worships "no-gods."[15]

In presenting the gospel to Western culture, we are "offering the only hope of conserving . . . the good fruits of these centuries into a future which might otherwise belong to the barbarians."[16]

REDEFINING MISSION TO THE WESTERN WORLD

If Western culture is truly a mission field as Newbigin contends, then the church in the West, he believes, will need to redefine its nature and mission, seeing itself as a holy community distinct from the wider society. Western theology will need to consider seriously the missionary nature of the church rather than perceiving the church as an institution of the culture and defined in static, institutional terms.[17]

If Western culture is a true mission field, then there must be an attempt to contextualize the gospel in a manner that would not make the gospel captive to culture nor compromise it. While a great deal of material on contextualization exists in many of the cultures of the world, there has been no comparable attempt to contextualize appropriately the gospel to

---

11. Newbigin, "Can the West be Converted?" 2.
12. Newbigin, *Open Secret*, 2.
13. Newbigin, *A Word*, 148.
14. Quoted in Wainwright, *Theological Life*, 284.
15. Newbigin, *A Word*, 150.
16. Newbigin, *To Tell the Truth*, 64.
17. Newbigin, *Trinitarian Faith*, 12.

reach the modern Western world.[18] Newbigin does not mean by this that the church must accept the assumptions of Western culture in order to adapt the message to the context; on the contrary, his idea of missionary encounter means, as we shall see, that the church refute some of the assumptions of Western culture.

Modern culture is spreading to every continent in an unprecedented way.[19] The phenomenon was clearly recognized in the 1960s, and Newbigin was well aware of it: "The most significant fact about the time which we are living is that it is a time in which a single movement of secularization is bringing all the continents into its sweep."[20] Thirty years later he sees it in a slightly different light, but fully understands its persuasive power. He assigns the cause of secularism to the scientific worldview. "What we call the modern Western scientific worldview, the post-Enlightenment cultural world," explains Newbigin, "is the most powerful and persuasive ideology in the world today."[21] It is changing the face of traditional cultures across the globe and adversely affects the response of the nations to the gospel. Western secularism can be seen, Newbigin asserts, in every major city of the world where Western culture is embraced and "is the most powerful, the most pervasive and (with the possible exception of Islam) the most resistant . . . of all cultures that compete for power in the global city."[22] Newbigin describes the influence of Western culture on the world:

> During most of the history of the world of which we have knowledge, the tribes inhabiting the western peninsulas of Asia have been surpassed in the arts of civilization by the peoples of India, China and the Arab world. Yet during the past three centuries the descendants of these same tribes have extended their culture into every part of the world, dominating and often destroying more ancient culture, and creating for the first time a common civilization which embraces the whole earth—not in the sense it includes everyone, but in the sense that it has a dominating role, at least in nearly all the great cities of the world.[23]

---

18. Newbigin, "Can the West be Converted?" 2.
19. See Newbigin, *Foolishness*, 1–20, but specifically p. 3.
20. Newbigin, *Honest Religion*, 11.
21. Newbigin, *A Word*, 67.
22. Ibid., 186.
23. Newbigin, *Other Side*, 5–6.

MODERN SCIENCE AND HUMANISM

The major tenets of modernism[24] are humanism and science. There has been a strong humanist tradition in Western culture going back to Greek and Roman times, but it resurfaced in the Renaissance and played a part in the Reformation.[25] This humanistic tradition has two main streams. The first stream is the rationalist tradition (with Greek and Stoic sources) that essentially believes that truth can be known through reason alone. The second stream is the spiritualist tradition from ancient Europe and India, where truth is known directly through mystical experience.[26]

These two streams share two ideas. First, they believe that historical events cannot be the source of truth, since reason or intuition alone is sufficient. Second, they believe that truth is that which is equally accessible to rational beings apart from the accidents of history.[27] Newbigin strongly insists that, despite these two ideas, it is important for Christians to maintain the importance of the fact that God's revelation is grounded in history.

Along with secularism and humanism is the emergence of pluralism, not just as a reality that is permeating Western culture but also as an ideology. In a secular society where there is great personal freedom because no official dogma is accepted as authoritative, pluralism emerges by default as the accepted prevailing dogma of culture. Newbigin is quick to point out that there is not the freedom in pluralism that is often purported. The dogma of pluralism becomes the authoritative dogma of culture, and any idea that does not submit to it is considered heretical. There is a "critical spirit which is ready to subject all dogmas to critical (and even skeptical) examination."[28]

---

24. Newbigin defines modernism or, more precisely, modernity as "the way of thinking that came to dominance in the intellectual leadership of Europe . . . that rejected appeals to revelation and tradition as sources of authority except insofar as they could justify themselves before the bar of individual reason and conscience." *Truth and Authority*, Newbigin (Valley Forge, PA: Trinity International Press, 1996), 3.

25. Newbigin, *Gospel in a Pluralistic Society*, 1–2. See also Küng, *Theology for the Third Millennium,* trans. Peter Heinegg, 213–14.

26. Newbigin, *Gospel in a Pluralistic Society*, 2.

27. Ibid.

28. Ibid., 1.

METHODOLOGY FOR ENGAGING AND CONFRONTING WESTERN CULTURE

The question arises concerning what approach the church should take toward Western culture if it is to engage it in mission. Newbigin insists that a theological understanding of the situation is the first priority, and then the reordering of structures will follow.[29] "We need," insists Newbigin, "a theological clarification of the issues involved in a global encounter with modernity."[30] Newbigin's method of engagement was not to write a systematic theology but to confront Western culture as a missionary, but to do so in a theological manner. V. Matthew Thomas has described Newbigin's unique approach in this manner: "Both theology and missiology find each other in their mutually enriching relationship in Newbigin's work."[31] The need for an effective missionary engagement with modernity is, for Newbigin, both an urgent and difficult task. The issues facing mission to the West are not methodological, but are the deeply imbedded presumptions of Western culture.[32]

Newbigin sees the scientific worldview, at least the radical, naturalistic side of this particular worldview more appropriately labeled *scientism*,[33] as causing Western culture ultimately to abandon the quest for truth because it has radically narrowed the parameters of where one can find truth. Newbigin describes this as "narrow positivism."[34] Truth is limited to that which can be verified only through scientific experiment. Newbigin sees the expression of this abandonment of the quest for truth in persons like Paul Knitter[35] and others who do not believe that any religious tradition has the answer to the world's problems. This, Newbigin says, is symptomatic of a "loss of faith in the possibility of knowing objec-

---

29. Newbigin, *Open Secret*, 11.
30. Newbigin, *A Word*, 194.
31. Thomas, "The Centrality of Christ," 25.
32. Newbigin, *A Word*, 186.
33. Newbigin makes a distinction between science and scientism. He is speaking positively of the process of authority and validation of truth in the scientific community, but he sees scientism as negative, since it views science as "simply a transcript of reality, of the 'facts' which simply have to be accepted and call for no personal decision on my part." *Gospel in a Pluralist Society*, Newbigin (Grand Rapids: Eerdmans, 1986), 49.
34. Newbigin, *Foolishness*, 15, 45.
35. Paul Knitter, *No Other Name?* Maryknoll, NY: Orbis, 1985.

tive truth, which is at the heart of the sickness of our culture."[36] "We are witnessing," Newbigin laments, "the collapse of the whole glorious enterprise of seeking to know the truth, to make contact with reality, to know God as God truly is."[37] His assessment of where this leads is negative: "We are in the midst of a dying culture."[38]

In the last twenty-five years of Newbigin's life, he wrestled with the question of the "meeting of the Gospel with the anti-traditional secularized societies of the West."[39] At the end of his career, there were many who commented on the influence of his life and ministry. Wilbert Shenk, American missiologist, said of Newbigin:

> Lesslie Newbigin was a frontline thinker because of his uncommon ability to sense the emerging issue that must be addressed at the moment . . . What makes Newbigin so compelling is his keen sense of context and his ability to identify his audience. He had the ability to articulate what for others remained only subliminal until he expressed it for them.[40]

Geoffrey Wainwright summarized his life by calling him "a holy man whose plain and humble character attracted many—not, ultimately, to him, but rather through him—to the Source of his and all holiness."[41]

H. Dan Beeby, Newbigin's lifelong colleague and friend, says there are three things necessary to understand what Newbigin was up to: first, one must have some knowledge of the Reformed tradition; second, some experience in cross-cultural mission; and third, a streak of nonconformity![42]

A MISSIONARY THEOLOGIAN

If one sees the work of theology as articulating the faith in the context of the ministry and mission of the church in a relevant manner, then Newbigin qualifies as a theologian. One writer has noted how easily

---

36. Newbigin, "Religious Pluralism," 50.
37. Ibid., 52.
38. Ibid.
39. Wainwright, *Theological Life*, 177.
40. Shenk, "Lesslie Newbigin's Contribution," 59–63; published in a special issue of the (British and Foreign) Bible Society's journal as "A Tribute to Lesslie Newbigin (1909–98)," *The Bible in TransMission*, 3–6; see also found in Wainwright, *Theological Life*, 393–94.
41. Wainwright, *Theological Life*, 392.
42. Ibid., viii.

Newbigin could live in the two worlds of intense practical ministry and that of theological debate with the world's leading theologians:

> Unlike many Christian leaders, Newbigin was never for any great length of time an academic, a church bureaucrat, or (never at all) a media savant. He has, however, done a great deal of street preaching before skeptical crowds. As a bishop in India, he set his priority on congregational ministry, traveling out to remote, illiterate villages, spending the night in local homes, conducting services in the open air. He could get on the next plane for Geneva to parley with the great theologians. (Beginning in 1952, for example, he chaired the "Committee of Twenty Five," an assemblage of feisty theologians, including Karl Barth, Emil Brunner, and Reinhold Niebuhr, leading them in drafting a statement on Christian hope.) Yet he came back to engage insistently the life of the church at the congregational level.[43]

George Hunsberger characterizes Newbigin's writings as essentially theological, produced in the anvil of active service of the church: "His theology," he writes, "has been produced 'ad hoc' . . . He did not set out to be a theologian nor to write extensively his theological reflections."[44]

Paul Knitter calls him a 'mission theologian'[45] while Geoffrey Wainwright says that Newbigin was a great man of God, theologian, and pastor,[46] as well as a 'bishop-theologian,' a figure of comparable stature with the Fathers of the Church.[47] Wainwright asserts: "Newbigin offers, I believe, an authentic representation of the scriptural Gospel and the classic Christian faith."[48] It is a theology forged in the midst of active ministry and mission, which, according to Newbigin, is a proper place for theological work:

> Theology is rightly done in the context of worship and discipleship. The central place of theological teaching is the place where, in the midst of the mystery of the Eucharist, the minister seeks to interpret the words of Scripture to those who, having partaken of the Eucharist, will then go out into the world to live out in prac-

---

43. Stafford, "God's Missionary," 3.
44. Hunsberger, *Bearing the Witness*, 36–37.
45. Knitter, *No Other Name?* 97.
46. Wainwright, *Theological Life*, viii.
47. Ibid., Preface, v.
48. Ibid., Preface, vii.

Missionary Theologian

tice the action of the broken body and shed blood. This kind of theological teaching certainly needs illumination and correction by the work of those whose whole time is given to the scholarly study of the Christian tradition, but it must not be allowed to lose its central place in the life of the Church.[49]

Newbigin does not attempt to produce a systematic theology in the sense of a singular work that fully develops his system of thinking. His book, *A Faith for This One World?*,[50] is not a systematic theology as such, but is a broad doctrinal study that Newbigin prepared for pastors while he was a Bishop[51] in India. Newbigin fits the model of an active practitioner of religion who, like John Wesley, developed his thinking in response to the deepest questions of the flock that he was shepherding.

HOW THE MISSIONARY BECAME A THEOLOGIAN

What caused Newbigin the missionary to become Newbigin the theologian? Some insight into his motivation for doing theology is seen in Hunsberger's assessment of how Newbigin approached his life and work:

> He has searched constantly for action based on a firm, undergirding theology. This forced over and over again the asking of ultimate questions of meaning and purpose, questions for which for him grew from practical issues and must produce practical guidance. He has always articulated his theology "to the point" which immediately faced him and the Christian church he cared so deeply to pastor.[52]

In the course of his formation as a missionary and as a theologian he was fortunate to have had contact with the great theological minds of the twentieth century. One of the first persons that Newbigin mentions that would directly influence his thinking was the missionary theologian

---

49. Wainwright, *Theological Life*, vii, 153. Wainwright is quoting from Newbigin's retrospective "reflections on the ministry of a bishop." The source of the quote is an undated typescript, probably dating from around 1980.

50. Newbigin, *A Faith for this One World?* London: SCM, 1961.

51. Newbigin went out as a missionary under the auspices of the Church of Scotland which does not use the terminology of 'bishop,' but, after the coming together of particular entities of various churches (including Anglican, Methodist, Congregational, and Presbyterian) to form the Church of South India, he became the Bishop in Madurai and Ramnad. His work as bishop was very pastoral in nature.

52. Hunsberger, *Bearing the Witness*, 36.

Hendrik Kraemer.[53] Kraemer had similar views to Karl Barth regarding revelation in other religions, but developed these ideas missiologically. "I had long talks with Kraemer," Newbigin recalls, "and was captivated by his strong yet open and flexible spirit."[54] Later he had a meeting with Barth and remarked: "It was a brief meeting and I had not yet learned to appreciate either Barth or his theology as I was to do later."[55]

Newbigin developed a number of his strongest theological convictions, not only in dialogue with the great theological minds of the twentieth century, but also in the midst of difficult and demanding missionary work. Between the years 1939–46 he served in Kanchipuram where the powerful evangelist J. H. Maclean[56] also served. He was a part of the famous class at Trinity College, Glasgow that produced some great missionaries. He labored in the Kanchipuram area for forty years, and in spite of the jeering and ridicule that was thrown his way when he was preaching in the streets, he was regarded as a holy man by those who rejected his message. Newbigin continued Maclean's work and the street preaching had a tremendous effect on his view of ministry and mission, culminating in his theological conviction regarding 'word and deed.' "What matters is that word and deed are not separated," exhorts Newbigin. "What matters more is that they are seen to flow from a centre where Jesus Christ is confessed and worshipped."[57] He goes on to explain:

> The value of street preaching may be questioned. The answer which I give in my own mind was that the people listening to us knew that we were also the people who taught their boys and girls in the schools and who cared for their sick at the Mission Hospital, so that the preaching was not disembodied words but had some flesh on it.[58]

---

53. Goheen, "*As the Father Has Sent Me,* 194.
54. Newbigin, *Unfinished,* 84.
55. Ibid., 115.
56. J. H. Maclean was on the Executive Committee of the newly begun Student Volunteer Missionary Union, which was constituted on 24 May 1892. His reputation for hard work was evident in his student years. Tatlow says of him: "J. H. Maclean had a first-class mind, was a fully equipped Scottish Presbyterian theological student, ready to work extremely hard for the cause and quite unready to be rushed into ill-considered action." *Story of the Student Christian Movement,* Tatlow (London: SCM, 1933), 32–33.
57. Newbigin, *Unfinished,* 56.
58. Ibid.

This perspective, articulated by someone within the ecumenical movement, shows that he was able to keep his theological balance while others were caught up in radical diversions that pitted evangelism against social activism.

Another experience brought him face to face with an issue that has played a major role in missiological and theological discussions in recent years. Instead of debating the issue of revelation and religions in a classroom isolated from contact with practitioners of other religions, Newbigin boldly engaged Hindu scholars in dialogue. Kanchipuram was the centre for Hindu learning, and there was in that place an openness to discussions with persons interested in such things. Newbigin confesses he spent many hours at the Ramakrishna Mission being schooled in the teachings of the school of Visishtadvaita, a part of the general school of Vedanta, a theistic belief that came from the teachings of Ramanuja. This experience brought him to the following conclusion:

> As I reflected on these long discussions on religious subjects with gracious and helpful Hindu friends, I became more and more sure that the "point of contact" for the Gospel is rather in the ordinary secular experiences of human life than in the sphere of religion. I had not then read Karl Barth and did not know that "religion is unbelief," but I was certainly beginning to see that religion can be a way of protecting oneself from reality.[59]

THEOLOGY IN THE 1960s

The 1960s proved to be a difficult time for Newbigin in regards to his hopes for the leadership of the ecumenical movement and for the affirmation of some of the theological convictions of the generation of leaders that he represented. Newbigin laments: "I did not yet know how far the decade that had just begun would take us from the lines on which my own theological development had brought me."[60] The issue at that time came to light at a conference held in Strasbourg in 1960 by the World Student Christian Federation,[61] where the topic of discussion was "The

---

59. Newbigin, *Unfinished*, 58. Interestingly, he mentions Barth on page 32 of his unpublished paper "Revelation," written while he was a student at Cambridge (1936).

60. Ibid., 175.

61. The World Student Christian Federation was first conceived by D. L. Wishard during a meeting of American and British leaders of the SVMU in 1892. A Second Summer

Life and Mission of the Church." Newbigin went to the conference with great hopes and expectations, believing (as did many of the leaders of ecumenical movement) that "there was an emerging theological consensus about the missionary nature of the church and that the coming generation of student leaders would be captured and fired by the vision."[62] Things turned out far differently than expected. Newbigin puts the issue in perspective:

> I had been pleading for a 'churchly' unity because I believed that God's purpose of reconciliation could not be achieved by a concatenation of programs and projects unless these were leading towards the life of a reconciled family in the household of God.[63]

Newbigin was not in agreement with the new theological thrust because the new vision was not for the church as he anticipated, but for the world, with Christianity being redefined as a secular movement. It would turn out to be a decade focused on the world, with the church essentially being by-passed.

The most intense period for theological endeavor prior to his retirement was the period of time he spent in Geneva as Director of the new Division of World Mission and Evangelism, 1962–65. At this time, he also took on the responsibility as editor of the *International Review of Missions*. The meeting in New Delhi in 1961 saw the merging of the International Missionary Council with the World Council of Churches and a new slogan, "the church is mission," accompanied the merger.[64] Newbigin took issue with the missiology that came out of New Delhi:

> Already at New Delhi I had recognized that the missiology of *One Body, One Gospel, One World* was not adequate. It was too exclusively church-centered in its understanding of mission. Only a full Trinitarian doctrine would be adequate, setting the work of Christ

---

conference was held at Keswick in 1894, under the auspices of both the Inter-University Christian Union (later the SCM) and the Student Volunteer Missionary Union. During this time the idea of a world-wide federation of students was on the minds of the participants. In 1895, representatives from six nations met in Sweden to form the World's Student Christian Federation. Dr Karl Fries of Sweden became the chairman and John R. Mott became the general secretary. See Tatlow, *Story of the Student Christian Movement*, 35, 62, 67–68.

62. Newbigin, *Unfinished*, 174–75.
63. Ibid., 175–76.
64. Glasser, "Conciliar Perspectives," 95.

in the church in the context of the over-ruling providence of the Father in all the life of the world and the sovereign freedom of the Spirit who is the Lord and not the auxiliary of the Church.[65]

His full-blown treatment of this subject came out later in his book *The Open Secret*.[66] It would appear that Newbigin contradicts himself by saying that it is unfortunate that the church was left out of the mix by the students meeting in Strasbourg in 1960 while appearing to say that the focus of New Delhi was too *church*-centered. In regards to Strasbourg, the move was toward the secularization of the church, which Newbigin saw as allowing the world to control the agenda of mission rather than the church determining its own course, informed by God's Word. The church has a mission to the world, but it must be the same as God's mission. Newbigin's argument is against the idea that the church can decide what that mission is without any reference to the Trinity, thus precipitating his critique of the New Delhi document.

The 'theological earthquake' that was shaking the English-speaking world at that time was the publication of John Robinson's book *Honest to God*.[67] Newbigin was compelled to respond to this book because he felt that it attacked the very center of the Christian faith.[68] He responded with a book titled *Honest Religion for Secular Man*.[69] Newbigin's definition of secularism, the topic of Robinson's book, is that it is "a system of belief... which in principle denies the existence... of realities other than those which can be measured by methods of natural science."[70] Newbigin asserts that existentialism, also popular at the time, was not the answer to the spiritual needs of secular man. The answer to mankind's spiritual need "is the declaration of God's cosmic purpose by which the whole public history of mankind is sustained and overruled."[71] The gospel can be known adequately only as it is affirmed in the public arena, and as Christ's death and resurrection are proclaimed as historical events open to public scrutiny. The church must break away from the cultural view that religion

---

65. Newbigin, *Unfinished*, 198.
66. Newbigin, *The Open Secret*. Grand Rapids: Eerdmans, 1978, 1995.
67. John Robinson, *Honest to God*. London: SCM, 1963.
68. Newbigin, *Unfinished*, 199.
69. Philadelphia: Westminster/London: SCM, 1966.
70. Newbigin, *Honest Religion*, 8.
71. Ibid., 46.

is a private matter and enter into public debate. His arguments in this book are a preview of some of the arguments that he will take up later.

His last assignment before retirement was as Bishop of Madras, from 1965–74. In 1966 he gave the Beecher Lectures at Yale Divinity School in New Haven, Connecticut and gave the same lectures later in Cambridge. They were published under the title *The Finality of Christ*.[72] The reason for the topic of his lectures was his assessment of the place of Christ in the theological thinking of some within the ecumenical movement. He explains:

> The subject was chosen because I was dissatisfied with what seemed to me a confused kind of 'ecumenism,' namely the inclusion of the 'interfaith' dimension in the ecumenical idea. I believed that the whole integrity of the Ecumenical Movement depended upon the acceptance of the centrality and finality of Christ, and that to move from this was not a legitimate extension of the Ecumenical Movement but a reversal.[73]

Upon retirement, Newbigin and his wife took two months to travel overland from India back to Britain. It was an arduous but rewarding journey. It was about that time that Newbigin began to realize that India and Europe are not as disconnected as one might believe. Newbigin observed:

> It was a vivid reminder of the fact that, for at least a thousand years before the rise of Islam, the whole region from India to Greece was one living space, and Europe was still essentially a peninsula of the one Eurasian continent.[74]

After the trip across the vast Indo-European continent, they settled in Edinburgh for the summer. It was then that Newbigin decided to read Barth's *Dogmatics* in its entirety. He writes:

> It was an immensely rewarding experience. Barth condensed and Barth quoted I had found unimpressive. But the real Barth, and especially his famous small-print notes, was enthralling. It was a needed preparation for the much more difficult missionary experience which (as I did not then realize) lay ahead.[75]

---

72. Newbigin, *The Finality of Christ*. Richmond, VA: John Knox, 1969.

73. Newbigin, *Unfinished*, 231. In an interview with H. Dan Beeby at Selly Oak on 28 April 2000, Beeby stated that Newbigin was in great conflict with the World Council of Churches when he died.

74. Ibid., 241.

75. Newbigin, *Unfinished*, 241–42.

Upon arriving back in Britain, Newbigin began one of the most productive periods of theological writing of his life.[76] He accepted a position at Selly Oak Colleges, Birmingham where he would teach 'Theology of Mission' and 'Ecumenical Studies' for those preparing for missionary work. Checking with other missionary training institutions, he discovered that most did not teach 'theology of mission' but usually taught a course in 'third-world theology.' Newbigin was not satisfied with this; he wanted to teach why the church needed to be missionary. Eventually his lectures ended up being published under the title *The Open Secret*.[77] Newbigin explains that his book was not written on a scholarly level, because that was not the intention of the lectures. Some of the themes of his mature theology of mission begin to be articulated, however. The radical secularization of Western culture, Newbigin observes, has placed the Western church in a true missionary situation.[78]

Missionaries expect things to change in their home culture while they are gone, but what Newbigin encountered upon his return to Britain in 1974 greatly unsettled his mind and heart. While spending time with ministers and lay persons in various conferences, he grew to understand that there was "much timidity in commending the Gospel to the unconverted in Britain."[79] Newbigin was used to the 'optimistic, evangelistic stance' of the Indian church, which was a significant minority yet enthusiastic about its faith. The church in England, however, seemed to not understand the message or its missionary calling.[80] Two thoughts regarding why this might be the situation of the church in England came to Newbigin's mind: first, was that the modern scientific worldview had influenced the church to where it could not believe in traditional Christian teachings; second, that the church needed to fashion the gospel message in terms of the requirements of modern thought.[81]

To Newbigin's astonishment, he was elected to be the Moderator of the United Reformed Church (URC)[82] for 1978–79. At the end of this

---

76. A review of Newbigin's bibliography reveals that over half of his writings appear after 1974.

77. Newbigin, *Unfinished*, 242.

78. Newbigin, *Open Secret*, 2.

79. Newbigin, *Unfinished*, 243.

80. Tim Stafford, "God's Missionary to Us," 2.

81. Newbigin, *Unfinished*, 243.

82. According to the *The Times* (London) obituary of Lesslie Newbigin on 31 January

tenure in office he planned to do some extensive reading and some writing, but another unexpected event changed the direction of ministry. At the 1979 meeting of the Birmingham District Council, the Chairman was absent and he was asked to preside. One agenda item concerned a small congregation across from the Winston Green prison. There had been no full-time pastor for forty years and a decision needed to be made whether it should be closed. Newbigin was very reluctant to preside over such a decision and he expressed his view that the church should not abandon such places to take up residence in the suburbs. The Council agreed to defer the decision, but Lesslie and Helen continued the discussion at home. The result was that they accepted a call to become the part-time minister of the congregation. He was installed as pastor in January 1980 and was the minister of this church until 1988.[83]

At the time of writing his autobiography, Newbigin was still pastoring this church. His statements regarding ministry in England are quite strong, but they are the assessment of a very experienced missionary on the front line of ministry. "There is a cold contempt for the Gospel," he writes, "which is harder to face than opposition."[84] Traditional British households seemed unconcerned about the gospel. Newbigin felt that God had been driven out of Britain, and other gods had come in the void, giving impetus to one of Newbigin's strongest missionary statements of his career:

> England is a pagan society and the development of a truly missionary encounter with this very tough form of paganism is the greatest intellectual and practical task facing the Church.[85]

This is a remarkable statement and an astute analysis of the contemporary situation of Western culture as seen by a veteran missionary with impeccable credentials. It ignited a passion that would continue until his death.

1998, Newbigin declined the invitation to be an assistant Bishop in the diocese of Birmingham and at that time "firmly identified himself with the United Reformed Church, into which the Presbyterian Church of England had flowed." Obituary of Lesslie Newbigin, *The Times* (London), 31 January 1998, 25.

83. Newbigin, *Unfinished*, 248.
84. Ibid., 249.
85. Ibid.

NEWBIGIN'S EVANGELICAL THEOLOGY

Earlier it was noted that Newbigin, during his Cambridge years (1928–31), was oriented toward the Student Christian Movement and not toward the 'evangelicals' because the latter group was always at him to believe. However, the term *evangelical* is used in a broader and wider sense than referring to a group of students at Cambridge.[86]

Karl Barth offers a definition of evangelical theology that would help to define Newbigin as an evangelical theologian. In his book *Evangelical Theology: An Introduction*,[87] Barth states that the theology contained in his book will be *evangelical* theology. He explains:

> What the word "evangelical" will objectively designate is that theology which treats the *God of the Gospel*. "Evangelical" signifies the "catholic," ecumenical (not to say "conciliar") *continuity and unity* of this theology. Such theology intends to apprehend, to understand, and to speak of the God of the Gospel . . . This is the God who reveals himself in the Gospel, who himself speaks to men and acts among and upon them.[88]

One of the most prominent characteristics of this evangelical theology is that this 'God of the Gospel' authenticates himself. "The dominant presupposition of its thought and speech is *God's* own proof of his existence and sovereignty."[89] In a statement that substantially reflects a view similar to Newbigin, Barth discusses theology and mission:

> Theology is no undertaking that can be blithely surrendered to others by anyone engaged in the ministry of God's Word. It is no hobby of some especially interested and gifted individuals. A community that is awake and conscious of its commission and task in the world will of necessity be a theologically interested community.[90]

For Barth, the community with the task of reaching the world and involved in theology is a community where faith is seeking understand-

---

86. The IVF saw themselves, for example, as 'conservative evangelicals' while the SCM people saw themselves as 'liberal evangelicals.'

87. The book is Barth's famous lectures given at the University of Chicago in 1962 with twelve additional chapters..

88. Barth, *Evangelical*, 5–6.

89. Ibid., 8.

90. Ibid., 41.

ing (*fides quaerens intellectum*). This is what theology "must embody and represent."[91] It is a theology which believes in order to understand (*credo ut intelligam*).[92]

NEWBIGIN'S THEOLOGICAL WRITING

As one reads Newbigin, it becomes clear that his writing style is vigorous, clear, and persuasive. Wilbert R. Shenk notes that "he early developed a characteristic style of discourse on which he continued to rely."[93] In a review of Newbigin's book, *The Gospel in a Pluralist Society*,[94] George Lindbeck notes: "The result is a significant recasting and expansion of the convictions articulated in the bishop's earlier writings, chiefly in the idiom of the biblical theology movement of the 1940s and 1950s."[95] While Newbigin was influenced by biblical theology, he does not fit formally in that category.[96] His early writings could be described best as biblical exposition, since his writing is aimed at a popular audience and not to the academic community. His style earlier on was to take an issue and develop his argument from a biblical standpoint.

While most of his earlier writings (such as *The Household of God* and *Sin and Salvation*, 1952 and 1956 respectively) are predominately biblical exposition, one can see the beginnings of an apologetic approach (as in *I Believe, Honest Religion, The Finality of Christ*—1946, 1966, and 1969), where he begins to engage cultural issues. His writings, it can be observed, become more argumentative, intending not only to teach (as in instructing Indian pastors how to do ministry) but also to persuade, often asking for a radical change of view.

REDEFINING APOLOGETICS

Newbigin utilizes what can be defined as an apologetic method, albeit apologetics on his own terms. He attempts to redefine apologetics by clearly setting the parameters of what he considers appropriate apologetics. He does

91. Barth, *Evangelical*, 42–43.
92. Ibid., 43.
93. Shenk, "Lesslie Newbigin's Contribution," 60.
94. Newbigin, *The Gospel in a Pluralist Society* London: SPCK, 1989.
95. Lindbeck, review of *Gospel in a Pluralist Society*, 182.
96. George Hunsberger discusses how Newbigin does and does not fit this category. See Hunsberger, *Bearing the Witness*, 38–42.

not accept the manner in which apologetics has been traditionally done and, as David Heim points out, Newbigin "exhibits a healthy suspicion of apologetics."[97] This issue will be addressed subsequently, but first we must see how others view and assess Newbigin's apologetic method.

Geoffrey Wainwright entitles chapter 10 in his book *Lesslie Newbigin: A Theological Life* "The Christian Apologist," and explains that Newbigin "is as an apologist to the doubting and to the unbelieving."[98] George Hunsberger, in a discussion of pluralism where he states that Newbigin's position on religions is more pluralistic than those who hold that all religions fit together into a unitary structure of thought, designates Newbigin's approach as 'apologetic':

> The value of this observation of Newbigin's is linked to the value of his overall apologetic, which stresses that every position begins from the standpoint of some fundamental axioms which are not proved and cannot be proved by any other set of axioms which are more ultimate. All thinking starts from some presupposed "faith-decision."[99]

A part of that "presupposed faith decision" for Newbigin is his affirmation of the uniqueness of Christ. Wainwright explains: "His own affirmation of the uniqueness of Christ will run through his work and thinking as . . . an apologist."[100]

Newbigin seeks to convince the church to be the church, advocating that the Christian community contend for the public truth of the gospel before the wider community. He is also trying to convince Western culture that the answers to its fundamental ideological problems can be found in Christian theology, specifically in the doctrines of Trinity and the Incarnation of Christ, both of which teach an understanding of reality far broader than the narrow parameters of Enlightenment scientism. Shenk sees in Newbigin an

> . . . attitude of readiness to fearlessly confront the intellectual and theological demands of each situation [that] continuously drew

---

97. Heim, *Christian Century*, 864.
98. Wainwright, *Theological Life*, 335.
99. Hunsberger, *Bearing the Witness*, 272.
100. Wainwright, *Theological Life*, 64.

him into dialogue with a range of viewpoints, regardless of whether or not he found them congenial.[101]

While Newbigin's apologetic method is straightforward and to the point, some may call it simplistic, implying that he is not willing to deal with the complexities of the modern situation. Wainwright sees it differently:

> The Christian apologist [Newbigin] is caught puzzling over the relation between Christianity and modernity and then cutting through the ambiguities in order to offer in the Gospel a new-old alternative to other worldviews that always end-up in either self idolatry or despair, if not both.[102]

The "cutting through the ambiguities" is what Newbigin does best, and that leads to his clear, precise theological prescription for Western culture's illness.

Apologetics, of course, is the branch of theology that seeks to defend or commend the Christian faith through reason. While Newbigin does not see reason as a source for faith, he does utilize reason to persuade the church and culture that to accept the convictions and premises of the Enlightenment is to fail to deal adequately with reality.[103] He defines apologetics as that which "seeks to respond to this question [How can we know that the Christian story is true?] and to demonstrate the 'reasonableness of Christianity.'"[104] He does not object to the use of reason to defend Christianity but refuses to submit to the use of reason as *dictated by culture* and which is subject to Enlightenment presuppositions. For Newbigin, reason is not the source of truth nor is it truth's final arbitrator. He adamantly resists the false ideal of indubitable knowledge set forth by Descartes. He believes that Christian apologetics has fallen prey to cultural expectations which he believes are not appropriate for maintaining the integrity of the gospel. This is most apparent "in the attempt of Christian apologetics to demonstrate the truth of Christianity on the basis of supposedly self-evident truths."[105] For Newbigin, true and necessary apologetics is demonstrating the truth of the gospel not grounded on

---

101. Shenk, "Lesslie Newbigin's Contribution," 59.

102. Wainwright, *Theological Life*, 27.

103. As J. Andrew Kirk has said, "modernism is far from dead." Kirk, in *Scandalous Prophet*, 119.

104. Newbigin, *Proper Confidence*, 93.

105. Newbigin, *Truth to Tell*, 51.

Western culture's standard for evaluating truth, but in the gospel itself.[106] "The assumption... is that the gospel can be made acceptable by showing that it does not contravene the requirements of reason as we understand them within the contemporary plausibility structure."[107] Newbigin does not seem to be concerned about whether the gospel is acceptable but that it be accepted, and that comes by faith not by reason. The role of the apologist is to tell the story and to bear witness to the truth.[108] Very early in his career he presented a significant paper entitled "I Believe" at a regional leadership conference at The American College in Madura, south India (1945). In this paper he affirms the importance of witness:

> The confessing Christian is not declaring the results of his research, reflection and speculation; he is speaking from a standpoint in which he has been placed by God's grace, and his confession is essentially a witness to grace.[109]

His apologetic stance sounds much like a prophet and a reformer. His prophetic voice calls the church back to its true faith and away from the presuppositions of culture.

It must be noted that essential to both Newbigin's apologetic and his theology in general is a strong disposition for a unitary view of life that permeates all that he did and thought. In a statement that reveals his passion for unity, he writes: "We have overdeveloped only half of our brains, and we need to recover what we have lost, the capacity to see things whole, not seeking to master everything by dissection... but accepting and rejoicing in the wholeness of things."[110] He strongly protests Western culture's dualism, seeking rather a unified understanding of the cosmos which includes God as the Creator and Sustainer of a contingent and dependent universe. There may be two dimensions but one reality.

---

106. Newbigin, *Proper Confidence*, 96.

107. Newbigin, *Proper Confidence*, 93. On page 28 Newbigin relates this assumption to what we would normally not doubt. The indubitable knowledge demanded by culture would be indisputable facts, which would lay the basis for belief. For Newbigin, "that is exactly what we cannot and must not do." Truth is known by faith. *Proper Confidence*, Newbigin (Grand Rapids: Eerdmans, 1995), 28.

108. Ibid., 94.

109. Newbigin, "I Believe," 73–88. In this paper, he introduces a number of themes that would later become some of his major tenets in his apologetic approach to the Western world.

110. Newbigin, *Truth to Tell*, 62.

His doctrine of salvation not only includes *human* redemption but also *cosmic* redemption. A basic theological conviction that Newbigin carries throughout his life is clearly articulated as early as 1945:

> Now religious faith is obviously of the nature of a synthetic apprehension of reality. Leaving aside lower forms of faith, we may at least truthfully say that theism is the apprehension, not just of some part of experience, but of all human experience, as a meaningful whole. Just as, in proportion to the development of our musical powers, we may appreciate a long a[nd] complex symphony as not merely a collection of miscellaneous sounds, but as a meaningful whole . . . And continuing this line of thought, we say that Christian faith is an apprehension of the whole of experience in terms of the clue which is given to us in the Fact of Christ. But . . . this apprehension is one that is given to us in so far as we . . . suffer a radical conversion, re-orientation of viewpoint.[111]

Newbigin's intense passion for a unitary view of reality is complemented by his advocacy of the concrete, organizational unity of the church, which he sought to accomplish through active participation in the ecumenical movement. At the same time, he does not believe in unity at any price. He is very clear that unity, whether it is in the church or in the universe, is wholly dependent upon agreement about the Trinity and the Incarnation as necessary for proper faith and for a correct understanding of the nature of the universe. It is in these two areas (in our understanding of the universe and in the organization of the church) where his passion for unity and a unitary view is most obvious.

The Trinity, in Newbigin's thinking, represents and models the relational aspect of life, exemplified on earth by the community of faith because God has revealed himself (and truth about himself) to humanity through relationship and community. Significant for Newbigin is the idea that truth is personal, not abstract and propositional. It is personal because it comes from God. Consequently, truth never stands alone but is always in relation to God. The Incarnation of Christ is the supreme example of God's involvement in the material world. The Incarnation of Christ brings eternity and temporality together where the spiritual and material are intertwined.

---

111. He argues earlier that scientific analysis takes that which is whole and breaks it down, but it cannot create "the experience of meaningfulness and value in the original object." "I Believe," Newbigin, in *I Believe*, ed. M. A. Thomas (Madras: SCM, 1946), 80.

The cosmos is not a purely mechanistic universe that slavishly follows rigid laws; it is a place where God and humanity meet.[112]

Newbigin redefines apologetics in two general ways, one being negative and the other positive. On the negative side, there are three things he will *not* do. First, his approach is not to answer the questions of the world. The gospel, he believes, must first be heard on its own terms.[113] Second, he seeks dialogue with various worldviews, with the willingness to learn but not to change his core convictions. The apologist is just an obedient witness. He writes in *The Open Secret* that "this [willingness to dialogue with people of other faiths] does not mean that the purpose of dialogue is to persuade the non-Christian partner to accept the Christianity of the Christian partner . . . The purpose of dialogue for the Christian is obedient witness to Jesus Christ."[114] Third, his approach is not to persuade through rational demonstration. He says that his method is confession. "It is a personal commitment to a faith that cannot be demonstrated on grounds established from the point of view of another commitment."[115] Newbigin states the 'starting point' for his apologetic in this way:

> We cannot accept the position that the ultimate norms for our thinking are provided by 'what modern men and women believe.' Our starting point is God's revelation of himself in Jesus Christ as this is testified in the Bible.[116]

---

112. "The Gospel," he writes, "comes to us not as a set of propositions which I can lay hold of and so stand as one who knows the truth among the multitude who do not, but rather as a truth which has laid hold on me." "I Believe," in *I Believe*, Newbigin, ed. M. A. Thomas (Madras: SCM, 1946), 75. "It [personal knowledge] cannot be apprehended in the way that a scientific theorem is apprehended. It can only be apprehended in the dimension of obedience and action, the dimension of the personal," ibid., 90. When asked the question: "But why should you choose on perspective rather than the other?" the only answer can be "You don't choose: you are chosen." "Context and Conversion," Newbigin *IRM* 68 (1979), 304.

113. Wainwright, *Theological Life*, 338.

114. Newbigin, *Open Secret*, 182. This statement seems contrary to his work as a missionary. Yet, a further look at the passage, seen within the context of Newbigin's thinking, reveals that it is not the apologist who persuades; it is God who persuades. The apologist is not witnessing to cause the other person to accept Christianity; it is God speaking through the apologist so that the person accepts God.

115. Ibid., 15.

116. Newbigin, *Honest Religion*, 42.

On the positive side, he believes, first of all, that an appropriate apologetic is confession or witness. His motivation is clear: "I have been laid hold of by Another and commissioned to do so." He continues:

> By ways that are mysterious to me, that I can only faintly trace, I have been laid hold of by one greater than I and led into a place where I must make this confession and where I find no way of making sense of my own life or the life of the world except through being an obedient disciple of Jesus.[117]

Newbigin's experience as a young student involved in an attempt to improve the social situation in the Rhondda Valley proves to be fundamental to his understanding of 'being laid hold of by Another.' A part of that confirming vision of the sufficiency of the cross of Christ is a statement that he makes regarding 'making sense of reality.' This idea finds its way into numerous places in Newbigin's writings. In *Journey into Joy* (1972), in an explicit reference to the Rhondda Valley experience, he testifies that the cross of Christ is a "reality great enough to span the distance between heaven and hell, and to hold in one embrace all the variety of humankind, the one reality that could make sense of the human situation."[118] This experience becomes the basis of his apologetic confession. He firmly believed that his commitment to the Christian view of the world was based on that fact that it is "an interpretation of the whole human experience more reasonable than any other."[119] Most importantly for Newbigin, "it authenticates itself as a true contact with reality."[120]

Another positive aspect of his apologetic is the necessity of confession in the public arena. Wainwright states that "Newbigin saw the task of the Christian apologist as to contend for the 'public truth' of the Gospel."[121] Wainwright says that for Newbigin, "it was the apologist's business to maintain the validity of the claims of Christ and the Gospel and to defend and advocate their universal range and scope."[122] Newbigin believes that

---

117. Newbigin, *Open Secret*, 17.

118. Newbigin, *Journey into Joy*, 14.

119. The source of this quote is Wainwright, page 337. It appears in an article Newbigin wrote for the *Spectator* ("Can I be Christian?") in 1938.

120. Newbigin, *Honest Religion*, 98.

121. Wainwright, *Theological Life*, 336.

122. Ibid., 336.

"confession implies a claim regarding the entire public life of mankind and the whole created world."[123]

Wainwright sees Newbigin as a role model for those who seek to engage culture in the future. In a summary statement about Newbigin's intellectual abilities, Wainwright sees value in Newbigin as a person to be consulted in future attempts to commend the gospel in culture:

> Throughout his life, his analytical penetration, his conceptual power, and his mental ability ensured the intellectual quality of his practical wisdom, and his ideas remain to be drawn upon by all those who still engage as he did in the task of commending the Gospel and defending the Christian faith.[124]

REDEFINING THE FOCUS OF THEOLOGY

As Newbigin began preparing for a course on the theology of mission at Selly Oak, he realized that 'theology of mission' meant many things to many people. So he set out to develop his own theology of mission, and this became the basis of his book *The Open Secret*. His theology of mission, however, is much broader than this book, since his post-1974 corpus of writing essentially sets forth his theology of mission to the Western world. His theological convictions, developed earlier, are recast into a theology of mission because this is what confrontation with Western culture required.

Newbigin's passion is to convince the church of its need for mission, something which is assumed by churches outside the West but not generally by those within Western culture. The Western church, he contends, bases its understanding of the church on the 'Constantinian' or 'Christendom' model. He seeks to convince the church to be freed from its captivity to the 'Christendom model.' "Newbigin developed insights," writes Wilbert Shenk, "from philosophy, history, sociology, and science to create a compelling analysis of the present situation, but his framework was theological and missiological."[125]

"Newbigin's mode of discourse," Shenk observes, "was theological, even though he consistently disclaimed any pretension to being a professional theologian."[126] Shenk reflects on the reason Newbigin's theology is

123. Newbigin, *Open Secret*, 16.
124. Wainwright, *Theological Life*, iv.
125. Shenk, "Lesslie Newbigin's Contribution," 152.
126. Ibid., 59.

hard to categorize: "The categories of theology and missiology are almost wholly irrelevant. Newbigin's theology is thoroughly missiological, and his missiology theological."[127] However, these categories are not "almost wholly irrelevant" if his work is categorized as a theology of mission.

Charles Van Engen says that the discipline of theology of mission was set in place by the publication of the book *The Theology of the Christian Mission*, edited by Gerald Anderson.[128] Newbigin, in the "Foreword" to Anderson's book, states his reason for his interest in theology of mission:

> The theology of the Christian mission is no longer a subject for specialists or enthusiasts. It has become a subject in which everyone who wishes to reflect seriously about the task of the Church in our time must interest himself. For the Church is now, in a sense which has not been true for many centuries, in a missionary situation everywhere.[129]

There is, however, some confusion regarding terminology, evidenced both in Van Engen's book and Shenk's article. Both tend to interchange "theology of mission" and "mission theology" with Van Engen showing a preference for "mission theology."[130] The 'theology of mission' terminology will be kept throughout this book for the sake of clarity.

Newbigin's theology of mission culminates in his ecclesiology, where he envisions the church as the instrument of mission to Western culture, including the radical conversion of the Western mind and the implementation of a new plausibility structure for the West. One aspect of Western thinking that particularly troubled Newbigin was the division of church and mission. Such a separation is, to Newbigin, theologically indefensible.[131] Newbigin was also troubled by the extent to which Western

---

127. Shenk, "Lesslie Newbigin's Contribution," 60.

128. Nashville: Abingdon, 1961. Van Engen's statement about this book being the first textbook of the discipline is found in *Mission on the Way*, 18. It is not that that this book by Anderson was the first theology of mission written, but it opened the door for theology of mission to become a part of the theological curriculum. Gustav Warneck is credited with writing the first theology of mission titled *Evangelische Missionslehre* (Gotha, 1897). Joseph Schmidlin wrote a theology of mission for Catholics in 1923 titled *Katholische Missionslehre* (Münster, 1923).

129. Newbigin, "Foreword," *Theology of the Christian Mission*, xi.

130. Van Engen, *Mission on the Way*, 17.

131. Newbigin, *Open Secret*, 60.

theologians have failed to challenge the assumptions of Western culture, failing therefore to influence culture's plausibility structure.[132]

DEFINING THEOLOGY OF MISSION

Generally, a theology of mission is an attempt to discuss mission from a theological perspective. David Bosch describes theology of mission as "the relationship between God and the world in light of the Gospel"[133] on the one hand, while it is a study of the "foundation, the motive and the aim of mission"[134] on the other. Roger Bassham offers a more specific definition of theology of mission: "[It] refers to those theological presuppositions, statements and principles which critically reflect upon and explicate God's purpose for the church in relation to the world."[135]

J. Andrew Kirk, in his book *Theology and the Third World Church*, insists that the permanent calling of the church is "to reflect theologically on its mission."[136] The goal and purpose of theological study and reflection, in the context of a theology of mission, is to provide guidance for the church in mission and to articulate theological convictions that can be implemented and incorporated into the methods, policy and strategy of the church in mission. Robert Calvin Guy writes:

> Mission arises from theological foundations. It is a projection of basic theological beliefs. Its vigor and form reveal what it is based on... Dynamic, growing churches do not spring from enfeebled or distorted theological roots. If the missionary enterprise, proliferating into many cultural and economic activities, would safe-guard its life, it must look closely to its theological foundations and make certain that they are found in the New Testament, commanded by Christ, and demonstrated in the growing churches of the 19 hundred years of church history.[137]

A theology of mission needs to be a well-thought-out, well-constructed, reasonably correlated discussion of the mission of God and the church's relationship to that mission. Arthur Glasser states that "never

---

132. Ibid., 152.
133. Bosch, *Witness to the World*, 10.
134. Ibid., 21.
135. Bassham, *Mission Theology*, 7.
136. Kirk, *Theology and the Third World Church*, 38.
137. Guy, "Theological Foundations," 56.

has there been such intense debate and radical difference of opinion within the church over the nature of her mission."[138] David Bosch feels that a crisis in mission is not unusual and is to be expected. The missionary enterprise "because of its very nature and being, will always be in dispute."[139] Missionary work, he says, in all situations, times, and places will be 'ambivalent.' The work of mission is never 'self-evident,' nor is it ever fully understood or devoid of confusion even though we have reflected upon it theologically.[140] He calls for the church to deal with issues appropriately:

> Merely repeating vigorous affirmations of the validity of the Christian mission without seeking to take the full measure of the present crisis in mission into account, would . . . certainly be culpable in God's sight.[141]

Theology of mission, then, is "a true correlation between mental and functional aspects" in mission.[142] What keeps theology of mission from being overly theoretical or merely a reiteration of practical methodology without any well thought out theological foundation is that it is "theology for action and theology in action . . . Paul, the greatest theologian of the Christian world, created his parts of the New Testament canon in the white heat of missionary expansion."[143]

Emil Brunner reminds us that

> . . . it is one thing to proclaim Christ to the world . . . it is quite another thing to remind the Church of the paramount importance of this duty and to urge her to fulfill it. Whatever else may be the task of theology, this is certainly its primary duty.[144]

It would certainly be the task of a theology of mission and it is very much a part of Newbigin's theology of mission to the Western world.

---

138. Found in Bassham, *Mission Theology*, xiii.
139. Bosch, *Witness*, 9.
140. Bosch, *Witness*, 10.
141. Ibid., 9.
142. Guy, "Theological Foundations," 42.
143. Ibid.
144. Brunner, *Mediator*, 14.

SOURCES OF NEWBIGIN'S POST-1974 THEOLOGICAL THOUGHT

Before engaging Newbigin's thought, it is good to provide the reader with some conceptual tools to more clearly discern Newbigin's unique theological approach to Western culture. While Newbigin draws on the thinking of numerous persons, he most specifically utilizes the thinking and writings of the following three persons, especially the latter two. Karl Barth is presented because of a particular view of Western culture that likely set the stage for Newbigin's thinking after reading Barth. The influence of Charles Cochrane and Michael Polanyi are much more apparent, as the reader will discover.

The Influence of Karl Barth

Reference has already been made to Karl Barth and the relation of his thought to Newbigin. As one reads Newbigin's theological writings, an occasional phrase will cause the reader to recognize the influence of Karl Barth on Newbigin. Newbigin's first attempt at reading Barth was quite unsatisfactory, yet his association with Barth over the years and his reading of Barth in the summer of his retirement in Edinburgh had an apparent influence on Newbigin's thinking. The influence of Barth is not always obvious and certainly not comprehensive. There is, however, some evidence that Newbigin shared some assumptions about Western culture with Barth.

In Barth's article "Evangelical Theology in the Nineteenth Century," there is a perspective that is shared by both Barth and Newbigin. This perspective has to do with the effect of culture on theology (and Christianity) in the eighteenth and nineteenth centuries. Barth comments:

> Nineteenth-century theology was burdened with the heritage of the eighteenth century. There was an all-pervasive rationalism and a retreat of vital or would be vital Christianity into undergrounds of many kinds.[145]

Newbigin believed that the church accepted this "all-pervasive rationalism" and also was guilty of retreating from the public arena, which has led to Christianity being considered strictly a private matter.

---

145. Barth, *The Humanity*, 15.

Barth's contention is that theologians, feeling the pressure of the eighteenth century Enlightenment, sought to prove the possibility of faith through the worldview of culture. This gave rise to the famous question: "Was it possible to win the 'gentiles' for the Christian cause by just accepting the 'gentile' point of view, in order to commend them to the Christian cause?"[146] Barth thinks not, and neither does Newbigin. The major error of Western Christianity, then, is that it has succumbed to the presuppositions of Enlightenment culture.

At one point in his short book *Truth and Authority in Modernity*, Newbigin refers to Barth in a discussion on faith. Faith, it is being said, is a gift of God and not the result of human achievement or autonomous reason.[147] Faith comes by the grace of God as does the revelation that faith recognizes and believes. Matters of faith, however, as an avenue of knowing provoke a deep hostility to the modern mind.[148]

When Newbigin mentions natural theology he is also indebted to Barth. Natural theology is rejected as an avenue of true knowledge of God because, as Newbigin states, it is "not merely a partial knowledge but is a distorted and misleading knowledge."[149] Natural theology attempts to use the methods dictated by Enlightenment critical thought to try to discover truth about God and is purported to be more reliable knowledge since it utilizes reason, a more dependable ground of assurance than God's own self-revelation in Jesus Christ. Obviously, Newbigin as well as Barth, would reject such a view. If humanity is to know God, it is only because God allows humanity to know him; it is a gift of God.[150]

The Influence of Charles Norris Cochrane

Newbigin was also influenced by classical historian and philosopher Charles Norris Cochrane. There are a number of ideas foundational to Newbigin's thinking about Augustine and the classical world that can be found in Cochrane. Newbigin explicitly mentions Cochrane in *The Other*

---

146. Ibid., 23.
147. Newbigin, *Truth and Authority*, 14.
148. Ibid., 15–17.
149. Ibid., 19.
150. Bowden, *Karl Barth*, 109.

Side of 1984 and alludes to Cochrane's thinking in his book *Truth to Tell*, even though he does not mention Cochrane's name.[151]

Cochrane's view is that the dominant influence of classical Greek philosophy was brought to an end (because it ceased to provide a workable philosophy for living) by Augustine's "post-critical philosophy." When Augustine put his faith in Christ and took the doctrine of the Trinity as a new starting point, it resulted in a radically new understanding of the cosmos. Quoting Isaiah 7:9, Augustine proclaims faith to be the starting point for knowledge (*credo ut intelligam*), not reason.[152] Michael Polanyi, noted scientist who became a philosopher of science, is another person who also recognizes Augustine's role in closing the classical age and inaugurating a new way of knowing, where belief precedes knowledge.[153]

Cochrane's argument is that the Early Christians radically revised the First Principles that were the foundations of the Classical Age of Western culture. These Early Christians devised a new set of first principles that had a more adequate cosmology and anthropology than classical culture, and their principles were able to answer the questions that the classical culture could not answer. In Christ, the *logos*, they believed they had found a principle of understanding and knowing far superior to anything that had existed in the classical world.[154] The Fourth Century church had a vision that included the regeneration of society by the acceptance of Christian truth. Such a vision would certainly resonate with Newbigin's passion for the conversion of Western culture. Since Newbigin insisted that the Enlightenment reintroduced into Western culture some of the problems classical culture had prior to Augustine's time, the cure for these problems would be the same—the re-acceptance of Augustinian thought. It would, Newbigin

---

151. Newbigin, *Other Side*, 24.

152. Ibid., 23–24. Frederick Mayer, in his book *A History of Ancient and Medieval Philosophy*, states that he believes that Augustine anticipates Descartes. Referring to *The City of God*, Book X, chapter 26, Mayer says: "Starting with his own existence, he explained why doubts verify beliefs." *History of Ancient and Medieval Philosophy*, Mayer (New York: The American Book Company, 1950), 358. Interestingly, Cochrane says that Augustine believed that 'next to myself, I know God,' which underlies the statement *crede ut intellegas*. *Christianity and Classical Culture*, Cochrane (London: Oxford University Press, 1944), 407. Newbigin does not pick up on this.

153. Polanyi, *Personal Knowledge*, 266.

154. Cochrane, *Christianity and Classical Culture*, vi.

believes, do away with classical dualism and give Western culture a more integrated and unified cosmology and epistemology.[155]

Cochrane recognizes the role Athanasius played in the reorientation of thought around Christian dogma. The replacement of the defective starting point of Graeco-Roman speculation began when Athanasius posited Trinitarianism as the first basic principle which was "inclusive enough to bear the weight of the conclusions derived from it."[156] The old Greek *arche* "was not found in nature or by pursuing the chain of natural causation to its limit."[157] Cochrane's analysis of the effect of the starting point is seen in these words:

> What he [Athanasius] offered them was an intellectual, no less than a moral and spiritual, release. This release was from the perplexities involved in pagan *scientia* and from the backwash of pagan obscurantism to which it inevitably led. It represented the fourth-century version of the promise: 'the truth shall make you free.'[158]

This Divine Principle was transcendent and immanent, "prior" to nature and yet operative within it as well.[159] From this perspective all of history could be conceived as the divine economy, the Spirit working in and through mankind.[160]

Since the Divine Principle integrated mankind with nature, they were no longer in conflict nor is the destiny of man the result of a mindless mechanism or capricious power external to mankind. The laws that govern humans and nature were also the laws of God.[161] The central idea of the Divine Economy was the Incarnation Principle. The redemption of mankind would be accomplished through the assumption of manhood by the Word of God. The invisible God would reveal Himself through the visible.[162] Instead of the invisible and the visible in dualistic relationship they are brought together and integrated in Christ. Athanasius created a strong foundation upon which Augustine would build.

---

155. Ibid., 359.
156. Ibid., 361–62.
157. Ibid., 362.
158. Cochrane, *Christianity and Classical Culture*, 363.
159. Ibid., 367.
160. Ibid., 367–68.
161. Ibid., 368.
162. Ibid., 369.

Missionary Theologian

Cochrane's description of Augustine's conversion (which was a radical turning from one life-style to another), and how this conversion worked out in his thinking, is what caught Newbigin's attention. Because of his conversion and embracing the Christian worldview, Augustine was able to see the deficiencies of Classicism, and come to a fuller understanding of man and the universe than Classicism could offer.[163] Augustine's view of faith is summed up in the dictum *fides quaerens intellectum*, which became the guiding maximum of his life.[164] "If faith precedes understanding," Cochrane writes, "understanding in turn becomes the reward of faith."[165] Augustine discovered a fresh foundation for his life and thought in the doctrine of the Trinity and his break with Classicism was quite radical.[166]

In Cochrane's discussion of the Trinitarian Principle, he explains that Augustine did not understand reality in terms of science (the classical word for knowledge) versus faith, but saw that faith was truly the precondition for both science and Christianity. In a lengthy passage, Cochrane lays out Augustine's view:

> The Trinitarian principle presents itself, not as a refinement of scientific intelligence, a tissue of metaphysical abstractions having no existence except in the imagination of theologians, but rather as an attempt to formulate what is 'imposed' upon the intelligence as the precondition of science; and its acceptance as such marks a rejection of the claim that the discursive reason can authenticate the presumptions which determine the nature and scope of its activity otherwise than in terms of their 'working and power.' Accordingly, the choice for man, as Augustine sees it, does not so much lie between science and superstition as between two kinds of faith, the one salutary, the other destructive, the one making for fulfillment, the other for frustration.[167]

Trinitarianism for Augustine was the quintessential starting point for all of life and thought. It provided a substantial basis for the true philosophy.

---

163. Cochrane, *Christianity and Classical Culture*, 368.

164. Ibid., 364.

165. Ibid., 400. Cochrane does not see *fides quaerens intellectum* as fideism. "In the case of Augustine . . . the revolt was not from scepticism to animal faith, a primitivism sustained by an arbitrary 'will to believe.'" 384.

166. Cochrane, *Christianity and Classical Culture*, 410.

167. Ibid., 412.

One also finds in Augustine the idea that the patterns of nature are comprehensible by the human mind. The human mind recognizes patterns in the materials in nature and, when looking outward, has the task of organizing these materials. Augustine calls this process of recognition and further organization *ratio scientiae*. *Ratio scientiae* is the rational apprehension of the temporal, which is the work of science. Reason, working in this manner, seeks to grasp what nature shows the mind. Both faith and reason are involved in science and religious belief, as they are in the many arenas of a unified life. Newbigin understands this to mean that since God is the creator of nature and the human mind, there would naturally be a correlation between the two.

Ratio sapientiae is also described as a "function" of reason (*actio rationlis*). It seeks to discover the creative principle upon which the possibility of reasoning ultimately depends. This principle facilitates the grasping of the "rules of wisdom" that are true and unchangeable, as are the principles of mathematics. So, for Augustine, reason probes the temporal world *and* the eternal world, and for one to be able to do science in the modern sense, both are necessary components of a true scientific approach.[168] This idea dispenses with the dualism of the classical world that put the temporal and eternal into two distinct categories because, in Augustine, there is an integration of the eternal with the temporal.

Augustine thought of himself as a member of the church and a possessor of truth as a part of this public body. In no way did he see his insights merely as private knowledge: he was merely a part of a greater whole.[169] One can see in Newbigin a similar need to see Christian truth as public truth and not as one's private possession only.

Augustine's new standard of objectivity, in contrast to the one proposed by classical *scientia*, was history. Augustine envisioned history as "a progressive disclosure of the creative and moving principle."[170] It ultimately depended upon the acknowledgement that the historic Christ embodied the "final and full revelation of the divine nature and activity."[171] Augustine's focus was on Jesus the mediator, the answer to the secular quest for a *logos*. Augustine's understanding of *logos* was that

---

168. Cochrane, *Christianity and Classical Culture*, 414.
169. Ibid., 416.
170. Ibid.
171. Ibid.

> ... through the revelation of God as the one supreme substance (*summa substantis*) underlying and sustaining all things visible and invisible; hence the source of actuality, truth, and value; capable ... of producing novelty without innovation of the will, and with potentialities which were inexhaustible.[172]

Augustine's vision of the Godhead constituted a new theory of the relationship between the body and the soul. Christ became the foundation of a new physics in that it solved the problem of dualism deeply embedded in classical thought.[173] Accepting Christ as Incarnate was important for a new theory of knowledge because it did away with the platonic idea of transcendent truth, and also affirmed the concepts of human science. God's truth and will could be revealed and understood in the world, through historical events. In the search for a principle of intelligibility, Augustine found his answer in the abandonment of the *logos* of Plato for the *logos* of Christ.[174] Augustine, therefore, saw this approach to knowledge as excluding the need for skepticism. Academic doubt was academic madness.[175]

As a result of the new interpretation of life under the Trinitarian principle, Augustine developed a unitary view of life. Life is seen as a whole, and not as an eternal dualism with a chasm between the spirit and the material. One evidence of this unitary vision (as mentioned earlier) is Augustine's understanding of *actio rationalis*, or the capacity for ordered knowledge that is peculiar to mankind. It ordered knowledge because it is the result of a reasoning mind dependent upon the creative principle (the *logos*), in correspondence with an ordered universe.[176] There is also continuity between what Augustine calls the "interior" and the "exterior of man:" There is an awareness of objects external to oneself while at the same time one is aware of being aware.[177] The world "out there" and the world "within" are not contrary to each other but are profoundly connected.

Mankind and the universe are expressions of the creative principle, which is also an expression of beneficent activity. This creative principle is the *summa substantia* which "manifests itself in the orderly movement of the cosmos and the source of truth, beauty, and goodness as these are

---

172. Ibid., 417.
173. Ibid.
174. Cochrane, *Christianity and Classical Culture*, 470.
175. Ibid., 431.
176. Ibid., 433.
177. Ibid.

progressively disclosed in the consciousness of mankind."[178] The world of nature is the theater of divine activity, pointing to a unitary view of reality where heaven and earth, God and mankind, body and soul are interconnected, and reflect a holistic view of reality rather than a dualistic view.

Also of concern to Augustine was the proper view of history. History is not cyclical as it was conceived to be in classical idealism, which had "a belief in the endless reiteration 'typical' situations, a belief which does the . . . injustice to the unique character and significance of the historical event."[179] Human history "does not consist of a series of repetitive patterns, but marks a sure, if unsteady, advance to an ultimate goal."[180] Newbigin sees the similarity of the classical view of history to the Asian view, both of which see history as cyclical. Newbigin believes that an Augustine-like conversion would correct Western culture's tendency to gravitate back to the classical and Asian view of history.

Related to history is the concept of time and space. Augustine's new orientation led to clear views of time and space. In Christianity, time is not a "thing" or an illusion. It is an "order of becoming," real and irreversible. Time is the sequence and space is the pattern in which events present themselves to human consciousness.[181] The concrete principle of interpretation for Christian historiography is the *logos*—the Christ who has come into this world.[182] The *logos* of Christ introduces a new principle of unity and division into human history and life.[183]

Since Newbigin makes specific reference to Cochrane's book, and because of Newbigin's belief that what modern Western culture needs is a radical conversion to a viewpoint like that of Augustine, one would have to conclude that it was Cochrane's book that provided the main interpretative viewpoint from which Newbigin's vision of a radically changed Western culture is derived.

---

178. Ibid., 436.
179. Ibid., 483.
180. Ibid., 484.
181. Cochrane, *Christianity and Classical Culture*, 482.
182. Ibid., 480.
183. Ibid., 487.

Missionary Theologian
The Influence of Michael Polanyi

Michael Polanyi further confirmed and solidified Newbigin's viewpoint, complementing Cochran's thought. The influence of Polanyi on Newbigin, in fact, is considerable. Polanyi, in turn, was powerfully influenced by J. H. Oldham. Polanyi acknowledges that Oldham expanded his intellectual concerns at a time when Polanyi's philosophical views and interests were broadening to include religion and culture. Polanyi's views were further shaped both by a group of intellectuals Oldham convened called the "Moot."[184]

Because of Germany's increasingly hostile view against Jews, Polanyi moved from the Kaiser Wilhem Institut for Fibre Chemistry in Berlin to the University of Manchester in 1933. While his area of interest was initially physical chemistry (he had been elected to the Chair of physical chemistry at Manchester), his interests changed to the philosophical assumptions of science.[185]

It was then that Polanyi's views regarding science began to change. With his move from practical science to philosophy of science, he began to challenge some of the most sacred assumptions held by scientists and Western culture. He set out to create a more realistic picture of what actually takes place within the scientific community. Some of his potent themes include the ideas that science is not neutral, that absolute objectivity is a delusion, that faith or belief is an essential part of the scientific process, that all knowledge is personal knowledge, that there is a tacit dimension to all knowing, that intuition plays a significant role in science, and that as a person indwells the plausibility structure of science one is able to move beyond it into another paradigm—one that cannot be explained by the previous paradigm. Polanyi writes:

> The popular conception of the scientist patiently collecting observations, unprejudiced by any theory, until he finally succeeds in establishing a great new generalization, is quite false.[186]

Polanyi is even more explicit in his refutation of the belief that there is complete objectivity in science. He comments: "complete objectivity as usually attributed to the exact sciences is a delusion."[187]

---

184. Mullins, "Michael Polanyi and J. H. Oldham," 179.
185. Puddefoot, *Michael Polanyi*, 1.
186. Polanyi, *Science, Faith, and Society*, 28.
187. Polanyi, Personal Knowledge, 18.

Faith, belief, and a critical presupposition play a role in science as well as in religion. Scientists profess faith in the continued progress of science as well as the "integrity of scientists in applying and amending their principles."[188] Polanyi believes that objectivism has misled Western culture in its search for truth. If our minds are restricted to only what is demonstrable, we fail to recognize the "a-critical choices which determine the whole being of our minds and has rendered us incapable of acknowledging these vital choices."[189]

Real knowledge is always personal because scientists are persons and personally participate in all acts of knowledge. Just because there is personal participation in knowing does not make it subjective because scientific knowledge is establishing contact with an objective, external reality. Polanyi is best known for his concept of "personal knowledge," which is, he says, a fusion of the personal and the objective.[190] Polanyi's concept of the tacit dimension of knowing and the role of intuition further support his view that all knowledge is personal.[191] Evidence of the tacit assumption in science is the assumption of an ordering principle and orderliness in reality.[192] "Science is a system of beliefs to which we are committed."[193]

Polanyi's concept of indwelling, which means that one accepts, commits to, and works within the parameters of a particular view, is significant in that he asserts that persons generally indwell a fiduciary framework uncritically. It is necessary to indwell some fiduciary framework in order to be able to know.[194] However, Polanyi sees the development of scientific truth happening within a structure of authority that every scientist indwells but must, if the new evidence requires, move beyond where the logic of the accepted fiduciary framework would allow. Polanyi describes it as "a transformation of the framework on which we rely in the process of formal reasoning. It is the crossing of a logical gap to another shore, where we shall never see things as we did before."[195] This would be described by Thomas Kuhn as a "paradigm shift" and by Newbigin as "conversion."

188. Polanyi, *Science, Faith, and Society*, 16.
189. Polanyi, *Personal Knowledge*, 286.
190. Polanyi, *Personal Knowledge*, viii, 286.
191. Polanyi, *Science, Faith, and Society*, 10.
192. Polanyi, *Personal Knowledge*, 34–35.
193. Ibid., 171.
194. Ibid., 59, 195.
195. Ibid., 189.

Newbigin sees what happens in the scientific community as analogous to what happens in the church when persons are converted to faith in Christ, initiating a whole new way of seeing the world.

Polanyi calls for the Western world (at least its scientists) to go back to Augustine to restore the proper balance in understanding our cognitive powers.[196] Polanyi recognizes the great heritage of the Enlightenment which has "enriched us . . . to an extent unrivalled by any period of similar duration."[197] This critical movement, however, seems to be nearing the end of its course: "But its incandescence has fed on the combustion of the Christian heritage in the oxygen of Greek rationalism, and when this fuel was exhausted the critical framework itself burnt away."[198] In Polanyi's view Augustine initiated a post-critical philosophy, and taught that all knowledge was really a gift of God. Consequently, we work under the guidance of antecedent belief. He quotes Augustine (*De libero Arbitrio*, Book I, par 4): *nisi credideritis, non intelligitis*—unless you believe you will not understand.[199] Polanyi seeks Augustine's support for restoring "the power for the deliberate holding of unproven beliefs."[200] Augustine's thinking ruled the minds of Christian scholars for a thousand years, but then faith declined and it was replaced by knowledge that is true if it can be demonstrated. Commenting on the thinking of John Locke, Polanyi describes the attitude that exemplified the change in Western epistemology:

> Belief is here no longer a higher power that reveals to us knowledge lying beyond the range of observation and reason, but a mere personal acceptance which falls short of empirical and rational demonstrability.[201]

Where once belief and reason were seen as two compatible aspects of the cognitive faculties, the two are now broken apart, and the latter is exalted while the former is discredited. Belief was shunted off to the category of subjectivity. Polanyi, however, believed that the scientific community (and Western culture as a whole) must recognize belief as the source of all

---

196. Ibid., 266.
197. Ibid.
198. Ibid.
199. Polanyi, *Personal Knowledge*, 266.
200. Ibid., 268.
201. Ibid., 266.

knowledge, which would essentially reinstate Augustine's understanding of human cognition.

CONCLUSION

This chapter has set the stage for the rest of the book by providing the context in which Newbigin began to recognize the need for a missionary confrontation with Western culture and began to develop his core conviction on how this was to be done. As he becomes aware of the critical need of Western culture and the crisis that it is experiencing in regard to its epistemology and its dependence upon Western science to formulate its belief system, Newbigin finds help in his quest for an answer to Western culture's problem is the writings of Karl Barth, Charles Cochrane, and Michael Polanyi. There writings give him valuable conceptual tools and a perspective from which to develop his theology of mission.

3

Grasping Truth and Reality

Beginnings of Newbigin's Theology

THROUGHOUT HIS CAREER, NEWBIGIN wrote on such theological topics as the doctrine of God, the Trinity, the doctrine of creation, Christology, sin and salvation, the church, and so forth. George Hunsberger observes:

> A survey of Newbigin's thought makes it obvious that at the most basic levels the major concerns to which he tended to give theological attention and the major insights which lie at the heart of his reflections were to a remarkable degree formed during his early years, particularly those spent as an undergraduate at Cambridge, as a staff worker for the SCM in Scotland, and at Cambridge again as a theological student.[1]

Newbigin steadfastly maintains his evangelical faith from his earliest years until his death in 1998. As his mind engaged Western culture, he would bring these theological convictions forward to meet the challenge of the new context, shaping the core presuppositions that would become the grid by which he evaluates modern Western Enlightenment culture.

GRASPING TRUTH: ULTIMATE REALITY AS KNOWABLE

The Development of Newbigin's View of Revelation

As early as 1936, while studying at Westminster College, Cambridge, Newbigin set out some of the main themes of his theological agenda in a paper on "Revelation."[2] In this paper can be found, in kernel form,

1. Hunsberger, *Bearing the Witness*, 37.
2. Theology paper presented at Westminster College, Cambridge, 1936.

Newbigin's particular view of God's revelation, and how these insights carry over into other theological concerns, particularly epistemology. He discusses such topics as the relationship between reason and revelation, the relationship between faith and revelation, and the contrast of theological dogma with the dogmatism of scientism. Revelation is, as Newbigin understands it, essentially the self-disclosure of God, so it is personal and focused on relationship rather than on the acquisition of abstract knowledge. It cannot be acquired through human reason alone, but is given to humanity by God, primarily through God's acts and activities in history. In the section on "The Patristic View of Revelation,"[3] Newbigin says that the Patristic writers appealed to certain evidences that validated that what happened at a particular time and place was indeed the revelation of God. Newbigin identifies this as the "self-evidencing power and sublimity of revelation" that is due to its "intrinsic grandeur and compelling rightness."[4] It is so compelling that "common men are capable of recognizing the divine revelation when they see it," as all the faculties of man lay hold of revelation "in the venture of faith."[5] Faith is the response to the divine self-disclosure, and that response sets up the possibility for revelation to be received.[6] Newbigin is not saying that humanity is capable naturally of recognizing divine revelation: the Holy Spirit is involved in this whole process, as we shall see subsequently. He is emphasizing at this point the human responsibility to respond to God.

Even though the Church Fathers point to evidence that validated what had happened was revelation, this revelation, he insists, is 'self-evidencing.' Newbigin does not say in what way it is self-evidencing, except that it 'seemed right' in some compelling way. It is compelling, one might say, to one who has faith. The Church Fathers had faith and believed because what they saw was validated by evidences. There is both the external events that take place in history testified to by witnesses and the internal confirmation by the Spirit that a particular event was truly a revelation from God. The external event and the internal confirmation are interconnected and not two separate paths to revelation.

---

3. Ibid., 23–26
4. Ibid., 25.
5. Ibid.
6. Ibid., 31.

Grasping Truth and Reality

Even from his student days it appears that Newbigin is dealing intellectually with the dualistic tendency that runs through Western culture. In the Middle Ages, theologians thought that the two bearers of revelation were the church (that interpreted the faith by means of the thought of Aristotle) and the Bible, representing *reason* and *revelation* respectively. According to Newbigin, although Augustine and Anselm did not draw the line sharply between reason and revelation, Aquinas did, thus causing the separation of these two spheres, which facilitated a movement back toward the dualism from which Augustine and Anselm had saved the church.[7]

In 1937, Newbigin reiterates his perspective on revelation, but in this case it is more specifically related to knowing God's will. He says that "we can only know it by a personal self-communication of God, something which comes from beyond nature, something in the strict sense supernatural."[8]

In 1946, in his article entitled "I Believe,"[9] Newbigin adds new elements deemed to press home his point and to provide more substance to his view on revelation. His *personalistic* view of revelation becomes evident in this piece of writing. Real knowledge, he writes, is only real knowledge if this knowing is our own.[10] Any knowledge of God is possible only if he chooses to reveal himself to humanity, and this revelation of himself must be received and accepted in trust.[11]

Knowledge of the gospel is wholly dependent for its meaning and content on certain historical events that are apprehended by our minds because humanity has been given the capacity to "recognize and respond to the personal," a capacity that is "in the very structure of our beings as persons."[12] He further clarifies these assertions by saying that the Bible cannot be understood "except by the inner witness of the Holy Spirit."[13] It is evident when reading Newbigin, especially in his earlier writings, that the Holy Spirit plays a critical role in knowing God and God's self-revelation. However, in a chapter in his book *Honest Religion for Secular Man* titled

---

7. Theology paper presented at Westminster College, Cambridge, 1936, 27.
8. Newbigin, *Christian Freedom*, 61.
9. Newbigin, "I Believe," 73–88.
10. Ibid., 73.
11. Ibid., 82–83.
12. Ibid., 83–84.
13. Ibid., 87.

"Knowing God,"[14] he does not explicitly mention the Holy Spirit, nor does he explicitly make reference to the Holy Spirit in much of his later writings. It is apparent, however, that his view of the work of the Holy Spirit in knowing God and reality is implicit to his theological thinking, but that he does not always state this explicitly.

Revelation, according to Newbigin, has the task of conveying the fact that there is purpose to our existence and that this purpose is "now wholly real in the will of the living God." It will not be fully realized in the present, however; a full understanding will come in the future.[15] At this point, Newbigin connects revelation and eschatology, emphasizing that what we apprehend now will not be known with absolute certainty until the end when all things will be known. We must now live by faith with reasonable assurance because our faith is in One who has come and who will come again.

The subject of 'infallible certainty' is an intellectual concern that comes up in his book *The Reunion of the Church* (1948).[16] His discussion revolves around the idea that people assert that if God gave revelation about himself, surely it would be done in such a way that it would be "infallibly certain of what that revelation is."[17] Somewhere in the Bible, the Creeds, or in the church, there *must* be, some would say, a standard of reference that would allow a person to know with infallible certainty what is the truth, and "it would be inconsistent with the character of God if that were not so."[18] Newbigin repudiates this sort of thinking, stating that there is no such certainty or infallible revelation that would "over-ride man's fallible insights." Such revelation is accepted and apprehended by faith and that it is risky.[19]

Revelation is mediated through the testimony of the witnesses to God's acts in history. "We believe . . . their testimony" and it is "the only basis of our knowledge."[20] This statement, coming so early in his career, is very significant for understanding Newbigin because it shows how we can

---

14. Newbigin, *Honest Religion*, 77–99.
15. Newbigin, "I Believe in Christ," 111.
16. This is his excellent apologetic for the union of various churches in South India.
17. Newbigin, *Reunion*, 126.
18. Ibid.
19. Ibid.
20. Ibid., 134.

know 'the facts' or truth of our faith and this becomes the first evidence of his approach to Western culture's epistemological problem.

In the William Belden Noble Lectures at Harvard University in 1958 (published as *A Faith for this One World?* in 1961), Newbigin presents a large amount of material on the presuppositions and content of Christ's revelation. One of the presuppositions discussed under the topic "The Biblical Doctrine of Creation" is the fact that God is a Creator God, an idea that does not seem so radical in the world of religions. However, when it is asserted that all things were created through Jesus Christ and that he is the "cause and cornerstone of the universe," it becomes a radical statement and one that distinguishes Christianity from other world religions. The One who wishes to reveal himself to humanity is also the Creator, and he has revealed himself most fully through Christ, whose humanity becomes the real point of contact between God and humanity.[21]

The second major presupposition discussed under the topic of "The Biblical Doctrine of Sin" is that "mankind is a fallen race," a truth and reality that precipitated God's need to reveal himself, both as judge and Savior.[22] The third presupposition is "The Biblical Doctrine of Election." At this point, he departs from the traditional Reformed exposition of this doctrine and focuses on its missiological implications. God chooses *one* to be the means of sharing the truth with *the many*. God chose ancient Israel for the sake of bringing salvation to the nations.[23]

The content of God's self-revelation is salvific. The kingdom of God is invading the world and the kingdom is being brought into the world through Christ.[24] The reason for the coming kingdom is to bring salvation to humanity. Those who believe in Christ and become a part of his kingdom become involved in his church. They are the first fruit of the Holy Spirit, and, as a community of those who have faith in Christ, are elected for mission to the world.[25]

In the book *Honest Religion for Secular Man* (1966), Newbigin repeats some of his earlier ideas. He includes a discussion of the Bible, universal history, and revelation, noting that these three important topics are inti-

---

21. Newbigin, *A Faith*, 63–67.
22. Ibid., 68ff.
23. Ibid., 77ff.
24. Ibid., 84ff.
25. Ibid., 87ff.

mately bound together. God has acted in history and these acts were witnessed to by individuals and nations, which is recorded in the Bible. It is this self-revelation of God as witnessed to in the Bible that opens the way for contemporary people to know God and reality.[26] Newbigin explains:

> Man can know God only in so far as God manifests himself in events which are accessible to man's observation and which are interpreted as God's doing. These events will enable man to know God in so far as man grasps them as occasions for trusting God and obeying him. Without this response there is no personal knowledge.[27]

Newbigin is very consistent in his insistence that God reveals himself, not in propositional statements of truth, but in what he *does*. God's personhood and character are revealed through his actions, and these actions have been observable in history.[28] At this point it is possible that Newbigin presses his point too far, because God did speak to individuals at times in propositional statements. It would appear that Newbigin is reacting against the idea that God's primary revelation of himself was in timeless and abstract statements. This, obviously, is not the case.

Newbigin's view of revelation also includes the idea that God has given us something radically new and unique:

> Something radically new has been given, something which cannot be derived from rational reflection on the experiences available to all people. It is a new fact, to be received in faith as a gift of grace. And what is thus given claims to be the truth, not just a possible opinion. It is the rock which must either become the foundation of all knowing and doing, or else the stone on which one stumbles and falls to disaster. Those who, through no wit or wisdom or godliness of their own, have been entrusted with the message can in no way demonstrate its truth on the basis of some other alleged certainties: they can only live by it and announce it.[29]

Newbigin had already articulated his view of revelation clearly in his earlier discussion of Dutch missiologist Hendrik Kraemer's view of revelation. Kraemer made a sharp distinction between religion and revelation,

---

26. Newbigin, *A Faith*, 91.
27. Newbigin, *Honest Religion*, 94.
28. Ibid., 95.
29. Newbigin, *Gospel in a Pluralist Society*, 6.

Grasping Truth and Reality

with Christianity placed in the category of religion. Since Christianity belongs to the world of religions, it cannot claim finality or absoluteness. Christian revelation, on the other hand, is the record of God's disclosure in Jesus Christ, and is absolutely *sui generis*.[30] Kraemer's assertion of the discontinuity between Christian revelation and human religion seemed so absolute that it could not allow any dialogue between Christianity and other religions.[31] Newbigin views Christian revelation as radically discontinuous, unique and original, but not so far removed from the world that there are no bridges to other religions.[32] Newbigin prefers to speak of *radical discontinuity* rather than *total discontinuity* because of his experience in India where some who converted to Christianity testified that it was God who was dealing with them prior to their conversion:

> This element of continuity is confirmed in the experience of many who have become converts to Christianity from other religions. Even though this conversion involves a radical discontinuity, yet there is very often the strong conviction afterwards that it was the living and true God who was dealing with them in the days of their pre-Christian wrestling.[33]

In the same way that Newbigin viewed the relationship between revelation and religion, he sees the relationship between Christianity and culture-produced world religions. There is a radical but not total discontinuity because, as the Apostle Paul experienced as a Pharisee within Israel, it was the same God who was dealing with him before he became a Christian.[34] Newbigin recognizes that some aspects of Christianity and other religions are compatible, because God is working in the hearts of all humanity:

> It is a relationship both of continuity and discontinuity. The Gospel demands and affects a radical break with, and conversion from, the wisdom that is based upon other experiences; yet mature reflec-

---

30. Newbigin, *The Finality*, 34.
31. Ibid., 40.
32. Ibid., 59. Kraemer was articulating a Barthian position in his missiology, but it was a modified Barthianism. Kraemer did not hold to total discontinuity, although he still seemed to hold to a wider chasm between revelation and religion than Newbigin. For Kraemer's view, see *Christian Message*, 118–20.
33. Newbigin, *The Finality*, 59.
34. Ibid.

tion by those who have experienced this break suggests that it is the same God who has been dealing with them all along.[35]

While religions may be seen as the realm of darkness (and Newbigin expounds this position, as we shall see subsequently), Newbigin here reflects a generally positive view of world religions in his discussion of continuity and discontinuity. These two views are incompatible except, perhaps, that Newbigin recognizes that the Gospel can be perceived somehow by persons even in the realm of darkness. This would not be *total* discontinuity but certainly a *radical* one. In his thinking, to be *radically* different does not mean to be *totally* different. Total discontinuity would mean that there is no possibility of some element of God's revelation coming into contact with another religion, whereas radical discontinuity recognizes that persons in other religions may have been influenced by revelation and that somehow it became incorporated in their religious thought. In neither case is salvation through other religions possible.

In two capstone statements, Newbigin summarizes his view of revelation.

The first is made eight years before returning to Britain. "The disclosure of God in Jesus Christ," he writes in 1966, "is determinative of his [the Christian's] interpretation of all the events of history."[36] Just a couple of years prior to returning to Britain for retirement, he writes the following:

> God shows himself as Saviour in concrete events of history—secular events, if you like to put it so—such as the deliverance from Egypt and the return from Babylon; yet God, the Saviour, is more than the one who does these things, for to know him and to have fellowship with him is greater than all possible earthly blessings.[37]

Newbigin's Later View of Revelation

ULTIMATE REALITY AS KNOWABLE

Newbigin's years in India made him fully aware of the ancient, venerable tradition that ultimate reality is unknowable. It is true that the human mind is limited and cannot *fully* comprehend God, but the idea

---

35. Newbigin, *The Finality*, 60.
36. Ibid., 83.
37. Newbigin, "Address on the Main Theme," 2.

Grasping Truth and Reality

that God is unknowable has been used to deny that humans can know *any* truth about God. While the human mind cannot fully comprehend God, it does not rule out the possibility that God may have made himself known to humans to some degree, and that they bear witness to what has been revealed to them.[38] In relation to mission to the West, Newbigin asks a pertinent question: "How do we escape from the pure subjectivity into which Descartes has led us, from a situation in which we have lost confidence in our capacity to know things as they really are?"[39] Human capacity to know things as they are is wholly dependent upon God giving us that ability. God, Newbigin believes, has, through personal revelation, allowed humanity to encounter true reality. Ultimate reality, as Christians know it to be, is not an impersonal philosophical principle; it is ultimately personal.[40] The only response to personal ultimate reality is personal faith, as Newbigin explains:

> . . . if the ultimate reality with which, or rather with whom, we have to deal is the being of the triune God, then the response of personal faith is to a personal calling is the only way of knowing that reality. To rule this out as unreasonable is to make an "a priori" decision against the possibility that ultimate reality is personal.[41]

While Newbigin has been influenced by Buber, John Oman, and Polanyi[42] in regards to a personalistic orientation, it seems that it is Newbigin's years spent in India that inform him here. Monistic thinking, the idea of ultimate reality as impersonal, would be counterproductive for the West, Newbigin believes, since it leaves no place for a personal God who reveals truth about himself and the nature of reality. From his student days Newbigin resisted the cosmology science has limited itself to, because it perpetuates an impersonal notion of the universe.

Newbigin sees all knowing as an adventure, and knowing God would qualify as the supreme adventure that would take us beyond what we can

---

38. Newbigin, "Religious Pluralism," 51.

39. Newbigin, *Gospel in a Pluralist Society*, 33.

40. The influence of John Oman's personalism has been noted by Thomas, "The Centrality of Christ," 116.

41. Newbigin, *Proper Confidence*, 95.

42. He mentions both Buber and Oman in his writings as early as 1946. See Newbigin, "I Believe," 82, 84. Polanyi is first mentioned in Newbigin's writings in *Other Side* on page 28.

know in a way dictated by culture.[43] God has provided a way that humans can know him; he has revealed himself through nature and history.[44] Newbigin does not explain how God reveals himself through nature. The idea of orderliness and rationality would, of course, be a possible explanation. In any case, the person would need, as previously stated, the help of the Holy Spirit to recognize the revelation of God.[45]

Knowing God means to be encountered by God, which suggests that mankind, through this encounter, is capable of perceiving the God who meets humanity in space and time.[46] "It is from this self-revealing of God," writes Newbigin, "that men and women can learn to discern the evidences of his presence and work through their daily experience of the created world."[47] Newbigin does not hesitate to posit the gospel as a valid framework for interpretation of experience within the terms of the loving and wise purpose of God.[48] The value of religious experience, in Newbigin's view, is only evident if it enables a person to make sense of the rest of reality.[49]

Knowing Truth, Reality, and God

Newbigin sees revelation not as a communication of a body of timeless truths that allows humans to know the mind of God, but as a disclosure of the way God is leading the world and his people, the church. This idea is carried over from his early thinking, but is now re-affirmed in the context of Western culture. The Bible, he says, is all about promise and fulfillment, a record of the action of God in real history.[50] The Bible, therefore, is as relevant for Western culture as it is for Indian culture.

---

43. Newbigin, *Honest Religion*, 99.

44. Ibid., 88. Also, "God shows himself as Saviour in concrete events of history" "Address on the Main Theme," Lesslie Newbigin, *South India Churchman*, February 1972:5.

45. Newbigin, "I Believe," 87.

46. Newbigin, *Gospel in a Pluralist Society*, 62. Newbigin cites Karl Barth, Church Dogmatics, Vol. III/2:399. The influence of Barth and Brunner (such as Truth as Encounter) is to be noted throughout this section. Also see Hendrik Kraemer's discussion in *The Christian Message in a Non-Christian World*, 130ff. In his early writing "I Believe" (1946), Newbigin says that we do not lay hold of truth but that it lays hold of us. See Newbigin, "I Believe," 75.

47. Newbigin, *Gospel in a Pluralist Society*, 62.

48. Newbigin, *A Word*, 95.

49. Ibid., 94.

50. Newbigin, *Good Shepherd*, 117.

Grasping Truth and Reality

While it is understandable that Newbigin would seek to avoid the idea of 'timeless eternal truths' that might point back to Greek philosophy, nevertheless the question must be asked if there is not truth about God that is not limited to space and time. Certainly there is such truth since God is greater than creation. The truth he has revealed, however, is limited by time and space because God has condescended to relate to us in this continuum. This would be the logical implication of the fact that God is distinct from creation and 'occupies eternity.' For humanity, the important thing is to know the truth of God that has been revealed.

God is the ground of truth and the source of the human understanding of reality. Most of all, however, God's self-revelation is the only source of knowledge of God available to us.[51] "In a world where God is not known," writes Newbigin, "he has made himself known."[52] Newbigin insists that God's revelation cannot be evaluated by anything more foundational or ultimate than God's own revelation of himself. "Are there grounds," he asks, "more trustworthy than those given in God's self-revelation?"[53] There is nothing prior to nor more basic than God's self-revelation that could be considered more reliable truth.[54]

The knowledge of God is personal knowledge,[55] because he has intentionally made himself known so humans not only may *know* him but also can have a relationship with him. Revelation in the Christian tradition is more than communication of information; it is also an invitation, a summons, a call.[56] The appropriate response, from a Christian point of view, would be belief and obedience.[57] Newbigin goes on to say, however,

---

51. See Newbigin, *Truth and Authority*, 14.

52. Newbigin, *Good Shepherd*, 63.

53. Newbigin, *Truth and Authority*, 6.

54. Ibid., 9–10.

55. In his 1936 student paper titled "Revelation," Newbigin lays down some considerations for the reason revelation is central to Christianity. The first one is that the "meaning of the world is personal" "Revelation," Newbigin (student paper, 1936), 1. He follows this with: "if the meaning of the world is personal then revelation is the only path by which it can be made known to us," Ibid., 2.

56. Newbigin, *Proper Confidence*, 65. "It is clear," he writes, "that we are here moving away from a view of revelation as the imparting of information, to one which sees it as the revealing of a purpose and the establishing of a personal relation" "Revelation," Newbigin (student paper, 1936), 31.

57. Newbigin, *Proper Confidence*, 65. In "I Believe" he says that "revelation which can only be accepted in trust" "I Believe." Newbigin, *I Believe*, ed. M. A. Thomas, (Madras:

that revelation is *more* than either invitation or information; it is about reconciliation, atonement, and salvation.[58]

REVELATION AND REASON

Revelation does not meet the criteria of the Enlightenment for knowing truth or facts since it cannot be experimentally or empirically proven.[59] Newbigin asserts that revelation and reason do not stand in opposition to each other; this opposition arises out of a tradition of rationality that sees the "whole of reality only as an object of investigation."[60] The conflict between reason and revelation emerges in the Age of Reason, which saw them as mutually exclusive,[61] requiring Western culture to put away its 'childish dependence' upon divine revelation and use the gift of reason to establish 'facts' independent of God and revelation.[62]

There is a tradition of thought, Newbigin observes, that has the experience of Moses as its basis and starting point, and continues to the present time in various forms within Jewish, Christian, and Islamic traditions. Reason operates in these traditions as rigorously as it does in the tradition that developed from the discoveries of Kepler. It is not that one system relies on reason and the other on revelation; both systems are inconceivable apart from rationality. The difference is their starting point: one says "I have discovered" while the other says "God has spoken."[63]

These two statements seem to validate the two approaches to knowledge. It is true that even scientific knowledge is personal knowledge since scientists are persons who apprehend knowledge but God has not revealed everything about creation in a relational manner; some things remain to be discovered. Newbigin falls into the same trap that he wishes Western culture to avoid: he speaks of God's revelation and knowledge gained by science as mutually exclusive. Newbigin does not seem to acknowledge

---

SCM, 1946), 83.

58. Newbigin, *Proper Confidence*, 67-68.
59. Newbigin, *A Word*, 92; *Truth and Authority*, 54-55.
60. Newbigin, *A Word*, 93.
61. This idea could at least be partially traced to Thomas Aquinas (1225-74) who believed that there were some things that can be known only through reason while there other things that can only be known by faith through revelation. See Newbigin, *Proper Confidence*, 17.
62. Newbigin, *Proper Confidence*, 55.
63. Newbigin, *Gospel in a Pluralist Society*, 60.

Grasping Truth and Reality

the validity of the method of science that seeks to know the natural world without undue reference to metaphysical assumptions that may prejudice the result of the investigation. Certain metaphysical assumptions would allow us to see the sun as the center of our cosmic system rather than the earth. He confuses 'scientism' (the radical, narrow, positivistic view of science) and the broader method of science. When he describes what should be called 'scientism,' he tends to use the nomenclature of 'the modern scientific worldview.' This makes it appear that he is against science *per se* when such is not the case.[64] Newbigin's view of revelation as the starting point, when viewed from the perspective of science, would necessarily require that he have a wider view of revelation than the fact that God has revealed himself in history; God's revelation, it would seem, must be extended to the cosmos as well.

When reason is set against revelation, Newbigin observes, the situation becomes confused. It is not that reason is set against something unreasonable but that it is really two traditions of rational argument in which one takes the starting point of divine revelation.[65] The Christian tradition does not base its understandings on 'self-evident truths' but on the God who has made himself known in particular circumstances in history and to historical persons, such as Abraham, Moses, the prophets, and the apostles. This revelation of God culminated in the incarnate Word of God, Jesus of Nazareth.[66]

Newbigin has a balanced view of reason, defining it as "the power of the human mind to think coherently and to organize the data of experience in such a way that it can be grasped in meaningful patterns."[67] Reason, therefore, is involved in every kind of knowing. The debate regarding the roles of reason and revelation is really a debate about how the data of experience is understood and interpreted.[68] "The true opposition is not," Newbigin insists, "between reason and revelation as sources of and criteria for truth. It is between two uses to which reason is put."[69]

---

64. Newbigin, *Gospel in a Pluralist Society*, 69.
65. Ibid., 62.
66. Ibid., 63.
67. Ibid., 10.
68. Ibid., 10–11.
69. Ibid., 62.

Grasping Truth and Reality

Revelation and History

God's revelation did not come through some special language or through heavenly beings; it came through historical people and actual events in history.[70] God's revelation, he writes, came through "the specificity of a particular historical revelation," yet it is universal and available to all. This is the theme of Scripture.[71]

While serving as a missionary in India, Newbigin, as mentioned earlier, would visit the Ramakrishna Mission where he would dialogue with Hindus scholars. They would argue that historical events are an illusion and certainly not a place to find ultimate truth.[72] Newbigin reminds us that this idea is not unique to India; there have been those in Western cultural history who have disputed the claim that truth can be found in particular events of history. Gotthold Lessing, German philosopher and dramatist in the eighteenth century, talked of the "great, ugly ditch" that separates history from science. "Lessing's great gulf which he confessed himself unable to jump," Newbigin writes, "[is] the gulf between accidental events of history and universal truths of reason.[73] Eternal truths cannot be proven through actual happenings of history.[74] Newbigin states that to assert that God's revelation comes through a historical Christ directly challenges the assumptions of Western culture:

> According to the ruling assumptions of our culture, human reason in its autonomy has direct access to truth; accidental happenings of history may illustrate this truth but can never prove it. To say that "God was in Christ," or to repeat the words attributed to Jesus, "I am the Way," is to challenge those assumptions. It is to make human reason dependent for contact with ultimate truth upon one particular happening among all the accidental happenings in

---

70. "God shows himself . . . in actual events of history." "Address on the Main Theme," Newbigin, *South India Churchman*, February 1972:5.

71. Newbigin, "Enduring Validity," 53.

72. Newbigin, *The Finality*, 50.

73. Newbigin, *Gospel in a Pluralistic Society*, 57. Colin Brown, in his *Philosophy and the Christian Faith*, explains that "since history was not of the same order as mathematics it would not provide the basis of a system. Between the two there was an 'ugly, broad ditch.'" *Philosophy and the Christian Faith*, Brown (Downers Grove, IL: InterVarsity, 1975), 88.

74. "Gotthold Lessing (1729-81) was a German dramatist and critic whose widely read writings disseminated an influential literary expression of the spirit of Aufklärung" *A History of Philosophy*, Martin J. Walsh (London: Geoffrey Chpaman, 1975), 300. See Newbigin, *Proper Confidence*, 71.

history. To say that the transcendent is to be truly known only by looking at one particular series of events with all their particularity of time, place, race, culture, and language, is to pose a direct challenge to the sovereignty of the autonomous reason as our culture has prized it.[75]

On the other side of this issue we find Nietzsche[76] and his contemporary disciples, the post-modernists.[77] Eternal truths and our 'metanarratives' are, according to the post-modernist view, only products of particular human histories and are part of a particular culture, with a particular language, using concepts, symbols, and models that have been developed in particular communities. So, they cannot be, it is reasoned, *eternal, universal* truths, and the stories of that culture cannot be a *meta*narrative.[78] To a limited degree Newbigin thinks Nietzsche and the post-modernists are correct: truth must be necessarily embedded in a particular culture since there is no 'supraculture' made up of humans who can receive and disseminate truth. Newbigin responds to this by saying that "the (true) assertion that all truth claims are not culturally and historically embodied does not entail the (false) assertion that none of them make contact with a reality beyond the human mind."[79]

The Significance of History

The idea that universal truth is revealed in particular historical events is part of the legacy of the Hebrews and clearly expressed in the Old Testament. What made the Hebrew view of history distinctive is its belief that history has a goal, in contrast to the Greek understanding of history that saw the "essence of perfection as changelessness," meaning that perfection cannot arise from changeable human history. The Old Testament looks forward to a glorious consummation of history, the goal

---

75. Newbigin, *Other Side*, 51.

76. Friedrich W. Nietzsche (1844–1900).

77. Newbigin appears to be skeptical about this term since he calls the followers of Nietzsche "so-called postmodernists," reflecting his reluctance to embrace this term. See Newbigin, *Proper Confidence*, 73. He does, however, deal with post-modern thinking. The topic will be dealt with in chapter 5 under the section titled Challenging the Enlightenment.

78. Newbigin, *Proper Confidence*, 73–74.

79. Ibid., 74.

of all of humanity united in Christ. This, Newbigin asserts, gives history its meaning.[80]

History, believes Newbigin, does not progress by forces innate within it but progresses as the result of the promises of God.[81] More specifically, history finds its meaning in Jesus Christ, for in him the end or goal has come.[82] World history is not meaningless because, in Christ, God has done something new and decisive.[83] It is within this framework that we can understand the decisiveness of the Christ-event, for all people and for all times.[84]

Newbigin criticizes modern historical consciousness as assuming a perspective that is, in their minds, superior to all other perspectives:

> There are certainly no grounds whatever for supporting that "modern historical consciousness" provides us with an epistemological privilege denied to other culturally conditioned ways of seeing.[85]

Newbigin would question what makes the modern view superior to other views, or what makes (more broadly) Westerners believe that they view reality in an unbiased manner, since their own presupposition is that no truth claim can be made from within a particular culture. Yet, this is precisely what they are doing.[86] Newbigin sees the difference between Christian historians and secular historians not in the nature of reality, but in the interpretation

---

80. Newbigin, *Gospel in a Pluralist Society*, 103. Newbigin reiterates the biblical picture of the goal of the ages: "It is a picture of Christ leading his whole creation and his whole human family towards the goal of unity in him." "The Secular-Apostolic Dilemma," Newbigin, in *Not Without a Compass*, ed. T. Mathias et al. (New Delhi: Jesuit Educational Association, 1972), 63. He adds: "we must think not only in terms of the destiny of individual souls, but also in terms of God's whole guidance of creation . . . through the long history of which we are a part" Ibid, 68.

81. Newbigin, *Gospel in a Pluralist Society*, 103, 105.

82. Ibid., 104.

83. Newbigin, *Good Shepherd*, 63.

84. Newbigin, "Christ and the World of Religions," 28.

85. Newbigin, "Religious Pluralism," 50. Newbigin's debate is with Gordon Kaufman, who says that "modern historical consciousness requires us to abandon the claim of Christ's uniqueness and . . . is the product of a particular culture." *Myth of Christian Uniqueness*, ed. John Hick and Paul Knitter (Maryknoll, NY: Orbis, 1997), 5–6. Newbigin's response is that even if all truth claims are culture-bound, it does not follow that they are necessarily untrue.

86. Newbigin, *Gospel in a Pluralist Society*, 160.

of actual historical events based on their particular presuppositions regarding what can be known through historical events.[87]

History is interpreted by persons who have made prior commitments to a certain perspective of history that, in turn, becomes the standard by which they evaluate and write history, pre-determining their conclusions. If this is so, there is then no absolute, objective history as historians of the era of modernity would have us believe. This illustrates that there must be recognition of the essential unity of the inward subjective element and the outward world of objectivity in modern Western historical scholarship. Newbigin believes that Western Christians do a similar thing by presupposing a dichotomy between internal spiritual experiences and the external world of facts.[88] Real spiritual experiences have their basis in actual historical events, he says. Stressing that faith is grounded in concrete historical events, Newbigin emphasizes the public nature of Christianity by asserting that it is open for inspection "as an ecumenical reality . . . in light of what it seeks to express and embody—God's actions for the creation and redemption of the world."[89]

Newbigin reminds Christians that in the context of the Bible it is not correct to interpret the work of Christ as 'excessively' concerned with the destiny of individual souls after death, "but must necessarily be seen in conjunction with God's purpose for the whole of history."[90] Newbigin emphasizes that even though God makes the divine known to each person's soul, reason, and conscience, this is not separate from God's self-revelation in public history, open for all to see and to experience.[91] In the person and work of Jesus Christ, ultimate reality, which is the object of the human

---

87. Newbigin, *Proper Confidence*, 77.

88. Newbigin, *The Finality*, 53; Newbigin, *Gospel in a Pluralist Society*, 164.

89. Newbigin, *Proper Confidence*, 52. This appears to be a reference to Romans 1:19 where Paul speaks of God's actions in the world being made plain to humanity so that they are without excuse when they rebel against God. It is God who makes His actions understandable to humanity.

90. Newbigin, *A Word*, 127–28.

91. Newbigin, "Religious Pluralism," 52. Newbigin does not believe that a person has the natural ability to recognize God's revelation. In his writings he makes it clear that the Holy Spirit is at work in the hearts of humanity, helping them to know and respond to the truth. In this particular article Newbigin emphasizes that God has made Himself known "not in a purely inward spirituality, which is separate from the public history that we share." Ibid. God works in the heart and public life of persons of various religious traditions and especially, Newbigin says, in the hearts and history of those who make no profession at all.

search for truth, has been present in history.[92] The central clue of history is the crucified Lord and "the horizon for all action in history is the advent of one who is to come."[93]

While Newbigin makes a necessary correction to an over-emphasis on the subjective character of salvation at the expense of a clear understanding of the role of history in salvation, nevertheless he tends to over-emphasize the historical and collective understanding of salvation at the expense of the subjective and individual salvation.

Revelation through Specific Culture

The Bible is a collection of writings that record the experiences of particular people and particular cultures to whom God has chosen to reveal himself in a profound and discernible manner.[94] Christian doctrine must also of necessity be expressed culturally, reflecting the concepts and specific cultural influences that contributed to their articulation and clarification. Christian doctrine is rational discourse that developed in specific faith communities over the centuries, in specific locations and among specific cultures. The fact that doctrine is rooted in 'one strand of the whole human story' does not invalidate its universal relevance. Every form of rationality requires that it be rooted in some particular cultural context.[95]

Newbigin makes no attempt to address the question of why God would choose the particular culture and people that he did. He takes the fact of God's revelation in history as a 'given,' a basic presupposition for his faith and subsequent thinking. While God revealed himself through specific historical events and particular cultures, these cultures did not create the biblical faith. They were the recipients of revelation, given the added responsibility to communicate it to other nations.

Newbigin sees the non-Christian world religions primarily as culturally generated religious systems and therefore, like any culture, they have a dark side.[96] Newbigin asks a penetrating question: "What ground is there for thinking that religion is the sphere of God's special working?"[97] There is little indication in the Gospels for believing, remarks Newbigin,

92. Newbigin, *Proper Confidence*, 63.
93. Newbigin, *Open Secret*, 177.
94. Ibid., 153.
95. Newbigin, *A Word*, 91.
96. Newbigin, "Christ and the World of Religions," 22.
97. Ibid.

Grasping Truth and Reality

that religion is the primary sphere of God's work on behalf of humanity.[98] Reflecting on the events where Jesus Christ was rejected by the key religious and cultural leaders, Newbigin reiterates that religion (and the religious establishment) can be powerfully influenced not by grace, as one would expect, but by darkness and sin. Newbigin reviews the circumstance of Christ's rejection:

> The same revelation in Jesus Christ, with its burning center in the agony and death of Calvary, compel me to acknowledge that this world which God made and loved is in a state of alienation, rejection, and rebellion against him. Calvary is the central unveiling of the infinite love of God and at the same time the unmasking of the deep horror of sin. Here not the dregs of humanity, not the scoundrels whom all good people condemn, but the revered leaders in Church, state, and culture, combined in one murderous intent to destroy the holy one by whose mercy they exist and were created.[99]

God, however, works in the hearts of persons, whatever their religion. There is no one, Newbigin asserts, who has not been affected in their mind and conscience by the 'whispers of God's Word.' Newbigin personally attests to knowing many "non-Christians who have a deep and often radiant sense of the presence of God."[100] In an article titled "Confessing Christ in a Multi-religion Society," Newbigin develops this point a little further. While he stops short of saying that other religions are a path to the true knowledge of God, he strongly affirms that all persons are illuminated by Jesus Christ, the light that lightens every person in the world. There is no human, he says, that is not touched by the grace of God.[101] This, he believes, is absolutely fundamental. What each person experiences is the gracious, tender, loving care of God.[102] He acknowledges signs of grace "which we see so movingly among people of other faiths."[103] In his book *The Gospel in a Pluralist Society*, he says that as humans we are all on a journey and need to know the road to travel, but not all roads lead to the top of the mountain. Some, in fact, lead us over the precipice. Newbigin is quite clear that in Christ we have been shown the road. We must share

---

98. Ibid., 23.
99. Newbigin, *Gospel in a Pluralist Society*, 175.
100 Newbigin, "Religious Pluralism," 51.
101. Lesslie Newbigin, "Confessing Christ," 128.
102. Ibid., 129.
103. Ibid.

with our fellow pilgrims the fact "that God has given us the route we must follow and the goal to which we must press forward."[104]

Revelation in Scripture

Newbigin's view of Scripture did not change over his career. The Bible is to Newbigin a record of God's revelational activity and a unique interpretation of history, both cosmic and human, in which the human person is a responsible actor who is called to respond to God, who is both Creator and Savior. This makes the Bible like no other sacred scriptures among the great religions of the world.[105]

Newbigin believes that the Bible ought to function as a guide in our attempt to understand the world. By indwelling the story of the Bible in the same way we indwell our particular language and culture, it becomes the orientation from which we view and evaluate the world.[106] While Western culture once embraced the biblical story, which functioned as the unchallenged grid by which Western culture viewed the world, the situation has steadily changed (beginning with the Enlightenment) with the Biblical narrative becoming less and less a part of that culture. This means, Newbigin laments, that the message of the Bible is becoming increasingly incomprehensible to Western culture.[107]

Newbigin insists that Christians must acknowledge the great debt to the Enlightenment by acknowledging that "the Bible and the teaching office of the Church had become fetters upon the human spirit" and needed to be removed. They were removed but against the resistance of the church. The removal of the cruelty and oppression of the church has led to developments in science and technology that has been a great benefit to all that followed.[108] Under Enlightenment tutelage, however, Western culture's epistemology shifted from story as the basis of truth to abstract, eternal laws. The Bible came under the scrutiny of Enlightenment prin-

---

104. Newbigin, *Gospel in a Pluralist Society*, 183.

105. Newbigin, *Proper Confidence*, 53. Newbigin sees the main thrust of the Bible as historical rather than mythological. This would make it different from much of the sacred scripture of Asia, where the story is not necessarily meant to be taken as factual history, but is mythological and embodies the truths held most dear. The stories are more illustrative than factual.

106. Newbigin, *Truth and Authority*, 42.

107. Newbigin, *Foolishness*, 51.

108. Newbigin, *Other Side*, 15–16.

ciples and was evaluated by criteria developed in modern scientific work as any other text of ancient literature.[109] The consequence of this is that the scholarly world began to distinguish between the confessional and the scientific approach to sacred literature.[110] Newbigin believes that the change to the critical method is really a change from one confessional stance to another, not from a confessional stance to a neutral, unbiased study as it purports to be.[111]

Putting the Bible under the same scrutiny as other ancient literature has the consequence, Newbigin observes, of making it difficult for many modern Western people to see the Bible as authoritative in the private or the public sphere.[112] So, Newbigin takes a critical view of the critical method. The Scriptures were written in faith and have the purpose of evoking faith. Therefore, to approach the Biblical text from a supposed neutral standpoint renders the scholar incapable of interpreting the text according to its original intention. To approach the text in a neutral fashion is, Newbigin believes, a decision against faith.[113] In reality, however, a claim of neutrality would be a false because the scholar approaches the text with modern scientific assumptions that will affect the conclusion.[114]

Newbigin refutes the assumptions of the historical critical method that are themselves not provable and are accepted by faith by the scientific community.[115] The principles of the historical critical method were set out by Ernst Troeltsch and may be outlined in the following manner:

1. The principle of critical or methodological doubt: Since any conclusion is subject to revision, historical inquiry can never achieve absolute certainty but only relative degrees of probability.

2. The principle of analogy: Historical knowledge is possible because all events are similar in principle. We must assume that the laws of nature in biblical times were the same as now.

---

109. Ibid., 43ff. See also *Gospel in a Pluralist Society*, 99. Newbigin notes that he was influenced in his thinking at this point by Hans Frei.
110. Newbigin, *Proper Confidence*, 79.
111. Ibid., 80.
112. Newbigin, *Other Side*, 43–44.
113. Ibid., 44, 47.
114. Ibid., 44–45.
115. Newbigin, *Proper Confidence*, 80–81.

3. The principle of correlation: The phenomena of history are interrelated and interdependent, and no event can be isolated from the sequence of historical causes and effects.[116]

Newbigin's view is that it is easy to deconstruct this whole argument by putting it under the scrutiny of its own method, because, in reality, any conclusion it would come to must also be doubted.[117]

Reading the Bible must necessarily be a critical activity within the Christian tradition, calling old beliefs into question as one reads and seeks to understand the text fully. These questions are to be asked, however, from within the Christian tradition, a tradition that is based on the fact that the Word of God is the Jesus Christ of history. This is the appropriate critical approach to the Bible according to Newbigin.[118] The primary approach to the Bible is to read it in such a manner that we understand Jesus in the context of the whole story and we understand the whole story in light of Jesus.[119] The critical factor is secondary and must remain secondary in our approach to the Bible since faith is the primary approach to be taken to Biblical study. If the critical factor is given priority, it will lead into nihilistic skepticism in which nothing can be known.[120]

On the other end of the spectrum is the view of Scripture held by Fundamentalism, which Newbigin describes as inadequate and culturally engendered. It is an appropriate concern to be faithful to the fundamentals of the faith, but not to fall into the trap of Fundamentalism "which treats Scripture as a 'scientific account' of the things recorded," where the

---

116. Ibid., 80. In one of the few places where Newbigin acknowledges his debt to another's thought. This summary of Troeltsch (whose thought is referred to) comes from an article "The Bible: Unexamined Commitments of Criticism." by Jon D. Levenson. The summary is by John J. Collins.

117. Ibid., 83.

118. Ibid., 87. "Newbigin might be considered vulnerable," writes V. Matthew Thomas, "in the very positive believing attitude he takes to the Bible. Many scholars and theologians would argue that he is far too uncritical and has not really heard or felt the force of biblical criticism, critique of the canon, ideological critique of biblical materials, etc. He often resorts to his own subjective experience of God to answer the question, 'How do we know?' a 'fideism' he wants to avoid." "The Centrality of Christ," Thomas (PhD diss., Toronto School of Theology, 1996), 167. Newbigin was particularly influenced by Hans Frei at this time. See Newbigin, *Proper Confidence*, 72.

119. Ibid., 88.

120. Newbigin, *Other Side*, 61.

objective facts from the past are dealt with by autonomous reason in an Enlightenment perspective.[121]

Newbigin also sees a problem of reducing Scripture to a series of doctrinal statements. Scripture must be allowed to speak for itself, not be forced to speak in categories that are not its own.[122] To turn the Bible into a "compendium of indubitably certain facts" is to change the Bible's fundamental character, attempting to reshape it according to the strictures of the Enlightenment.[123] The variety of voices in the Bible should be allowed to speak in their different ways and not be synthesized into a series of propositions that can become solidified truth that is set against the kind of knowledge one can get through the study of nature and its laws.[124]

The Bible, unlike the other religious literature of the East, is different in that it speaks of human life in the context of a vision for universal cosmic history, which it views from the creation of the world to its consummation. The Bible is universal history because it speaks of one nation that was chosen to be the bearer of the meaning of history for all humanity, and it speaks of one Person who was chosen to be the bearer of meaning for that nation.[125]

For some in Western culture, to see the Bible as a source for cosmic history and the record of God's action is not logically defensible, at least not from the Enlightenment point of view. Newbigin refutes this idea:

> There is nothing logically incoherent about recognizing the Bible as embodying the long and patient struggle of the living God to lead a people into true knowledge of his purpose for creation, or in believing that the same living God has become part of the story in Jesus Christ, addressing a personal call to men and women to find in following him the way into the fullness of truth.[126]

The story of the Bible is about a real God who deals patiently with sinful and fallible people.[127] The essence of the Bible, then, is not propositional truth but narrative, a story of which the community of the Christian

---

121. Newbigin, *Proper Confidence*, 97–100.
122. Newbigin, *Other Side*, 48.
123. Newbigin, *Proper Confidence*, 99.
124. Newbigin, *Other Side*, 4, 49.
125. Newbigin, *Gospel in a Pluralist Society*, 89.
126. Newbigin, *Truth and Authority*, 71.
127. Newbigin, *Proper Confidence*, 99.

Church understands itself to be a part.[128] This story reveals the character of God so it is important that we allow the story to fill our minds and to shape our lives.[129] As one allows the biblical story to be the 'all-surrounding ambience of daily life,' one discovers that it allows for a continuous dialogue with the One whose character is revealed in the biblical story.[130] We may grow in our knowledge of God "by allowing the biblical story to awaken our imagination and to challenge and stimulate our thinking and acting."[131] To those who indwell[132] the story, the Bible becomes authoritative for them.[133] The *Religionsgeschichte* School, representing the sociological view of religious knowledge, would require one to say of the biblical story that this is what 'Israel thought' rather than 'I believe.' To submit to this idea means to submit to the reigning plausibility structure, but to confess belief calls this structure into question.[134]

Since we are not at the end of history, we cannot know what is yet to come. Consequently, we cannot have indubitable certainty.[135] The only possible response to Biblical claims is belief or unbelief. Newbigin writes: "It must be, as the Church has always said, a matter of divine revelation accepted by faith (John 1:18)."[136] There is no way to test Biblical claims, no way to satisfy the demands of the Enlightenment in this matter.[137] Perhaps, Newbigin suggests, we should reverse the order and view the world (and the critical method) through the standards and lenses of the Bible. There is no reasonable means to determine the superiority of the critical method over faith. There is also no reasonable means to discount

---

128. Newbigin, *Proper Confidence*, 52–53. Hans Frei is mentioned on page 72 (as noted in footnote 118), but his influence is clearly seen throughout the book.

129. Ibid., 72–77.

130. Ibid., 88.

131. Ibid., 91.

132. Newbigin is being influenced by Michael Polanyi's thought at this point. See Newbigin, *Proper Confidence*, 39ff. On page 40 Newbigin explains what it means to 'indwell' a tradition. He does not, however, mention Polanyi's name until page 48.

133. Newbigin, *A Word*, 86.

134. Newbigin, *Gospel in a Pluralist Society*, 93.

135. Newbigin, *Proper Confidence*, 54–55.

136. Ibid., 55.

137. Ibid.

reversing this and making the Bible the standard by which to measure the critical method.[138]

In a somewhat different manner, the question may arise regarding a possible dichotomy between the objective historical events of the Bible and the subjective religious experiences of the writers. Newbigin's discussion, at this point, is concerned about the supposed dichotomy between subjective and objective ways of knowing. Newbigin does not see these two realms as distinct so there is no need to choose between the two ways of understanding Scripture. The prophets of the Old Testament and the Apostles of the New lived in the same world as we do, where "knowing is a matter of the commitment of a personal subject to the clearest possible understanding of reality."[139]

The Bible is not only a record of God's acts in history, but it is also the testimony of persons who were a part of this history. According to Newbigin, "testimony, or witness, is a kind of utterance different from a statement of fact which is self-evident or can be demonstrated from self-evident premises."[140] The content of the testimony is a witness to the 'traces' of the living God whose presence and action are being recounted in the events being witnessed to. They are only traces because the living God cannot be enclosed or confined to any statement that is made.[141] God invites humanity to trust him as we meet him in the events of history, not with an idea among many ideas.[142]

Interpreting the text, however, involves the realization that what is presented in the Bible in relation to God seems paradoxical. There is a tension between the love and wrath of God that can only be resolved in understanding the atoning death and resurrection of Jesus. "When this is accepted," writes Newbigin, "the whole Bible is seen as a unity whose coherence is found in the total fact of Christ."[143]

In an early article, Newbigin states that the Bible cannot be understood "except through the inner witness of the Holy Spirit."[144] This state-

---

138. Newbigin, *A Word*, 111; Also see Newbigin, *Foolishness*, 41.
139. Newbigin, *Proper Confidence*, 90.
140. Newbigin, *Other Side*, 50.
141. Ibid.
142. Ibid., 51.
143. Newbigin, *Truth and Authority*, 72.
144. Newbigin, "I Believe," 87.

ment clearly reveals Newbigin's view that the Holy Spirit is involved in helping persons, both inside and outside the church, to recognize the truth. The Bible, while it is a public document open for public scrutiny and examination, was written by the church for the church, so it must be read in the church. He writes:

> . . . the Bible has to be read in the Church because the Church is the sphere of the working of the Holy Spirit, the place where Christ is received and obeyed, the place where the love of God is shed abroad in our hearts through the Holy Ghost which was given unto us, and where therefore all that is said about the Bible 'comes alive.'[145]

GRASPING REALITY: CREATOR GOD AND A CONTINGENT UNIVERSE

Newbigin's Early View of God and Reality

In an article titled "The Student Volunteer Missionary Union" (1933), the first glimpse of Newbigin's thinking regarding God, reality, and the cosmos appears. All humans assume that a certain reality exists and that they are part of it. Newbigin realizes that it is important for the creature to adjust to this reality. The question about religion, for Newbigin, is whether it is an illusion or whether it causes the creature to make a true adjustment to reality.[146] Newbigin is emphatic that Christ's testimony to God is the way of understanding true reality.[147] In the same article, Newbigin speaks of God's deep longing for fellowship with humans. This is a deep mystery for humans trying to understand the nature of God.[148] This early insight into the nature and character of God becomes a starting point in Newbigin's understanding of the motivation for mission. Even before the challenge of encountering the philosophies of India (that view ultimate reality as non-personal), Newbigin speaks of ultimate reality in terms of being personal. His view is articulated in his unpublished student paper on "Revelation."[149] There is a reality, he says, that exists independently of

---

145. Newbigin, "I Believe," 86–87.
146. Newbigin, "Student Volunteer Missionary Union," 101.
147. Ibid., 102.
148. Ibid., 104.
149. Newbigin, "Revelation," 1.

our knowing.[150] The religious approach to reality, he writes, is of the nature of a synthetic apprehension[151] of reality. More specifically, the Christian faith is the "apprehension of the whole of experience in terms of the clue which is given to us in the Fact of Christ."[152]

T. F. Torrance, a theologian who studied under Barth and has specialized in comparing methodologies in natural science and theology, takes the occasion of the Preface to his book *Theological Science* to share his experience with God and how that influenced his faith:

> If I may be allowed to speak personally for a moment, I find the presence and being of God bearing upon my experience and thought so powerfully that I cannot but be convinced of His overwhelming reality and rationality. To doubt the existence of God would be an act of sheer irrationality.[153]

This is an affirmation of what Newbigin describes as synthetic apprehension, which becomes the basis of a life-long pursuit of understanding. Newbigin's experience becomes the door to his faith-seeking-understanding, but it is also the point where there is a critical acceptance of the revelation of God as authoritative for his faith.

Newbigin's theological view of God is spelled out in more detail in the article "I Believe in God" (1946). Generally, God is the ground of all existence, the source of all truth, the very basis of rationality itself. To deny this would be irrational.[154] Newbigin's insight into the value of the Trinitarian model for understanding ultimate reality also comes early in his career. In "I Believe in God" he writes: "The doctrine that the three are one is a refutation of every philosophy which makes an ultimate distinction between God and history, between time and eternity, between mind and matter."[155]

Newbigin makes a reference to the vision of the prophet Isaiah, where God is seen as high and lifted up, and his glory fills the Temple.[156] It is a

---

150. Newbigin, "I Believe," 73.

151. A synthetic apprehension of reality is immediate and does not come about by the process of rational analysis.

152. Newbigin, "I Believe," 80.

153. Torrance, *Theological Science*, ix.

154. Newbigin, "I Believe in God," 89.

155. Ibid., 99–100.

156. Newbigin, "I Believe in God," 89.

majestic picture of God and as such stands opposed to any philosophical construction of the being of God. We cannot, Newbigin warns, speak *about* God as if he were not present, because he is always present. He is living and personal, and therefore not a mere object of our investigation. We do not know him by talking about him, but "by dealing with Him and letting Him deal with us."[157] "So," Newbigin insists, "we are not speaking and hearing about an object we can dispassionately discuss, but standing before the Holy One and called upon to hear Him and obey Him."[158] This being true, it must be asked whether, in fact, the desire to know God does not somehow ignite the hearts and minds of some persons to seek to understand the philosophical implications of God's being and of reality.

There are some evidences of God in the very make-up of the universe, certain characteristics that cause the human mind to find reasons to explain. The universe is not, according to Newbigin, self-explanatory and as rational beings we seek to know the ground of the coherence. There is a certain orderliness that evokes the mind of humanity to discover its origin. "There are principles of coherence running through the universe," writes Newbigin, "there are unities embracing even apparently disconnected phenomena, laws upon the basis of which men can rationally plan for the future."[159] "All that exists," he says, "is the creation of God."[160]

Newbigin ends his treatise with a short discussion of the Trinity. We cannot escape the doctrine of the Trinity, Newbigin says, which is a perfect unity and the personal source of our being as humans.[161]

Newbigin's next chapter, "I Believe in Christ," is a significant declaration of the heart of Newbigin's Christology. The tone of the piece bears the marks of one who is exhorting his doubting friends to face the facts. What is recorded in the Bible must either be accepted as fact, which would circumvent modern categories of what is plausible, or one must say that it

---

157. Newbigin, "I Believe in God," 90.

158. Ibid., 90. This sentiment is very closely allied to Karl Barth's view of theology, as explained by John Bowden in his book *Karl Barth*. In making a distinction between religion and theology, Barth would identify theology as 'God-talk', a term that Bowden goes on to clarify as follows: [It is] "not talk about God, for God is not an object that can form the content of our discourse, but the human response to the word of God that has already spoken to man before theology begins" *Karl Barth*, Bowden (London: SCM, 1971), 13.

159. Newbigin, "I Believe in God," 90.

160. Ibid., 95.

161. Ibid., 99.

is absurd. If it is factual, then it cannot be taken in a casual manner.[162] In words intended to bring an emotive response, Newbigin reiterates the essence of the story:

> And yet these incredible claims, made in the very city where Jesus had lived and died as a man only a few weeks before, were believed by multitudes and became the basis of a movement that burst the bonds of Judaism and of the Roman Empire itself. Something had happened: Christ had risen from the dead.[163]

The centerpiece of this discussion is the resurrection of Christ, an event that contradicts our experience but has become the very foundation of the church.[164] From this discussion of the resurrection, Newbigin's exhortation moves backwards to the death of Christ and the meaning of the Cross as a deliberated act of love of Jesus and a revelation of the mercy of God.[165]

Most significantly, Newbigin sees the belief in the resurrection not as delusional, but as the means to be released from delusion. The theme that real faith in Christ puts us into contact with reality permeates much of Newbigin's early writings, a theme that is pronounced with clarity in the following:

> To understand this is to be released from a world of make-believe into a world of reality, into a daylight world where all facts can be faced, into a world where we do not need to 'cook' our accounts because He has made all our debts His own.[166]

It is impossible, writes Newbigin, to understand these words unless the Spirit "takes them and makes them live in you."[167] To believe in the revelation of God in Christ, crucified and risen, "is the starting point for the only possible rational view of the universe."[168] "Our redemption," he writes, "is the work of our Creator and of none other."[169]

---

162. Newbigin, "I Believe in Christ," 103.
163. Ibid.
164. Ibid.
165. Ibid., 105.
166. Ibid., 107.
167. Ibid., 108.
168. Newbigin, "I Believe in God," 89.
169. Ibid., 113.

Newbigin continues his Christological discussions in his book published in 1948 entitled *The Reunion of the Church: A Defense of the South India Scheme*. He focuses on the atonement[170] of Christ as the only means by which humanity is reconciled to God, and clearly affirms that Christ is the only redeemer.[171] Once again expounding the cosmic dimension of the work of Christ, he reiterates his strong conviction that salvation is far more than an individual affair:

> Our faith is that the word of the Cross is in very truth the power of God unto salvation—and that does not mean just the rescue of each of us separately, but the healing, making whole of the whole creation and the fulfilling of God's whole will.[172]

His Christological focus continues undiminished in his book *A Faith for this One World?* Here he connects the work of Christ with the biblical understanding of creation. The 'fact of Christ' is to be understood in this context.[173] This Christ is the One through whom all things were created, the cause and cornerstone of the universe.[174]

It is this Christ that is the fulfillment of God's purposes for the universe. He writes:

> It is the declaration of God's cosmic purpose by which the whole public history of mankind is sustained and overruled, and by which all men without exception will be judged. It is the invitation to be fellow workers with God in the fulfilment of that purpose through the atoning work of Christ and through the witness of the Holy Spirit.[175]

This theme is carried on into the 1970s in an article titled "The Secular-Apostolic Dilemma" (1972), where he says that when we think of salvation, we must not think of it in terms of the destiny of individual souls only, "but also in terms of God's whole guidance of creation, through all the unimaginable eons of the evolution of the physical world."[176]

---

170. A discussion of Newbigin's doctrine of the atonement is found in chapter 4 under The Way of Salvation.
171. Newbigin, *Reunion*, 13ff.
172. Newbigin, "The Summons," 185.
173. Newbigin, *A Faith*, 61.
174. Ibid., 62.
175. Newbigin, *Honest Religion*, 46.
176. Newbigin, "The Secular-Apostolic Dilemma," 68.

Grasping Truth and Reality

Newbigin's View of God and Reality after 1974

God is the Creator of a rational and contingent universe. It is rational, Newbigin writes, because it is a creation of God "who is the light and not darkness," and it is contingent[177] because "it is not an emanation of God... who has endowed it with a measure of autonomy."[178] Any attempt to interpret the cosmos comprehensively without the recognition that ultimate and fundamental reality is God is doomed to failure. Any theory that fails to recognize that this God has made himself known in history with Jesus Christ at its centre will end in illusion.[179]

Newbigin does not depart from the traditional Christian view of God as Creator and therefore his doctrine of creation assumes ultimate reality to be personal.[180] Newbigin's doctrine of creation rests on the belief that God has placed the evidence of his existence in creation. This evidence cannot be recognized without Christ giving humanity "the eyes through which we can begin to understand our experiences in the world."[181] It is not, however, a matter of God creating the universe and then leaving it to run on its own. God maintains a relationship to the cosmos and interacts with it at will.[182] The biblical vision of creation allowed for the development of science because the universe is rational and contingent; it is connected to God but is not in itself 'necessary being.' It is a reality that stands in relation to God and has an objective existence, supported, nourished, and governed by God.[183] Newbigin sees this contingency as a particularly important viewpoint in the context of Western culture's understanding of the cosmos. Many cultures world-wide are *ontocratic*,[184] meaning that the

---

177. See Torrance's book *Theological Science*. He has many references to creation as contingent (separate and dependent). His interest is in the relationship between theology and science.

178. Newbigin, "Can the West be Converted?" 4.

179. Newbigin, *Truth and Authority*, 10.

180. Newbigin, *Proper Confidence*, 95.

181. Ibid., 97.

182. Newbigin, *Foolishness*, 88.

183. Ibid., 70–71.

184. Newbigin acknowledges the source of this concept as being from a book by Dutch scholar A. T. van Leeuwen titled *Christianity in World History*. Van Leeuwen's thesis is that the process of secularization is destroying the type of cultures that deify the orders on earth because they reflect, in their thinking, the order of heaven. This kind of thinking deifies, for example, earthly kings. Van Leeuwen says that the main theme of the Bible is the prophetic confrontation of this pattern. Consequently, reasons van Leeuwen, secularism is doing to-

patterns of society presume to "rest upon the total identification of the orders of society with the order of the cosmos."[185] Newbigin believes that the 'desacralization' of culture is a necessary precondition for the development of science in any given society.[186] If secularism has a positive side, it is in the fact that when it confronts an ontocratic society, it delivers it from its bondage to elemental powers.[187] This desacralization allows persons, once bound by elemental powers of the natural world, to be free to investigate and to experiment, which is the essence of science.[188]

The Reality of God

For Newbigin, God is the both Creator and Sustainer of the universe as well as the source of truth and reality. Western culture has denied the existence and hence the necessity of God to explain reality. Not only is Western culture's view of the cosmos affected by its acceptance or rejection of the biblical view of God, its view of the value and place of humans in the cosmos is also affected. If the biblical view of God has been eliminated, for example, there "can be no final safeguard for the human person."[189]

Since God has revealed himself as a Trinity and the Trinitarian model is ultimate, it cannot, Newbigin asserts, be founded or grounded upon *more* ultimate principles or by a standard constructed by a culture.[190] Newbigin states that the 'inexhaustible power' of the prophetic tradition of the Bible was derived from "the affirmation of the reality and power and holiness of God who is other than, greater than, and more enduring than any human institution or achievements."[191] The new starting point for understanding God, truth, and the cosmos is the Person of Jesus Christ, God's revelation to mankind, and not an abstract idea or a first principle.[192]

---

day what the prophetic religion of the Hebrews did in ancient times.
185. Newbigin, *Honest Religion*, 28.
186. Ibid., 33.
187. Ibid., 29–32.
188. Ibid., 32.
189. Ibid., 52.
190. Newbigin, *Truth to Tell*, 37.
191. Newbigin, *Honest Religion*, 38.
192. Newbigin, *Truth to Tell*, 37, and *Foolishness*, 6.

Grasping Truth and Reality

The witness of the church is that Jesus Christ is the Lord of all of life,[193] the center around which all history and all creation revolves.[194] This truth cannot be demonstrated by references to some more ultimate reality or standard.[195] To attempt to prove that Jesus is Lord is to give in to the plausibility structure of society.[196] The new starting point needs no such support: Christ is His own authority. Authority resides in the one who is the Author of all being.[197]

The Apostle Paul was not the teacher of a new theology but only a messenger commissioned by the authority of the Lord to proclaim a new fact in history, "that in the ministry, death, and resurrection of Jesus God has acted decisively to reveal and affect his purpose for redemption of the whole world."[198] Paul asserted this as the truth, not as one possible option among many.[199]

A Contingent Creation

An important aspect of Newbigin's pre-1974 theological thinking is his viewpoint on a contingent universe. T. F. Torrance argues that the classical mind saw the universe as an expression of an unchanging and eternal Divine Person, but that the Fathers of the church and the Reformation changed the understanding of the relation between God and nature by positing the idea of a contingent creation.[200]

At issue is the difference between monism and monotheism. One cannot absolutely prove the ultimate nature of reality, whether it is monistic or the contingent creation of a Creator God, although evidences could be brought forward to try to show that one or the other might be the case. Nevertheless, the ultimate decision is a matter of faith, of deciding which view of reality seems to fit the experiences of life. Newbigin makes the assumption, based on his belief in God and the revelation of Scripture,

---

193. Newbigin, *Foolishness*, 102.
194. Newbigin, *Truth to Tell*, 64.
195. Ibid., 34.
196. Ibid., 28.
197. Newbigin, *Truth and Authority*, 1–2.
198. Newbigin, *Gospel in a Pluralist Society*, 5.
199. Ibid., 6.
200. Torrance is cited in Thorson's chapter titled "Scientific Objectivity and the Listening Attitude" in *Objective Knowledge*, 69. Regarding the Church Fathers, see Gunton, *Christ and Creation*, 78–79.

that creation is an objective, contingent reality that exists apart from but is still dependent upon God. This would imply that God has objectivity apart from creation. Barth writes: "Biblical faith lives upon the objectivity of God."[201]

In the taxonomy of epistemological positions there is the category of the nature of knowledge that is generally called 'critical realism.' Critical realism, as an epistemological model, is surfacing in a variety of contexts. Paul Hiebert, anthropologist and missiologist, defines critical realism in this manner:

> The external world is real. Our knowledge of it is partial but can be true. Science is a map or model. It is made up of successive paradigms that bring us closer approximations of reality and absolute truth.[202]

Van Huyssteen takes this epistemological model and applies it to theology. Scientists who use the critical realist model believe their theories to be representations of the world as a reality, holding that their theories are valid, provisionally true, and useful.[203] So,

> In theology, critical realism will imply, on the one hand, a model of rationality where theological concepts and models are indeed provisional, inadequate, and partial, but, on the other hand, also necessary as the only way of referring to the reality that is God, and the reality of His relation to humanity.[204]

Theological reflection "takes place within the context of an ultimate faith commitment to God as a personal but transcendent Creator."[205] The commitment is based on the reality of a God who is there and who has communicated to humanity. It is not an irrational retreat into subjective, inward commitment, but is a commitment to a reality outside the mind. Newbigin remarks that when conservative Christians assert that their faith refers to objective realities, they are rightly denying the position that faith is merely subjective feelings or experiences, but believe in a reality beyond the self.[206]

---

201. Barth, *Church Dogmatics*, vol. II part 1:13.
202. Hiebert, "Epistemological Foundations," 23.
203. van Huyssteen, *Theology and the Justification of Faith*, 157.
204. Ibid., 158.
205. Ibid., 159.
206. Newbigin, *Proper Confidence*, 43.

Grasping Truth and Reality

John Polkinghorne links science, theology, and critical realism:

> Neither science nor theology can be pursued without a measure of intellectual daring, for neither is based on incontrovertible grounds of knowledge. Yet both can, I believe, lay claim to achieving a critical realism.[207]

Torrance says that the universe is an open system dependent upon factors that are transcendent to it. He explains:

> ... the contingent nature of the universe can be taken with the fullest seriousness only if we realise its utter dependence on determining factors utterly beyond it, and that the interaction of God with the universe can be taken with full seriousness only if we think of him as the transcendent ground of the creation and as the transcendent integrating factor that lends depth to all our human experience including natural science.[208]

Colin Gunton notes that Torrance stresses the idea of the relatedness of God and creation as complementary to the idea of a radical separateness and distinction that could be implied by the idea of objective reality:

> Thomas Torrance has argued that the christological thinking of the Fathers enabled them to break free of ancient views of space and time as a container externally related to God, and to generate in place of them a relational view which enables a dynamic inter-relatedness of God and the world to come to expression.[209]

Newbigin, as well, keeps the balance between the objectivity of creation with the idea of the inter-relatedness of God and creation in his view of contingency.

CONCLUSION

Newbigin approaches his theology of mission from a theological basis and his theological thinking begins early and remains fairly consistent throughout his life. We have presented a somewhat chronological overview of his thinking in two areas, his view of revelation and his view of God and reality, with the realization that these two fundamental areas set the tone for the rest of his theological thinking.

---

207. Polkinghorne, *Reason and Reality*, 1.
208. Torrance, *Theology in Reconciliation*, 100.
209. Gunton, *Christ and Creation*, 78–79.

His view of revelation emphasizes the personal aspect of God's revelation of himself to humanity. He also emphasizes the role of faith in understanding revelation and recognizing truth. It is not an infallible certainty based on reason alone, as required by Cartesian method, but a certain belief in God. While there is a significant disconnect between religion and revelation, his does not go as far as some who claim that it is total discontinuity; he prefers to say it is a radical discontinuity. It is essentially different but not completely unrelated to religion.

Newbigin's views God as Ultimate Reality and the Creator of a rational and contingent world. While God is separated from creation he nevertheless can interact with it and has done so significantly in history, the culmination of such interaction being the incarnation of Jesus Christ, and continues to act in the human events.

Newbigin's theological thinking is broader than his view of God and revelation. In the next chapter we will continue the discussion of his theological thinking.

4

Humanity's Need for Salvation and the Call for Radical Conversion

HUMANITY'S NEED FOR SALVATION

The Predicament of Humanity

NEWBIGIN'S VIEW OF HUMANITY is one that acknowledges human sinfulness while maintaining the value and worth of human persons as God's creation. His methodology is to discuss Christian doctrine in dialogue with the Enlightenment and post-modern thinking. The Enlightenment sought to free humanity from the 'dogma' of original sin because they believed that "the most dangerous and destructive of all the dogmas which have perverted human reason is the dogma of original sin."[1] Enlightenment thinkers saw the significance of the doctrine of original sin as central to the whole Christian 'system.' If humanity is not, in fact, sinful, then humanity is free to dismiss God and the whole scheme of redemption.[2] So, Enlightenment thinkers saw the destruction of the dogma of original sin as the first and most essential step to destroying the whole system of dogmas that prevented the liberation of human reason and conscience.[3]

---

1. Newbigin, *Other Side*, 12.

2. Newbigin does recognize the important contribution of the Enlightenment. See *Gospel in a Pluralist Society*, 187, *Other Side*, 15–16, and "The Bible and Our contemporary Mission," 12. When generally referring to the Enlightenment, however, he is speaking to issues he sees in connection with the missionary confrontation and is not focusing on the accomplishments of the Enlightenment, but only those areas that have created a problem for Western culture.

3. Newbigin, *Other Side*, 12.

The Doctrine of Original Sin

Humanity is a fallen race and the human heart, which was originally created by God for intimate fellowship with God, is the source of the evil that defiles humanity.[4] Newbigin has a rather interesting view of what constituted the first sin. The problem was not, as often understood, the true knowledge of good and evil, but *how* it was obtained. The true knowledge of good and evil can only come from God and should have been obtained from God. Adam and Eve in the Genesis story, however, sought this knowledge through illegitimate means and, as a result, it was distorted knowledge.[5]

Newbigin believes that the doctrine of original sin is at the heart of New Testament teaching. Christ challenged his culture's belief that they were free when, in fact, they were slaves to their own corrupt assumptions. "This radical judgment on human nature is a part of the very marrow of the New Testament witness."[6] "Sin," writes Newbigin

> is such a radical corruption of the nature of man that even his 'goodness'—that is his attempt to obey what he understands to be the will of God—becomes the quintessential sin, the spearhead of his attack upon God.[7]

The strongest indication of the seriousness of an illness is what is required to cure it. Newbigin says that there is no ground for speaking of the radical sinfulness of human nature until one has seen what God has done in Jesus Christ and through the cross.[8] Similarly, it is only in the light of the gospel that one can see the darkness of unredeemed human nature.[9]

It is precisely because of the radical corruption of human nature that humanity cannot conceive that God could find the whole human race guilty of rebellion and sin. Our sin, explains Newbigin, "blinds us to that possibility."[10] "Because sin is based on a lie," remarks Newbigin, "it breeds lies."[11]

---

4. Newbigin, *A Faith*, 68.
5. Newbigin, *Sin and Salvation*, 19.
6. Newbigin, *Proper Confidence*, 69.
7. Newbigin, "I Believe in God," 98.
8. Newbigin, *The Light*, 206. Also see Newbigin, "Cross-currents," 151.
9. Newbigin, "Cross-currents," 149.
10. Newbigin, *A Faith*, 69.
11 Newbigin, *Sin and Salvation*, 34.

Humanity's Need for Salvation and the Call for Radical Conversion

The nature of sin is self-love, which stands in defiance of God's fundamental law to love God.[12] Sin is disobedience,[13] a disobedience that begins with a distrust of God.[14] The root of sin, Newbigin believes, is unbelief, which is a refusal to believe and take God seriously.[15] But most of all it is a spiritual disease, which he calls an evil heart.[16] Evil deeds and words are really only the outward evidence of a much deeper problem.

Newbigin's most comprehensive treatment of sin is found in his book *Sin and Salvation*, written for the Tamil diocese. "Mankind," he says, "is full of self-contradiction—not at peace with himself or with the world."[17] Humanity suffers from inner self-contradictions, from being in contradiction against creation, against fellow humanity, and against God.[18] "A radical self-contradiction has been introduced into human nature" and man, notes Newbigin, is in "a perpetual state of self-contradiction, of revolt, against his own constitution."[19] Man is in revolt against the Creator and is a creature cut off from the roots of his own being.[20] Humanity is no longer free but a slave to hostile forces within and without. Newbigin writes:

> He is no longer free, but is confronted and limited at every turn by hostile forces which are too strong for him, the power of sin in his own soul, and finally the powers of death to put an end to his life, all combine to rob him of his freedom. And no power of his is enough to overcome these hostile powers and free him.[21]

The source of human alienation, Newbigin believes, is sin as a condition of the human heart, a heart set against God and the world.[22]

---

12. Newbigin, *A Faith*, 73.
13. Newbigin, *Sin and Salvation*, 16.
14. Ibid., 25.
15. Ibid.
16. Ibid., 24.
17. Ibid., 13.
18. Ibid., 11–13.
19. Newbigin, "I Believe in God," 95.
20. Newbigin, *Sin and Salvation*, 13.
21. Ibid., 14.
22. Ibid. 33.

The Alienation of the Whole Created World

The coming of Jesus and his death are outward signs of the depths of the alienation of the whole created world from God.[23] There are within creation evidences of powers alienated from God who became powerful as they become concentrated. The most concentrated form of evil is the figure of the antichrist who stands (though not equally) over and against Christ. This evil one opposes Christ and the Kingdom: he becomes the rejection and negation of Christ. The last and final effort of this antichrist and the powers of this world is to attempt to organize human history apart from obedience to Christ.[24]

Spiritual principalities and powers that exist in the world, Newbigin recognizes, stand against God.[25] God is the creator of the structural elements of the world, as well as the potential in humanity for social and political structures. Yet it was these very things that stood in murderous hostility to Christ, even though God continues to uphold these structures. These spiritual powers have somehow been infiltrated by evil and therefore are in need of redemption. When God raised Jesus from the dead, however, these structures were unmasked but not destroyed.[26] Newbigin says human life is impossible without these structures, so it is the place of the church to influence these structures while God mercifully delays judgment. The church, therefore, has a two-fold relation to these structures, one of judgment and one of patience:

> We are rather patient revolutionaries who know the whole creation, with all its given structure, is groaning in the travail of a new birth, and that we share this groaning and travail, this struggling and wrestling, but do so in hope because we have already received, in the Spirit, the first fruit of the new world (Romans 8:19–25).[27]

The early Christians realized that they were not fighting against persons but systems of evil that were to be combated on the spiritual level. Through prayer and obedience to Christ they were able to unmask and render powerless the Roman Imperial system.[28] Although the world

---

23. Newbigin, *A Faith*, 99.
24. Ibid., 100–101.
25. Newbigin, *Gospel in a Pluralist Society*, 198–210.
26. Ibid., 208.
27. Ibid., 209.
28. Ibid., 210.

Humanity's Need for Salvation and the Call for Radical Conversion

seems to be in the grip of evil and is destined to pass away, God's ultimate purpose is not to destroy the earth but to recreate it. At the end of history, he will create a new heaven and a new earth.[29]

Some People will be Lost

The presence of evil in the world and sin in the hearts of persons means that, in the economy of God, people are alienated from Him and ultimately lost. Newbigin explicitly affirms that there are passages in Paul's writings that sound universalistic (e.g., Rom 5:18) but others point to the possibility of persons being lost (e.g., 1 Cor 9:27).[30] There are some who will be castaways. Newbigin does not believe that we can exclude this possibility without departing completely from "the gravely realistic teaching of the New Testament, with its insistent reminders that there is a broad . . . way leading to destruction and many go therein."[31] Newbigin says that it is in the light of the grace of God that was given to humanity through Jesus Christ that we can know the "terrible abyss of darkness into which we . . . fall if we put our trust anywhere but in that grace."[32] While the idea of judgment is often thought of as focused primarily in the prophets, there is hardly anything in the Old Testament to match the terrible severity of some of the words of Jesus on the possibility of being lost.[33]

In discussing Raymundo Panikkar's book about the *Unknown Christ of Hinduism*,[34] Newbigin responds to Panikkar's suggestion of universal salvation by saying that the revealed character of God precludes the idea of salvation for all. He believes that the gospel, which is centered on the story of the cross, reveals the terrible estrangement of humanity from God. This excludes forever any deduction that salvation will be a reality for all persons.[35] Interestingly, the threat of eternal loss, Newbigin notes, was directed primarily toward those who were confident of being among

---

29. Newbigin, *A Faith*, 101.
30. Newbigin, *Gospel in a Pluralist Society*, 88.
31. Newbigin, *The Household*, 140.
32. Newbigin, "Cross-currents," 151.
33. Newbigin, "Confessing Christ in a Multi-religion Society," 129.
34. Panikkar's book is an example of those who wish to reshape Christianity into the mold of the world.
35. Newbigin, *The Finality*, 42.

the saved.[36] God alone is the judge and Christians are not to presume to anticipate God's judgments.[37]

Newbigin recognizes that there is always a tension between the love and the wrath of God.[38] We are to be witnesses to Christ in whom alone humanity can find its unity, who has promised to draw everyone to himself.[39] This of course does not mean that everyone will respond in a positive way. The grace and the judgment apply to the whole range of existence.[40] Between now and the end of history, Christians have a responsibility to the world to share the gospel of the Kingdom so that those who are not a part of the Kingdom of God may repent and believe and turn to God.[41] There is urgency because there is not infinite of time before us.[42] The final day and hour of the revelation of God's Kingdom is in God's hands.[43]

Judgment

Newbigin traces the necessity of judgment to the 'total fact of Christ.' It is Christ who "brings the world under judgment and makes the biblical doctrine of sin not only possible but inevitable."[44] While there were specific persons involved in the arrest, trial, and crucifixion of Christ, these persons represented all humanity, and the judgment for all humanity was that Christ should be crucified.[45] There is a marvelous aspect to what happened there, that it would not be the kind of moral judgment that humanity would pass on each other: it would be a judgment of a different dimension. This would be the all-embracing judgment of God. It would be "the judgment of him who has judged us by taking our judgment upon himself and bearing with us and for us and as one of us the doom which we have deserved and to which we have been blind."[46] The 'total fact of

36. Newbigin, "Cross-currents," 151.
37. Ibid.
38. Newbigin, "Confessing Christ," 129.
39. Newbigin, "Common Witness and Unity," 158.
40. Newbigin, "Cross-currents," 149.
41. Newbigin, *A Faith*, 102.
42. Ibid., 103.
43. Ibid.
44. Ibid., 68.
45. Ibid., 70.
46. Ibid., 70–71. The influence of Barth on Newbigin is possible at this point, since the ideas are similar to those found in *Church Dogmatics*. vol. IV, part I:211–283. He was asso-

Humanity's Need for Salvation and the Call for Radical Conversion

Christ' implies that in him the total rejection of humanity against God is "unmasked, judged and forgiven."[47] Newbigin does not explicitly connect judgment with the holiness of God or the wrath of God based on his moral character. It is love that in the end claims victory, and it is love that brings man to judgment. Newbigin sees in John 3:16–17 that Jesus is the one who "leads men to the point where they must accept him as Lord or absolutely reject him." It is done tenderly because God never crosses the boundary of freedom that he has put around us.[48]

Newbigin describes the gospel story as the shining of a light that brings all things into the light, compelling people to accept or reject it. In this story we see "Jesus tenderly but inexorably leading persons to the point where they must either accept or absolutely reject him as Lord."[49] From this Newbigin draws the inevitable conclusion that every person must be in the end "wholly given to Christ or wholly given to the devil."[50]

Referring to Christ's action in the Temple when he drove out the money-changers, Newbigin interprets this as not only a judgment against corrupt religion but a judgment upon the "whole apparatus of organized religion—at least in form."[51] It was more than just an example of a prophetic protest against religion that had degenerated and become corrupted: it was the sign of the end of organized religion."[52] This is interesting coming from a man who spent his whole life as a leader in the institutional church and who advocated concrete organizational unity as God's will for the church. In spite of the tendency for organized religion to become sinful, he nevertheless believed strongly that disunity also fell short of God's will:

> . . . a divided Church in the New Testament sense of the word Church is something illogical and incomprehensible—as illogical and incomprehensible as human sin.[53]

---

ciated with Barth as a part of "the Twenty-five" theologians and churchmen who worked together to produce the "Report of the Advisory Commission on the Main Theme of the Second Assembly" of the World Council of Churches at Evanston (Illinois), 1954.

47. Newbigin, *A Faith*, 71.
48. Ibid., 104.
49. Ibid.
50. Ibid.
51. Newbigin, *The Light*, 31.
52. Ibid., 33.
53. Newbigin, *Reunion*, 24.

THE WAY OF SALVATION

Newbigin's Early Doctrine of Salvation

Newbigin remarks in an article in 1971 that the word 'salvation' has little meaning to contemporary man, who, in fact, is not aware of the need to be saved.[54] The earliest glimpse of his doctrine of salvation appears in an article on the Student Volunteer Movement in 1933. He makes reference to the statement in the gospels regarding those standing near the cross who remarked that Jesus could save others, but he could not save himself. Newbigin says that this should also be the mark of the church, that it spends its life to save others and is not concerned about saving itself.[55]

In his student paper on "Revelation," he states that the purpose of revelation is for salvific purposes. Paul, Newbigin notes, was called to the Gentile world to announce the "saving act of God."[56] Newbigin's particular position on salvation, as mentioned earlier, involves de-emphasizing individual salvation and greatly emphasizing the corporate and cosmic dimensions of redemption.[57] In his book, *The Finality of Christ*, Newbigin states unequivocally that the meaning of the word 'saved' should not be restricted to what will happen to the individual soul after death, a concept he feels is widespread among Christians but does not fully represent the teaching of the New Testament. He writes:

> The New Testament picture is dominated by the great corporate and cosmic completion of God's work in Christ, whereby all things will be restored to the unity for which they were created in Christ, and God will be all in all. In that final consummation the whole history of the world, as well as the history of each human soul, will find its true end. To be saved is to participate—in fore-taste now and in fullness at the end—in this final victory of Christ. According to the New Testament, the coming of Christ, his dying and rising and ascension is the decisive moment in God's plan of salvation.[58]

Reacting against the ecumenical movement's substitution of the doctrine of social or political salvation from oppression for the doctrine of salvation from sin, Newbigin is very clear to say in his writings that salvation

---

54. Newbigin, "Salvation," 537.
55. Newbigin, "The Student Volunteer Missionary Union," 98.
56. Newbigin, "Revelation," 21.
57. Newbigin, "The Summons," 185.
58. Newbigin, *The Finality*, 61.

Humanity's Need for Salvation and the Call for Radical Conversion

from sin is the reason for Christ's coming.[59] While Newbigin agrees that salvation from political oppression is one element of salvation broadly understood, the biblical doctrine of the cross is central to the redemption of humanity from sin and judgment.[60] He does not rule out the broader definition of salvation that includes "deliverance from the powers that oppress men—from enemies, pestilence, storms, and disease"[61] and that "salvation has to do with all men and with men in all their needs."[62]

Newbigin's Doctrine of Salvation

In order for humanity to be redeemed, God must make a way for humanity to be forgiven and restored. God's method was to make a covenant with and for the benefit of the whole human race through Noah in Genesis 9, as well as through Abram in Genesis 12:1–3. All the nations would benefit by the renewing and sealing of this covenant forever in the sacrifice of Jesus on the cross (1 Cor 11:25). This covenant is one of free, unconditional grace.[63] Central to this covenant of grace and to the redemption of humanity is Christ the Redeemer. Through his atoning work Christ has become the Lord of both the church and the world.[64]

THE INCARNATION AND AUTHORITY

The full revelation of God has come through the Living Word, the incarnated Christ. Commitment to Jesus, Newbigin believes, is the clue to the understanding of reality, seen and unseen, and all that is yet to be discovered.[65] In Jesus Christ the Word was made flesh and this is the "central and decisive event of universal history."[66] Ultimate reality has made its appearance in history in the person and work of Jesus Christ.[67] The Logos, by which and for which all things exist, became flesh and a part of human history, accessible to human knowledge. Newbigin explains:

---

59. Newbigin, "Ecumenical Amnesia," 2–5.
60. Ibid., 5.
61. Newbigin, "Salvation," 537.
62. Newbigin, "Address on the Main Theme," 6.
63. Newbigin, "Cross-currents," 151.
64. Newbigin, "Ecumenical Amnesia," 4–5.
65. Newbigin, *Proper Confidence*, 91.
66. Newbigin, "Reply to Konrad Raiser," 51.
67. Newbigin, *Proper Confidence*, 63.

"The Logos, the ultimate reason in which all that is coheres, the light that lightens every man, took flesh"[68] He continues to press the point: "The final secret of reality was given among men in the form that every man could see and hear and handle."[69] While he makes the point of the Logos becoming human, he also wishes to make another important point: "Jesus in his concrete reality . . . is the actual presence of life of God in the midst of the contingent happenings of human history."[70]

The incarnation dissolves the dichotomies that have plagued Western culture. There is no ultimate division of reality into 'material' and 'spiritual' because in the incarnate Christ they are fully unified.[71] The coming of Christ into the world means the Kingdom of God has also come into the world.[72] We preach Jesus the Creator, says Newbigin, because through him all things have been made, "the cause and cornerstone of the universe."[73] Newbigin sees the issue in terms of authority. Christ's authority, the substance of his Lordship, is based on his sovereign will to which all of creation owes its existence.[74] It has a great practical value for Christian action in the world. The authority of Jesus is absolute, and this means that it has priority over every other claim to authority.[75] Since Jesus is the ultimate authority for all humanity, it cannot be ratified by other authority.[76] If religion seeks a true vision of union with God, then it would be a gift of God and that gift is Jesus Christ. Christ, then, is the end of religion in the same way that he is the end of the Law.[77] A Christian cannot make an exclusive claim for possessing truth but can make an exclusive claim for the 'total fact of Christ,' which provides the point at which the critical and final issues of human life are both exposed and settled.[78] All of this is

---

68. Newbigin, "I Believe," 76.
69. Ibid.
70. Newbigin, *The Light*, 86.
71. Ibid., 3.
72. Newbigin, *A Faith*, 84.
73. Ibid., 62.
74. Ibid., 61.
75. Ibid., 64.
76. Ibid., 31.
77. Ibid., 74.
78. Ibid., 46.

Humanity's Need for Salvation and the Call for Radical Conversion

dependent upon the act of God where the Word became flesh and became a part of history.[79] Newbigin puts it into perspective:

> Without His incarnation there would be no cross and no salvation. Without His words and works we should not know who it was that died for us then. Without his resurrection the cross would not be known to us as victory but as defeat. Without His ascension to the Father and the gift of the Spirit, we who live at other times and places could have no share in Christ.[80]

Resurrection Faith

Newbigin turns to the writings of St. Paul in his discussion of final victory and resurrection faith. He says:

> the resurrection of Jesus from the dead is more than the guarantee of our individual resurrection; it is the first fruit, the sign and guarantee of God's new creation . . . This means that the resurrection faith . . . concerns not only . . . our ultimate status as persons, but also the ultimate status of humanity and of the cosmos.[81]

The Easter story is the starting point, says Newbigin, for a new way of understanding. The crucified Jesus was the first fruit of the new creation, signified by being raised from the dead. In a true sense, the Easter story is dogma, something asserted as true that is offered for acceptance by faith.[82] The Easter story challenges the contemporary worldview and the Enlightenment way of thinking.[83] Yet, the liberation of our rational faculties from religious dogma as the Enlightenment desired has not led the world into a more rational or more meaningful existence. We are again at the point in Western culture, writes Newbigin, "where accepted 'explanations' no longer explain."[84]

While the life and death of Jesus Christ have a significant place in the story of the redemption, Newbigin sees the resurrection as the defining event of Christianity. It was this resurrection belief that launched

---

79. Newbigin, *The Light*, xii.
80. Newbigin, *Sin and Salvation*, 61.
81. Newbigin, "The Secular-Apostolic Dilemma," 70.
82. Newbigin, *Gospel in a Pluralist Society*, 12.
83. Ibid.
84. Newbigin, *Other Side*, 117–18.

Christianity into the world with spiritual power.[85] Those who witnessed this marvelous event were witnesses to the breaking into this world of a new order of being. It was the lifting of a corner of the curtain that divides this world from the eternal world. It was a foretaste and first fruit of the true end of history.[86] The resurrection is also our assurance that God, Newbigin writes, has not withdrawn from life; God is very much a part of the phenomenal world. It is the ultimate security for the belief in the goodness and the reality of the created world.[87]

The Atonement of Christ

The purpose for Christ's coming into this world was to bring about reconciliation between God and humanity, estranged and alienated by sin. Newbigin, we recall, was influenced by James Denney's treatment of Paul's Letter to the Romans. The central doctrine for Denney was the atonement of Christ or the 'finished work of Christ,' referring to the completion of the purpose for Christ's incarnation. Newbigin insists in the centrality and (especially) the objectivity of the atonement.[88] In reading Denney's commentary on Romans (especially chapters 3–5),[89] four things stand out as representing his thought on the atonement: first, humanity needs to be freed from the condition that it was exposed to when the wrath of God was revealed from heaven against sin; second, it is the love of God that provides the propitiation; third, Christ's blood vindicates God's character and makes it possible to justify those who believe; fourth, his preference for the word *propitiation*[90] in describing what Christ's death accomplished.

The concept of the atonement has, of course, a whole history of meaning that has informed the New Testament concept of the atonement. The history of Israel's religion is the story of a developing concept of how God desired sin to be atoned for. Newbigin states that "God has provided

---

85. Newbigin, *A Faith*, 44.
86. Ibid., 99.
87. Newbigin, *Honest Religion*, 56.
88. Newbigin, *Unfinished*, 30–31.
89. Denny, "St. Paul's Epistle to the Romans," 555–725.
90. Denny writes: "Christ a propitiation is the inmost soul of the Gospel for sinful man." "St. Paul's Epistle to the Romans," Denny, in *The Expositor's Greek Testament*, Vol. II., ed. W. Robertson Nicoll (Grand Rapids: Eerdmans, reprinted, September 1976), 609.

Humanity's Need for Salvation and the Call for Radical Conversion

in Jesus Christ one mercy-seat where man's total rebellion is judged and pardoned."[91] Newbigin summarizes the benefits of the atonement:

> This is the time for the bold and tireless preaching of Jesus Christ as Lord, central, sovereign, final, of the Cross as the one place in all human history where the full measure of evil has been taken, where sin, guilt and death have been met and mastered; of the resurrection as the first-fruit of a new creation, as the birthplace of a hope which nothing can destroy; of Jesus as one name given under heaven, the one in all the human story who could be obeyed and loved as king and head of the human race, as the one in whom alone all our thinking and acting in the world can find its starting point and reward.[92]

"Christ's sacrificial death," he writes, "has expiatory value for us, and avails for our justification, only when it evokes in us the response of faith."[93] He puts special emphasis on the atonement as the gift of God to humanity and springs from God's love for us. Christ's work was representative and substitutionary.[94]

In his book, *Sin and Salvation*, Newbigin has an extensive discussion of the atonement as a part of his discussion of the work of Christ.[95] He says that the character of God cannot simply ignore sin, because he is holy love, which repels and resists sin. If this were not so, all of creation would be destroyed by sin.[96] Newbigin develops his thinking on the atonement from certain premises: first, that God is the author of salvation; second, that God's acts that bring about atonement also preserve his character; third, that *no one theory* truly represents what was accomplished in the atonement; fourth, that even though Newbigin acknowledges that Christ ransomed humanity, he is not sure how it was accomplished. "This word of Jesus [Mark 10:45]," Newbigin observes, does not tell us "how His life is a ransom for many."[97] Newbigin's purpose is not to develop a theory of

---

91. Newbigin, *A Faith*, 77.
92. Newbigin, "Centrality of Christ," 28.
93. Newbigin, *Reunion*, 86.
94. Ibid., 84–90.
95. Newbigin. *Sin and Salvation*, 56–90.
96. Ibid., 41.
97. Newbigin, *Sin and Salvation*, 66 (repeated on page 67). Later (on page 71), he says that the ransom idea cannot be pressed too far; he is not willing to say that ransom was paid to God or Satan.

the atonement but to point to it as a basis for new understanding of reality and God.

The Holy Spirit applies the work of Christ to the benefit of humanity. Newbigin explains:

> The Spirit could only be given when Jesus had completed His atonement, when He had provided the ransom, the sacrifice whereby sinful men could come near to Holy God. Until He had done that, there could be no union between God and man, and therefore no sharing for man in God's Spirit.[98]

The scope of Christ's work is universal, which according to God's "forbearance" (Rom 3:23 and following), is even efficacious for those who lived (and died) before the time of Christ's ministry on earth.[99]

The Saving Power of God through Real History

Sin, Newbigin realizes, is a terrible historical reality that could only be overcome by mighty acts of God.[100] According to Romans 8, God has delivered those who believe in Jesus Christ from the dominion of darkness and sin. While salvation is intensely personal and individual, Newbigin observes that the church has put so much emphasis on personal salvation that it has neglected public witness. This very deliverance makes us long for an even greater deliverance, not just for personal salvation but for all of creation to be delivered. The present anguish is the anguish of childbirth, a new world struggling to be born.[101] The Bible does not just see the person as a *soul* but more realistically as a *living body-soul*. This person cannot be understood isolated from the network of relationships that are a part of every person's life, a network of family, tribes, nations, and "all the progeny of Adam."[102] The New Testament is faithful to its Old Testament roots in speaking of salvation in terms of the resurrection of the body, a new creation, and even a heavenly city. The vision of this

---

98. Newbigin, *Sin and Salvation*, 96–97.

99. Newbigin, "Christ and the World of Religions," 27. See Michael W. Goheen, "*As the Father Has Sent Me, I Am Sending You*," 147, for a discussion of Newbigin's doctrine of atonement.

100. Newbigin, *Sin and Salvation*, 43.

101. Newbigin, *Good Shepherd*, 67.

102. Newbigin, "Cross-currents," 149.

Humanity's Need for Salvation and the Call for Radical Conversion

heavenly 'polis' does not allow us to exclude politics from salvation. It has concrete ramifications and implications.[103]

Salvation in the Old Testament, however, is never fully a secular vision. It is never only justice, social peace, or political liberation; it is the restoration of a relationship with the living God. The outward result of salvation is the result of inward realities. Behind and beyond both of these is the eschatological vision of a totally new order, which goes far beyond anything that can be imagined in this world. Salvation has an inward and an outward manifestation as well as a present and future application.[104]

SALVATION INCLUDES COSMIC RESTORATION

Newbigin articulates this comprehensive vision as follows:

> The salvation of which the Gospel speaks and which is determinative of the nature and function of the Church is—as the very word itself should teach us—a making whole, a healing. It is the summing-up of all things in Christ. It embraces within its scope the restoration of harmony between man and God, between man and man and between man and nature for which all things were first created. It is the restoration to the whole creation of the perfect unity whose creative source and pattern is the unity of perfect love with the being of the triune God. It is in its very essence, universal and cosmic.[105]

Christ is at the center of the restoration of the cosmos as he is in the redemption of the individual believer.[106] While the Bible's main focus is upon the salvation of the nations, the restoration of the cosmos is a part of the restoration of the broken relationship between God and mankind, for the fall of mankind had a catastrophic influence on the cosmos as well.[107]

---

103. Newbigin, "Cross-currents," 149.

104. Newbigin, *Good Shepherd*, 106.

105. Newbigin, *The Household*, 140.

106. Newbigin was very much influenced by W. A. Vissser 't Hooft, which he acknowledges in an article, "The Legacy of W.A. Visser 't Hooft" in *IBMR*, 78–82. Visser 't Hooft writes: "Many Christians can only conceive of Christianity as a matter of individual edification and personal salvation and are completely blind to the universal aspects of the biblical message. The churches have not clearly proclaimed that the Christian faith has to do with the ends of the earth and the ends of time, with mankind, with universal history, with total 'cosmos.'" *No Other Name*, Visser 't Hooft (London: SCM, 1963), 93–94.

107. T. F. Torrance touches on the idea of evil in nature, but phrases his sentences to seem more rhetorical than an assertion of his thinking. He writes: "the question must

The Eschatological Dimension of Salvation

The eschatological dimension that is behind the scenes in the Old Testament becomes explicit in the New.[108] All things will be summed-up in Christ and all things will be made new.[109] The Kingdom of God, which will be made manifest to all humanity in the future, presently remains hidden. The resurrection of Christ and the post-resurrection words of Christ promise to his followers that the Kingdom will manifestly rule over all creation.[110] Salvation is both a present and a future reality.[111] What is experienced now is a 'foretaste' of complete salvation which lies ahead.[112]

The eschatological dimension of salvation does not mean that we do not engage in God's battle with evil in the present. Salvation means that we have taken sides, and we are participants in this struggle that already is won in Christ.[113] "Action for social justice," Newbigin asserts, "is salvation in action."[114]

Newbigin sees two alternative views to biblical eschatology evidenced in Western cultural thinking. On the one side are those who have replaced the biblical idea of the Kingdom of God and an eschatological order consummated in Christ with the utopian idea of building a perfect earthly society. The real meaning of history is not that great act of God of recreating the heavens and the earth, but of building a better social order.[115] On the other side, there are those who have strongly reacted against seeing salvation exclusively in terms of social betterment by seeing salva-

---

be posed whether moral disorder or evil is rooted in the expansion of the universe. In other words, we have to reckon with the reality of natural as well as moral evil, and with some interconnection between them." *Christian Frame of Mind*, T. F. Torrance (Colorado Springs, CO: Helmers & Howard, 1989), 100. Later he says: "if in some inexplicable way there is evil at work in the universe, giving disorder a crooked twist so that it is not just a neutral feature of nature on the way toward order, but is fraught with distinctive tendencies, then the redemption of the universe from disorder requires more than a rearrangement of form like the resolving of dissonance in music, namely, the radical undoing and defeat of evil." Ibid., 103.

108. Newbigin, *Good Shepherd*, 106–7.
109. Newbigin, *The Household*, 140.
110. Newbigin, *Good Shepherd*, 66.
111. Ibid., 107.
112. Newbigin, *Sin and Salvation*, 115.
113. Newbigin, *Good Shepherd*, 108.
114. Ibid., 109.
115. Newbigin, *A Faith*, 97.

tion exclusively as personal spirituality. They are preoccupied with the destiny of the individual soul.[116] Neither of these views is tenable, according to Newbigin.

A THEOLOGY OF RADICAL CONVERSION

The Call for Radical Conversion

Central to Newbigin's theological convictions is his concept of radical conversion,[117] which he believes is absolutely necessary to pull Western culture out of its downward spiral and place it on firm footing once again. Newbigin says that apprehending the whole of experience in terms of the fact of Christ is meaningful to us only if we "suffer a radical conversion, re-orientation of viewpoint."[118]

Newbigin recognizes that the conversion experience coincides with one's relationship with the church. In a chapter titled "How Salvation Becomes Ours" in *Sin and Salvation*, Newbigin explains that salvation becomes ours "when we become part of this society, the fellowship, He left behind to be the continuation of His life on earth."[119] The most notable example of Newbigin's early view of conversion is his statement in *The Household of God* (1952) that conversion is a radical break with the whole of non-Christian culture.[120] In his article, "Conversion" (1966), he defines conversion primarily as a moral and spiritual change, a turning around, and a recognition of and participation in "the dawning reality of God's rule."[121]

Radical Repentance

The gospel is a radical judgment upon all human wisdom and requires a new way of salvation.[122] Commenting on *The Logic of Evangelism* by

---

116. Newbigin, *A Faith*, 97.

117. This section is a summary of numerous passages where Newbigin speaks of a radically new starting point that implies a radical conversion from one plausibility structure to another. He writes: "To accept it means a new beginning, a radical conversion." *Foolishness*, Newbigin (Grand Rapids: Eerdmans, 1986), 148.

118. Newbigin, "I Believe," 80.

119. Newbigin, *Sin and Salvation*, 93.

120. Newbigin, *The Household*, 15.

121. Newbigin, "Conversion," in *Religion and Society* 31–32.

122. Newbigin, *The Finality*, 57.

William Abraham,[123] Newbigin remarks that Abraham defines evangelism as "initiation into the Kingdom of God."[124] Acceptance of Jesus Christ as Lord of one's life involves, according to Newbigin, a radical repentance.[125] The call to repent is not (as the T. E. V. translates it) to "turn away from your sins."[126] "To repent," writes Newbigin, "means to turn around and face in a different direction."[127] Repentance is a call for *metanoia*, a complete change of the mind. Without this *metanoia*, it is impossible to recognize the reign of God in Jesus Christ or in the event of Good Friday.[128]

In his discussion of Mark 1:14–15, Newbigin says that the people were waiting for the Kingdom of God, but that it came from a direction different from the one expected. In order to see the coming kingdom, the people would be required to turn around and face the other direction.[129] The initial call of the gospel was to repent and be converted, which means having a radically new mind-set. To be able to recognize the new reality requires facing the opposite direction.[130]

The emphasis must remain, however, on God's initiative because humans cannot put themselves right with God through their own effort.[131] "The great evangelical doctrine of justification by faith remains basic," insists Newbigin, "and we must never stray away from it."[132] The reign of God is not obvious to everyone; otherwise there would be no need for faith. Those who have faith will see it: this is why Jesus answered questions with parables and stories of everyday life. Christ's announcement of the coming of the Kingdom is a challenge to faith.[133] By faith, we see

---

123. Abraham is the Albert Cook Outler Professor of Wesley Studies at Perkins School of Theology, Southern Methodist University.

124. Newbigin, "Episcopacy and Authority," 336.

125. Newbigin uses the term in connection with the ministry of John the Baptist. See "Conversion," 30. Later in the article, he ascribes it to a call from Christ. See "Conversion," 34.

126. Newbigin, "Episcopacy and Authority," 337.

127. Newbigin. *Good Shepherd*, 64.

128. Newbigin, "Episcopacy and Authority," 337.

129. Newbigin, *Good Shepherd*, 64.

130. Newbigin, *Gospel in a Pluralist Society*, 6. While Newbigin was wholly involved in the Ecumenical movement, his view of conversion is very evangelical.

131. Newbigin, *Good Shepherd*, 108–19.

132. Ibid.

133. Ibid. 108–9, 64.

Humanity's Need for Salvation and the Call for Radical Conversion

the enormity of our sin against God and it is then we see God's judgment. We acknowledge our guilt and shame and then surrender our will to him. That surrender, which Newbigin describes as the 'Amen,' is faith and it too is the work of the Holy Spirit. Conversion is a turning that allows a person not only to believe in, but also to participate in the coming reign of Christ.[134] The free gift that is offered is the restoration relationship with God and, consequently, a renewed and redemptive relationship with other human beings based on the model of God's love.[135]

The Meaning of Conversion to Christ

When one is converted, it is not in a vacuum;[136] conversion always involves a concrete decision at a particular moment in history.[137] Conversion is, among other things, a change in the loyalty to the kingdom of light rather than the kingdom of darkness. Persons must forsake all other claims to ultimate loyalty and be converted to Christ. It is at this point that the claim to the finality of Christ becomes actual and therefore threatening to the old loyalties and securities.[138] It involves "the abandonment of every intellectual and spiritual security in order to 'come to Jesus.'"[139] The convert accepts a pattern of conduct that reflects God's will and the fulfillment of God's reign at a particular time and place in history.[140]

God leads persons to conversion by doing a secret work in their heart.[141] This secret work is not enough to save; a person must follow the lead and respond to God's initiative.[142] "The union of the believer with Christ is," writes Newbigin, "the work of the Spirit quickening and using these visible means [the church and fellowship] which Christ has given to

---

134. Newbigin, *The Finality*, 113.
135. Newbigin, *Good Shepherd*, 179.
136. In an article in 1966, Newbigin is making a point regarding the purpose of conversion, an idea that coincides with his doctrine of election. "God converts a man not just that he may be saved, but that he may be the sign, earnest and instrument of God's total plan of salvation for the world." "Conversion," Newbigin *Religion and Society* 13, no. 4 (1966), 41.
137. Newbigin, *The Finality*, 94.
138. Ibid., 87.
139. Newbigin, *The Light*, 96.
140. Newbigin, *The Finality*, 91.
141. Newbigin, *The Light*, 81.
142. Newbigin, *A Faith*, 45.

his people."[143] It is the Holy Spirit working in our hearts that causes us to understand what Christ has done for us.[144] It is at the cross (the recognition of what Christ has done at the cross) that people die and are then made alive. This whole experience is described in the Bible as being *born again*. It is the regeneration of spiritual life brought about by the Spirit.[145] It is at that moment that Christ's mind is formed within the person and it is in believing that we receive the righteousness of God:

> That believing, obeying, loving mind towards God is righteousness. It is the only true righteousness. True righteousness is not a possession of my own which I can have apart from God; that is self-righteousness, and it is the very essence of sin. True righteousness is a relation of loving trust and obedience toward God.[146]

Radical conversion means also a radically new starting point. It is impossible to find such radical renewal within the framework of the presuppositions and assumptions of the Enlightenment. There must be a new starting point, Newbigin insists, beginning with trust in divine grace, something to be received in faith and gratitude.[147] Radical conversion means not only a conversion of the will but also of the mind. It would entail a transformation by the renewing of the mind so that it is no longer conformed to this world, not seeing things, in other words, from the non-Christian aspect of Western cultural perspective but from an entirely new set of lenses in a radically different way.[148] It is not seeing things from a 'heavenly' viewpoint, it means seeing the human situation as it really is.[149]

Newbigin confesses that his view of conversion had changed by the end of 1980. It came about in part by his reading of Alasdair MacIntyre's book *Whose Justice? Whose Rationality?*[150] Conversion, Newbigin says, cannot be thought of merely in moralistic terms, where one turns away from sin only. Something more radical must happen. It must involve a

---

143. Newbigin, *Sin and Salvation*, 96.

144. See Newbigin, "Context and Conversion," 304 and 307, for a discussion on the work of the Holy Spirit in conversion.

145. See Newbigin, *Sin and Salvation*, 99–101.

146. Ibid., 105.

147. Newbigin, *Other Side*, 25.

148. Newbigin, *Gospel in a Pluralist Society*, 38.

149. Newbigin, "Episcopacy and Authority," 337.

150. MacIntyre, *Whose Justice?* London: Gerald Duckworth & Company, 1988.

Humanity's Need for Salvation and the Call for Radical Conversion

complete transformation of the mind.[151] Newbigin calls true conversion a radical subversion of the world's order that opens the door for a person to accept the new order where Jesus Christ is the head.[152] Accepting him means to "undergo a radical and total re-orientation of being by which the centre is shifted from self to him."[153]

The Extent of Conversion

Conversion requires a "considerable, perhaps even radical, rearrangement of our mental furniture."[154] It means converting from one fiduciary framework to another, reflecting the new truths that are foundational to one's new world view.[155] Newbigin believes that the Christian must seek to convince people of the superior rationality of the new plausibility structure, and also must demonstrate its adequacy.[156]

While Newbigin focuses his critique on Western culture, he is not saying one thing in the West and another in the East. He believes that radical conversion in the Hindu context would require a radical break with those non-Christian aspects of culture in the same way that it is necessary in the West. The uniqueness of Newbigin's position is that he applies the same principle to both contexts. He did not always hold this to be the case. In his book *The Household of God* (1952) he explains the difference between the situation of the churches in the West (Christendom) that exists in a culture that has become secularized but still has a memory of things Christian. At that particular time in his career he described Western culture as "semi-Christian."[157] By this he implied that the demands upon Christians in a non-Christian culture like India are different and more radical than that of Western Christians because of the nature of the context. However, his view of the situation in the West changed significantly after he retired back into Britain. His experience as a part-time pastor in Winston Green brought home the reality that Britain is a pagan society that must be dealt with by a missionary encounter not unlike the manner

---

151. Newbigin, *A Word*, 142.
152. Newbigin, *The Light*, 169.
153. Newbigin, *A Faith*, 62.
154. Newbigin, *Truth to Tell*, 10.
155. Newbigin, *A Word*, 108.
156. Newbigin, *Truth and Authority*, 53–54.
157. Newbigin, *The Household*, 15.

in which missionaries have confronted Indian culture.[158] So, his message is the same for the West as for the East: radical conversion means turning around, changing one's mind, and breaking with aspects of culture that are not Christian. Ultimately, it requires a radical shift in perspective.[159] While it is understood that Newbigin is focusing on the epistemological problem exacerbated by the Enlightenment, he nevertheless fails to give enough consideration to the moral dimension of conversion.

Radical Conversion as a Paradigm Shift

Drawing on the thinking of Michael Polanyi,[160] Newbigin describes a paradigm shift as a new perspective that requires new language to communicate because it cannot be demonstrated in terms of the old paradigm, nor is an over-arching logical system that can adequately explain the change from one vision to another.[161] At one point Newbigin describes the change as a 'leap,' but in a very restrained sense. This 'leap' takes place when there is no logical bridge between the old paradigm and the new. He explains: "This understanding is only possible after the paradigm shift has occurred, and this shift is a sort of leap which cannot be justified by reasoning based on the Newtonian principles. I suggest this as an analogy—nothing more."[162]

The terminology of a paradigm shift is a more contemporary way of expressing his doctrine of radical conversion and it comes from Thomas Kuhn as well as Michael Polanyi.[163] Kuhn's view is that before a person would change paradigms, there must be significant evidence and persuasion to warrant leaving behind long-held convictions and believe something new to be true.[164] Since the new paradigm cannot be demonstrated in terms of the old, the only test for its validity would be its adequacy to

---

158. Newbigin, *Unfinished*, 249. His view is strongly presented in *Foolishness*, 1.
159. Newbigin, *A Word*, 112.
160. Polanyi's thinking is dealt with in more detail in the chapter 6.
161. Newbigin, *A Word*, 91.
162. Newbigin, "Context and Conversion," 303.
163. There is some debate regarding whether there may be a connection between Kuhn and Polanyi. At the least, they were familiar with each other's work and had similar ideas. See Fuller, *Thomas Kuhn*, 149. Also see Kuhn, *Structure of Scientific Revolution*.
164. Newbigin, *Truth and Authority*, 53.

Humanity's Need for Salvation and the Call for Radical Conversion

the reality that is to be interpreted.[165] Such language would resonate with Newbigin.

Newbigin explains the manner that the worldview becomes changed in the new convert. Once a person has made the critical step of changing paradigms or experiencing conversion, there comes a time for a reassessment of the paradigm of the culture from which the person has come. The convert looks at culture with a new, discriminating eye, seeking to retain what is good but necessarily discarding that which would contradict or oppose this new paradigm. The assessment of the person's culture is done within the context of the new faith community, which adheres to a different set of principles from the culture. While dwelling in this community, the new convert will make decisions from within this new environment, enveloped in the new atmosphere.[166]

This new context is radically different, Newbigin asserts, from the Western cultural context that the convert comes from. For example, the common belief in Western culture is that personal knowledge is somehow inferior to knowledge based on pure induction from data supplied by the senses. Such a belief, Newbigin insists, has no foundation in reality.[167] In the Christian community, faith is not a substitute for knowledge; it is "the indispensable precondition for knowledge."[168]

Another point of contention between the convert's new paradigm and Western culture is seen in the fact that over half of the Gospel of Mark deals with the miracles of Jesus, which means that spiritual powers can operate directly to change the material world. Such a view, Newbigin notes, is generally excluded from Western cultural thinking.[169] The paradigm change is eventuated when the convert makes the paradigm shift by faith from what was not plausible in terms of the old understanding to a new understanding of reality.

---

165. Ibid.
166. Newbigin, *The Household*, 15.
167. Newbigin, *The Light*, 20.
168. Ibid.
169. Ibid., 24.

The Role of the Holy Spirit in Conversion

As noted above, conversion is a new act of the Holy Spirit in the heart of human being.[170] The witness of the Spirit brings a person to the point of decision, one that is informed by a story of reality and of God that the person is asked to believe.[171] Newbigin recognizes that this work of the Spirit is seldom explicit or observable, but it is always mysterious. It is mysterious how men and women come to adhere to and live by a different story from the one that operates in society.[172] It is also mysterious in the way that the Holy Spirit takes all the scattered acts and words of faithful witnesses and uses them to bring about conversion.[173] God uses a variety of persons, words, and witnesses to bring about the marvelous *metanoia*.[174] It is always a free and supernatural work of the Holy Spirit[175] and is always beyond our control or even our understanding.[176]

Newbigin says that it is the work of the Holy Spirit in the heart of persons that gives them the faith they need to respond to the overtures of God. Salvation seen from God's side is the work of the Holy Spirit, while from the human side it is faith. Faith is not something that is conjured up by the human heart but is the work of the Holy Spirit in the heart. At the same time, we may say that it is through faith in Christ's completed work that we receive the Holy Spirit.[177]

The initiative for salvation and regeneration is always on the side of God. The work of the Holy Spirit begins in the heart of a person even before they are conscious of it. Newbigin writes: "Conversion is a miraculous work of God. It is by his calling that the paradigm shift occurs which makes the story of the cross the power of God to salvation."[178] The end result is not just individual salvation but persons becoming incorporated into the faith community that bears witness to Christ.[179] This is signifi-

---

170. Newbigin, *The Finality*, 104.

171. Newbigin, *Trinitarian Faith*, 45. Newbigin writes: "But the . . . witness which brings men to the point of decision is the witness of the Holy Spirit himself."

172. Newbigin. *A Word*, 96.

173. Lesslie Newbigin, "Integration—Some Personal Reflections," 247.

174. Newbigin, "Context and Conversion," 306.

175. Ibid., 304.

176. Newbigin, *A Word*, 42.

177. Newbigin, *Sin and Salvation*, 99.

178. Newbigin, "Context and Conversion," 306.

179. Newbigin, *Gospel in a Pluralist Society*, 119.

Humanity's Need for Salvation and the Call for Radical Conversion

cant for Newbigin, who believed identity with the visible church to be crucial.[180]

Newbigin makes an interesting and somewhat controversial observation when he asserts that, while conversion is most certainly brought about by the Holy Spirit, it "seems to bear little visible relationship to organized missionary efforts."[181] This disproportionate view of the connection between missionary effort and conversion is suggested, he believes, in the parable of the sower and the seed.[182] While massive evangelistic campaigns seem to produce little or nothing, he says, a quiet word spoken in the course of an ordinary caring human relationship is the seed that produces a great harvest.[183]

The question remains: What would cause a person to choose one perspective available in the world over another one? "The Gospel comes to us," Newbigin writes, "as a truth which has laid hold of me."[184] It is, for those who are called to believe, the strange story of a crucified Christ who is the power for salvation, for the individual and the world.

The Question of Continuity and Discontinuity

Newbigin addresses the ethical implications of radical conversion in terms of continuity and discontinuity. He emphatically states that "conversion implies a real discontinuity," between the old life and the new one in Christ.[185] Conversion has always had ethical implications and content. It means not only joining a new community but also a new pattern of conduct, one that is relevant for doing God's will and feeling his reign at a particular point in world history.[186] The idea of conversion as a purely

---

180. Newbigin, "Context and Conversion," 307.

181. Newbigin, "Integration—Some Personal Reflections," 254.

182. Newbigin, "Context and Conversion," 306.

183. Ibid. While the quiet word may be effectively used by the Holy Spirit, it does not necessarily rule out the possibility that the Holy Spirit can and does work in large campaigns as well. It would appear that Newbigin is basing these comments solely on his experience in India. Certainly he would have been cognizant of the influence that persons like Dwight L. Moody had on the early leaders (Robert Speer in America and J. H. Oldham in Britain, for example) of the Student Christian Movement and the formation of the ecumenical movement. See Tatlow. *The Story of the Student Christian Movement*, 6–7.

184. Newbigin, "I Believe," 75.

185. Newbigin, *The Finality*, 90.

186. Ibid., 91.

inward experience without any change in concrete conduct is an erroneous concept, because conversion intrinsically involves certain decisions about conduct.[187] "This inward turning," he writes, ". . . involves both a pattern of conduct and a visible companionship. It involves membership in a community and a decision to act in certain ways." [188]

The effect of true conversion goes far beyond the life of the individual; it can call into question, Newbigin believes, the existing manner of life in the community. The dynamic of God's intervention into the life of the individual would also influence the life and structure of the community.[189] Those who have been brought to new life by the resurrection of Jesus are those who are truly free.[190] They also gain assurance that what happened in Jesus Christ at a specific point in history has significant relevance for their lives today. Newbigin writes: "The resurrection of Jesus, and the gift of the Holy Spirit, provide us with unshakeable assurance, outward and inward, that our hope in the Kingdom is not a dream, but is based on God's sure promise."[191]

Such an assurance should cause Christians to witness to such a wonderful hope. Christians, however, have often withdrawn into a private sphere to enjoy the benefits of personal salvation. Newbigin repudiates such an action. In his student paper on "Revelation" (1936), he noted that there is "an individualistic mysticism very remote from the genius of Christianity."[192]

CONCLUSION

In this chapter Newbigin's theology of radical conversion is discussed. By radical conversion he means not only the conversion of the heart but also of the mind. It is radical because it results both in a complete change of direction and loyalty, but also a total change of the mind from the worldview of the world to the worldview of the Kingdom of God.

In the process of discussing his theology of radical conversion Newbigin's doctrine of salvation was expounded. His view of salvation includes individual salvation but also extends to cosmic redemption as

187. Newbigin, *The Finality*, 93.
188. Ibid., 97.
189. Ibid., 109.
190. Newbigin, *Proper Confidence*, 69–70.
191. Newbigin, *Sin and Salvation*, 116.
192. Newbigin, "Revelation," 3.

Humanity's Need for Salvation and the Call for Radical Conversion

well. Salvation is initiated, obtained, and offered by God. It is the Holy Spirit who leads persons to salvation and who seeks to bring about the paradigm shift where one's belief in the cognitive system of the world is exchanged for the mind of Christ.

In the next chapter we will discuss Newbigin's critique of Western culture, which has imbedded within it a cognitive system that is in defiance of God and the biblical view of reality.

5

Newbigin's Critique of Western Culture

NEWBIGIN UTILIZES THE THEOLOGICAL convictions he developed over the years as a standard of evaluation when confronting contemporary Western culture. "The gospel," he writes, "provides the stance from which all culture is to be evaluated."[1] What emerges in Newbigin's engagement with Western culture is a theology of mission that meshes his theological convictions with the post-critical assumptions of Charles Cochrane and Michael Polanyi.

WESTERN CULTURE FROM THE CLASSICAL ERA TO THE MIDDLE AGES

The Earliest Development of Western Culture

It was the gospel story, Newbigin believes, that distinguished Europe from Asia. In the gospel, truth is taught by way of a story, a series of historical events that were a part the history and tradition of Israel, and that culminate in the life and ministry of Jesus Christ. In Asia, by way of contrast, there is no real place for history in the discovering of truth, for truth is timeless and eternal, not found in the material world or in the events of history.[2]

Western culture is further distinguished from Asia by the idea of a contingent creation, a biblical idea that allows humanity to view the cosmos objectively and be the object of curiosity and discovery. It is a cosmos separated from God, but God still interacts with it and sustains it.[3] Newbigin's critique of the development of Western science and its

---

1. Newbigin, *Foolishness*, 21.

2. Newbigin says the rationalist tradition of the West and the spiritualist tradition of the East share the same belief that "historical events are not a source of ultimate truth." *Gospel in a Pluralist Society*, Newbigin (London: SPCK, 1989), 2.

3. While there is some evidence that Newbigin read T. F. Torrance (see McKinney,

Newbigin's Critique of Western Culture

influence on culture is that it moved Europe back toward Asia in that it re-introduced, although in a different form, a movement from a culture based on story to one based on a 'set of timeless laws.' If the cosmos has no history, truth could be stated in the 'timeless formulae of mathematics.'[4]

The biblical story shaped the mental pictures of early Europeans after the gospel was introduced to the barbaric tribes. Newbigin describes the process by which these tribes incorporated biblical ideas into their cultures:

> In the constant remembering of the great events of creation and salvation through the liturgical year, in the popular drama of the streets, and in the pictures that surrounded the congregation as they gathered for worship, it was this story that was their mental framework, the story that defined human life and its meaning and destiny. It was this story that shaped those barbarian tribes into the cultural and spiritual entity that made Europe something other than simply a peninsula of Asia.[5]

For a thousand years, successive waves of people from Asia went to Europe and were schooled in the biblical story, so much so that the biblical story[6] became the framework for life for the culture. The development of the cultural worldview and the creation of a material culture were based on a Christian cultural ideology.[7] During these thousand years, the church, the bearer of the gospel story, lived out the narrative and gave shape to culture and public life.[8] The distinctive character of Europe,

---

Creation, Christ, and Culture), Torrance does not appear to be major source of Newbigin's thought. One can see the idea of contingent creation in Torrance, See T. F. Torrance *Theology in Reconciliation*, 100.

4. Newbigin, *Truth and Authority*, 75.

5. Newbigin, *Proper Confidence*, 13. See also Newbigin, *A Word*, 164.

6. Newbigin's use of the terms 'biblical story' and 'narrative' suggest that he was influenced by contemporary hermeneutical and homiletical thinking which reflect a shift away from metaphysical thinking and propositional statements. Newbigin mentions Hans Frei in *The Gospel in a Pluralist Society*, 99. He does not mention which book he is referring to, but most likely it is *The Eclipse of Biblical Narrative*. Newbigin never liked the idea of biblical teachings being thought of as propositions, see also "I Believe," 74–75. He preferred to talk of biblical truth as story. As early as 1948 he says the Bible is not the story of ideas about God, the story of the people of God and God's action in history. See Newbigin, *Reunion*, 27.

7. Newbigin, *Proper Confidence*, 12, 53.

8. Newbigin, *Proper Confidence*, 9, 53. Christopher Dawson, in his book *Religion and the Rise of Western Culture*, writes: "The Latin fathers—Ambrose, Augustine, Leo and

Newbigin insists, is based on the uniqueness of God, the chief character in the biblical story.⁹

Christianity and Classical Thought

Newbigin's interest in the relationship of Christianity to classical thought is focused primarily on the areas of cosmology and epistemology. There are two streams of thought that have formed the deep roots of European intellectual history: the philosophy of antiquity and the history of Israel.¹⁰ There has always been tension between these two streams. Newbigin asserts that while the intellectual leaders of the European tribes were educated in Greek and Latin (with the respective cultural and philosophical ideas attached), it was the biblical story that subsequently shaped their thinking at the deepest levels.¹¹

Classical philosophy, for all its enormous contribution to modern Western culture, struggled with certain dichotomies that Western culture still contends with, in spite of the fact that Augustine introduced a worldview into Western culture that could resolve these dichotomies.¹² Newbigin explains:

> Classical thought, for all its splendid achievement, had been unable to overcome dichotomies between being and becoming, between reason and will, between the intelligible or spirit world and the material world known by the senses.¹³

Introduction of a New Arche

The overriding question for the theologians of antiquity was how the Christian message could be communicated in classical thought without

---

Gregory—were in a real sense the fathers of Western culture, since it was only in so far as the different peoples of the West were incorporated in the spiritual community of Christendom that they acquired a common culture. It is this, above all, that distinguishes the Western development from that of other world civilizations." *Religion and the Rise of Western Culture*, Dawson (London: Sheed & Ward, 1950), 26.

9. Ibid., 53.
10. Ibid., 2.
11. Ibid., 3.
12. The source of Newbigin's ideas regarding Augustine comes from Cochrane's *Christianity and Classical Culture*.
13. Newbigin, *Truth to Tell*, 15–16.

Newbigin's Critique of Western Culture

being absorbed into it. Newbigin believes they found a way because at the heart of the Christian message is a new 'fact.' The original word for 'fact' in Latin is *factum*, 'something done.' God had acted and this is a 'fact.' What God has done has changed the way we understand the world. According to Athanasius,[14] what God has done has created a new starting point (a new *arche*) for human understanding of the world.[15] In using the word *arche*, Athanasius was using the language of classical philosophy.[16] God's actions in history provided a new model for the understanding of reality, and more importantly, "it provided a framework within the ancient dichotomies were overcome and a new 'plausibility structure' was created."[17]

Newbigin elaborates on the change that ensued in human thinking as a result of the new *arche*:

> There is no more an ultimate dualism of matter and spirit, because God has taken our flesh in such a way that he who has seen Jesus has seen the Father. History is no longer an endless and hopeless struggle of virtue and fortune, of the human spirit against the power of fate, for the one who created and rules all things in heaven and earth, and the one whose Spirit is given to those who are in Christ, is one with the man who went his way from Bethlehem to Calvary, and we can therefore say that God works all things together for good to those who love him.[18]

This new *arche* would require a radically new way of thinking about God.[19] If the *logos* had truly become a part of history in Jesus Christ, then the dualism between the *material* and the *spiritual* (the 'sensible' and 'intelligible') and between *being* and *becoming* are made untenable. The Incarnate Christ, being the same substance as God the Father, destroys the first dualism. That God, Perfect and Ultimate Being, transcendent above

---

14. Athanasius (ca. 293–373) was Christian theologian and bishop who defended the cause of orthodoxy against Arianism.

15. Newbigin, *Proper Confidence*, 4.

16. T. F. Torrance refers to *arche* in *Trinitarian Faith*: "In linking it together with the uncreated *arche*... which God is in his transcendent being, Athanasius clearly regarded the created *arche*... which Christ constituted in our human being both as the Beginning of a new beginning with the creation and as the fundamental Principle or archetypical Pattern of God's gracious provision for his Creation" *Trinitarian Faith*, T. F. Torrance (Edinburgh: T. & T. Clark, 1988), 83.

17. Newbigin, *Truth to Tell*, 17.

18. Ibid.

19. Newbigin, *Proper Confidence*, 7.

creation, could also be one with Jesus of Nazareth, who was a part of the historical process and changing historical reality (*becoming*), overcomes the second dualism.[20]

Newbigin explains the positive consequences of such a radical change of thought:

> It [the new *arche*] provided the starting point for a whole new chapter in human thought and action, a new beginning which was destined to shape what we call Europe. Ultimate reality was no longer unknowable; it was available to us in the person of Jesus Christ, who was made known to us in the New Testament and the preaching of the church. By faithfulness to this reality, we would be led by the work of the divine Spirit to full knowledge of the Father, a knowledge partial *in via* but promised in its fullness at the end.[21]

Newbigin connects not only a change in the way of understanding reality, but also a change in how one can know reality. Closely aligned to Newbigin's discussions of cosmology is his concern with epistemology.

Augustine and Western Culture

What Athanasius began Augustine continued. Augustine of Hippo was a significant figure in Western thought. He was a credible classical scholar, a professor of rhetoric at the imperial university, a "brilliant product of the classical world," and "a master of the finest classical thought."[22] As he worked through his own moral and intellectual struggles, he was strongly influenced by the Christian bishop Ambrose. Subsequently he became a Christian, and accepted, as a consequence, a tradition that had the biblical story as its center.[23] This tradition radically changed his viewpoint. Newbigin writes:

> He [Augustine] took the Biblical story as the starting point for a way of understanding, which required a radical reconstruction of his former ways of thought. In his famous slogan *credo ut intelligam* (I believe in order to know), he defined a way of knowing

---

20. Newbigin, *Proper Confidence*, 6.
21. Ibid., 7.
22. Ibid., 9.
23. Ibid.

that begins with the faithful acceptance of the given fact that God revealed himself in Christ.[24]

Augustine lived while the classical world was crumbling and the barbarians were sacking Rome. In his *Confessions* he talks about seeking truth and not finding it, but, on the contrary, *was found* by the One he sought. Once he found God (or God had found him) he had a new starting point for answers for his deepest questions. It was not found through dialectics: it was found in the biblical story:

> The story of God's mighty acts in the creation and redemption of the world through the Word made flesh in the actual history of Jesus Christ, not a belief in the Idea of Good, would henceforth be the foundation for all the great intellectual and spiritual striving which filled the remaining years of his life.[25]

Newbigin explains the difference between classical and biblical ways of knowing:

> If the place where we look for ultimate truth is in a story and if (as is the case) we are still in the middle of the story, then it follows that we walk by faith and not by sight. If ultimate truth is sought in an idea, a formula, or a set of timeless laws or principles, then we do not have to recognize the possibility that something totally unexpected may happen.[26]

The classical view, for example, divided knowledge into *theoria* and *praxis*. True knowledge is vision or *theoria* of eternal truth. Once the vision is grasped then one must find ways of putting it into action or *praxis*, thus making a distinction between *theoria* and *praxis*. The biblical view is that ultimate reality is personal, that God speaks to us regarding his will and purpose, and that his words can be obeyed or ignored. It is a unitary view of knowing since there is reciprocity where the eternal is heard and acted upon.[27]

Newbigin's interpretation of the radical change in Augustine has a direct bearing on how he believes the Christian church must deal with the contemporary crisis in Western culture. In agreement with philosopher

24. Newbigin, *Proper Confidence*, 6.
25. Ibid., 12.
26. Ibid., 14.
27. Ibid.

of science Michael Polanyi, Newbigin believes that Augustine brought the history of Greek philosophy to a close by initiating the first "post-critical philosophy."[28] It was a post-critical philosophy because it started with God's revelation in Christ and asserted that faith in this revelation was the starting point for understanding and knowing. It also provided a framework for grasping experience, and it overcame the dichotomies that classical thought could not escape.[29]

A MEDIEVAL PARADIGM CHANGE

As Western culture entered the Middle Ages, the medieval worldview embraced, Newbigin notes, a unified view of society, with no dichotomy between public and the private life because it was based on Christian dogma that integrated these two aspects of life. Nor was there a dichotomy between what can be known by faith and what can be known by reason.[30] This was about to change, Newbigin declares, because of the influence of Aristotle's thinking on the Medieval Church.

Aristotle and Medieval Culture

Nestorian Christians, Newbigin explains, translated Aristotle into Syriac, the language of the 'Church of the East' or the Middle East. When that region was overpowered by Islam, the Nestorian Christians became the teachers of their Arab captors and masters. Aristotle was translated into Arabic, and Islamic theology embraced Aristotelian rationalism. In the eleventh and twelfth centuries in Spain, Jewish, Muslim, and Christian scholars enjoyed much interaction. Aristotle was translated into Latin, as were the writings of two Islamic thinkers Avicenna (980–1032) and Averroes (1126–1198), whose influence brought into the thinking of Western Christianity "a new kind of rationalism that challenged the traditional ways of thought."[31] The influence of the teachings of Averroes at the University of Paris caused the Pope in 1263 to reinstate the ban on the study of Aristotle. In spite of the ban, however, Aristotle's influence still greatly influenced Christian scholars of that era, the most prominent of whom was Thomas Aquinas.

---

28. Newbigin, *Other Side*, 23–24, and Polanyi, *Personal Knowledge*, 266.
29. Newbigin, *Other Side*, 24.
30. Newbigin, *A Word*, 182.
31. Newbigin, *Proper Confidence*, 16–17.

Thomas Aquinas

Thomas Aquinas (ca. 1225–74) was, according to Newbigin, the key figure in the paradigm shift that took place in the Middle Ages. Influenced by the writings of Aristotle, he attempted a synthesis of the new ideas that had been introduced through a revival of Aristotle with the biblical tradition.[32] The restatement of the Christian faith in the face of the new intellectual situation made a distinction between what can be known by reason alone and what can be know by revelation and faith.[33] The source of this view was Averroism, which made a sharp distinction between faith and reason, holding to the doctrine of 'double truth,' whereby a believer could hold to doctrines by faith that a philosopher, who must rely solely on reason, would have to deny. The response of Aquinas was that, while he attempted to refute the idea of a 'double truth,' he accepted the distinction between things that can be known through reason alone (which he believed were the existence of God and the immortality of the soul) and that which can be known through faith (by means of divine revelation). Doctrines such as the Trinity and the Incarnation, in this scheme, can only be known through revelation and faith. Aquinas had the right motive; he sought to meet the challenge posed by Averroes. Averroes introduced a new kind of rationalism that would challenge the traditional ways of thinking in the church and culture. Aquinas had begun in his *Summa contra Gentiles* to utilize Aristotle's thought in an attempt to synthesize the new learning with the old biblical tradition. What he did would shape Christian thinking in the West to the present time. While his motive may have been right, the consequences of his thinking led to the bifurcation of knowledge that Newbigin views as troublesome.[34]

Aquinas believed that all human knowledge came through the senses and that the mind can recognize the forms and principles inherent in what the senses encounter. Further, the mind is able to isolate the universal aspects found in particular things and to abstract them from their particular material setting and restore them to their pure intelligibility. This view is based on Aristotle's notion of abstraction as the source of knowledge.

---

32. Newbigin, *Proper Confidence*, 17.
33. Newbigin, *Truth and Authority*, 4–5.
34. Newbigin, *Proper Confidence*, 17.

Newbigin observes that, in Aquinas, "faith and reason had been pried apart," rather than creating the synthesis that Aquinas had hoped for.[35] The separation of faith and reason pulled apart what Augustine had been able to hold together. Newbigin explains the practical results of this split:

> Certain knowledge is one thing; faith is something else ... Certainty is a matter of knowledge, not of faith ... Here one can see the origins of that split which runs right through contemporary Western thought, the split which gives rise to what C. P. Snow called "the Two Cultures" and which runs through every university campus separating the buildings devoted to science from those devoted to other pursuits.[36]

The biblical distinction between faith and unbelief was replaced, Newbigin observes, with the classical distinction between theory and practice, which split knowing into two distinct categories.[37]

There were further, and perhaps more damaging, effects of this cleavage. Aquinas taught that the existence of God could be proven by reason alone.[38] F. C. Copleston interprets Aquinas and believes he would say the following: "Revelation confirms the truth about God which the metaphysician can attain without it, though only with difficulty; and it also sheds on man's way to his final goal a light which is unattainable by philosophy alone."[39] Newbigin points out that the 'God' that emerges through the effort of philosophical argument hardly resembles the God we encounter through the Bible. It would be hard to imagine the 'god' of philosophy becoming incarnate.

---

35. Newbigin, *Proper Confidence*, 18. Herman Dooyeweerd says that when Thomas attempted a synthesis, the result was a dichotomy of reason (that could function autonomously) and faith (where truth can be known through revelation). See *Twilight of Western Thought*, 44–45. Further he writes: "As soon as we, on the basis of the central biblical standpoint, arrive with Augustine at the insight that philosophical thought cannot be self-sufficient, since it is always dependent on a religious starting-point, the entire Thomistic criterion for the distinction between philosophy and theology breaks down." *Twilight of Western Thought*, Dooyeweerd (Nutley, NJ: The Craig Press, 1980), 13.

36. Ibid., 18.
37. Ibid., 15.
38. Ibid., 18.
39. Copleston, *Aquinas*, 60.

THE LIGHT HAS DAWNED

Descartes and Modern Rationalism

Newbigin cites Michael J. Buckley in *Proper Confidence* (p. 80 and following) as his primary source for his discussion on Descartes. Buckley's extensive discussion of the context in which Descartes felt compelled to discover a way to indubitable knowledge gives evidence that Descartes' motive was to repel Michel de Montaigne's assertions that nothing is certain or probable except what comes by way of revelation. "The philosophy of Descartes was a desperate struggle to emerge from Montaigne's skepticism."[40] Descartes was a renowned rationalist,[41] the source of the rationalistic tool known as 'Cartesian doubt,' which refers to the acceptance as true only that which is clearly true and to which any doubt was excluded from serious thought. While observation or experience could be deceptive, rational argument could not be, so it could be utilized to discover truth.

Descartes' thinking, according to Newbigin, "symbolized a retreat into the individual self-consciousness as the one sure starting point in philosophy."[42] "He pictured the human mind," Newbigin observes, "as though it were a disembodied eye looking at the cosmos from a god-like vantage point outside it (*sub specie aeternitatis*)."[43] Descartes was preoccupied with answering one question: "How can one have certain knowledge?"[44] Newbigin notes:

> From the asking of this question . . . there followed the program of the last three hundred years of European history, a program of systematic skepticism. Every supposed truth must be critically

---

40. Gilson, *Unity*, 127, quoted in Buckley, *Origins*, 69.

41. "Descartes operated with the assumption that the relation of God to the universe has given it an objective intelligibility which makes it accessible to rational inquiry, and indeed makes possible scientific attempts to grasp reality by pure thought apart from our observations, so that the observations "through" which the mind penetrates may themselves be judged for their truth or falsity in the light of that reality." *Trinitarian Faith*, Torrance (Edinburgh: T. & T. Clark, 1988), 9.

42. Brown, *Philosophy and the Christian Faith*, 52.

43. Newbigin, "Modernity," 7.

44. Or, "that which is perfectly known and indubitable (*perfecte cognitis, et de quibus dubitari non potest*), a knowledge that is both certain and evident (*omnis scientia est cognito certa et evidens*)." In this, Descartes rejected all knowledge that is probable. *Origins of Modern Atheism*, Buckley, S.J. (New Haven, CT: Yale University Press, 1987), 75.

examined afresh. Old Traditions and dogmas must be exposed to the acids of critical doubt, and only what survives is to be retained. The rest can be thrown away. That is the only safe path from the darkness of superstition to the clear light of truth.[45]

Descartes found his starting point in the certainty that since he had the capacity to doubt, he was thinking and if he was thinking, he must exist. Consequently the famous dictum, *cogito ergo sum*;[46] "I think, therefore I am."[47]

The centerpiece of Descartes' method for ascertaining certain knowledge was the 'critical method,' where reliable knowledge is obtained by starting from indubitable certainties, and building on them with arguments that have the clarity and certainty of mathematics. All claims of truth or knowledge must pass through critical questioning, so the way of knowledge is through doubt, not faith.[48] Every truth claim must be open to scrutiny and criticism, and all beliefs, no matter how venerable, are subject to doubt, and only those that are indubitable can be accepted.[49] Everything that cannot be shown to be certain must be doubted.[50]

Newbigin describes Descartes' method in the following manner:

1. Begin with something which is self-evident and indubitable. In the skeptical climate of his time, Descartes began with what was common to him and to the skeptics: skepticism involves thinking. Inasmuch as I doubt, I think. If I think, I am. Here is an indubitable starting point.

---

45. Newbigin, *Gospel in a Pluralist Society*, 28.

46. Hannah Arendt believes that this statement "contains a logical error, that, as Nietzsche pointed out . . . should read: *cogito, ergo cogitationes sunt*, and that therefore the mental awareness expressed in the *cogito* does not prove that I am, but only that consciousness is." *The Human Condition*, Arendt (Chicago: The University of Chicago Press, 1958), 280, see footnote.

47. Newbigin, *Gospel in a Pluralist Society*, 18. Descartes "early decided that his contemporaries and teachers were in a muddled state of mind about the universe, and that he was born to set it right. He has himself described the steps he went through in his progress from repudiation of all authority to his discovery of what he thought was a solid, absolutely certain, rock-bottom truth on which to build.", *The Shaping of Modern Thought*, Brinton (Englewood Cliffs, NJ: Prentice-Hall, Inc., 1963), 94.

48. Newbigin. *Truth and Authority*, 7.

49. Newbigin. *Proper Confidence*, 23.

50. Newbigin. *A Word*, 182.

2. From this Descartes proceeded by deductive reasoning having the clarity, precision and indubitability of mathematics. By such rational means he would construct a world of indubitable facts.

3. All claims to knowledge are to be tested by the criteria here provided. What fails the test of certainty is not knowledge, but only belief. The critical principle is the key to certain knowledge. The way to certainty is to question every claim to knowledge and accept only what can be shown to be indubitably certain. Descartes has thus reversed Augustine. The way to certain knowledge is not faith but doubt.[51]

This approach has defined Western culture's approach in seeking and validating truth.[52] "The method of Descartes," remarks Newbigin, "has cast a deep shadow of skepticism over the subsequent history of European thought, even in the midst of the superb technical achievements it has made possible."[53] "We are witnessing," Newbigin laments, "the collapse of the whole glorious experience of seeking to know the truth, to make contact with reality, to know God as God truly is."[54]

In spite of his intentions,[55] Descartes reintroduced a radical dualism into Western culture similar to the Greek distinction between the world of ideas (known directly by the mind) and the world of objects (known

---

51. Newbigin, "Certain Faith," 342–43.

52. "The skeptical method, calling everything into doubt, became the initial *via negationis* to a foundation which was self-justifying and self-authenticating, principles intuitively so justified that they admitted no denial and were ever sustained by the experience of doubt. From there one could build by a proper *art de bien raisonner*, a metaphysics of the self which carefully deduced the existence of God and the world, and thus lay the foundations for physics, mechanics, and morals." *Origins of Atheism*, Buckley, S.J. ((New Haven, CT: Yale University Press, 1987), 73.

53. Newbigin, *Proper Confidence*, 24.

54. Newbigin, "Religious Pluralism," 52. T. F. Torrance writes that, adhering to post-Cartesianism, "with a subject/object relation in which the object is regarded as standing opposed to the subject, and therefore with an impersonal model of thought, we become trapped in detached, objective relations to what is other than ourselves. Thus the very model of thought we use inevitably tends to exclude 'the place of personal agency' in our knowing and in the nature of what we seek to know. That is why in dualist modes of thought it is impossible to take seriously any understanding of God as personal active Agent in the universe." *Reality and Scientific Theology*, Torrance (Edinburgh: Scottish Academic Press, 1989), 132–33.

55. "In the system of Descartes, God was another of those clear ideas that are clearer and more precise in the mind than anything seen by the actual eye. Furthermore, everything hung on this existence of a perfect and righteous God." *Origins of Modern Science*, Butterfield (NY: The Free Press, 1957), 124.

through the senses). Descartes' dualism has dominated European thinking since his time, and eventually led, not to certainty, as he had hoped, but to skepticism:

> This dualism, expressed in Descartes' distinction between *res cogitans* (thinking reality) and *res extensa* (reality extended in space) created a situation in which it was necessarily doubtful whether the gap between these two worlds could be bridged. A skepticism about whether our senses give us access to reality is the background of the philosophical thinking ever since.[56]

According to Newbigin's thinking, this dualism has caused problems in at least two critical areas: it has led to a further split in the medieval dichotomy of faith and reason, as well as causing a further cleavage between public and private truth. Reason, on the one hand, has become the source of truth, *the* means by which science discovers truth. Faith, on the other hand, is a matter of personal opinion that is confined to the private realm. The dichotomy between the public and private worlds is a distinctive characteristic of Western culture.[57] This dichotomy led, early on, to the idea that God could influence the mind of individuals, but could not act upon the material world.[58] God, then, was essentially excluded from the concrete world, shunted off into a realm away from the realm of observable truth.[59]

The problem of the dichotomy in Western thinking went even further; it separated the objective and subjective realms of knowing. The consequences for Western culture were ongoing:

> It created on the one hand the idea that there is a world of objective facts that we can know without the involvement of any subjective commitment, and on the other hand the idea that what falls outside this category is personal opinion and unreliable. It created a dichotomy between public doctrine and personal opinion.[60]

---

56. Newbigin, *Gospel in a Pluralist Society*, 18.
57. Newbigin, *A Word*, 64.
58. Newbigin, *Truth to Tell*, 26.
59. Crane Brinton concurs: "Rationalism tends... to banish God and the supernatural from the universe." *Shaping of Modern Thought*, Crane (Englewood Cliffs, NJ: Prentice-Hall, 1963), 82.
60. Newbigin. *A Word*, 160.

Newbigin's assumption is that there is both an objective and subjective element in knowing, and that *both* aspects are valid.[61]

Even though Descartes' thought has been largely abandoned in intellectual circles, it continues to influence popular culture on a very practical level.[62] Newbigin describes what he believes to be three major consequences of Descartes' thinking. First, it reinforced the dualism of mind and matter that was prevalent in the classical worldview. Descartes separated the thinking mind from the whole person, and from human and cosmic history. A huge gap re-opened between the world of thought and the material world of historical events. Second, as has already been noted, he separated the objective and subjective aspects of knowing, causing a polarization between objectivity and subjectivity. Descartes' thinking created the popular image that science is totally objective, free from any subjectivity. Third, Descartes reinforced the dichotomy between theory and practice, prying them apart rather than viewing them as integrated and complimentary. "The Cartesian program," Newbigin remarks, "has run into difficulties."[63]

The Enlightenment

Descartes was only the beginning of something that would dominate Western culture to the present day. The reintroduction of Aristotelian thinking and classical ideas into Western culture in the eleventh and twelfth centuries, combined with the flood of classical ideas introduced at the time of the Renaissance, the great debates of the Reformation, and the beginning of modern science in the seventeenth century, led to the formation of movement of thought that came to be known as the Enlightenment.[64]

The Enlightenment came as a result of an intellectual revolution of the seventeenth and eighteenth centuries. Traditional ideas about God, the universe, and humanity were challenged and, in many cases, replaced with an impersonal, mechanistic construct fuelled by new self confidence and belief in progress.

---

61. Newbigin. *A Word*, 161.
62. Newbigin, *Proper Confidence*, 22.
63. Ibid., 22–23.
64. Newbigin, *Other Side*, 6–7.

The progenitors of the revolution were Francis Bacon, René Descartes, John Locke, and John Newton. All assertions of truth were to be met with doubt, and the direct observation of nature was valued over authority and tradition. Breaking free from the old restraints of culture and religious dogma, they sought to discover truth without the constraints of religious authority. The focus was upon the natural world, a world to be explored and exploited. There was significant advance in science and the dream of creating a utopia on earth began to emerge. It set the stage for both the French and American revolutions and the rights of men began to see the light of day.

By the middle to the eighteenth century, there was the general feeling among Europeans that Europe had reached a point of 'clarification' that was called an 'enlightenment.' "Light had dawned. Darkness had passed away. What had been obscure was now made clear."[65] Europe was conscious that it had turned a corner, exchanging one paradigm for another, one that seemed to offer new freedom and a new horizon.[66] It appeared to be a time of great promise and progress.

Newbigin, however, believes that the Enlightenment was a move backwards.[67] The introduction by Newton of timeless laws that govern the modern understanding of the universe (that could be expressed in mathematical formulae) was a step back toward the timelessness evident in Asian thinking, as well a concept of history that is cyclical rather than linear and teleological, greatly affected culture's view of the cosmos and reality.[68]

Newbigin is not unaware of the positive effects of Enlightenment culture on Europe.[69] It would, he says, be "perverse and misleading" to look critically at the paradigm shift that brought the contemporary Western worldview into existence, "without first acknowledging our enormous debt to the Enlightenment."[70] Newbigin writes: "No one, surely,

---

65. Newbigin, *Other Side*, 7.
66. Ibid., 10.
67. Newbigin, *Truth and Authority*, 68.
68. Ibid., 68, 75.

69. Ramachandra criticizes Newbigin for his generalizations: "Anyone who writes sweepingly of the 'Enlightenment' and 'Post-Enlightenment culture' is liable to generalizations and one-sided distortions. Newbigin, unfortunately, is no exception." *Recovery of Mission*, Ramachandra (Carlisle, Cumbria: Paternoster, 1996), 156. Ramachandra holds both the bachelor and the doctoral degrees in nuclear engineering from the University of London and is well-acquainted with the writings of Newbigin.

70. Newbigin, *Other Side*, 15.

can fail to acknowledge with gratitude the achievements of this period of human history."[71] Newbigin recognizes that the Enlightenment was a corrective to the abuse of power and freedom condoned and practiced by the church.[72]

Reaction against Christendom

Since the Enlightenment was, at least in part, a reaction against the medieval arrangement of church and state, Newbigin is not advocating in any way the reinstatement of old Christendom where the Christian faith and political/cultural powers were blended together.[73] This arrangement resulted in the corruption of the Christian faith and a misuse of its power in both the spiritual and civil realms. Newbigin's view is explicit:

> For Christians it is particularly necessary to acknowledge that the Bible and the teaching office of the Church had become fetters on the human spirit; that the removal of barriers to freedom of conscience and of intellectual inquiry was achieved by the leaders of the Enlightenment against the resistance of the churches; that this made possible the ending of much cruelty, oppression and ignorance; and that the developments in science and technology which liberation has made possible have brought vast benefit to succeeding generations.[74]

Enlightenment thinkers felt that they had cast-off an old framework of thought that was inadequate, and had adopted another way of thinking

---

71. Newbigin, *Gospel in a Pluralist Society*, 223.

72. Oman wrote a book titled *Grace and Personality* a few years before Newbigin arrived in Cambridge on the topic of the Enlightenment. It begins with a very crucial statement about what Oman believed to be the supreme crisis of Christianity, the result of what the French call "Illuminisme" and the Germans call "Aufklärung." Oman called it "Rationalism" but it is more commonly known as the Enlightenment. Oman saw it primarily as an attack on external, traditional authority. At the heart of this attack is the assertion of individual autonomy. Oman explains that the new and revolutionary development was the positive assertion that nothing is either true faith or right morality which is not our own; and that, in consequence, external authority is, in principle, an unsound basis, and individual judgment, not merely a right, but a duty. It is possible that Newbigin heard Oman critique the Enlightenment at an early stage in his undergraduate training. The theme of individual autonomy is one of the crucial issues in Newbigin's critique of the result of Enlightenment thinking.

73. Newbigin, "Can a Modern Society be Christian?" 11.

74. Newbigin, *Other Side*, 15–16.

that was, in their minds, more satisfactory.[75] To Enlightenment thinkers, dogma represented the closed minds of persons who had no appreciation for what science, loosed from the grip of such restraints, could do for humanity. By liberating societies from the bondage to dogma and superstition, science could, they believed, unlock the secrets of nature for the benefit of all.[76] In the place of dogmatic or unscientific explanations that would no longer satisfy the mind, it was strongly believed that the true explanation of things was coming to light. Old superstitions would be banished and the real nature of things would become apparent.[77]

Newbigin acknowledges that there was a genuine failure of institutional Christianity in the Middle Ages, a failure that Christians must admit:

> The Enlightenment was in part a legitimate and proper revolt against an authority claimed in the name of revelation. The battle which was fought by those of the Enlightenment, and by the pioneers of modern science, for freedom of conscience and freedom of inquiry, was one in which Christians were often on the wrong side. This must be acknowledged.[78]

Newbigin has pointed out that the liberation from dogma was the repudiation of ecclesiastical authority over the whole of life.

Religious Wars and the Enlightenment

The era prior to the Enlightenment was dominated by religious wars in Spain, France, the Netherlands, Denmark, and Germany. The Thirty Years' War (1618–48) played a part in opening the way for the Enlightenment. Newbigin acknowledges this:

---

75. Newbigin, *Other Side*, 10. "As a matter of principle, tradition is declared to be epistemologically bankrupt, a source of intellectual enslavement rather than liberating knowledge." *The Genesis of Doctrine*, McGrath (Oxford: Basil Blackwell, 1990), 179.

76. Newbigin, *Other Side*, 13–14.

77. Newbigin, *Other Side*, 8. "The Enlightenment both freed us from the weight of certain oppressive traditions and taught us, as Kant insisted, that we must dare to speak for ourselves. But as the dialectic of the Enlightenment unfolded, it became trapped in even narrower models of what could count as truth...The once emancipatory concepts of the Enlightenment, as Adorno suggested, became mere categories. Reason retreated into a formal and technical rationality." *Plurality and Ambiguity*, Tracy (San Francisco: Harper & Row, 1987), 31.

78. Newbigin, *Other Side*, 52.

Newbigin's Critique of Western Culture

> The division of western Christendom at the Reformation did not end the territorial principle, in spite of the Anabaptist protest against it. Lutherans, Calvinists, Anglicans, and Roman Catholics each made territorial claims on the principle of *Cuius regio, eius religio*. But the terrible religious war of seventeenth century Europe opened the way for the conversion of western Europe to the new faith of the Enlightenment, and so for the ending of territorial religion.[79]

Wolfhart Pannenberg shares the same view regarding the immediate effect of the religious wars upon Europe just prior to the Enlightenment, and believes that the reason that Europeans embraced secularism[80] was because thoughtful people decided that if there was going to be social peace, religion and the ever-raging controversies would have to be bracketed.[81] The rise of modern culture, in Pannenberg's view, was not an ideological process but came about because of the desire for social peace and the cessation of religious wars.[82] While Newbigin sees religious wars as contributing to coming of the Enlightenment, he believes that ideological issues rather than religious wars were primarily responsible for its commencement.

Restructuring the Cultural Mind

The Enlightenment purported to have the secret of knowledge and mastery over the world; two things in which any culture would be interested.[83] The nature of reality could be opened by science since, as Newton asserted, the real world is not governed by purpose but by natural law, so the way to understand reality is through the natural world. All causes are adequate to the effects they produce, so to discover the cause of something

---

79. Newbigin, "Can a Modern Society," 5.

80. Wolfhart Pannenberg has said that the strong emphasis on the human person, a characteristic of secularism, had its origin in Christianity. He writes: "No break with Christianity was intended by those who based public culture on conceptions of human nature rather than religion. In fact, Christian ideas continued to be socially effective, although they were gradually transmogrified into secularized beliefs, and it is not surprising that, in time, many people forgot where the ideas came from in the first place." "How to Think about Secularism," Pannenberg (*First Things* June/July 1996), 30. See also Pannenberg, "Christianity and the West, 18–23.

81. Pannenberg, "How to think About Secularism," 28.

82. Ibid., 29. See also Pannenberg, "Christianity and the West, 21.

83. Newbigin, *Foolishness*, 23.

is to explain it.[84] Teleology has no place in physics or astronomy because purpose is not observable in nature. It is through reason (analytical and mathematical) that humanity is able to have complete mastery over nature and all forms of reality.[85]

The abandonment of teleology is, according to Newbigin, a decisive feature of our culture.[86] "Questions of ultimate purpose are excluded from the public world," observes Newbigin, "because Western culture believes they have no place in science."[87] There is no viable way, in view of the limitations placed on Western culture by Enlightenment thinking, of moving from what *is* to what *ought to be*.[88] The Enlightenment set the parameters of what was an acceptable avenue to truth, and reason alone became that avenue. "Reason," Newbigin says, "was used to denote conformity with a set of assumptions derived from the science and philosophy of the time."[89]

The Enlightenment also caused the restructuring of the cultural understanding of the nature of reality. Newbigin comments on this change:

> The replacement of "God" by "Nature" involved a new understanding of "Law." There is no longer a divine lawgiver whose commands are to be obeyed because they are God's. Laws are the necessary relationships which spring from the nature of things (Montesquieu). As such they are available for discovery by human reason. Reason is a faculty common to all human beings and is in principle the same everywhere. Provided it is not perverted by the imposition of dogmas from without, reason is capable of discovering what the nature of things is and what—therefore—are "Nature's laws."[90]

While the Enlightenment sought to dislodge dogma from its place in society, it managed to replace it with another dogma, the dogma of human rationality, capable of comprehending reality completely unaided by God. The Enlightenment was a "great burst of confidence in European civilization" and at the heart of this confidence was the belief in the power of reason: "Reason, in contrast to faith, was the avenue of reliable knowl-

---

84. Newbigin, *Foolishness*, 24.
85. Ibid., 25.
86. Ibid., 34–35.
87. Ibid., 30.
88. Ibid., 37.
89. Newbigin, *A Word*, 90.
90. Newbigin, *Other Side*, 12.

Newbigin's Critique of Western Culture

edge. Faith, in the classic definition of John Locke, was a persuasion that fell short of certainty."[91]

As a consequence, the human being is not subject to an 'external law-giver' whose existence one must recognize and whose ways require one to submit and be obedient. Breaking free from these restraints, the Enlightenment set out on a course where reason became the ultimate method of discovery. Discovery was possible without outside interference, be it God or dogma or faith.[92]

Since Descartes' day, Western culture has been dominated, we noted, by the search for knowledge that cannot be doubted.[93] This idea has been applied to science. Truth that cannot be doubted is, in fact, discovered through modern scientific method:

> ... the secular societies that have developed in Europe since the seventeenth century share the common belief that reliable knowledge about human nature, and therefore about how life should be managed, is to be found not by reliance upon divine revelation and grace but by reliance upon the methods of empirical science.[94]

Reason can reveal reliable and certifiable facts because these facts are verifiable through scientific method.[95] Scientific methodology requires that truth be considered somewhat tentative, since there is the possibility that new information could prove to alter a previously held truth. Yet, while these convictions are held tenaciously, providing a grid or standard by which to evaluate any new information or findings, they are always open for challenge and, if the new information is found worthy, modification.[96] The progress of knowledge according to this method must be systematic and incremental.

Newbigin is careful to point out that in the scientific method there is an assumption that there is a reality about which we can know.[97] This opens the door, Newbigin believes, to other assumptions by scientists that

91. Newbigin, *A Word*, 182. Stephen Williams, in his book *Revelation and Reconciliation*, takes exception to Newbigin's interpretation of Locke's statement. See Williams, *Revelation and Reconciliation*, 24–55.

92. Newbigin, *Other Side*, 12–13.

93. Newbigin, *A Word*, 103.

94. Ibid., 150 and *Truth and Authority*, 75.

95. Newbigin, *Truth to Tell*, 22.

96. Ibid., 26.

97. Ibid., 57.

are unverifiable and not provable. While science has assumed and advocated neutrality of observation in finding facts, they have done so based on certain assumptions that could be considered subjective by their own definition of the term. Science is based on faith and, one might say, on 'dogma' in the most positive sense of the word.[98]

An Earthly Utopia

The dichotomy of faith and reason has also led to the development of the idea of two realms in Western culture. Reason and scientific method contribute to the public realm, while faith is shunted off to the private realm of personal opinion.[99] In the public realm, there emerged in eighteenth century philosophy, the possibility of an 'earthly utopia.' Western cultural confidence based on Enlightenment ideas and principles led to great expectations of what was possible through human reason and science. It was eighteenth century philosophers, notes Newbigin, who translated the Christian vision of a heavenly city into a future and earthly utopia.[100] They urged their contemporaries to dispense with God, and to put their hope in a future on earth, where everyone has the right to happiness, something God could not provide.

The concept of an earthy utopia came, Newbigin acknowledges, when society became disenchanted with the church and all that it represented. Not only did the Enlightenment seek to dethrone the church from power, it sought to remove the influence of God from society. The real world can be explained scientifically by laws of cause and effect, and in mathematical terms. God was not necessary to the equation.[101] The *real world* became the focus of the Enlightenment and humanity's future lay in society's ability to create here on earth what was once thought of as heaven.[102] Science, it was widely believed, could create the heavenly city now, because humans are the bearer of history's purpose and solely responsible for their own well-being. When society seeks blessedness in another world, the present world tends

---

98. Newbigin, *A Word*, 72, 103.
99. Newbigin, *Truth to Tell*, 25–28; *A Word*, 160.
100. Newbigin, *Other Side*, 3.
101. Newbigin, *Foolishness*, 65.
102. "In the broadest terms, the change in the attitude of Western man toward the universe and everything in it was the change from the concept of supernatural heaven after death to the rationalist natural heaven on this earth now—at least very shortly." *Shaping of Modern Thought*, Brinton (Englewood Cliffs, NJ: Prentice-Hall, 1963), 114.

Newbigin's Critique of Western Culture

to be neglected. So, society should seek its own good through the benefits of science, which can create blessedness now.[103]

The apocalyptic books of the Bible, Newbigin insists, do not speak to the notion of earthly progress, and do not picture the emergence of justice and peace on earth. If anything, they call for patience and endurance to the end. Apocalyptic thinking did not fit the doctrine of earthly progress or the new vision of an earthly utopia, so the Bible was seen as not relevant to the Enlightenment proper.[104] "The practical corollary of this vision is . . . the privatization of religion."[105] The church became a haven for those who would seek blessedness in another world. This led to the virtual demise of the vision of the church as a part of public history, a vision that has all but faded away.[106]

Newbigin partially blames eighteenth century pietism for the split of the public and private realms, where the church and religion are delegated to the private realm. He sees Protestantism in the eighteenth century gravitating toward inward religion, while the culture became secular.[107] Culture has intentionally dismissed religion as a source for certain truth, while Christianity has seemingly and, perhaps even unwittingly, allowed it to happen.[108]

Newbigin recognizes that it was not just a matter of neglect on the part of Christians; many Enlightenment thinkers attacked Christianity. He writes:

> Although most of the philosophers and other writers who were the leaders of the movement of Enlightenment in the eighteenth century were quite consciously setting out to attack and destroy the Christian belief-system, the churches have to a large extent conceded the ground they claimed.[109]

Enlightenment philosophers saw history as a struggle between two mentalities: Hebrew and Hellene, Christian and pagan.[110] The most glaring

---

103. Newbigin, *Other Side*, 35.
104. Ibid., 52.
105. Ibid., 35.
106. Ibid.
107. Ibid., 22.
108. Ibid., 22, 35.
109. Newbigin, "Mission in a Pluralist Society," 10.
110. Gay, *Enlightenment*, 36.

defect of the Enlightenment, writes one scholar, is "its unsympathetic, often brutal, estimate of Christianity."[111]

CHALLENGING THE ENLIGHTENMENT

Immanuel Kant and the Challenge to the Enlightenment

The Enlightenment, which created Western culture's distinctive self-consciousness, was a movement, according to Newbigin, which essentially rejected tradition and the authority of tradition.[112] Immanuel Kant articulated the main theme of the Enlightenment with the phrase 'dare to know.' "It was," according to Newbigin, "a summons to have the courage to think for oneself, to test everything in the light of reason and conscience, to dare to question even the most hallowed traditions. That robust determination remains operative as . . . the central thrust of our culture."[113]

Kant, however, also demonstrated the limits of reason. He concluded that reason could not see beyond the appearance of things (the *phenomenal*) to ultimate reality (the *noumenal*).[114] We can only know what appears to our senses, while the real or *noumenal* world remains impenetrable by our senses.[115] The manner in which we understand, organize, and structure is the way we make sense of the phenomenal world.[116] Newbigin explains Kant's meaning as follows: "The rational structure of the created world, which science seeks to understand, is not given to it by its Creator; it is furnished by the necessities of human thought."[117] It is not possible to find guidance for living through knowledge of things as they are, be-

---

111. Gay, *Enlightenment*, 37
112. Newbigin, *Gospel in a Pluralist Society*, 39.
113. Ibid., 39.
114. Newbigin, *Proper Confidence*, 25. "Since Kant it has been very widely believed that you cannot know reality; you can only know phenomena." "Christian Witness in a Pluralistic World," Stromberg *IRM* 76, no. 307 (July1988), 416–17. T. F. Torrance comments that "in spite of empiricist criticism he was able to provide on-going science with a working objectivity, but at the expense of any hope of being able to apprehend things in themselves in their interior relations independent of the way they appear to us and of our observations of them." *Reality and Scientific Theology*, Torrance (Edinburgh: Scottish Academic Press, 1989), 74.
115. Newbigin, *Gospel in a Pluralist Society*, 18.
116. Ibid.
117. Ibid.

cause that knowledge is not attainable.[118] Kant taught that ultimate reality is unknowable, at least *through reason*.[119] However, Newbigin interprets Kant as saying that while there are limits to reason, there are ways to move beyond the boundaries or limits of reason:

> In his two succeeding works [succeeding the *Critique of Pure Reason*], *Critique of Practical Reason* and *Critique of Judgment*, Kant sought to show how our moral experience and our aesthetic experience can lead us beyond the boundary that defines the limits of reason. He showed how our moral experience requires us to acknowledge the reality of God, of judgment, and of immortality.[120]

Kant concluded that God exists because of the sense of the absolute character of the moral law. For this reason, he affirmed not only the existence of God, but also the *necessity* of the existence of God. Kant reasoned that God and freedom are necessary postulates (practically necessary presuppositions) of practical reason (practical reason being the rational grounds on which we act). We must, Kant asserts, assume God because God must be the cause of the whole of nature and the integrating factor that harmonizes morality (virtue) and happiness, the essence of the *summum bonum*. The *summum bonum* is possible in the world only on the supposition of a Supreme Being having a causality corresponding to moral character. Freedom, on the other hand, comes from the necessary presupposition of independence from the sensible world and of the faculty of determining one's will according to the law of an intelligible world.[121]

The Enlightenment, however, took a different view; it emphasized that reason is the only path to reliable truth, thus by-passing Kant's idea of the sense of the moral absolute. The Enlightenment view has led to the idea that if there is no God, there is no moral law.[122]

Germane to our discussion of Newbigin is the fact that Kant perpetuated the dualism reintroduced into Western culture by Descartes. Kant's

---

118. Newbigin, *Gospel in a Pluralist Society*, 18.
119. Ibid.
120. Newbigin, *Proper Confidence*, 25.
121. Kant, "The Postulates of Practical Reason" in *Critique of Practical Reason*, 476–83.
122. Newbigin, *Proper Confidence*, 25–26.

dualism led to a split between science and faith, a dualism that continues to the present day.[123]

Nietzsche's Critique of Descartes

The critique of Descartes' thinking and method continues into the nineteenth century with the philosopher, Friederich Nietzsche. Newbigin explains Nietzsche's position:

> [Nietzsche] . . . drew with inescapable clarity the necessary conclusion of the method of Descartes . . . the critical principle must necessarily destroy itself. Rational criticism rests on beliefs which are themselves liable to critical questioning. If the critical principle is exalted to the supreme place in the enterprise of knowing, then the possibility of knowing anything is destroyed. "True" and "false," "right" and "wrong"—these are now words that have no objective reference. They are simply expressions of the will. The will to power is the driving force in history.[124]

Nietzsche was the first to realize that the modern critical principle would make it impossible to speak of right and wrong.[125] "The factual, ontological basis for using such language has been removed," concludes Newbigin, because the possible ultimate reference point for knowing truth and reality is lost.[126] In spite of the role of the Supreme Being in Descartes' thinking, the critical principle removed God from the realm of certain knowledge, because certain knowledge could be attained without reference to God.[127]

---

123. Dooyeweerd writes: "the inner conflict between the nature-motive and the freedom-motive in the religious starting point of Humanism led Kant to a strongly dualistic world and life view. Nature and freedom were sharply separated from one another. And this separation corresponded to Kant's separation between science and faith." *In the Twilight of Western Thought*, Dooyeweerd (Nutley, NJ: The Craig Press, 1980), 71.

124. Newbigin, *Proper Confidence*, 26.

125. Newbigin's source is Bloom, *Closing of the American Mind*, (no page number given). Newbigin makes reference to Bloom in his discussion of Nietzsche in *Gospel in a Pluralist Culture*, 17.

126. Ibid.

127. Newbigin, *Proper Confidence*, 28.

Newbigin's Critique of Western Culture

The Post-modern Challenge

Newbigin recognizes the line of critique of modernism that follows from Nietzsche to what has become known as *post-modernism*.[128] In the middle 1990s Newbigin recognizes that there was another important challenge to modernism that was emerging and he begins to address it. He defines post-modernism as:

> ... the abandonment of any claim to know the truth in an absolute sense. Ultimate reality is not single but diverse and chaotic. Truth claims are really concealed claims to power, and this applies as much to the claims of science as to those of religion.[129]

Newbigin concedes that he is an ally of post-modern thinking but only up to a certain point. He agrees with post-modern thinkers who say that all "human beliefs are rooted in particular histories."[130] Human thought is always embodied, "but this does *not* mean that there is no such thing as truth."[131] Newbigin asserts that there is truth, that a story (even though it is a part of a particular culture) could be a true story, and that the story of Christ has universal relevance.[132]

What has taken place is the fulfillment of Nietzsche's observation that all would devolve into each person asserting his/her will. The practical result is that there is no history nor is there a reality beyond the self. "This development," Newbigin remarks, "must be surely recognized as a sign of impending death."[133] Newbigin connects Nietzsche's observation about the will to power with Foucault's[134] idea of successive 'regimes of truth.' Both of these ideas are critical of Enlightenment thought and support post-modernism. Newbigin does not advocate these views but agrees with Nietzsche that the result of Enlightenment thinking produces what Nietzsche envisioned, and that the results of these regime changes will produce nihilism and narcissism. "There is," observes Newbigin, "pro-

---

128. Newbigin, *Proper Confidence*, 27.
129. Newbigin, "Religious Pluralism," 23, quoted in Goheen, "*As the Father Has Sent Me*," 372.
130. Newbigin, *A Word*, 202.
131. Ibid., 202–3.
132. Ibid., 203.
133. Newbigin, *Proper Confidence*, 35.
134. Michel Foucault (1926–84) was French philosopher who was influenced by German philosophers Nietzsche and Martin Heidegger.

found irony in this story: the relapse into nihilism and narcissism is the end product of the search for indubitable knowledge."[135]

Newbigin discusses the collapse of modernity into post-modernity in his unpublished paper titled "New Birth to a Living Hope."[136] Modernity and post-modernity, he writes, coexist in the minds of people in contemporary European society, creating a difficulty for evangelists.[137] Newbigin feels, however, that modernism continues to be the major threat to Christianity because it is embodied in the institutions of Western culture.[138] His critique of modernity also gives the church important insights for "interpreting and responding with a missionary encounter to the post-modern condition in western culture."[139]

Newbigin's refutation of the ideology of pluralism is, in reality, a part of this critique of post-modernist thinking.

The Loss of Dogma and the Coming of Nihilism

One area of significant loss in the change from Medieval to Enlightenment thinking was, Newbigin believes, in the understanding of the word *dogma*, which in the older Christian tradition was a good word, not having the negative connotations that are associated with it today. Dogma, throughout church history, stood for reliable truth, because it came from God's revelation and a community of faith that sought to understand and interpret this revelation. *Doubt*, on the other hand, had a different history in Christian thinking. It was associated with evil, partly because it was linked to Adam's doubt regarding God's goodness in relation to eating fruit of the tree of the knowledge of good and evil.[140]

The Enlightenment, however, changed the attitude of culture toward these two words. Doubt, Newbigin observes, was elevated to a high position, and given the prerogative of questioning all accepted beliefs. 'To doubt' became the first principle of knowledge, because doubting became the primary and preferred method of ascertaining truth. Doubt was the

---

135. Newbigin, *Truth and Authority*, 9.

136. Newbigin, "New Birth into a Living Hope," 5.

137. Newbigin, *New Birth*, 5.

138. See Newbigin, *Modern, Postmodern and Christian*, Chapter 1, "Modernity in Context," 8.

139. Goheen, "*As the Father has Sent Me*," 372.

140. Newbigin, *Other Side*, 19.

tool used to demolish superstition, or any belief that refused to submit to rational doubt.[141] Western culture has prided itself in subjecting every dogma "to fearless criticism in the light of reason and experience."[142] This fearless criticism was utilized to insure that what was believed was true by verifiable standards. This, however, completely dismisses the possibility that one could believe something by faith that may actually be true, but is unverifiable according to modern scientific standards. This does not slip past Newbigin, and it becomes a focal point of his criticism of Enlightenment thinking.[143]

Dogma, on the other hand, became a bad word because it was seen as synonymous with a closed mind, and opposed to the free exercise of reasoning for discerning truth. This reversal of roles helped to usher in the modern scientific worldview.[144] Questioning dogma is seen in the contemporary world as one of the marks of intellectual maturity and competence; it has become the hallmark of the educated and critical mind.[145]

Since Western culture has categorically rejected dogma, any assertion of truth by a Christian is going to be met with resistance. Christians can expect a sharp encounter because, Newbigin warns, any assertion of faith is viewed as an arrogant assertion of power.[146] Long-established dogma does not give way to critical attack unless that attack comes from some other belief that seeks to replace it. The criticism, as Newbigin notes, "does not come out of a vacant mind."[147] Dogma, then, gives way only to another dogma seeking to replace it.

Newbigin notes that dogma is not peculiar to the church; every system of thought has dogma as its basis and starting point. Coherent thinking is not possible without some system of dogmatic belief. In Western culture, as in any culture, these assumptions are taken for granted. In Christian thinking, if it is valid and coherent, the primary dogma is "that God has acted to reveal and affect his purpose for the world in a manner made known in the Bible."[148] Western culture does not realize that it has cast

141. Newbigin, *Other Side*, 19–20.
142. Newbigin, *Gospel in a Pluralistic Society*, 6–7.
143. Newbigin, *Truth to Tell*, 35–36.
144. Newbigin, *Other Side*, 19, and *Gospel in a Pluralistic Society*, 5.
145. Newbigin, *Gospel in a Pluralistic Society*, 5.
146. Ibid., 19.
147. Ibid., 1.
148. Newbigin, *Gospel in a Pluralistic Society*, 8.

out Christian dogma based on its own dogmatic assertions. Since dogma is indispensable for a well-functioning of culture, the limitations Western culture has placed upon itself is debilitating; it cannot live up to or live by the dogma that it has posited in the place of Christianity. It has not found certain truth. In fact, it has succumbed to nihilism. Newbigin observes:

> We are heirs of the Age of Reason which claimed it could dispense with dogma and with tradition, using the tools of critical thought to dissolve what had hither been taken for granted. This has led us into nihilism.[149]

Western culture fails to recognize its own reliance upon dogma. Newbigin maintains that the difference is not between those who rely on dogma and those who do not, but is between those who are explicit about their presuppositions and those who are unaware of their underlying presuppositions. In regard to Western culture, people generally accept the reigning dogma without ever seriously questioning its validity; it is not critical of its own presuppositions.[150] Dogma is the most powerful critical agent in society, and yet it is deemed to be beyond criticism itself.[151]

Newbigin's answer to Western culture's epistemological dilemma is to throw-off the Cartesian criteria of truth, and replace it with one that is workable:

> What is now required is that we openly acknowledge that we accept as given, as dogma, that which "can" be doubted, that we have the courage to affirm as true what does "not" pass the Cartesian test of indubitable certainty.[152]

Since the Enlightenment program has become unworkable because of its failure to be in contact with reality, the pressing need, in spite of the mistakes of Christendom, Newbigin believes, is to affirm the gospel as truth, even if it cannot be proven with indubitable certainty:

> We must affirm the gospel as truth, universal truth, truth for all peoples and for all times, the truth which creates the possibility of

---

149. Newbigin, "Certain Faith," 347–48.
150. Ibid., 347.
151. Newbigin, *Truth to Tell*, 67.
152. Newbigin, "Certain Faith," 378.

Newbigin's Critique of Western Culture

freedom; but we negate the gospel if we deny the freedom in which it alone can be truly believed.[153]

The dogma that is believed is the biblical story with Jesus at the center.[154]

Confronting Pluralism

Newbigin is clear to distinguish between the *fact* of plurality and the *ideology* of pluralism. Western society is open and free, so there are many religions, philosophies, and ideologies, making it pluralistic. That in itself does not disqualify one particular religion or philosophy from having truth, while others may have partial truth or no truth at all. The ideology of pluralism, however, holds "the view that since no one can really know the truth we must be content with the multiplicity of opinion."[155] Such an ideology provides no incentive to search for truth, since the underlining assumption is that it is impossible to find truth amidst all the possible alternatives. In the spirit of tolerance and respect for the diversity of opinion in Western culture, it is culturally unacceptable to assert publicly that one knows truth and that others may not have it or have it in an inferior form. Western culture insists that such opinions remain in the private realm, and that only facts (things verified by science) be understood as truth for public discussion. In the face of this particular challenge, Newbigin exhorts: "It will no longer do to accept the dichotomy between a public world of so-called 'facts' and a private world of so-called 'values.'"[156] Newbigin suspects that this dichotomy is culture's way of keeping the church out of the public debate, so the church must not accede to culture's demands. He instructs the church to defy culture:

> We shall have to be bold enough to confront our public world with the reality of Jesus Christ, the word made flesh, the one in whom

---

153. Newbigin, *Gospel in a Pluralist Society*, 10.

154. Charles S. McCoy writes: "transformation will recover the impulse toward saga, story, and parable prominent in . . . the Hebrew and Christian scriptures. The paradigm which has informed Western theology tends to discount the importance of artistic narrative in favor of dogmatic formulations . . . As a result, the theology of Europe and North America has not only become excessively rationalistic . . . but also has become mired down in a bifurcated world of Western philosophy." *When Gods Change*, McCoy (Nashville: Abingdon, 1980), 37.

155. Newbigin, "Can the West be Converted?" 6.

156. Ibid.

the eternal purposes of almighty God has been publicly set forth in the midst of our human history, and therefore to affirm that no facts are truly understood except in the light of him through whom and for whom they exist. We shall have to face, as the early church faced, an encounter with the public world.[157]

Newbigin reminds the church that Christ's ministry was public and a part of human history, so it is a part of the public record and can be investigated, discussed, and dealt with in the public forum. Writing with unusual passion, as one embracing a counter-cultural rhetoric, Newbigin implores the church to be decisive at this point:

> we must reject the ideology of pluralism. We must reject the invitation to live in a society where everything is subjective and relative, a society which has abandoned the belief that truth can be known and has settled for a purely subjective view of truth—"truth for you" but not truth for all.[158]

This confrontation should include challenging the notion that religious experience is a separate form of cognition when, in reality, rationality and spirituality are a part of one, unified whole. The dogmas of the Incarnation and the Trinity, Newbigin asserts, are the starting points for seeing reality as a whole.[159]

CONCLUSION

The heart of Newbigin's confrontation with the Western world begins with his critique of Western culture. The heart of his criticism is that Western culture has allowed the great story of the gospel, which shaped the culture for a thousand years, to be set aside for a rationalistic dogma that has not served it well. It is rooted in doubt and has led to skepticism. Newbigin has a response to the Western culture's unsatisfactory situation. This is the substance of the next chapter.

---

157 Newbigin, "Can the West be Converted?" 6.
158. Newbigin, *Gospel in a Pluralist Society*, 244.
159. Newbigin, *Foolishness*, 88–94.

6

Newbigin's Response to Western Culture's Crisis

AN ANSWER TO WESTERN CULTURE'S DILEMMA

NEWBIGIN'S ANSWER TO WESTERN culture's dilemma is essentially a theological response based on the theological convictions presented earlier in this book. In this case, he turns his attention toward Western culture which he believes to be in need of a radical conversion of both spirit and mind.

The Need for Radical Conversion

Newbigin begins by asking questions that go to the heart of his desire to see Western culture experience a missionary confrontation:

> Who will confront this culture of ours with the claim of absolute truth, the claim that Jesus Christ is the truth? Who will be bold enough to say, not that the Christian message can be explained in terms of the facts as we know them, but rather that all so-called knowledge must be tested against the supreme reality: God incarnate in Jesus Christ, present yesterday, today, until the end, in the power of the Spirit? What will it mean to call for a missionary confrontation with this culture?[1]

If the church accepts the call to confront culture, "it must call unequivocally," insists Newbigin, "for radical conversion," a conversion of both the mind and the will. It must be a change of worldview rather than a mere change of allegiance. This, however, cannot be done if the biblical vision

---

1. Newbigin, *A Word*, 72.

of reality is adjusted to the assumptions of culture.² The conflict that will come as the result of missionary confrontation will not be between Western culture and the Bible but between two communities, one that indwells the biblical story of humanity and the other that indwells the cultural story.³ This 'indwelling,' a term borrowed from Michael Polanyi,⁴ means that the Christian community and culture will see reality from very different perspectives that will inevitably come into conflict. It will not be a matter of words only, but "will entail actions which bring conflict and suffering."⁵ There is no 'peaceful coexistence' since such a confrontation that challenges the deeply held fiduciary framework of the culture will inevitably bring conflict.⁶ Newbigin offers a definite answer to Western culture's moral chaos: "Only the revelation of God in Jesus Christ, only the living Word of the Creator," insists Newbigin, "can bring light out of darkness, order out of chaos."⁷

A missionary confrontation of Western culture (as a missionary would do in any culture) must include unmasking the ideology that supports, permeates, and drives the culture, and then offering a more rational model for understanding the human situation.⁸ Newbigin suggests a remedy to heal Western culture's sickness:

> The ideology which we have to recognize, unmask, and reject is an ideology of freedom, a false and idolatrous conception of freedom which equates it with the freedom of each individual to do as he or she wishes. We have to set against it a Trinitarian faith which sees all reality in terms of relatedness. In explicit rejection of an individualism which puts the autonomous self at the center and sees other selves as limitations on our freedom, we have to set the basic dogma entrusted to us, namely that freedom is to be found by be-

---

2. Newbigin, *Other Side*, 53.
3. Newbigin, *Truth to Tell*, 48.
4. Newbigin specifically cites Polanyi's use of the term 'indwelling' in *Truth and Authority*, 44. Polanyi, a Hungarian, was a philosopher of science who began as a professor of physical chemistry at the University of Manchester in the 1930s and authored *Personal Knowledge*.
5. Newbigin, *Other Side*, 54.
6. Newbigin, *Foolishness*, 66–67.
7. Newbigin, "Enduring Validity," 52.
8. Newbigin, *Truth to Tell*, 77.

ing taken into that community of love given and received which is eternal reality from which and for which all things exist.[9]

Newbigin makes a radical suggestion to the church: it needs a radical conversion as well! Since the church tends to measure itself by the standards of the world rather than by God's Word and will, such a change as Newbigin suggests would seem radical under these circumstances.

One example of the way that the church has accommodated itself to Western cultural strictures is found, Newbigin notes, in the way the church interprets Scripture. It attempts to understand the biblical message in the light of modern thought.[10] Newbigin thinks the church needs to reverse the process: "What we are required to attempt is the much more difficult enterprise of trying to understand modern thought in the light of the biblical story."[11]

Newbigin sets forth several answers to the question of how the church should recover its proper distinction from contemporary Western culture.[12] Newbigin calls for the church to offer a radically new starting-point for culture, which would essentially entail a radical conversion from its present fiduciary structure to a radically different fiduciary structure, one that the church must articulate in the public arena.[13] What Christians must propose in the public realm would be open to critical questioning, as would any assertion made in the public realm, but it would soon become apparent that what the church proposes cannot be proved to be true by the present presuppositions or axioms of Western society.[14] Hence, there is the real possibility of confrontation and refusal.

The central belief of Christianity, the Easter story, makes more sense in regards to human experience, Newbigin asserts, than the current plausibility structure of the Western world. It is an actual event in history, but it is "as mysterious to human reason as the creation itself."[15] The Easter story does not fit the contemporary worldview because it must be ac-

---

9. Newbigin, *Truth to Tell*, 75–76.

10. Newbigin, *Gospel in a Pluralist Society*, 95.

11. Ibid.

12. Newbigin, *Foolishness*, 134–50. T. R. Milford, a chaplain of Cambridge University, also wrote a book titled *Foolishness to the Greeks*. He was the force behind the beginning of the SCM study conferences at Swanwick. See McCaughey, *Christian Obedience*, 110.

13. Newbigin, *Foolishness*, 148.

14. Newbigin, *Foolishness*, 148, and also in *Truth to Tell*, 65.

15. Newbigin. *Gospel in a Pluralistic Society*, 11.

cepted by faith. If it is accepted, Newbigin insists, "it becomes the starting point for a wholly new way of understanding our human experience, a way which—in the long run—makes more sense of human experience as a whole than does the reigning plausibility structure."[16] Newbigin views Augustine as a model of how a Christian thinker can influence the course of culture, and encourages the church to emulate Augustine:

> . . . we can, I believe, follow the example of Augustine in being ready, boldly and without embarrassment, to offer to our dying culture the framework of understanding that has its base in the work of Jesus and to invite our contemporaries to join with us in a vigorous attempt to understand and deal with our experiences afresh in the light and in the power of that name.[17]

The church must proclaim the whole gospel, one that requires a commitment to discipleship and a new way of looking at reality:

> A preaching of the gospel that calls men and women to accept Jesus as Savior but does not make it clear that discipleship means commitment to a vision of society radically different from that which controls our public life today must be condemned as false.[18]

This radical conversion requires a paradigm shift, Newbigin insists, that will involve the will, feelings, and the mind. It will lead to the vision of a new plausibility structure, to a new of vision of how things are and of who God is, resulting in a much more adequate system of belief than is currently believed in Western culture.[19]

To be able to truly grasp truth and reality, we must break from the confines of Enlightenment ideology:

> If we are to escape from the ideology of the Enlightenment . . . we must recover a doctrine of freedom of thought and conscience not founded on the ideology of the Enlightenment but on the gospel.[20]

---

16. Ibid., 12.
17. Newbigin, *Other Side*, 63.
18. Newbigin, *Foolishness*, 132.
19. Ibid., 63–64.
20. Newbigin, *A Word*, 74.

Newbigin's Response to Western Culture's Crisis

The Radical Alternative

Newbigin believes that Western culture, "without possibility of question, is the most challenging missionary frontier of our time."[21] Everywhere Western culture goes, it tends to make the population less responsive to the gospel. Highly conscious of the effects of the ideology of modernity in global areas, Newbigin envisions a Christian response to this malady:

> What I think has been lacking, and what I hope the next decade will provide, is a serious and sustained effort to articulate the Christian message vis-à-vis this globally dominant Western culture, which has become the shared culture of at least the urbanized part of humankind.[22]

Western culture must reconsider God, and the starting point for this reconsideration is not found in immutable principles, but in the actual story of the apostles that has been told from the beginning.[23] The challenge for Western culture is a new way of thinking, a new understanding of reality. Newbigin invites Western culture to see the Easter story as a new way of understanding of reality, a new way of thinking that is incompatible with the dogma of the Enlightenment. The old must be replaced by the new.[24] The church must recognize "with fresh clarity" that it is the community that God has entrusted with a fiduciary framework that could be the starting point that would help Western culture to regain its balance and stop its downhill slide.[25]

Although much of the discussion regarding the ideology of Western culture is theological and philosophical in nature, the real issues have to do not with timeless truths, but with the acceptance of the living Lord, the One who lived among us and who leads us into fullness of truth as it is present in him.[26]

Most importantly, however, "the church's mission is not primarily our program; it is the manifestation of the reality of the present, though hidden, reign of Jesus Christ through the presence and power of the Holy

---

21. Newbigin, "Can the West be Converted?" 6.
22. Newbigin, "Mission in the 1990s: Two Views," II:101.
23. Newbigin, *Proper Confidence*, 6.
24. Newbigin, *Gospel in a Pluralist Society*, 12.
25. Newbigin, *Other Side*, 31.
26. Newbigin, *Truth and Authority*, 70.

Spirit."[27] The goal of mission is to bring glory to God, not glory to our own program.[28] The deepest motive for mission comes from the desire to work on "the frontier between the reign of God and the usurped dominion of the devil."[29] It will not be without a price, however. Newbigin sobers any triumphalism that might arise by reminding the church of the necessity of suffering. It was true of Christ, and it will be true of his disciples as well:

> The point is that this active and uncompromising challenge to the dominion of evil takes Jesus to the cross. And when the risen Lord commissioned the disciples to go on the same mission as he received from the Father, he shows them the scars of his passion to remind them of the way the mission must take them.[30]

A CHALLENGE TO SCIENTISM

Introduction to Newbigin's View of Science

Newbigin's interest in science is limited to the philosophy of science and the effect that the scientific method has had on Western culture over the last few centuries. His rebuttal of 'scientism' begins quite early in his career. Newbigin is not opposed to science *per se*, but is opposed to *scientism*, that is, a narrow view of science that limits reality and truth to what can only be validated by the scientific method. In 1936, while a student at Cambridge, he wrote in a student paper that science enjoys the reputation of having infallibly guaranteed dogmas that are accepted "with a credulity which might have been the envy of past theologians."[31] In 1958, still well before his retirement in Britain, he says that science has become a new kind religion, since it purports to be a source for ultimate truth.[32] From the very beginning of his writings, he has shown a disdain for a scientism that claims ultimacy and that seeks to dispose of other avenues of truth as illegitimate detractors for the true quest for factual knowledge.

---

27. Newbigin, *A Word*, 141.
28. Newbigin, "Mission in the 1990s" II:102.
29. Newbigin, *A Word*, 129.
30. Newbigin, "Cross-currents," 148.
31. Newbigin, "Revelation," 33.
32. Newbigin, *A Faith*, 15.

Newbigin's Response to Western Culture's Crisis

The Rise of Modern Science in the West

THE BIBLICAL VISION AND THE RISE OF MODERN SCIENCE

Newbigin believes that science developed in Europe because "it was willing to take as its starting point affirmations rooted in the biblical revelation of God as Creator and redeemer."[33] Newbigin observes how two beliefs have been instrumental to the phenomenal development of science in the West. The first belief is that the universe is rational, while the second is that the universe is contingent, something created and standing apart from the Creator. These two ideas were the 'precondition' for the birth of science in the West.[34] The rationality of the universe is a faith commitment on the part of science, because it must be assumed to proceed with scientific inquiry.[35] The biblical vision that the universe is rational and contingent[36] supports the ideas that the universe is orderly, that it is capable of being understood, and that it is capable of being seen objectively because it is separate from God.[37] The Christian view is that God is the cause of creation, but that creation is distinct and contingent, standing apart from God in an objective sense.[38]

The cyclical worldview of Asia embraces a rational world but not one that is contingent. Such a context could coexist with science, Newbigin observes, but would not give birth to it. Likewise, for science to proceed, it must have a contingent universe. If the cosmos is an emanation of an absolute spirit (as in Indian thinking), we could know ultimate reality

---

33. Newbigin, *Proper Confidence*, 11.

34 Newbigin, *Foolishness*, 71.

35 Newbigin, *Gospel in a Pluralist Society*, 20.

36. See T. F. Torrance, *Divine and Contingent Order*.

37. Newbigin, *Foolishness*, 70–71.

38. Torrance explains: "Christian theology rejected the determining presuppositions of Greek science and philosophy, a necessary relation between the world and God and the bifurcation between matter and form, and opened the way for a realist natural science in which factual knowledge of the universe can be established under the objective control of its independent reality and its divinely conferred inherent intelligibility. This Christian outlook upon the created universe had the effect of liberating the understanding of nature from the iron grip of necessary forms of thought extrinsically clamped down upon it, and called for an open empirical investigation of its intrinsic process and their hidden patterns of order." *Theology in Reconciliation*, Torrance (London: Geoffrey Chapman, 1975), 2. Torrance is much more positive in his approach to science than Newbigin.

only through contemplation, and would not need to test a hypotheses by laboratory equipment.[39]

Good Soil for the Growth of Science

It was not superior intelligence or unusual gifts that made Europe move in the direction that it did. It was, Newbigin says, the biblical worldview that freed Europe from the Aristotelian worldview and allowed it to embrace science.[40] Aristotle's worldview was that of an unmoved mover, a static God who is the final cause in a long progression of causes to the ultimate cause.[41] Christopher Kaiser summarizes the four principles established by the Cappadocian Fathers in the fourth century that shaped the development of science for centuries:

1. That the cosmos is coherent and comprehensible by the human mind because it was created by a rational God.

2. The cosmos is relatively autonomous because it is not an emanation of God, but has a separate reality. It can be known, not by mystical contemplation but through empirical investigation.

3. Since God created the heavens and the earth, heavenly bodies are of the same substance as the earth, contrary to what Aristotle taught.

4. Christ's Incarnation implies that we may use material means for the advancement for human salvation.[42]

These four principles provide a grid for understanding on what basis science developed.[43] Newbigin explains:

> These four principles, which were to provide the foundation for the subsequent development of science in Europe . . . were based on faith in the biblical revelation. They were part of the whole re-

---

39. Newbigin, *Gospel in a Pluralist Society*, 20.

40. Newbigin, *Foolishness*, 23.

41. Aristotle also stressed the capabilities of human reason to understand the principles of reality. Reason alone, then, became the avenue of truth and reality. Newbigin would object to this. Aristotle also held that the first principles of science are presupposed and cannot be demonstrated but must be taken for granted, something with which Newbigin would concur, stating that science is not neutral or free from assumption as it purports itself to be. See Mayer. *A History of Ancient and Medieval Philosophy*, 151.

42. Kaiser's *Creation and the History of Science* is quoted in Newbigin, *Proper Confidence*, 7–8.

43. Newbigin, *Proper Confidence*, 7.

construction of thought necessitated by the new fact, the action of God, the incarnation of the Word in Jesus Christ.[44]

Newbigin goes on to elaborate on the significance of each principle for the growth and development of science. The first principle states that because the cosmos is the creation of a rational God, it is understandable to the human mind. The cosmos is coherent and not a collection of random events, so there is no ultimate self-contradiction between the cosmos and the human mind. "It has an ultimate coherence, a coherence of which the central secret is made known in the Incarnation."[45] The second principle states that the cosmos is a free act of God's will, not an emanation or overflow of the Being of God. The cosmos has a relative autonomy, meaning that not everything that happens is the ultimate will of God. The way to know the cosmos is not through mystical contemplation, but through investigating the empirical facts by careful observation.[46] The third principle regards the substance that comprises 'heavenly bodies' and the earth. Since God created both the heavenly bodies and the earth, the heavenly bodies are not made from "a substance different from the elements that compose the earth," as Aristotle taught.[47] The fourth principle relates to the incarnation of Christ. Because of Christ's incarnation, it is legitimate to use material 'means' for the advancement of the salvation of humans. The church, for example, did not follow the Hebraic tradition of rejecting Greek medicine, but used it in the development of a healing ministry.[48] The incarnation destroyed the old classical categories, both Platonist and Aristotelian, since God became man yet maintained a distinct existence, interacting with creation, but not being absorbed by it.

Referring to the Second Law of Thermodynamics (that every closed system runs down into randomness), Newbigin notes that if the cosmos is believed to be a closed system that can be fully explained without reference to anything beyond it, then the conclusion that the cosmos must decay in chaos is inescapable.[49] John Polkinghorne says that science "presents us with the picture of a universe that, despite its present fruitfulness,

44. Newbigin, *Proper Confidence*, 8.
45. Ibid., 7–8.
46. Ibid., 8.
47. Ibid.
48. Ibid.
49. Newbigin, *Truth to Tell*, 63.

will eventually end in the futility of cosmic collapse or decay."[50] Since the cosmos is not, Newbigin asserts, a closed system, the Second Law does not have the last word. God created the cosmos and is continually active in creation, renewing and creating new patterns of order.[51] God the Father raised the body of Jesus from the dead, and he continues to renew the earth and humanity.[52]

In his book *The Natural and the Supernatural* (1931), John Oman begins with a concept of the unitary nature of the cosmos that is identifiable in Newbigin. Oman writes: "Seeing that the world is one and our experience of it 'one universe of discourse,' there is no ultimate separateness either in what we study or how we study it."[53] Dualism is not necessarily imbedded in the cosmos. It is truly one world, although it can be approached from various viewpoints. The spiritual and the physical aspects are not ultimately separated, nor are they in opposition to each other.[54] On the same page, Oman makes another significant observation: that natural science has purposefully limited its field of inquiry to the parameters of that which can only be quantitatively measured. Consequently, it does not have a real grasp of reality but has, in fact, a very narrow grasp.[55] Such an idea resonates with Newbigin, who views the Enlightenment as narrowing the scope of Western culture's understanding of reality to the physical world, and to the strictures of cause and effect. Scientists, however, cannot live according to their own view, Oman believes. Even the most natural-

---

50. Polkinghorne, *God of Hope*, xviii. Polkinghorne is a scientist and a theologian. He is the past President and now Fellow of Queens' College, Cambridge, and Canon Theologian of Liverpool. He was formerly Professor of Mathematical Physics in the University of Cambridge and is a Fellow of the Royal Society.

51. Polkinghorne writes: "We need to embrace a cosmic hope as well as a personal hope, for it would be far too anthropocentric simply to regard this vast universe as being of concern of God only as a backdrop for a human drama which started after an overture lasting fifteen billion years. It is, of course, beyond our feeble powers of imagination to conceive what that act of cosmic redemption will be like, but if there is a true hope it lies in God and not in physics." *Reason and Reality*, Polkinghorne (London: SPCK, 1991), 81–82.

52. Newbigin, *Truth to Tell*, 63.

53. Oman, *Natural and the Supernatural*, 2. Oman was a teacher of Newbigin at Cambridge and a family friend.

54. Ibid., 111.

55. Oman, *Natural and the Supernatural*, 2.

istic scientist deals with the world as if it has meaning, and not as if it is only constituted by natural causes.[56]

NEWBIGIN'S CRITIQUE OF SCIENCE

Again, Newbigin's argument is against scientism, not the work of science generally, which he recognizes as benefiting humankind. The issues are not so much in the details as they are in the controlling philosophy of science. V. Matthew Thomas says that

> Newbigin might be misunderstood as an enemy of modern science and an inadequate interpreter of Western culture, because he tends to ignore major positive elements that are intrinsic to its stability. Newbigin spurs some misunderstanding with the vigor of his argument against the ideology that is so pervasive in his culture. He could have been clearer in his presentation and more attentive to the positive elements in science. However, his attack on modern scientific culture is not seen as an attack on science itself, but on the tendency to absolutize science without any reference to its origin and purpose.[57]

Newbigin's critique of scientism could be classified into five categories. The first category is the assumptions of scientism. Among these would be that the universe is purely a mechanical, closed universe where there can be no supernatural intervention. These assumptions formed the plausibility structure of the scientific community, and categorically eliminated God from the equation. The second category is the methodology of science, which is reputed to be totally objective. It cannot be totally objective, Newbigin observes, because scientists must make decisions regarding the validity and importance of scientific findings, and that indicates a personal involvement in science. The third area is the loss of teleology. Science has categorically rejected the notion of purpose. Newbigin questions whether the rejection of purpose is necessary or even possible. The fourth category is that of the autonomy of reason. The Enlightenment not only sought the autonomy of man from God and the church, it has also separated reason from faith. Newbigin believes that this is not possible, and that scientists have faith in certain presuppositions that cannot be proven. Finally, Newbigin objects to the replacement of God with science as the answer to mankind's problem. Up to this point, science has not

---

56. Oman, *Natural and the Supernatural*, 236.
57. Thomas, "Centrality of Christ," 208–9.

delivered all that it has promised. By the eighteenth century, the idea of Providence was being eliminated in favor of mankind's ability to direct its own future. It was Francis Bacon who accomplished this major shift away from teleology in science.[58] Strongly reacting to Aristotelian speculation regarding purpose, Bacon asserted that science should be concerned only with value-free facts. Things are to be understood in relation to their cause.[59] Isaac Newton[60] reiterates the idea that the real world is not ruled by purpose, but by nature through cause and effect, signaling a shift from story (the biblical narrative) to timeless laws as the basis of culture. The cosmos, as Newton conceived it, has no history:

> This was to become a model for reliable truth, the kind of truth for which the word science is now reserved, truth that could in principle be stated in timeless formulae of mathematics. For truth in this sense, accidental happenings in history have, as Lessing said, no relevance.[61]

Newton had an enormous influence on the eighteenth century mind and his thinking would dominate European thinking for the next two hundred years. Newton did not begin with revelation or the innate ideas within the human mind, but rather sought to formulate general laws that would describe the largest possible range of phenomenon. He pictured the real world as moving bodies that have an objective existence apart from any observer. Analysis is the tool by which humans are able to move beyond appearances to discover reality. Analyzing the data of experience in its smallest components the laws that govern the movements and natural relations of those components can be discovered.[62]

Nature, then, is the sum total of all observable phenomena and, in essence, replaces God, who is no longer an essential part of the picture.[63] This being the case, Newbigin concludes, the scientist has become the priest who mediates between nature and humanity, helping people to un-

---

58. Francis Bacon (1561–1626) was an English philosopher and statesman, considered to be one of the pioneers of modern science. See Newbigin, *Foolishness* pages 24–25 for Newbigin's lengthy discussion of the nature of modern science. Torrance gives a number of pages to Bacon in *Theological Science*, 69 ff.

59. Newbigin, *Foolishness*, 76.

60. Isaac Newton (1642–1727) was an English philologist and mathematician.

61. Lesslie Newbigin, *Truth and Authority*, 75.

62. Newbigin, *Other Side*, 10.

63. Ibid., 11.

derstand nature and to benefit from it. There is no other authority except observable facts. This excludes speculation or revelation, and it essentially disallows God.[64] The most fundamental of Newton's laws are mathematical, which are applicable to all of reality.[65]

As noted before, Newbigin cites Frederick Nietzsche as one of the most influential thinkers of the nineteenth century. Nietzsche, Newbigin says, was able to understand with unusual clarity the ultimate conclusions of the rationalistic premises that were held in his day. His argument is that if there is no hope of finding truth, then truth is merely an assertion of the will. Descartes, Nietzsche believed, set up criteria for knowing truth that were impossible to fulfill, and science could no longer be seen as a means to wisdom but as a means to power.[66] Science claims to know truth exclusively, and has become dominant in Western culture, thus, according to Newbigin, fulfilling Nietzsche's observation regarding the will to power.[67]

Newbigin's Critique of the Premise of Total Objectivity

Newbigin argues that *total* objectivity is an illusion, because persons and personal judgments enter into the methodology of science at just about every significant point.[68] To support his argument, Newbigin points to Bertrand Russell's assertion that scientists work with 'significant facts.'[69] What Russell allowed into this assertion was a statement of value by using the term 'significant.' It is a statement of personal evaluation. The scientist must determine that, based on some criteria external to the facts, certain facts are 'significant' and certain ones are not. Such a distinction is made on the grounds of a scientific judgment that, since scientists are persons, must be a personal judgment, necessarily informed by the plausibility structure that is accepted and assumed by faith to be true by the scientist.[70] Russell's statement is based on a personal evaluation. There is

---

64. Newbigin, *Other Side*, 11.
65. Ibid., 10.
66. Newbigin, *Truth and Authority*, 8.
67. Ibid., 9.
68. Eminent scientist and philosopher of science Karl Popper rejected the idea of total objectivity in science. "Popper's concept of the critical approach [means] he totally rejects any possibility of naked, neutral, or objective observation." *Theology and the Justification of Faith,* van Huyssteen (Grand Rapids: Eerdmans, 1989), 27.
69. Russell, *Scientific Outlook,* 58.
70. Newbigin, *Gospel in a Pluralist Society*, 30.

not, Newbigin insists, a body of value-free facts that have become a standard of measurement for science or religion. Such an idea, prevalent in Western culture, that requires religion to be evaluated by scientific truth that rests on the premise of an objective and neutral standard, is therefore an illusion.[71]

Far from impersonal or cold indifference, the scientist approaches the search for and recognition of significant facts with passion, high motivation, concentration, and energy. This passionate search is a venture of faith for the scientist:

> This passionate search is the only context in which the scientist can begin to discuss which facts are significant. It is venture of faith, believing where one cannot see. Without the faith and this "intellectual love," science cannot begin.[72]

Science, then, is neither impersonal nor dispassionate, and it is most assuredly, according to Newbigin, not totally objective. Newbigin continues: "The idea that brute facts simply imprint themselves on our minds apart from our deliberate and fallible efforts to grasp them is an illusion."[73] Newbigin explains the process of scientific discovery to show that it is not a matter of pure objectivity:

> Scientific discovery involves such gifts as intuition, imagination to project possible patterns, prudence coupled with a willingness to take risks, and courage and patience in pursing a long arduous curse of investigation. At every point along this course, there is need of personal judgment in deciding whether a pattern is significant or merely random. None of these can be covered by formal rules. They all involve the personal commitment of the scientist, and it is absurd to pretend that the findings of science can be understood without taking into account all these subjective factors.[74]

Our formal and explicit knowledge depends greatly on what is not formal or explicit, but provides us with a grid to evaluate, process, and critically judge what we are exposed to. It is called *tacit knowledge* because we know it tacitly rather than explicitly.[75] Tacit knowledge allows us to see beyond

71. Newbigin, *A Word*, 72.
72. Newbigin, *Gospel in a Pluralist Society*, 31.
73. Newbigin, *A Word*, 72; also *Truth to Tell*, 4.
74. Newbigin, *Proper Confidence*, 41.
75. Ibid., 41–42. Newbigin credits Michael Polanyi with this phrase but does not

Newbigin's Response to Western Culture's Crisis

just looking at clues but to really *see* them within the parameters of our acquired understanding. Newbigin says "we do not look at them, but from them to the object of our attention."[76] A Western scientist will interpret information according to the prescribe guidelines of Western culture.[77]

A part of the tacit knowledge of the Western tradition is the biblical worldview. It is in the collective mind of Western people and informs their perspective, expectations, and decisions. For many in the West, it is not explicitly understood nor could it be articulated, but is a part of the latent consciousness of culture. Enlightenment thinkers, being a part of the Western cultural tradition, referred to 'self-evident' truths, which were, in reality, the residue of a biblical heritage, a part of the latent consciousness of the biblical worldview. Newbigin observes: "With hindsight, it is now easy to see how many of the self-evident truths of the Enlightenment were self-evident only to those who were heirs of a thousand years of Christian tradition."[78]

The consequence of false objectivism is false subjectivism. "From the disastrous consequences of a false objectivism," Newbigin writes, "we are in danger of collapsing into a false subjectivism where there are no criteria but everything goes."[79] It would appear that this is the basis for the emergence of the ideology of pluralism that recognizes the only standard of truth as being that there is no standard. If there is no standard, as Nietzsche and post-modernists assert, then truth is what is asserted by those who happen to be in power at the moment.[80]

The Authority of Tradition in Science

In science, each discovery or assertion of newly discovered truth is evaluated by persons who have, as their standard of measurement, a tradition of knowledge that is, at least in theory, cumulative. Certainly scientists seek for truth, and, when a specific discovery is made, this new understanding or fact is scrutinized according to this tradition.[81]

---

specifically reference Polanyi's writings in this case. The term can be found in Polanyi, *Tacit Dimension*, 69–245.

76. Newbigin, *Truth to Tell*, 46.
77. Newbigin, *Gospel in a Pluralist Society*, 34–35.
78. Newbigin, *Proper Confidence*, 48.
79. Newbigin, *Truth to Tell*, 56.
80. Newbigin, "Enduring Validity," 52.
81. Newbigin, *Gospel in a Pluralist Society*, 44. This explanation is taken from Michael

Newbigin makes the point: persons create the tradition by deciding that discoveries or facts are significant to be apart of that tradition. The tradition (the accumulated wisdom of previous scientists), in turn, becomes the standard for measuring new facts. The scientific tradition is not codified or embodied in a set of formal rules, but must be passed through personal contact between teachers and learners. Pressing his point a little further, Newbigin says that there are no logical rules that a scientist can learn to make new discoveries. There are processes and procedures, but the recognition of something that may be new and startling comes from within the scientist. Newbigin notes that there are no logical steps by which one can argue logically from the premises of Newton's physics to the formulations of the general and special theories of relativity.[82] Newbigin explains:

> It has much more to do with intuition and imagination—the intuition that there is a problem waiting to be tackled, a configuration of things waiting to be discerned, an orderliness not yet manifest but hidden and waiting to be discovered. And it is a matter of personal judgment between alternative possibilities for experiment and research, personal judgment also in distinguishing between a meaningful pattern and a set of random of events.[83]

There are objective criteria by which to judge the work of a scientist, but it is the scientific community that determines the criteria for success.[84] Without the a-critical acceptance of a tradition, the dynamic of discovery would be lost.[85]

A paradigm shift, Newbigin notes, can only take place "when a new and more compelling paradigm is offered, a vision of reality which commends itself by its beauty, rationality, and comprehensiveness."[86] Generally, there is a long period of reflection, of brooding over the observation until at some point there is "an imaginative leap with a new vision of coher-

---

Polanyi. Newbigin cites Polanyi, *Knowing and Being*, 66. This is an idealized picture of the scientific community that some have questioned. Whether scientific knowledge is cumulative or not, it is a much more complex situation than Newbigin recognizes.

82. Ibid. As mentioned earlier, Newbigin is dependent upon Polanyi for this argument.

83. Ibid. On page 31 Newbigin credits Einstein with affirming that intuition is an important factor in new discoveries.

84. Newbigin, *Gospel in a Pluralist Society*, 45.

85. Ibid., 46–47.

86. Ibid., 47.

ence." It is something that "compels assent by its beauty, its simplicity, and its comprehensiveness."[87] The acceptance of this new vision is a personal act, an act of judgment whereby the scientist is committed to this new vision with the likelihood that others may disagree with it. This involves personal commitment, but it is not entirely subjective because the scientist commits to the new vision with, as Polanyi calls it, "universal intent." The scientist believes that the new explanation is objectively true, and therefore desires to publish widely the new ideas, inviting and expecting discussion, seeking ultimately to persuade fellow scientists of the truth of the new vision of reality.[88] At no point is this considered merely personal opinion since it is held with universal intent, meaning that it is held to be valid and true account of reality, an account that ought to be accepted, and an account that will prove itself to be not only verified by further experiment, but will open the way to fresh discovery. In other words, the new ideas are offered as public truth.[89]

A major paradigm shift, however, does not come about easily. When scientists work for generations within a certain paradigm, it is not easily abandoned. The conversion of scientists to the new view begins the process of long debate that may eventuate in a major shift in perspective.[90] Science rests, Newbigin observes, on a circular argument, where what one believes to be true may eventually be proven to be true.[91] Scientific tradition rests on its own authority, not on something outside itself. Science assumes from the beginning the truth that it seeks to prove. If the scientist sets forth ideas that are truly innovative, the scientist must challenge the authoritative tradition, not with the intention of undermining it, but with the intention of altering it or radically changing it if the facts prove sufficient. If the innovative ideas prove acceptable, these new ideas will be incorporated into scientific tradition as well.[92]

All of this is based on the assumption that scientists can know truth about reality, that reality itself can be known, and that it will ultimately prove to be rationally coherent. "The commitment," writes Newbigin, "is

---

87. Newbigin, *Gospel in a Pluralist Society*, 59.
88. Ibid., 47.
89. Ibid., 48.
90. Ibid., 46.
91. Ibid., 94.
92. Newbigin, *Gospel in a Pluralist Society*, 48.

a personal matter; it has to be my commitment. In that sense it is subjective. It is, however, a commitment that has an objective reference, so it is not subjectivism."[93] Philosophers and historians of science have shown that "the whole work of modern science rests on faith-commitments that themselves cannot be demonstrated by the methods of science."[94] The scientist holds to the new vision of truth by faith, believing it to be true before it is proven to be true. This faith is justified if, in fact, the theory proves to work. The analogy to Christian faith, in Newbigin's view, hardly needs to be pointed out.[95]

One might question whether using the idea of a paradigm shift in science to explain religious conversion as a radical change of perspective is adequate. Of course, an analogy is only approximate, sharing *some* likeness to the thing compared. There are, also, different factors involved in religious conversion that are not present in a scientific paradigm shift. The spiritual dynamic of religious conversion is not fully comparable to the inspiration of an aesthetic experience or the intuitive insight of the scientist. Newbigin admits to the need for the work of the Holy Spirit in the heart of a person, convincing them of the truth. Perhaps this analogy is as close to the experience of conversion, as Newbigin conceives of it, as one can get *outside* the spiritual or religious realm. The paradigm change in science is seen primarily a change of mind, whereas the spiritual conversion is thought of as primarily a change of heart. Newbigin sees spiritual conversion also as a change of mind, which is more comprehensive than just a change of heart.

Newbigin, as such, emphasizes the cognitive aspect of religious conversion to counteract the over-emphasis by some Christians upon the 'spiritual' aspects of conversion that do not require any real change in thinking about reality beyond one's own individual spiritual realm. In this case, I believe, Newbigin's use of the analogy of a paradigm change in the scientific field makes good sense. It is also apparent that, in spite of Newbigin's dislike of the term *contextualization*,[96] he practices it by using a model that is understood by society to explain conversion.

93. Newbigin, *Gospel in a Pluralist Society*, 35.
94. Ibid., 20.
95. Ibid., 46.
96. Contextualization is, generally, the attempt to communicate truth to a particular culture in a manner that would allow the hearers to understand the truth as the communicator intended it to be understood. To a certain degree, then, one must use the

Newbigin's Response to Western Culture's Crisis

Those who popularize science have given the impression that science is a world of 'facts,' quite apart from the world of imagination, intuition, or even faith. "There is no knowing without believing, and believing is a way to knowing," writes Newbigin.[97] Science rests on a host of personal judgments that are based on a host of assumptions. "No critical act is possible," writes Newbigin, "except on the basis of a whole complex of beliefs which are assumed a-critically as the grounds on which one can criticise the belief under discussion."[98]

CHALLENGING THE SCIENTIFIC WORLDVIEW

The first and most fundamental challenge for the church must be to confront the prevailing worldview of Western culture, which Newbigin believes is the scientific worldview.[99] The scientific worldview has become the 'fiduciary framework' of Western culture, and it must be called into question.[100] This fiduciary framework, the system of beliefs that drive Western culture, can be thought of as the 'plausibility structure,' a term Newbigin borrows from Peter Berger.[101]

Newbigin, however, disagrees with Berger on whether there is a plausibility structure in Western culture. Berger defines a plausibility structure as a set of beliefs that are taken for granted and accepted without argument, best represented by non-modern cultures. When persons dissent from the cultural plausibility structure, they are considered heretics. Berger believes that all Westerners are forced to be heretics because Western culture has no fixed plausibility structure. In fact, he observes, when modern culture comes into contact with these traditional cultures, it tends to radically change them.[102]

---

epistemology of the culture.

97. Newbigin, *Gospel in a Pluralist Society*, 32–33. Paul Ricoeur thinks that this should be understood in a way that reinforces the circular argument: we must understand in order to believe and we must believe in order to understand. See Polkinghorne, *Reason and Reality*, 6.

98. Newbigin, *Gospel in a Pluralist Society*, 82.

99. Newbigin, *Foolishness*, 14, 41.

100. Newbigin, *Other Side*, 30.

101. Professor Emeritus Religion, Sociology, and Theology at Rutgers University.

102. Newbigin, *Foolishness*, 10–13.

Newbigin, however, believes that Western culture *does* have a plausibility structure, and that modern people make choices within the parameters of this structure. They are not as free as they might think:

> My point is simply this: while Berger correctly shows how the traditional plausibility structures are dissolved by contact with this modern world-view, and while he correctly reminds us that the prevalence and power of this world-view gives no ground for believing it to be true, he does not seem to allow for the fact that it is itself a plausibility structure and functions as such.[103]

This modern Western plausibility structure has determined that we must live on two levels: one is the level of facts (public) and the other is the level of beliefs and values (private). This dichotomy of life, Newbigin believes, is leading to the disintegration of Western culture much in the same way that ancient dualism destroyed classical culture. If the church is to have an effective missionary encounter of the gospel with Western culture, the church must understand and appropriately confront this dichotomy.[104]

The Reality of Principalities and Powers

One way of confronting the modern scientific worldview is to assert the inter-penetration of the natural world by the supernatural, which includes not only God's intervention into history and society, but also the presence of 'powers' that are evident to those with spiritual acumen and discernment. Newbigin affirms his belief in such supernatural intervention: "The principalities and powers are realities. We may not be able to visualize them, or to say exactly what they are. But we are foolish to pretend they do not exist."[105] Newbigin takes the biblical view of the presence of evil spirits, angels who have changed loyalties, who come to us as evil 'embodied,' that is, visible and tangible in people, institutions, and nations. They were defeated at the death of Christ and the church is, Newbigin believes, the agency through which Christ's victory over them is fully realized.[106] No doubt, Newbigin's many years as a missionary in India reaffirmed his belief in these principalities and powers. If they exist in India, it stands to reason that they also exist in the West as well but are not recognized as

---

103. Newbigin, *Foolishness*, 13–14.
104. Ibid., 15.
105. Newbigin, *Gospel in a Pluralist Society*, 210.
106. Ibid., 207–8.

readily in the West since the West is blinded by a worldview that does not allow these to be an actual part of the universe.

CONVERSION TO ANOTHER PLAUSIBILITY STRUCTURE

The purpose of challenging the prevailing plausibility structure is to convince Western culture that it needs to convert to another plausibility structure. "A serious commitment to evangelism, to the telling of the story which the Church is sent to tell," Newbigin exhorts, "means a radical questioning of the assumptions of public life."[107] While the most essential beliefs of Christianity cannot be proven within the parameters of the scientific worldview, believing them, then, would mean to accept another plausibility structure that challenges the prevailing cultural worldview of reality. Just because a plausibility structure is culturally acceptable, Newbigin insists, does not mean that it is in touch with reality.[108]

The most fundamental task of Western Christianity, according to Newbigin, is to question contemporary assumptions of what it means to know.[109] Newbigin describes what he thinks is at stake:

> What is at stake is the meaning of "knowing." It is a question of the way in which human beings are enabled to come to a true understanding of and a practical relation to the realities with which human life is set. Science does not give and does not pretend to have a complete answer to that question. But the scientific achievements of the past two hundred years have been so awe-inspiring that we have been tempted to believe that the methods of science are the sufficient key to knowledge in all its fullness. That belief has led us to the brink of disaster.[110]

For Newbigin, the question of epistemology is more than just an academic discussion; it is a missionary problem in that a civilization is on the brink, and the gospel, he believes, is a more than adequate answer for the dilemma facing Western culture.

The issues at stake are more than philosophical questions; they involve the very practical realm of public values. The worldview or core ideology of a culture determines the values of the culture. These values are lived out in society, and are concerned with very practical things such

107. Newbigin, *Truth to Tell*, 2.
108. Newbigin, *Foolishness*, 63.
109. Newbigin, *Other Side*, 60.
110. Ibid., 60–61.

as cultural priorities, the nature of relationships, and the parameters of what is allowed and what is forbidden. Cultural values are based on some ultimate visions that have traditionally been rooted in religion. Western culture, because of its acceptance of the scientific worldview, has excluded purpose from its system of values. Within the parameters of the scientific worldview, it is not possible to move from 'what is' to 'what ought to be.'[111] Newbigin believes that this has made Western culture less than adequate as a comprehensive guide to a meaningful life.

Determining what is right and wrong, or what is acceptable and not acceptable is the prerogative of every culture, and is the basis of stability and consistency of culture. Newbigin believes that Western culture, because of its plausibility structure and the acceptance of the scientific worldview, has fallen into moral chaos.[112] On the basis of modern critical thought, it is impossible to determine truth from error or right from wrong.[113]

A Call for New Understanding

The situation in Western culture in regard to its attitude toward science has significantly changed over the last few decades. Science and technology are now seen as a threat to civilization, clearly faulting on their role as a ground of hope for Western culture.[114] It is becoming apparent that the problems of Western culture will not be solved within the terms provided by Western culture itself. Western culture is becoming skeptical about the viability of its approach, since it continues to struggle with many of the same problems that have plagued the culture since the Enlightenment.[115] There are, however, few voices that provide an alternative viewpoint to what is presently being rejected. Newbigin challenges Western culture to rethink its framework of understanding: "The question has to be asked whether we do not need new models for understanding our human situation. This means that we need to examine our accepted framework of understanding."[116]

---

111. Newbigin, *Foolishness*, 34–38.
112. Newbigin, "Enduring Validity," 52.
113. Ibid.
114. Newbigin, *Other Side*, 2.
115. Ibid., 18.
116. Ibid.

Newbigin's Response to Western Culture's Crisis

The Need for God

Newbigin believes that since Western culture has dwelt in the biblical narrative for over a thousand years, biblical culture cannot be dismissed altogether. God is at least in the memory of culture:

> No one who has been immersed in the biblical narrative could ever again entirely escape from the presence of that One, God, so tender and yet so terrible, so passionate in his wrathful love and his loving wrath, forever calling on those who turn their backs on him, forever humbling himself in tender appeal, forever challenging his children to the heights of utter purity, and finally accepting the shameful death of a condemned sinner in order to open for us the gate of glory. There is absolutely nothing in all the world's sacred literature that can be compared for a moment with this. And a society that has linked with this God for more than a thousand years can never, even when revolting against him, wholly cast off that memory.[117]

It is a memory that needs to be revived. Newbigin asserts that the purpose of God is being worked out in the entire history of the cosmos:

> We cannot have total understanding of things without the cultivation of that particular kind of understanding which is conceived with knowing the nature and purpose of the One whose purpose is being realized in the entire history of the cosmos.[118]

Christianity, as a system of thought, gives a much more reasonable and rational explanation for the universe and human experience than the Enlightenment paradigm.[119]

A New Understanding of the Universe

The mechanical understanding of the universe and the value-free understanding of science that emerged has been challenged, according to Newbigin, not only by thinking Christians, but by the radical viewpoint of the advocates of the new physics as well. The advancement of particle physics has shown that ultimate elements, which Western science had assumed to be matter, is not matter at all, but a "pattern of relationships between non-material entities—relationships which can be represented mathemati-

---

117. Newbigin, *Proper Confidence*, 54.
118. Ibid., 59.
119. Newbigin, *A Word*, 173.

cally but cannot be visualized."[120] In the development of quantum physics, it was recognized that a picture of the cosmos that does not include the observing subject is not accurate, since the scientist, a person with purpose and personal judgment, is also a part of the picture.[121] Unfortunately, these developments in physics have not penetrated popular thinking, so most ordinary people (as well as many practitioners of the human sciences), far from understanding the importance of these far-reaching changes, still operate on the myths and assumptions of Newtonian physics. Western culture must recognize that "the concept of a purely mechanical system operating without any place for purpose is mistaken."[122]

A NEW RATIONALITY

Epistemology emerges as the fundamental issue for Newbigin. In two of his earliest writings, there are explicit references to epistemological themes that reappear after 1974, especially his extremely important chapter "I Believe" in *I Believe* by M. A. Thomas[123] and his unpublished student paper titled "Revelation."[124] Knowing, Newbigin contends, is not just cognition, but is relational, and not confined to the narrow limitations of scientific positivism. The Western cultural plausibility structure limits what is accepted as truth or factual, and, as such, shuts the door to certain aspects of reality and truth that are also valid sources of truth.

The Need for Another Rationality

Newbigin's most fundamental critique of the Western way of knowing is that the methods of science are not a sufficient key to understand the whole of reality.[125] This failure has spawned such reactionary movements as New Age. He explains:

---

120. Newbigin, *Gospel in a Pluralist Society*, 37.

121. Ibid.

122. Ibid. Newbigin acknowledges his dependence on Drusilla Scott's, *Everyman Revived: The Common Sense of Michael Polanyi*. Consequently, he is dependent upon Polanyi's thought for this paragraph.

123. Newbigin, *I Believe*. Madras: SCM, 1946.

124. Newbigin, "Revelation," 73–88. The 'personalist' theme becomes more explicit after Newbigin reads Polanyi.

125. Newbigin, *Other Side*, 61.

Newbigin's Response to Western Culture's Crisis

> ... we need to recover what we have lost, the capacity to see things whole, not seeking to master everything by dissection, analysis, and the experimental method that force nature to answer questions we put to her but accepting and rejoicing in the wholeness of things.[126]

Western culture needs another kind of rationality, another plausibility structure that is broad enough to include the whole of reality, and this would require a radical epistemological shift for Western culture.[127] It must begin, however, with a "radical critique of the reigning epistemology, the way in which we regard any claim to know the truth."[128]

The New Role for Reason

From our previous discussion, we can deduce that the scientific tradition and its specific rationality is the construction of scientists within a particular cultural context. "The idea (dominant in our culture)," comments Newbigin, "that there exists a supracultural rationality that can stand over all the culturally conditioned forms of rational discourse is an illusion."[129] Reason, then, is not an autonomous authority that judges the discourse of culture, but is the product of a cultural tradition of rationality.[130] Knowing involves a subject who is inducted into a tradition of knowing that is embodied in the literature, language, symbol, and story of the culture, which Newbigin calls a fiduciary framework.[131] "Reason," writes Newbigin, "operates within a specific tradition of rational discourse, a tradition that is carried by a specific human community."[132] We only experience the world within the framework of understanding that we receive as a part of a

---

126. Newbigin, *Truth to Tell*, 62.
127. Ibid.
128. Ibid., 50–51.
129. Newbigin, *A Word*, 142; also see Newbigin, "Religious Pluralism," 50.
130. Newbigin, *A Word*, 142.
131. Newbigin, *Truth and Authority*, 35. This would seem to imply relativism, that each culture develops its own 'truth' and can only be understood within that culture. What Newbigin is saying, however, is that we 'know' through a whole cluster of avenues (multidimensional) that are far more instructive than mere reason. Every culture has its way of connecting to and interpreting reality, and reason is but one way among many ways of knowing. Western culture has tried to limit itself to just one dimension: reason.
132. Ibid., 52.

living tradition.[133] Reason operates with a particular cultural worldview that is embodied within the language, concepts, and models of culture.[134] Therefore, "all rationality is socially embodied"[135] and all truth claims, therefore, are culturally conditioned.[136]

Newbigin views the function of reason as the ability to grasp different elements in ordinary experience in a manner so that they make sense to us.[137] In other words, reason is a function of the mind, not a separate source of knowledge. Newbigin, in contradistinction to the Enlightenment, reduces the role of reason to a functional rationality:

> ... reason only works with something given, with data, with things which are accepted as a starting point. Reason is not a source of information about what is the case; it is the faculty by which we seek to discover the order and coherence in what is presented to us. All rational discourse takes place within a tradition which accepts some things as given.[138]

Reason is subject to the test of adequacy, whether it really engages, understands, and copes with reality.[139] The mental activity that is involved in trying to make contact with reality, remarks Newbigin, only functions by indwelling a tradition that functions as a lens through which one can find what is actually there.[140] Even the most acutely critical reason cannot, for all its functional value, actually establish truth.[141] Reason can only tell us if what we experience matches the presupposition or preconception of what constitutes truth. It is not an autonomous authority that can be the source of truth; it can only recognize it within the parameters of culture's

---

133. Newbigin, *A Word*, 95.
134. Ibid., 91 and "Religious Pluralism," 50.
135. Newbigin, *A Word*, 142.
136. Newbigin, *Truth to Tell*, 4.
137. Newbigin, *A Word*, 90.
138. Newbigin, "Certain Faith," 347.
139. Newbigin, *A Word*, 91.
140. Newbigin, *Proper Confidence*, 47–48.
141. Newbigin, *Truth to Tell*, 30. This idea appears in the Newbigin's discussion of Descartes' assertion that reliable knowledge (see page 29) comes only through the critical method. The critical method would be thought to approach a subject without presuppositions. Nietzsche repudiates this view. Any assertion of truth is based on a person's presuppositions is an assertion of power over against the truth assertions of others.

fiduciary framework and plausibility structure.[142] All genuine learning is also guided by a tradition whose authority is accepted, often uncritically, by the one who seeks to know.[143] Newbigin says that most of what we know is not what has our attention; tradition is that invisible framework we use to make sense of our experience.[144]

Newbigin recognizes that biblical thought is embodied in a particular cultural tradition that utilizes human language.[145] This in no way disqualifies it from being true.[146] All cultures have a fiduciary framework that is held to be true by each community.[147] Every tradition rests upon presuppositions and assumptions that Newbigin observes "cannot be verified by reference to some reality external to it."[148] This is true of mathematics, physics, and psychology as well as religious thinking.[149] Knowing any reality is not possible except on the basis of a cultural framework that is generally accepted uncritically, and which cannot be proven by reference to a more "ultimate ground of belief."[150]

Revelation was given to the people of Israel and, through Christ, to the Christian Church. Revelation, then, came to be known and understood within a rational as well as religious tradition. The fact that truth comes through a particular tradition does not make it untrue. Newbigin writes:

> All knowing of reality, and supremely when the reality in question is God, is the work of people nurtured in a tradition of rational discourse. The fact that the Christian affirmation is made from one such socially embodied tradition in no way discredits its claim to speak truth.[151]

---

142. Newbigin, *A Word*, 142.
143. Newbigin, *Gospel in a Pluralist Society*, 12.
144. Newbigin, *A Word*, 83.
145. Newbigin, *Open Secret*, 153.
146. Newbigin, *Proper Confidence*, 50.
147. Newbigin, *Other Side*, 29–30.
148. Newbigin, "Religious Pluralism," 52.
149. Newbigin, *Proper Confidence*, 50.
150. Newbigin, *Other Side*, 28, and Polanyi, *Personal Knowledge*, 267.
151. Newbigin, "Religious Pluralism," 52–54.

The Critique of Epistemological Dualism

The epistemological question that Newbigin addresses has a number of practical consequences beyond the fundamental question of how one knows. The most critical problem, as mentioned earlier, is that Enlightenment epistemology, with its dualist orientation, has created a number of dichotomies in various realms that are essential to culture. Earlier we noted that Descartes' thinking has produced three distinct dualisms, those of mind/matter, subject/object, and theory/practice.[152] Newbigin, as we have already seen, sees the subject/object dichotomy in human knowing as a key to understanding its failure to come to terms with the whole of reality. In the first place, there has been a breakdown of that unity into a dichotomous relationship between the objective and subjective poles of knowing.[153] He explains:

> What seems to have happened in our culture is a falling apart, a disconnection between the subjective and objective poles. We have on the one hand the ideal, or shall I call it the illusion, of a kind of objectivity which is not possible.[154]

Newbigin believes this illusion threatens Western culture with disintegration.[155] The paradigm structure of Western culture is based on faulty and incorrect assumptions that do not allow Western culture to see reality as a whole, and disbars faith as a way of knowing, even though science utilizes faith in its method. There is one inconsistency in this regard, according to Newbigin, in the plausibility structure of Western culture. He points out that devaluing belief statements as merely subjective is logically absurd because it "presupposes the possibility of an 'objective' knowledge which is not knowledge as believed to be true by someone."[156]

Newbigin suggests that one way of resolving the subject/object problem is to utilize George Lindbeck's cultural-linguistic model.[157]

---

152. Newbigin, "Certain Faith," 344–345.
153. Newbigin, *A Word*, 104.
154. Newbigin, *Gospel in a Pluralist Society*, 23; see also *A Word*, 82.
155. Newbigin, *A Word*, 160–61.
156. Newbigin, *Gospel in a Pluralist Society*, 22.
157. Lindbeck, *The Nature of Doctrine*, 18, 20. Ramachandra believes that Newbigin is vulnerable at this point because of "his uncritical stance toward George Lindbeck's 'cultural-linguistic' model of Christian doctrine." It gravitates toward relativism. Ramachandra details his view: "For Lindbeck, doctrine serves as the regulatory grammar of the Christian language, ensuring the internal consistency of the narrative. But he sits

Stories, not propositional truth, structure human experience and help us understand ourselves and our world. All knowing involves a subject that has been included into a tradition of knowing that is embodied in the language and stories of a culture. It is through this tradition of knowing that we look at the world, the object of our attention. The tradition of knowing is, Newbigin says, a 'faith,' which is a system of assumptions and beliefs that are accepted without proof. It becomes a mechanism by which we are able to perceive and understand our world. Doctrine, which is a statement of faith to be believed, is something you look *through* to understand reality.[158]

The result of the subject/object dichotomy of human knowing is the problem of the public/private dichotomy in Western culture, where certain things are seen as public facts and other things merely as personal opinion. As a result of Cartesian thinking and then the rise of scientific method, Western culture, as has been mentioned before, has chosen to accept as factual only those things that can be proven by reason or experiment. Any truth that is unproven or unable to be proved is considered personal opinion, and not allowed as valid information in the public realm, and not considered serious enough to be concerned about heresy. The empiricist concept of experience (that it is uninterpreted sense data) is a cultural invention of the late seventeenth and eighteenth centuries. For Alasdair MacIntyre, "it is a concept of experience which has a short history and surely has no future."[159]

Newbigin points out that pluralism, which is highly valued in Western culture, is selectively relegated to the area of personal opinion, where it is celebrated. In the public arena, no such pluralism is allowed. Newbigin explains:

> We do not teach as public truth any particular belief about the purpose of human life. But this pluralism does not extend to the world of "facts." When there is disagreement about what are called "facts," we do not take it as an occasion for celebrating our pluralism! No! We argue, we conduct experiments, we try to convince each other of

---

far too lightly on the issue of the extra-linguistic referents of the narrative and so reduces all questions of truth to purely 'intrasystemic' (or 'intratextual') cohesion. His model... tends to sever Christian language from its historical anchoring." *Recovery of Mission*, Ramachandra (Carlisle, Cumbria: Paternoster, 1996), 170.

158. Newbigin, *Truth and Authority*, 34–35.

159. Quoted in Newbigin, *Gospel in a Pluralist Society*, 58–59.

error, and we do not rest until we reach agreement about the facts. In the public world of "facts," pluralism does not reign.[160]

Newbigin observes that while there may be significant changes in the scientific community as to what constitutes reality, on the folk level of Western culture the idea of what constitutes factual knowledge still dominates. Facts are neutral, neither good nor bad.[161] Every child in the Western public education system is introduced to this concept of facts, and it becomes the agreed plausibility structure of culture. The expectation is that everyone will agree with this view and this forms the parameters of what individuals are allowed to believe.[162]

While in the public realm the rational system of culture is imposed on the populace, in the realm of private opinion no one has the right to impose truth on others. In this context, the proclamation of the church is seen as arrogant:

> In this cultural milieu, the confident announcement of the Christian faith sounds like an arrogant attempt of some people to impose their values on others. As long as the Church is content to offer its beliefs modestly as simply one of the many brands available in the ideological supermarket, no offence is taken. But the affirmation that the truth revealed in the gospel ought to govern public life is offensive.[163]

While culture has relegated the church to a place of irrelevancy in regards to public truth, the church, Newbigin believes, has more or less accepted this role.[164]

Another area this dichotomy affects is the division of the human person into *soul* and *body* that is, according to Newbigin, "a reversion to the ancient pagan dichotomy from which the biblical vision delivered the classical world."[165] Newbigin insists that, according to the biblical view, there is no dichotomy between the outward aspect and the inward aspect of humans. Of course, we can see others from without (as we are ourselves are seen) and we can see inwardly, but this does not mean that the person

160. Newbigin, *A Word*, 101.
161. Newbigin, "Can the West be Converted?" 5.
162. Ibid.
163. Newbigin, *Gospel in a Pluralist Society*, 7.
164. Newbigin, "Can the West be Converted?" 4.
165. Newbigin, *Other Side*, 38.

is split into two separate entities. Each of us is a whole person, and these two ways of knowing and being known are complementary ways of seeing humans.[166]

If culture is unable to decide, based on factual evidence alone, what is right and wrong or truth and error, it is headed for moral chaos. Newbigin's answer to this dilemma is the revelation of God in Jesus Christ, because "only the living Word of the Creator can bring light out of darkness, order out of chaos."[167]

The Critique of Impersonal Truth

As mentioned earlier, Descartes' attempt at certitude is based on the clarity of mathematics. This faith in mathematics as a way to certain knowledge has the concealed assumption that it is possible to know the truth of things without the dependence on any revelation from the Creator. This is an "astounding assumption," declares Newbigin, but it sets the tone of Western culture for centuries.[168] If there was any assumption of God in the mind of Descartes it was quickly lost by subsequent generations who could see no essential necessity for God based on Descartes' assumptions about the nature of knowing. The modern scientific worldview, insists Newbigin, excludes the possibility that the Creator of the universe has made himself personally known.[169]

As with every other aspect of the Cartesian program of impersonal knowledge, it has led to skepticism about the possibility of knowing truth. "We do not seek to convince one another of the truth of what we believe," observes Newbigin, "because truth is unknowable."[170] If a possibility of divine revelation exists, it would necessarily be, under the overarching assumption of Cartesian methodology, subject to the test of human reason. One of the intellectual assumptions of free Western societies is that everyone has the right to know the truth, and that this truth must come without the interference of dogma or divine intervention:

> Free inquiry, unfettered by any dogma, is seen as the way to establish truth. If there is divine revelation, it must produce its creden-

---

166. Ibid., 39.
167. Newbigin, "Enduring Validity," 52.
168. Newbigin, *A Word*, 159.
169. Newbigin, "Can the West be Converted?" 4.
170. Newbigin, *A Word*, 161–62.

tials before the bar of full inquiry. The human person, apart from divine grace, has the freedom to know and also the right to know the truth.[171]

The use of inductive methods to find truth about the human situation and the meaning of life ends in failure because this method is not able to see the end of human history, which is revealed now in Jesus Christ but will become more explicit at the end of history:

> If . . . "reason" means the use of inductive methods to discover the truth about our situation by observing all the "facts" and drawing conclusions from them, then it is clear that this kind of inductive process is not applicable to the question of the meaning of the human story as a whole, for the reason that the data for the valid induction are not available until cosmic history has reached its end.[172]

The way to knowing the meaning of the human story and the purpose of human history is by faith, and never by indubitable knowledge.[173]

Truth as Personal Truth

Newbigin's argument in support of personal truth is two-fold: one, is that God has revealed himself to humanity, which we must recognize as legitimate truth even though we may not be able to prove it in a laboratory or through logic; second, that knowing truth has a personal aspect, which means that we do not know truth just as neutral 'facts' nor are we confined to just what we can observe in the empirical world.

Newbigin reacts negatively to the Enlightenment belief that knowledge is impersonal and does not involve a commitment on the part of the knower. Newbigin believes, as we have noted before, that such an idea is an illusion.[174] Knowing, including the knowledge of a scientist, comes through personal experience.[175] It is neither absolute nor exhaustive, but it is true knowledge for it is possible to know persons truly. What if, Newbigin asks, the ultimate reality behind what we experience is personal, and what if the best way to know this ultimate reality is not through

---

171. Newbigin, *A Word*, 160.
172. Newbigin, *Gospel in a Pluralist Society*, 91.
173. Ibid., 95.
174. Newbigin, *A Word*, 95.
175. Ibid., 94.

laboratory experiment but is related more to the way we know persons in a personal relationship? Personal knowledge of that reality would be available to us in much the same way that we would know other people.[176] Newbigin explains:

> If ultimate reality is best understood in the analogy of personal being, or, to put it in more familiar terms, if God has created all things and has made all human beings in his image, and has never left himself without a witness in the mind and conscience of any people, then it will follow that data are available from which it is possible to arrive at the hypothesis that God exists.[177]

Newbigin compares the Indian tradition of knowing to the Enlightenment tradition, both of which claim that ultimate reality is impersonal. Newbigin says that there is a fundamental difference between a worldview that sees ultimate reality as personal and one that sees it as impersonal.[178] The question arises as to whether there is a possible universal principle that might adjudicate between these two views. There is none, Newbigin retorts, so the matter must be decided by faith as to which system is truly in contact with reality.[179] For Newbigin, the evidence points to ultimate reality being personal, and that knowing is based on knowing a Person. Since Western culture's bias to confining true knowledge to the purely 'objective' impersonal method of natural science has proven to be unsatisfactory, the biblical way of knowing must be reinstated as the primary way of knowing truth and ultimate reality.[180]

Martin Buber, in his book *I and Thou*[181] drew a distinction between the world of autonomous reason and reason as a "listening and trusting openness." Buber labeled these two kinds of knowing as "I-it" and "I-you." The former is the experience of autonomous reason, where one can look

---

176. Newbigin, *Gospel in a Pluralist Society*, 61.

177. Ibid.

178. The fact that Newbigin spent over three decades in India, working closely with Indian communities and dialoguing with Indian scholars on a regular basis, makes him uniquely qualified to see the issues related to the West slipping into monism and seeing ultimate reality as impersonal.

179. Newbigin, *Proper Confidence*, 13–14.

180. Ibid., 4.

181. Buber (1878–1965) was a Jewish religious philosopher, born in Austria, who developed a philosophy of encounter. See also Friedman, *Encounter on the Narrow Ridge* and Werner Manheim, *Martin Buber*.

at the world (even persons) objectively as 'things.' It is a world where "I am in control," where I decide what questions to ask. In fact, I force the world to answer the questions I ask.[182] The second form of knowing is more open and receptive to the world. Newbigin observes that if one moves from the first (I-it) attitude to the second (I-you), reason has not been abandoned, but there is a distinction in the role of reason. In the former relationship, reason is the servant of the self, which is sovereign; in the latter relationship (I-you), reason is the servant of a trusting openness, and a person is in a mutual relationship with other selves. It is truth, therefore, in the receptive mode.[183] Newbigin also recognizes that the idea of two different ways of knowing can easily lead to a false separation of the idea of knowing into two parts.[184]

Knowing has both objective and subjective aspects. The objective aspect is well understood in a culture where science dominates. The subjective aspect does not mean that knowing is robbed of its objective reference: to know someone is an objective experience with a subjective element.[185] Knowing is subjective, Newbigin writes, when it requires personal commitment and personal responsibility for one's beliefs.[186] Faith, then, is not an act of pure subjectivity because the person is focusing on Someone who is outside the person, an objective reality that in this case is God.

Real knowing, writes Newbigin, is an activity that "involves the whole person in a passionate commitment to make contact with reality."[187] Knowing, then, is not only an epistemological issue: it is also ontological. Ultimate reality, which is the object of our search for truth, has entered history in the person and work of Jesus Christ.[188] "If that is true," Newbigin reasons, "then it must define the nature of our search for truth, including our search for truth in a world of impersonal entities."[189]

---

182. Newbigin, *Gospel in a Pluralist Society*, 60.
183. Ibid.
184. Newbigin, *Proper Confidence*, 60.
185. Newbigin, *A Word*, 83.
186. Newbigin, *Gospel in a Pluralist Society*, 23.
187. Newbigin, *Proper Confidence*, 50.
188. Ibid., 63.
189. Ibid.

Newbigin's Response to Western Culture's Crisis

Biblical Way of Knowing God

Knowledge in the Bible is based on a relationship of trust, a relationship of trust in a personal reality greater than ourselves. Without this kind of trust, knowledge of reality and truth will forever remain hidden from us.[190] Western culture, as has been noted, is based on Enlightenment presuppositions, which insist that freedom is necessary for the attainment of truth. Europe claims to be free, but there is, Newbigin insists, a profound skepticism regarding the possibility of knowing truth. One can conclude that the Enlightenment has not really produced the necessary freedom to discover truth.[191] Jesus reverses the Enlightenment axiom that freedom of inquiry is the only way to truth. Commenting on John 8:31 (where Jesus said that if you continue in his teaching, you will know truth and that truth will make you free), Newbigin concludes that truth is not the fruit of freedom; it is the precondition of it. The hearers of these words, who thought they were free because they saw themselves as the children of God due to their birth and national heritage, were greatly angered because Jesus was telling them that they were, in fact, not free.[192] Newbigin believes that these would bring the same reaction today as it did then:

> Here we have the most radical attack possible on the assumptions of modernity. To state the situation straightforwardly, this attack can hardly fail to rouse the same kind of anger in contemporary society as it did among those who heard those words of Jesus.[193]

The biblical story of Jesus Christ cannot provide the indubitable certainty that was idealized by Descartes.[194] If the biblical story is true, it will rest on the fidelity of God, not on the competence of the human knower. "It will be," writes Newbigin, "a kind of certainty that is inseparable from gratitude and trust."[195]

The idea of certainty has become a problem even for Christians, for it "hopelessly confuses Christians about the certainty of their faith."[196] Christians need to consider whether they are not operating on a false idea

---

190. Newbigin, *Other Side*, 61.
191. Newbigin, *A Word*, 159.
192. Newbigin, *Proper Confidence*, 68.
193. Ibid., 68.
194. Newbigin, *Proper Confidence*, 54.
195. Ibid., 28.
196. Ibid., 44.

of certainty, one created by culture rather than the Bible.[197] One of the ways Christians have tried to develop a system of indubitable truths is to try to summarize and condense Christian truth into propositional statements, seeking to make them timeless and universal by abstracting them from stories. Newbigin sees the value in re-positing 'story' as the primary means by which truth is conveyed.[198] For Christians, of course, the 'story' is the biblical story set within the realm of one that will ultimately come to an end. When it does, what humanity now knows in part will be made clear.[199]

Because Christians do not know the end of the story, at least not experientially, they cannot claim to know with absolute certainty all the dimensions of God's revelation in Jesus Christ. Newbigin paraphrases the Bible by saying that now we know in part, but we will know much more when we see him face to face.[200] In the meantime, we continually seek to comprehend more.[201] Christians, however, do not have to resort to agnosticism, but must articulate their faith with humility:

> To pretend to "possess" the truth in its fullness is arrogance. The claim to have been given a decisive clue for the human search after truth is not arrogant; it is the exercise of our responsibility as part of the human family.[202]

In another passage, Newbigin talks about agnosticism from a different perspective. He says that there is, indeed, a proper place for agnosticism in the Christian life, properly understood. Christians are witnesses to truth but not *possessors* of all truth. In a sense, Christians are like all other seekers after truth who are "learners to the end of their days," since they have been placed on a path leading toward truth. The apophatic tradition in theology has always believed that no human image or concept has ever been able to grasp the full reality of God, so Christians can, at best, know God truly but not fully.[203] It would seem that even knowing God truly would give a Christian the certainty of hope and faith, a certainty that God will bring this age to consummation and will prevail.

197. Newbigin, *Proper Confidence*, 44.
198. Newbigin is clearly influenced by the thought of Hans Frei at this point.
199. Newbigin, *Gospel in a Pluralist Society*, 12–13.
200. 1 Cor 13:12.
201. Newbigin, "Religious Pluralism," 52.
202. Ibid., 54.
203. Newbigin, *Gospel in a Pluralist Society*, 12.

Newbigin's Response to Western Culture's Crisis

There is a longing in the human heart, Newbigin believes, for complete mutual understanding. The model for true mutuality is the Trinity, because in the Trinity there is complete reciprocity. This is, Newbigin says, a model for human relationships and for knowing other persons. This kind of knowledge, knowing through reciprocity, is fundamental to the biblical concept of knowing.[204]

The Role of Faith and Belief in Knowing

"All understanding of reality involves a venture of faith," writes Newbigin, in the spirit of Augustine's *credo ut intelligam*.[205] The acquisition of knowledge is begun by "openness to a reality greater than ourselves,"[206] and faith is not a substitute or alternative to knowledge, but is the starting point and pathway to knowledge.[207] "One cannot learn anything," Newbigin asserts, "except by believing something."[208]

Newbigin utilizes science as a case in point. Scientists, as noted before, base their work on certain assumptions they take by faith because they cannot be proven.[209] These commitments may seem self-evident but they are, in fact, ultimately unprovable: "Scientists themselves know that science rests on faith—commitments that cannot be demonstrated, on the faith that the universe is both rational and contingent."[210] Newbigin cites Michael Polanyi's work as an "attempt to demonstrate that knowledge of reality rests upon faith-commitments."[211] Newbigin is significantly dependent upon Polanyi in his discussion of science. Polanyi primarily attacks the notion prevalent in science of "objective truth," that truth is arrived at without any subjective or personal elements and is neutral fact. Polanyi's argument is that in spite of what science may claim "personal commitment in faith and personal judgment about evidence are required at every

---

204. Newbigin, *Foolishness*, 89. Newbigin does not mention his source at this point. The idea is, as he says, most clearly expressed in the prayer of Jesus recorded in John 17:23.

205. Newbigin, *Truth and Authority*, 3–4.

206. Ibid., 4.

207. Ibid., 3; *A Word*, 103; "Certain Faith," 340.

208. Newbigin, "Certain Faith," 340.

209. Newbigin, *A Word*, 103.

210. Newbigin, *A Word*, 71.

211. Newbigin, *Other Side*, 23.

stage."[212] Newbigin reiterates Polanyi's fundamental claim: "All knowing is a personal commitment."[213]

Scientists not only trust certain assumptions that form and shape their work, they also trust in the tradition of science. This becomes the foundation upon which they stand, as well as the grid through which they perceive and analyze the world. Tradition guides the progress of science, even when that scientist may be attempting to prove something that is a radical departure from that tradition.[214]

Even with tradition to monitor and to guide the scientist, there is still an element of risk. Personal knowledge, as Polanyi has argued, is impossible without risk, because it begins with an act of trust and trust is something that can be betrayed. For a scientist whose discoveries suggest a theory quite different from the traditional view, it requires a fundamental decision in which there must be the risk of everything to put one's faith in a new possibility.[215]

While this trust may be risky, it is not irrational. When, as a young person, Newbigin read *The Will to Believe* by William James, he realized that belief is not irrational.[216] Newbigin is not advocating an irrational belief where the intellect is rejected, but insists that knowledge requires both faith and an element of risk because, in spite of the view that factual truth is essentially neutral, all knowledge is personal. This personal knowledge includes knowledge stored as facts in an electronic computer and knowledge shared in a living community.[217] So, a person makes a commitment to what appears to be the best representation of reality.

Doubt and Certainty

Newbigin concedes that doubt is, in a certain sense, necessary for proper critical thinking, but its role is secondary and derivative. Doubt assumes a certain set of presumptions, and these assumptions are believed to be true even though they may not be capable of proof. This is the basis of Newbigin's statement that "rational doubt depends on faith," but "rational

212. Newbigin, *Truth to Tell*, 32.
213. Ibid., 33.
214. Newbigin, *Proper Confidence*, 40–41.
215. Ibid., 14.
216. Newbigin, *Unfinished*, 6.
217. Newbigin, *Honest Religion*, 87.

faith does not depend on doubt."[218] Rational faith, however, requires some risk. In a similar way to the role risk plays as a part of the process of paradigm change in science, it can be said to be a factor in one's belief in God. Knowledge is never complete, Newbigin explains, because of the transcendence, mystery, and fullness of God, so one's knowledge of God is essentially based on risky faith.[219] There is no possibility of absolute certainty in human knowing, and final certainty, remarks Newbigin, will come on the Day of Judgment![220]

Nevertheless, there can be, according to Newbigin, a reasonable amount of certainty in life, but it is not based on indubitable knowledge. It is, in fact, based on faith. "Faith," Newbigin asserts, "is the only certainty because faith involves personal commitment."[221] So the Christian can proceed with confidence, but a confidence different from that defined by the Enlightenment:

> The confidence proper to a Christian is not the confidence of one who claims possession of demonstrable and indubitable knowledge. It is the confidence of one who has heard and answered the call that comes from the God through whom and for whom all things were made.[222]

Newbigin says "the Christian faith is not a matter of logically demonstrable certainties," but is putting one's trust in a faithful God.[223]

The only way that a Christian can affirm the objectivity of the Christian truth claim, Newbigin writes, is by committing oneself to live and act in accordance with this claim.[224] Such a commitment focuses the attention on the ultimate authority for all truth claims, not on logically demonstrable truth by reference to something more ultimate than God.[225] For humanity, caught in the grip of history that is moving toward

---

218. Newbigin, *Proper Confidence*, 25.
219. Newbigin, *Honest Religion*, 94.
220. Newbigin, *Truth and Authority*, 54.
221. Newbigin, *Proper Confidence*, 105.
222. Ibid.
223. Newbigin, *Proper Confidence*, 98.
224. Ibid., 75.
225. Newbigin, *A Word*, 79.

consummation in God, the justification for the faith of the Christian will occur at the end of history.[226]

In all of this, it becomes apparent that knowledge, since it is connected to God, revelation, and faith is really a gift of grace.[227] Real understanding of truth and reality is not found by trying to find certitude apart from grace.[228] The search for knowledge without the grace of God, Newbigin affirms, is doomed.[229] Faith, as the ability to recognize and receive God's gift of revelation, is not a human achievement but comes as a gift of grace.[230]

Not only is faith a gift of God's grace but so is freedom, something that Enlightenment thinkers hold dear. To Enlightenment thinkers, freedom is a natural endowment of every being. Newbigin, however, asserts that freedom comes by the acknowledgement of the truth, "something given in the sheer grace to be received by faith."[231] "The gospel," he says, "is not a matter of indubitable certainties; it is the offer of grace that can only be accepted by faith, where heart and intellect are joined."[232]

Speaking from within the Reformed tradition, Newbigin says that Calvinism has been affected by the idea of absolute certainty. In Calvinism, the desire for an absolute truth took the form of belief in God who elects and regenerates persons by the secret working of the Holy Spirit. This belief, Newbigin observes, moves Christ's work in history from the "determinative centre," which Newbigin believes is an error on the part of Calvinism.[233] Newbigin explains his view:

> If instead of taking as the starting point of our thought the fact of Christ, we take the undoubted truth that God can choose and regenerate by the secret working of the His Spirit whomsoever He will, it will inevitably follow that the actual work of Christ in history will come to take a place other than the determinative centre.[234]

---

226. Newbigin, *Gospel in a Pluralist Society*, 74.
227. The source of this idea is Augustine. See Newbigin, *Open Secret*, 29.
228. Newbigin, *Truth to Tell*, 36–37.
229. Newbigin, *Truth and Authority*, 15.
230. Ibid., 14.
231. Newbigin, *Truth to Tell*, 61.
232. Newbigin, *Proper Confidence*, 100.
233. Newbigin, *The Household*, 102.
234. Ibid.

Newbigin's Response to Western Culture's Crisis

Knowing God and Truth

It is not possible to have a clear and substantive grasp of reality, Newbigin insists, without knowing the nature and purpose of God, which is being realized in the whole history of the cosmos.[235] In one sense, God has given us ultimate revelation and truth in his Son, a qualitative revelation that cannot be surpassed. In another sense, God's activity continues to work within history to bring about his ultimate purposes. Consequently, the Christian community claims that Jesus Christ is absolute truth (seen in the light of the relative truths of human cultures), not in the spirit of dominance or imperial power but as one without power, manifested in weakness and suffering. The church does not claim to 'possess' absolute truth, but is able to point persons to the One for whom they are searching.[236] To point to Jesus Christ as the source and ground for truth would mean that Western culture must accept a new starting point, as well as seeing Christ as the definitive basis for knowing and understanding God and reality.[237]

It is not just a matter of truth: it is a matter of meaning and purpose for life. People cannot live without meaning in their lives, and the only place where one can find ultimate meaning is in Jesus Christ. Newbigin expounds on this idea:

> . . . there is no other place in human history where the ultimate issues of man's existence—his interior personal life and his public political and social life—are finally exposed and settled, except in the living and dying and rising again of Jesus Christ.[238]

Ultimate meaning implies ultimate reality and ultimate reality, as Newbigin has asserted, is a personal, triune God, to whom the only appropriate response would be personal faith or commitment.[239]

Newbigin affirms the validity of theological inquiry in the quest for knowing truth but does not deny the validity of what he calls "the lower levels of explanation," by which he means the natural and human sciences. Theological inquiry is an "essential part in the whole enterprise of human

---

235. Newbigin, *A Word*, 59.
236. Newbigin, *Gospel in a Pluralist Society*, 163.
237. Newbigin is influenced here by Charles Cochrane and his Divine Principle. See Cochrane, *Christianity and Classical Culture*, 367.
238. Newbigin, *A Word*, 38.
239. Ibid., 95.

knowing,"[240] because, unlike science, it is able to discern and affirm purpose and meaning in life and the universe.[241] It is on the theological level that "we can seek for the purpose for which they exist."[242]

CONCLUSION

Newbigin's answer to Western culture's critical need is a radical conversion, which means a new rationality for a culture that has lost its understanding of truth. Newbigin sees Western culture's belief in the parameters set by science to determine facts and truth as being too narrow and falling far short of a correct view of reality. The new rationality he calls for will resolve, he believes, the dualism that plagues Western culture and will provide the culture with truth that truly connects with reality.

The question arises as to how Newbigin envisions Western culture becoming convinced of the truth of the gospel story. Newbigin believes the agent of that change is the church.

---

240. Newbigin, *Proper Confidence*, 59.

241. Ibid., 61–62.

242. Ibid., 61. Purpose does not 'necessarily' follow the category of the personal, but Newbigin would say that only persons create things for a purpose.

7

Living in Truth and Reality

The Church in Mission to Western Culture

Throughout the previous chapters, there have been numerous references to the church, usually in connection to some task or action that Newbigin believes the church must perform to confront Western culture. While the emphasis thus far has been on the substance of Newbigin's theology in the face of the challenge of the Enlightenment ideology, it would be incorrect to conclude that what Newbigin envisions is somehow confined to mere words, as important as words are. His theology includes, in fact *culminates in*, his vision for a community of faith that would live out its faith in contemporary Western culture.

While he refutes the *ideology* of pluralism, he recognizes the *fact* of plurality, and sees it as an opportunity for the church to reassert itself into the public arena alongside other communities. Newbigin believes that the church has the right to be heard alongside others who may be advocating their belief systems. It would be for the hearers to determine which belief system truly puts them in contact with reality. Newbigin is confident that the Holy Spirit works in the lives of persons who hear the gospel, not only persuading the heart, but also helping the mind comprehend the superior rationality of the biblical worldview.

In no way, Newbigin insists, is this to be taken as a return to Christendom.[1] The resurrection of Christendom presupposes the idea of coercion, especially on those who would not accept the new starting point, and there is no hint of the idea of coercion in any of Newbigin's writings. His method of converting culture is based on witness, which would be

---

1. For a discussion of his view of Christendom see Newbigin, *Other Side*, 32ff.

persuasive only because God is acting in the hearts of the hearers. It has nothing to do with the alignment of political power with the church.

In Craig Van Gelder's five-point summary of Newbigin's theology of mission, the fifth point refers to the mission of the church:

> The church is the hermeneutic of the gospel. It is the reality of God's people living in faithful love and obedience to God that becomes the compelling evidence to a postmodern world that this God is, in fact, the living and true God. In this sense, salvation, although it may be accepted individually, must be understood in social and corporate terms. God is at work in the world in and through a community that is sign, foretaste, and instrument.[2]

The last point is where Newbigin's theology of mission moves from being merely a theological alternative to culture's ideology to the embodiment of this theology of mission in the community of faith.

A DIDACTIC AND HERMENEUTICAL COMMUNITY

As we have just noted, Newbigin's theology of mission to the Western world is to be lived out in the community of faith. This is the constructive aspect of his theology of mission, and all his theological convictions converge at this point. His thinking comes full circle because it revolves around his dynamic understanding of revelation. Newbigin's ecclesiology incorporates his understanding of revelation. Revelation is still 'alive' today in the community of faith that indwells the story of the Living Christ. This community of faith is the living evidence of the existence and purpose of God in this world. Importantly, it also functions as a location for a rational tradition that articulates and supports the faith epistemologically, and desires to replace Western culture's fiduciary framework with a wider rationality that encompasses all of reality.

Newbigin's ecclesiology developed early in his ministry, and was quite evident when he gave the Kerr Lectures in Trinity College, Glasgow in November 1952. The book that came out of these lectures was *The Household of God*. The church (and Newbigin means every congregation of the church as well as the whole church) is the first-fruit, sign, and instrument of God's new creation. It is the congregation of the faithful, the body of Christ, and the community of the Holy Spirit. Newbigin's doctrine of the church was born out of his attempt to think systematically about

---

2. Van Gelder, "Postmodernism and Evangelicals," 501–2.

his experience of the participating in the life and ministry of the newly-formed Church of South India. The last two chapters of the book point to what would eventuate as substantial themes in his post-retirement years. In these chapters he discusses the church from an eschatological and missionary perspective, "the perspective of the end of the world and the ends of the earth."[3]

At the writing of his work *Trinitarian Faith and Today's Mission* (1964), Newbigin felt the stress should be on what God is doing in the life of mankind as a whole, which paralleled much of the thought in ecclesiastical circles at the time. Knowing what God is doing allows Christians to communicate in a way that is relevant.[4] God is at work in the lives, thoughts, and (even) prayers of persons *outside* the church as well as inside it. Since it is the same God working in both places, Christians can learn as well as teach. Specifically, Christians must learn what God is actually doing in the world[5] and must hear the voice of the Good Shepherd wherever he speaks in the world.[6] This thought is explicitly stated by Newbigin as follows:

> The inexhaustible power of the prophetic spirit in the tradition of biblical faith was derived from a tremendous affirmation—namely the affirmation of the reality and power and holiness of God who is other than, greater than, and more enduring than any human institution or achievement.[7]

Newbigin draws the conclusion that the church is not the exclusive possessor of salvation, nor is it something *owned* by the church.[8] This does not mean, however, that the church is not important nor has an important role to play in the world.

The emphasis in the middle of the twentieth century in the International Missionary Council was on what God was doing outside the institutional church. They believed this idea could best be served by restating theology of mission in terms of *Trinitarian* theology, which began in earnest after the World Council of Churches meeting in Amsterdam in

---

3. Newbigin, *The Household*, 9.
4. Newbigin, *Trinitarian Faith*, 28.
5. See Newbigin, *Open Secret*, 175.
6. Ibid., 183. This is a paraphrase of a statement that Newbigin attributed to Karl Barth, although he does not use quotation marks nor does he cite the exact source.
7. Newbigin, *Honest Religion*, 38.
8. Newbigin, *Open Secret*, 180.

1948. The fruit of this labor came out at Willingen (1952), and was subsequently radicalized by students at the Strasbourg (1960) meeting of the World Student Christian Federation, where mission was recast in secular terms, not in terms of the mission of the church. Newbigin strongly reacted against this radicalization.[9]

While it would seem necessary to recognize and affirm the concrete reality of the church as a part of human history (and Newbigin does this), it is necessary also to recognize the *hiddenness* of the kingdom of God. There seems to be a contradiction in the New Testament between statements that the kingdom is present while it is also seen as coming in the future. It is not, Newbigin says, the difference between the incomplete and the complete, but is the difference between the hidden and the manifest.[10] The kingdom remains hidden so that it remains possible for the nations to be converted. If the glory of God's kingdom were unveiled with all its terrible majesty, it would leave no further room for the free acceptance of salvation by faith. It is necessary for the glory to be veiled so that persons can respond to the lowliness of the incarnation with repentance and faith.[11]

The idea of the kingdom of God as hidden leads to the thought that, while there is a visible church made up of people who have been called by God into fellowship with His Son, there is some validity to the idea of the invisible church. What is invisible about the church is the work of the Holy Spirit in the hearts of people, hidden from view and somewhat behind the scenes.[12] However, notes Newbigin, the kingdom is *explicit* in Jesus Christ. In the Gospels, the kingdom is present in the man Jesus, and comes near so that it confronts people with its reality. God desires that people radically turn around and recognize the truth of the kingdom.[13] Christ's ministry was a public ministry, Newbigin observes, so the kingdom of God confronts culture in the public square. Newbigin calls for the church to reclaim the public sector for the gospel by escaping its rather long domestication in culture. By reclaiming the public sector, Newbigin does not mean a return to what he calls the 'Constantinian Trap,'[14] a res-

---

9. For a conservative evangelical view of these events, see Glasser and McGavran, *Contemporary Theologies of Mission*, 82–99.
10. Newbigin, *Gospel in a Pluralist Society*, 105.
11. Ibid., 108.
12. Newbigin, *The Household*, 29.
13. Newbigin, *Gospel in a Pluralist Society*, 133.
14. He does not explain the meaning of this phrase, but it would appear that he sees

toration of the church to a position of secular and political power. What is required is that the church return to the biblical vision of the last things that should govern the church's obedience in the public realm.[15] In a more recent publication, Newbigin articulates what this vision is about. The New Testament envisions a goal, he explains, toward which the church must progress. With eager expectation on almost every page, the Bible points to a vision of the city of God where all evil is excluded and where all nations will bring their treasures. Such a vision of a reality that will come is a strong motivation for the church.[16] This is what the church is to explicitly share in public witness.

In the *The Good Shepherd* (1977), Newbigin writes that the church is where believers have real fellowship with God through Jesus Christ, but this is only a foretaste of a greater and fuller reality that God intends for his people and for his church.[17] He sees the role of every congregation of the church as a people separated out for service to God much in the same way the Old Testament describes the role of ancient Israel. The congregation is to be a humble servant of Jesus Christ, not for its own benefit but for the sake of its neighbors. It is to be a witness to Jesus and to his kingdom, pointing past itself to the One for whom it was created, articulating to the neighbors all about this Jesus whom they serve. In the same way that Christ came as the great High Priest for all humanity, so the congregation of believers are to fulfill and carryout his priesthood on behalf of its neighbors. The priesthood has a two-fold responsibility: it has the responsibility of representing God before persons who do not know Him and it has the glorious task of offering up to God worship, prayer, and obedience for all humanity that is due to God.[18]

The Problem of the Church

What troubles Newbigin is that the church is so much a part of culture that it seems indistinguishable from it. Instead of adopting Western culture's

---

any attempt by Christians to try to restore Christendom, would be a serious mistake. Forsaking the public domain is also, in his view, a serious mistake. The church should not control the public domain, but it should have a voice in it.

15. Newbigin, *Other Side*, 36.
16. Newbigin, *Gospel in a Pluralist Society*, 110.
17. Newbigin, *Good Shepherd*, 87.
18. Ibid., 89. While this material was published in 1977, after Newbigin came back to Britain for retirement, it was prepared and used as Bible studies in India in the late 1960s.

worldview and plausibility structure, the church must begin to distinguish itself from the trappings of culture, because it is difficult for it to challenge culture's presuppositions if it sees no need for such a challenge.[19]

As we have noted, Newbigin's holistic view of reality includes the natural and supernatural, seeing both realms as real and not radically disconnected. The downside of the secularization process in Western culture has been the narrow confinement of reality to nature without reference to the supernatural realm.[20] Further, humanity, in the spirit of secularism, demands autonomy from God, which, causing culture to lose its reference for truth, has led it into a devastating agnostic pluralism. In a tone more representative of a prophet than a scholar, Newbigin cuts through the superficial to come to the heart of the problem: "A society in which any kind of nonsense is acceptable is not a free society. An agnostic pluralism has no defense against nonsense."[21]

Consequently, the church has been tempted to withdraw into the private realm and avoid confrontation:

> We have been tempted either to withdraw into an intellectual ghetto, seeking to preserve a kind of piety in church and home but leaving the public world . . . to be governed by another ideology. Or we have been tempted to regard the "modern scientific worldview" as though it were simply a transcript of reality which we must . . . accept as true. We then try to adjust our Christian beliefs to the requirements of "modern thought" and to find room for ideas . . . suggested to us by the Christian tradition—but always with the framework of the "modern scientific world-view."[22]

Newbigin believes the church should be authentically Christian, which in itself would be a challenge to the cultural worldview. "The Church should by this time have learned," observes Newbigin, "that it is normal for it to work 'against the stream.'"[23] This leads Newbigin to ask a very penetrating and perceptive question:

> From whence comes the voice that can challenge this culture on its own terms, a voice that speaks its own language and yet

---

19. Newbigin, *Truth to Tell*, 65.
20. Newbigin, *Honest Religion*, 33–34.
21. Newbigin, *Truth to Tell*, 60.
22. Newbigin, *Other Side*, 32.
23. Newbigin, *Trinitarian Faith*, 27.

confronts it with the authentic figure of the crucified and living Christ so that it is stopped in its tracks and turned back from the way of death? . . . From whence can the voice, not of doom but of deliverance, be spoken so that the modern Western world can hear it as the voice of the Savior and Lord?[24]

Newbigin sees the remonstration against the categories of culture as an exceedingly challenging frontier that the church must engage.[25] Newbigin, however, asks a perceptive question: "How can the European Churches, whose life and thought is shaped so completely by this post-Enlightenment culture, become bearers of a mission to that culture?"[26] Speaking specifically to North America, Newbigin says that 'main-line' churches have a mission before them of incomparable challenge and complexity, yet they cannot respond because they are so entwined in Enlightenment thinking. "It is now typical to find in the old 'main-line' churches an acute embarrassment about missions . . . partly a fundamental loss of nerve which manifests itself in all aspects of 'Western' culture outside of its science and technology."[27]

Newbigin's concern is for the church as a corporate body to become a prophetic voice in culture. "What I am pleading for," Newbigin writes, "is a genuinely missionary encounter with post-Enlightenment culture."[28] This missionary approach would recognize that Christian dogma has a fiduciary framework that is much different and, at certain points, incompatible with modern Western culture.[29] A genuine missionary encounter would take Western culture seriously, but not take it as the final truth by which the Bible would be evaluated. It would, rather, require that the modern world would be evaluated its assumptions according to the Bible. "This is, I believe," confesses Newbigin, "our present task."[30]

Christians in the West face the temptation of trying to live in two separate, distinct worlds, the world of faith and the secular world. This separation of life into two realms is generally assumed by Western culture and it becomes an acute problem when each 'world' demands things

24. Newbigin, *Foolishness*, 10.
25. Newbigin, *A Word*, 67.
26. Ibid., 69.
27. Newbigin, "A Missionary's Dream," 5.
28. Newbigin, *Other Side*, 31.
29. Ibid., 32.
30. Ibid., 47. See Wainwright, *Theological Life*, 260.

that are contradictory. It is apparent that some Christians resolve this by living by the ethic of the context they are in at the given moment, often without realizing that these ethical demands are contradictory to their faith.[31] Because there are two worlds in which Westerners must live, Western culture teaches two languages, one of culture and one of God, but, as Newbigin insists

> There are not two worlds, one sacred and the other secular. There are differing ways of understanding the one world and a choice has to be made about which is the right way, the way that corresponds to reality, to the reality beyond all the show which the ruler of this world can put on.[32]

If a Christian accepts the Lordship of Christ, then God's sovereignty cannot be confined to the private sector of life, while acknowledging a different sovereignty for the public side of life. Christ, Newbigin exhorts, is Lord of all of life.[33] This is not just a *religious* statement, but a statement of *fact*, but one that cannot be proven by the dictates of scientific method. It is, however, a statement in favor of a unified view of the cosmos and reality. "You cannot divide the natural world into two parts, one open to divine influence and the other not."[34]

Newbigin observes that during the two centuries that gave rise to Enlightenment culture, the primary concern of the church was to adjust the Christian message to fit the new framework of thought. Hundreds of volumes were written to demonstrate the 'reasonableness' of Christianity, which meant, to Newbigin, a certain compatibility with the Enlightenment framework of thought.[35] One of the most explicit examples of this methodology is seen in theology, which, Newbigin says, separated theology into two categories. On the academic level, there is a distinction made between 'confessional theology' and 'scientific theology,' where scientific theology represents a kind of study where one approaches the subject with a totally open mind to whatever truth may emerge. The truth is, Newbigin asserts, that both confessional and scientific theology presuppose what every ra-

---

31. Newbigin, *A Word*, 96.
32. Newbigin, *Truth to Tell*, 49.
33. Newbigin, *Gospel in a Pluralist Society*, 220.
34. Ibid., 93.
35. Newbigin, "Episcopacy and Evangelism," 336.

Living in Truth and Reality

tional inquiry presumes, "a long tradition of thought and practice that determines which beliefs are plausible and which are not."[36]

Those who defended the faith in the eighteenth century, observes Newbigin, overly-accommodated themselves to the assumptions of culture with little thought given to challenging those assumptions.[37] The mistake these Christian thinkers made was that they sought to defend a "system of timeless metaphysical truths" about God, nature, and man, but these truths cannot be discovered by reflection upon innate human ideas or the direct observation of nature, as one would do in science. The truth sought for is found in the narratives of the Bible, stories of the interaction of God and people.[38]

Even in the Fundamentalist/Liberal debates of the early twentieth century both theological positions actually accepted Western cultural precepts regarding truth, but utilized them in different ways. Liberal theology embraced the scientific method with its presuppositions, while Fundamentalism, usually thought of as anti-cultural, incorporated Cartesian thinking into its criteria for discerning truth.[39] Newbigin writes:

> ... the attempt of a certain kind of Christian to claim for the gospel the kind of indubitable certainty which was Descartes' claim must be seen as mistaken. It is a surrender to a false rationalism. We must walk by faith, not by sight.[40]

The modern compromise is realized in the objective/subjective dichotomy of Western culture, which takes two forms. On the one side, there are those who affirm the Christian faith as a series of objectively true propositions drawn from an infallible Scripture, and are, therefore, recognizable upon investigation. They become the standard for and the parameters of truth. On the other side, there are those who see the essence

---

36. Newbigin, *Proper Confidence*, 46.
37. Newbigin, *Gospel in a Pluralist Society*, 3.
38. Ibid., 12–13.
39. Newbigin sees in the Fundamentalist's desire to posit an infallible Bible that would allow for indubitable certainty as being grounded in Cartesian thinking. See also chapter 5, "Beyond Modern Liberalism and Fundamentalism," in *Anglo-America Postmodernity*, 87–112, where Nancey Murphy sees Liberalism and Fundamentalism sharing the same cultural assumptions.
40. Newbigin, "Certain Faith," 347. Also see Newbigin, *Other Side*, 47, for the Fundamentalist view of Scripture, which Newbigin says is also a product of Western culture.

of Christianity as an inward experience that is personal to each believer, so the doctrines that are formulated and developed through the process of church history are really only symbolic representatives of this personal inward experience.[41]

Newbigin recognizes that there are conservative Christians who do have a balanced view of objectivity and subjectivity of the faith. Newbigin says that

> ... it is obvious ... when conservative Christians insist that their faith refers to objective realities, they are (rightly) seeking to deny the opinion that these Christian beliefs are simply expressions of subjective feelings or experience and to affirm that they make contact with a reality beyond the self. But it is also clear that it is futile to deny the subjective elements in the Christian confession.[42]

Syncretism or Contextualization

The church, Newbigin observes, has been domesticated in Western culture, an example of a syncretism that reflects the inappropriate combination of contradictory ideas into one system.[43] Newbigin came to this realization while visiting the Ramakrishna mission in India. He saw a picture of Jesus that represented him as just one figure in the endless cycle of *karma* and *samsara*, the wheel of being in which humanity allegedly is caught. He comments:

> It was only slowly, through many experiences, that I began to see that something of this domestication had taken place in my own Christianity, that I too had been more ready to seek a "reasonable Christianity," a Christianity that could be defended on the terms of my whole intellectual formation as a twentieth-century Englishman, rather than something which places my whole intellectual formation under a new and critical light. I, too, had been guilty of domesticating the gospel.[44]

The church has experienced a peaceful coexistence with Western culture because it has accepted the culture's view of reality, thus rendering it un-

---

41. Newbigin, *Gospel in a Pluralist Society*, 24, and *Truth to Tell*, 42.
42. Newbigin, *Proper Confidence*, 43.
43. Newbigin, *A Word*, 130, 139, 152, 164.
44. Newbigin, *Gospel in a Pluralist Society*, 3.

Living in Truth and Reality

able to challenge radically that vision of reality held dear by culture.[45] It is difficult for the church to face modernity because culture has made such inroads into the life and thinking of the church.[46] Newbigin is making a generalization that cannot be verified in a detailed study of Western theology. There are some who do not share Western culture's worldview but who also value a reasonable explanation of the gospel as one avenue of witness.

The motive to engage culture and to speak to it in a meaningful way is what contemporary missiologists call *contextualization*.[47] The problem, as Newbigin observes, is the age-old question of how far the church should go to accommodate culture. There are those who advocate that the best approach to culture must be *from within the culture* where 'gospel issues' arise.[48] Newbigin questions whether the program of contextualization actually solves the problem because it requires at least a provisional acceptance of the thought-world of the culture. There is no logical way to argue from the context to the gospel.[49] Newbigin's view of contextualization begins with the realization of the need to be sensitive to the needs of people and to understand their situation, but none of these or even an analysis of the cultural situation based on a principle other than Scripture should become the starting point for mission. The starting point for mission is God's revelation of himself, to which Scripture is a powerful witness.[50] Mission begins by paying close attention to what God has done in the story of Israel and especially in the story of Jesus Christ. When we are indwelling that story, we can, Newbigin argues, attend to the needs of the people in a way that Jesus attended to them. The real needs of people, whatever the culture, "can only be satisfied by everything that comes out of the mouth of God (Matt 4:4)."[51]

True contextualization, for Newbigin, only happens when the gospel is made primary, for it has the power to penetrate every culture and to speak

---

45. Newbigin, *A Word*, 173, and *Other Side*, 22–23.
46. Newbigin, "A Missionary's Dream," 7.
47. Contextualization was defined earlier as the attempt to communicate truth to a particular culture in a manner that would allow the hearers to understand the truth as the communicator intended it to be understood.
48. Newbigin, "Context and Conversion," 301.
49. Ibid., 302.
50. Newbigin, *Gospel in a Pluralist Society*, 153–54.
51. Ibid., 151.

from within each culture the 'no' and 'yes' of judgment and grace.[52] True contextualization only happens when there is a community that is faithful to the gospel, and also truly identified with the people in a manner that is costly as modeled in the ministry of Jesus. It is when these pre-conditions are met that the Holy Spirit is free to do his own surprising work.[53]

The assumption of culture is that the culture itself possesses the standard by which to evaluate the gospel story, as if it were or had an absolute standard that stands in a superior position to the gospel story. Newbigin sees this as an unfortunate accommodation of the church to the dictates of culture:

> It is an illusion to suppose that we can find something more absolute than what God has done in Jesus Christ. It is an illusion to suppose that we can find something larger, greater, more inclusive than Jesus Christ.[54]

Western Christendom's inappropriate accommodation to culture has led to its decline because it has aligned itself with a culture that dissolves "the most enduring of religious beliefs including the beliefs of Christians."[55] Those religious bodies that have accommodated as much as possible to the rationalism of the Enlightenment are in decline, while those that have a strong emphasis on the supernatural aspect of religion, Newbigin notes, flourish.[56]

The theology of the Reformation took Western culture for granted and therefore did not see the Western culture as a missionary situation. The theology of the Reformers reflects this, and their theological doctrines are defined in relation to other churches rather than over against the pagan world. "It is not necessary," remarks Newbigin, "to point out how profoundly this affects the structure of their thinking."[57]

Eventually this accommodation by the church became unacceptable to certain forces within Western culture, and these forces launched "a full scale attack upon the whole ethical tradition of Western Europe," seek-

---

52. Newbigin, *Gospel in a Pluralist Society*, 152.
53. Ibid., 154.
54. Newbigin, "Enduring Validity," 53.
55. Newbigin, "Can the West be Converted?" 2.
56. Newbigin, *Gospel in a Pluralist Society*, 213.
57. Newbigin, *The Household*, 11.

Living in Truth and Reality

ing to replace it with something totally different.[58] Newbigin interprets culture's turn upon the church as evidence of a pruning that is promised to the church so that it may bear more fruit (John 15:1ff.). For decades in the future, the church in Europe, unlike the churches in other parts of the world, may continue to be a small and shrinking minority because God is pruning it.[59]

The acceptance of Western cultural assumptions negatively influences the witness of the church, which has been dampened, Newbigin thinks, by the cultural attitude that sharing one's faith is an act of arrogance.[60] No one person or religion can know absolute or ultimate truth, culture says, so to assert that one knows it essentially makes the claims of other religions and philosophies relative.[61] Further, those who see unity as the paramount need of our day (in the face of the possibility of nuclear war, the global ecological crisis, and the need for the world to draw together for economic and cultural reasons) view the claim of the knowledge of truth in Christ as a threat to world peace and unity. This view, Newbigin believes, is widely held and is considered to be culturally orthodox and any violation of it would be culturally censored.[62]

This concern seems to be limited to religion, Newbigin observes, because Westerners seem eager to witness to the world about science without embarrassment. He writes:

> There is an absurd irony in the fact that we are busy exporting our scientific culture to every corner of the world without any compunction about arrogance, but we think that humility requires us to refrain from offering to the rest of the world the vision of its true goal, which is given in the gospel of Jesus Christ.[63]

Newbigin sees the Western church's embarrassment about mission as stemming not from an excess of humility but an expression of the relativism that dominates Western culture.[64] With the collapse of confidence in the great project called the Enlightenment, it seems inevitable that the

---

58. Newbigin, *The Household*, 12.
59. Newbigin, *Gospel in a Pluralist Society*, 244.
60. Newbigin, *A Word*, 122–23.
61. Newbigin, *Gospel in a Pluralist Society*, 9–10.
62. Ibid., 155–56.
63. Newbigin, "Enduring Validity," 52.
64. Newbigin, *A Word*, 129.

church, so connected to Western culture, would experience a similar collapse of confidence in the church's mission to the world.[65]

Another concern for Newbigin is the distinction make between personal righteousness and justice. He believes the church must also challenge the artificial separation of these two important aspects of Christian experience and witness. In Western culture, and even in the church, there is generally a focus on personal righteous *or* on social justice, but they are seldom integrated. Such a dichotomy, Newbigin reminds the church, is unbiblical and unnatural.[66]

While Newbigin sees the church as over-accommodating itself to Western culture, he nevertheless realizes that the church has outlasted civilizations, civilizations that have tried to extinguish the church. He reminds those who seek to dismiss the church as irrelevant and relegate it to the fringes of culture that "the Church is an anvil that has worn out many hammers."[67]

A Visible Community

Newbigin writes that Christ did not leave behind a body of teachings in a book like the *Quran* nor a program or an ideal; he left behind a community.[68] It is in this community that God's desire for unity among the peoples of the world is realized. Jesus said that by being lifted up on a cross he would draw all people to himself. The cross is where sin that divides humanity is dealt with and put away. So, the community of believers should reflect the unity that comes about as a result of sin being dealt with.[69] The whole thrust of biblical history, according to Newbigin, is the story of the calling of God's own people to be a visible community that functions as His royal priesthood on earth, bearing his light to the nations.[70] Newbigin believes that a visible fellowship is at the center of God's plan of salvation in Christ.[71] God's purpose is fulfilled in a visible community made up of

---

65. Newbigin, *Proper Confidence*, 33.
66. Newbigin, *Foolishness*, 132.
67. Newbigin, *Truth to Tell*, 67.
68. Newbigin, *The Light*, 228–29.
69. Newbigin, "Enduring Validity," 52.
70. Newbigin, *The Household*, 27.
71. Newbigin, *The Finality*, 97.

Living in Truth and Reality

those whom he has chosen,[72] and where persons become related to God by being related to God's people.[73] A part of a person's calling to salvation is the joining of God's visible congregation on earth, a visible community, a congregation of God constructed by the Holy Spirit.[74]

Conversion and Community

It is in the life of the new community created by God, and the story they indwell, that the saving power of the gospel is known, and it is in such a community that will be where the miracle of conversion takes place.[75] This inward work of the Holy Spirit the people of God have experienced continues today. The community is a reconciled fellowship of persons who have experienced a restored relationship with God and with each other.[76] The gospel that is embodied in this community is a gospel of reconciliation, both corporate and cosmic, and is the foretaste of the restored harmony that the gospel promises. Newbigin believes a new convert must become a part of the community of faith because it is this community that will nurture the convert in the faith narratives that will alter the convert's world view.[77] Newbigin, therefore, ardently advocates membership in the institutional church.

The disappointment Newbigin felt at the 1960 World's Student Christian Federation in Strasbourg, which tried to negate the importance of the church, seemed to affect Newbigin for the rest of his life. It appeared to Newbigin that the ecumenical dream of a unified church (for Newbigin, a visible, organizational unity), would be forever lost. The church was always at the center of his theological thinking, but increasingly he saw the church as a local fellowship of converted people who hold to a different fiduciary framework from the culture around them. This dynamic community was a door to knowing God in a way that would radically change the lives of the converts.[78] Membership in a visible community is a commitment to act in certain ways in accordance to the worldview and lifestyle

---

72. Newbigin, *Sin and Salvation*, 45.
73. Newbigin, *A Faith*, 54.
74. Newbigin, *The Household*, 26.
75. Newbigin, "Context and Conversion," 304. Also see *The Household*, 37.
76. Newbigin, *The Household*, 141.
77. Newbigin, *The Finality*, 98.
78. See Goheen, "As the Father Has Sent Me," 238ff.

of the Christian community.[79] Newbigin explains the three ways that new converts are incorporated into the historically continuous church:

> The first answer is, briefly, that we are incorporated in Christ by hearing and believing the Gospel. The second is that we are incorporated by sacramental participation in the life of the historically continuous church. The third is that we are incorporated by receiving and abiding in the Holy Spirit.[80]

So, for Newbigin, putting on the 'new man' means participation in the life of fellowship with God's people and in the means of grace available in community.[81] By way of the Spirit and participation in the fellowship of believers, one becomes a partaker in Christ.[82]

It is not altogether automatic that a new convert would seek to identify with the visible community, but Newbigin acknowledges that people are drawn into Christian community when they have a meaningful contact with members of the community.[83] People in the neighborhoods surrounding the church are constantly brought in touch with the Christian not so much through organized campaigns as through the multitude of relationships in the daily life of the people of God.[84] The Holy Spirit works through these relationships to bring persons to Christ and to the church.

The Work of the Holy Spirit in the Church

The work of the Holy Spirit, Newbigin says, is very comprehensive in relation to the community of faith. It is the work of the Spirit to help the church to see all things in relation to Christ who is the head of all things. The Spirit will lead the church into the fullness of truth in Christ Jesus to the point where all things become subject to him.[85] The same anointing of the Holy Spirit that was given to Christ at his baptism is available also to his chosen disciples. From the Day of Pentecost forward, the Holy Spirit is at work in these disciples to bring forth the same fruit. The new reality,

---

79. Newbigin, *The Finality*, 97, 109.
80. Newbigin, *The Household*, 30.
81. Newbigin, *Sin and Salvation*, 113.
82. Ibid., 100.
83. Newbigin, *Proper Confidence*, 87.
84. Newbigin, "Context and Conversion," 309.
85. Newbigin, *Good Shepherd*, 116, 121.

Living in Truth and Reality

the coming of the Spirit, is let loose in the world and is ever-expanding as the gospel is carried to the ends of the earth.[86]

It is the presence of the *arrabon* (foretaste) that makes it possible for the church to be a witness to the gospel.[87] The Holy Spirit points people to the coming Kingdom of God and leads the church until God's purposes for the whole of creation is complete, and all things are brought into unity with Jesus Christ as the center.

The Question of Authority

The church faces a serious question of authority, according to Newbigin. What, in fact, is the final standard of arbitration regarding truth? There are many in the Western world who believe that culture must posit the criteria by which we decide what is true or factual. For the Christian, however, the question is not *what* but *who* is the final arbitrator of truth. Authority, Newbigin writes, emerges from the inner workings arising from different aspects in the life of the community of faith. There is authority, as long as it is a living tradition, where the community indwells the narratives of faith. The written Word becomes a living Word as the Holy Spirit works in the hearts of the people of the community.[88] For Newbigin, then, the Holy Spirit is the final authority for Christians. Newbigin explains:

> There can be no ultimate authority except the authority of the Spirit of God speaking in the heart and conscience of a man or woman. But the presence of that Holy Spirit is promised to the community that "indwells" the story of which the incarnation, ministry, death and resurrection of Jesus is the central key.[89]

While the Holy Spirit affirms the truth in the heart of believers in community, there is no way that the community can claim that Christianity is final. While the corporate life of the community, which is based on apostolic teaching, is committed to Christ and is enabled to interpret correctly God's work in history, it points to the end of the story when all things will be affirmed and seen as true. In the meantime, it lives by faith that this will eventuate, strengthened and fortified by the witness of the Holy Spirit.[90]

---

86. Newbigin, *A Faith*, 85.
87. Newbigin, *Gospel in a Pluralist Society*, 134.
88. Newbigin, *A Word*, 96ff.
89. Ibid., 97.
90. Newbigin, *The Finality*, 80, and also *The Other Side*, 46.

The Convert in the Didactic Community

Once the convert is firmly established in the community of faith, the community disciples the convert, shaping his or her mind and heart in conformity to the person in Christ. Christian discipleship is only understood within the Christian tradition, the cherished memories, shared practices, and rituals of the community. These are things that truly define what it means to be a Christian.[91] As the convert begins to read Scriptures and the story unfolds, it is then that the assumptions of the old life will have to be changed.[92]

Newbigin also sees the community of faith as a community of praise, where one experiences the "radiance of the supernatural."[93] On the horizontal level, it is a community that is enriched by shared hospitality. This is especially essential in the context of a multicultural and multireligious community where the church resides.[94] There is a growing recognition of the role played by the community in the healing of persons, both the body and the soul, and healing is as much a part of the ministry as preaching and teaching, Newbigin believes, for healing is an authentic sign of the presence of God's Kingdom and should be seen as a legitimate part of ministry.[95]

A Tradition of Rationality in Community

The community assists the new convert to enter into a deeper inward experience of God's love by participating in the rational discourse of the community. This tradition enables the convert to make sense of the world, "to grasp its real nature."[96] The only real validation for choosing and living in a particular rational tradition is if that tradition gives one the ability to understand and cope with reality.[97]

Christianity has a rational tradition that reflects its basic assumptions. Every form of rationality is, as has been noted before, socially embodied in a particular language and tradition, and is based on presuppositions that cannot be proven but are accepted by faith. At the heart of Newbigin's

---

91. Newbigin, *Proper Confidence*, 87.
92. Ibid.
93. Newbigin, *Foolishness*, 149.
94. Newbigin, "Confessing Christ," 131.
95. Newbigin, *Good Shepherd*, 72.
96. Newbigin, "Religious Pluralism," 52.
97. Newbigin, *Truth to Tell*, 48.

epistemology is his belief that indubitable knowledge is impossible, and that real knowing is essentially personal.[98]

The truth is, explains Newbigin, that there is no alternative to working within a specific community, and that there is no rational ground (at least based on Enlightenment thinking) for insisting that it be one community over another, like Israel over Japan. This sounds like a post-modern statement and appears not to give normative status to the Hebrew culture through which God revealed himself to humanity. It is not the culture that is normative but the revelation and, historically, it was given through the Hebrew culture. The key idea, though, is that there are no *rational* grounds for believing that the truth given to Israel is normative; it is accepted by faith. There is rational ground, however, for asserting that it must be in a specific community, and that Christianity, whose rational tradition developed surrounding events in which God has acted to disclose his nature and purpose, has the right to assert that its viewpoint is valid and should be seriously considered.[99] Christians, Newbigin exhorts, are responsible for convincing people of the superior rationality of the new paradigm, and should do so with intellectual vigor and courage. The 'superior rationality' would be a rational system that has a wider rationality than the narrow positivist rationality of Enlightenment scientism and it would be a system that accounts for all of reality, not just the material world of nature. That system would be Christianity. The Christian vision is a new and alternative structure to the cultural construct and Christians must be keen to demonstrate its adequacy.[100]

There is a clear analogy, from Newbigin's viewpoint, between the kind of imaginative leap (which is, in reality, a change of commitment based on what seems to be the reasonable assertions of the new viewpoint) explained by the witnesses and participants of the great events of the Bible and that which marks the birth of a new vision of scientific discovery. These great new visions flash into the mind of a scientist or are

---

98. Newbigin, "Religious Pluralism," 52.

99. Newbigin, *Gospel in a Pluralist Society*, 74.

100. Newbigin, *Truth and Authority*, 53–54. While Newbigin does not speak of himself as an apologist, Geoffrey Wainwright devotes one whole chapter (appropriately titled "The Christian Apologist" in *Theological Life*, 335–89) where he details that aspect of Newbigin's work.

disclosed to a prophet, and can become the basis of a new rational tradition.[101] Newbigin explains:

> Both the discovery by Kepler of a new pattern in the movement of heavenly bodies and the disclosure to Moses of a personal calling become the starting points of a tradition of reasoning in which the significance of these disclosures is explored, developed, tested against new experience, and extended into further areas of thought.[102]

A Christian congregation is a specific community among other communities, but it is a community that seeks to understand what was disclosed to the witnesses and participants in the historical events that form the content of the biblical record.[103]

Indwelling a Tradition

It is evident that Newbigin reshaped his view of the community of faith in dialogue with Michael Polanyi's concept of a scientific community indwelling truth.[104] Newbigin's use of sociologists and philosophers of science distinguish him from most missiologists who have traditionally utilized the methods and concepts of anthropology, primarily because of the predominance of missionary work in less developed, animistic societies. Since Newbigin is seeking to confront modern Western culture, it seems appropriate for him to utilize the conceptual tools of sociology and science.

The community of faith indwells the biblical stories, and these become the elements of a fiduciary framework from which it views the world. The development of Newbigin's ecclesiology is the subject of a

---

101. Newbigin, *Gospel in a Pluralist Society*, 59. This statement has much in common with T. F. Torrance's view of intuition. Torrance writes: "Polanyi has shown that where Einstein speaks of intuitive insight or apprehension we operate with an anticipatory grasp or a preliminary inkling of the rational pattern of things which is essentially an inarticulate movement of thought or a tacit form of apprehension." *Reality and Scientific Theology*, Torrance (Edinburgh: Scottish Academic Press, 1989), 78. Torrance states his own view: "it is possible for the human mind, in reliance upon the inner connections between its laws and the laws of nature, to penetrate intuitively into the intelligibility imbedded in nature." *Christian Frame of Mind*, Torrance (Colorado Springs, Colorado: Helmers & Howard, 1989), 50.

102. Newbigin, *Gospel in a Pluralist Society*, 60.

103. Ibid., 57–58.

104. Newbigin specifically cites Polanyi's use of the term 'indwelling' in *Truth and Authority*, 44.

dissertation by Michael Goheen.[105] Regarding Newbigin's use of Polanyi, Goheen also notes how Newbigin utilizes Polanyi's idea of the way truth is dealt with within the scientific community and the church (faith community). Goheen comments: "The structures of both are similar."[106]

Newbigin, as we have already noted, borrows the concept of *indwelling a tradition* from Polanyi. When one remembers, ponders, and celebrates the critical events of biblical history, it becomes, Newbigin observes, like a personal language, providing models and concepts through which one understands life.[107] One cannot validate the *indwelling* by judging it against some external standard or criteria but it can be scrutinized to see if it helps persons make sense of the world that confronts them.[108] Our faith is that it does make sense because the Incarnate Word of God is the One by Whom and for Whom all things were made.[109]

There are limitations, of course, to the comparison between the Christian and scientific communities. The scientific community is a tradition of human learning while the Christian community has a special structure of knowing that goes beyond the mere human tradition of science.[110] This special structure of knowing involves a living community with a rational tradition based on revelation, a tradition that always has access to the continuing work of the Holy Spirit who points to the validity of that divine revelation.[111] Newbigin describes the function of tradition:

> Tradition is not a separate source of revelation from Scripture; it is the continuing activity of the Church through the ages in seeking to grasp and express under new conditions that which is given in Scripture. The study of Scripture takes place within the continuing tradition of interpretation.[112]

The Christian life is lived by indwelling the biblical story, a story that is also shared by the whole community of faith. At the heart of the mes-

---

105. The title is: *"As the Father has Sent Me, I Am Sending You,": J. E. Lesslie Newbigin's Missionary Ecclesiology.*
106. Goheen, "As the Father has sent me," 385.
107. Newbigin, *Truth to Tell*, 47.
108. Ibid., 48.
109. Ibid.
110. Newbigin, *Gospel in a Pluralist Society*, 50–51.
111. Newbigin, *Truth and Authority*, 29.
112. Newbigin, *Gospel in a Pluralist Society*, 53.

sage is the story of the incarnation, life, death, and resurrection of Jesus Christ.[113] When persons trust this tradition, it becomes the authority for their life.[114] In chapter 15 of John's Gospel, the disciples are exhorted to 'dwell' in Christ. As they indwell him, they will gain an ever greater understanding of truth.[115]

Newbigin summarizes the importance of the community to the faith of the new convert. It is in the community of faith where the faith of the convert is nourished, as the Bible is *indwelt*, and as the community of faith dialogues with Scripture.[116] The boundary between culture and the community of faith is breached by a paradigm shift called conversion,[117] and because it requires such a paradigm shift to enter the faith community, it implies that the community lives by a different plausibility structure from culture.[118] The community testifies to a rational, finite, contingent world, where God has left his mark.[119] Finally, the church must not allow itself to be relegated to mere personal opinion, but must witness to the Lordship of Christ over all of life.[120] God's work of salvation for humanity is not a "series of private transactions within a multitude of individual souls," but is something that is worked out in public history, concrete and specific.[121]

The Christian story provides Christians with a set of lenses, not something to look *at* but something to look *through*. As the Christian community indwells the story, the story shapes the way it understands the world.[122] There are six implications of *indwelling* the biblical story, according to Newbigin. In the first place, it means to inhabit a different plausibility structure from the one in the society in which one lives. Secondly, it is the narrative of actual historical events recorded in the Bible that gives Christians the clue for understanding contemporary history. Thirdly, the Bible does not give answers to questions that would cause a person to be relieved of personal responsibility. Fourthly, when a person is asked why a

---

113. Newbigin, *Gospel in a Pluralist Society*, 99.
114. Ibid., 49.
115. Ibid., 99.
116. Newbigin, *Foolishness*, 58–60.
117. Ibid., 61–62.
118. Ibid., 62.
119. Ibid., 88.
120. Ibid., 79–102.
121. Newbigin, "Religious Pluralism," 54.
122. Newbigin, *Gospel in a Pluralist Society*, 38.

Living in Truth and Reality

particular plausibility structure is chosen, there are two possible responses: one is that we make decisions from within a plausibility structure and, two, it is not that one chooses it, it is the fact that one is chosen. Fifthly, the distinguishing mark of the community where plausibility structure is shaped by the biblical story will be hope. Sixthly, the Christian will look forward to the advent of Christ and when he comes, the Christian offers whatever she does, whether it is private prayer or political action.[123]

It is only as a person truly indwells the gospel story, and is deeply involved in the life of the community that is shaped by the biblical story, that one develops the hope that allows a person to understand and cope with reality. The essence of the Christian testimony is that God has acted in such a way through Jesus Christ that humanity can know that he loves us and that that knowledge is confirmed in the events of daily life.[124] This is radical hope and Newbigin believes that the church must be the bearer of hope in the midst of a famine of hope.[125] A part of the great hope for humanity is for unity and this is only possible, Newbigin is convinced, when it is based on the crucified and risen Jesus.[126]

Newbigin has pointed out that what constitutes the Christian plausibility structure contradicts society's plausibility structure. Consequently, the new convert will be indwelling a story that will be quite different from the cultural story that shaped him or her, so the new convert will experience a radical shift in the way he or she views the world.[127]

The church not only indwells the story, but it is also a part of the ongoing story. As the church moves through history, it has a double character, it is a suffering church but also one marked by mighty works.[128] These works are not marks of the church moving *toward* the kingdom but are a witness that the kingdom is *already present* but is hidden.[129]

---

123. Newbigin, *Gospel in a Pluralist Society*, 99–102.
124. Newbigin, *Honest Religion*, 89.
125. Newbigin, *A Word*, 45.
126. Newbigin, *Truth to Tell*, 4.
127. Newbigin, *Gospel in a Pluralist Society*, 232.
128. Ibid., 107.
129. Ibid., 108.

Grasping Truth and Reality

Understanding in Terms of the Story

By indwelling the biblical story, the objective revelation of God is internalized and becomes the subjective experience of the Christian.[130] What is true of the convert is true for the whole community. The Christian community of faith understands itself and its history in terms of this story.[131] In the context of post-modernism that asserts that there are many stories, the church affirms the validity of this one story for all humanity.[132] The Christian community not only knows the story, but it rehearses and celebrates it. The church goes back again and again to the place where God revealed Himself and the words and acts of Jesus are read and explained, his baptism is re-enacted each time a believer is baptized, and his sacrificial death and his victorious resurrection are recalled each time the community breaks bread and shares the cup. The community of faith relives the moment of revelation, renews the community's participation in that moment of revelation, and reaffirms its faith in the truth.[133] Weekly the community returns to the place where God and the world are known as they truly are.[134]

The Hermeneutical Community

The Christian community indwells the biblical story and has done so for two thousand years, so it is the most qualified to interpret the meaning of the story. Newbigin believes that the local congregation is really the only effective hermeneutic of the gospel,[135] a congregation of persons who believe it and live by it.[136] "The originally given revelation," writes Newbigin, "had to be continually reappropriated and reinterpreted in the light of new situations."[137] The church interprets the Scriptures from within a context of commitment, faith, and obedience, while Scripture, in turn, constantly calls the church and its interpretation into question.[138] The question that

---

130. Newbigin, *The Light*, 190.
131. Newbigin, *Proper Confidence*, 52.
132. Ibid., 76.
133. Newbigin, *Honest Religion*, 95.
134. Ibid., 150.
135. Newbigin, *A Word*, 175.
136. Newbigin, *Gospel in a Pluralist Society*, 227. Also "Episcopacy and Authority," 339.
137. Newbigin, *Gospel in a Pluralist Society*, 63.
138. Newbigin, *Other Side*, 46.

Living in Truth and Reality

is continually addressed by the church is whether God's revelation can continue to provide coherence and meaning for each new era.[139]

The Local Church: the Church for That Place

In words reminiscent of Karl Barth,[140] Newbigin describes the church as the church *for that place*. Newbigin believes that the preposition *for* must be understood Christologically; in other words, it is to be defined by what Jesus has done, is doing, and will do as the Redeemer of the world. The church for that place is really a church *for* mankind.[141] The church "in each place is to be a sign of the true end for which everything in the secular reality of that place exists."[142] Even though it is a particular community, it is one chosen and sent by God for a universal mission.[143] The actual sphere of redemption, of which Jesus is the historical center, is the historical community of faith and from this center, the word of redemption goes out to all the earth through the sovereign working of the Holy Spirit.[144] The gospel can only be communicated, says Newbigin, to Western pluralistic society by the community of faith that utilizes the Bible as the basic framework for its theology, understanding the world and the human story through the biblical perspective.[145] The church, however, can only reach the world if it maintains a certain 'radical other-worldliness,' which is possible if the church maintains its commitment to the holy name of God, a commitment that is outside the comprehension of a culture that rejects such a notion.[146]

The nature of the community of faith consists in love that expresses itself in very concrete ways. The deep appreciation for what God has done must lead to a welcoming embrace of every human being. It is a place where the love of God flows out to everyone, a place where the stranger, whatever their race or life situation, is welcomed, loved, and embraced.

---

139. Newbigin, *Gospel in a Pluralist Society*, 63.
140. Barth, "The Community for the World," 762–95.
141. Newbigin, "What Is a 'Local Church Truly United?'" 118.
142. Ibid., 119.
143. Newbigin, *Gospel in a Pluralist Society*, 87–88, and also *A Faith*, 58.
144. Newbigin, *The Household*, 131.
145. Newbigin, *A Word*, 165.
146. Newbigin, *The Light*, 231.

This is done in the context of celebration of the amazing things God has done, celebrating his overwhelming and amazing generosity.[147]

The deepest problem of Western culture is an individualism that fails to acknowledge that human nature is given by God. To counteract this problem, Christians only grow into true humanity in relation to each other, in a relationship of natural faithfulness and responsibility. The local congregation is called to be that kind of community, a community of mutual responsibility.[148] It is from this robust mutuality in the local congregation, where the new creation is known and experienced, that persons go into every sector of life to claim it for Christ, "to unmask the illusions which have remained hidden and to expose all areas of public life to the illumination of the gospel."[149]

ENGAGING WESTERN CULTURE

Mission of the Church

Central to Newbigin's ecclesiology is the theological principle that the church exists not for itself but for the world. More specifically, it exists for the purpose of fulfilling God's purpose for the world. The mission of the church is evidence of the meaning and end of world history, and it is precisely in the concreteness and particularity of the people of God that makes them the bearers of salvation to the whole world.[150] Each local congregation is a part of the home base for mission to the whole world. Each congregation is related in mutual dependence and responsibility with every other part of the church in fulfilling God's mission to the world.[151]

The church's mission is dependent upon the fact that it comes from God, and, therefore, has a missionary dimension.[152] The church must remain constantly aware of the fact that its mission is really the mission of God, and that the church is not so much the agent of mission as the focal point or locus of mission.[153] Newbigin explains:

---

147. Newbigin, "Confessing Christ in a Multi-religion Society," 127.
148. Newbigin, *Gospel in a Pluralist Society*, 231.
149. Ibid., 232–33.
150. Newbigin, *A Faith*, 81.
151. Ibid., 109.
152. Newbigin, "Cross-currents," 149.
153. Newbigin, *Gospel in a Pluralist Society*, 117, 119.

Living in Truth and Reality

> The mission of the church is in fact the Church's obedient participation in that action of the Spirit by which confession of Jesus as Lord becomes the authentic confession of every new people, each in its own tongue.[154]

This confession of Jesus as Lord must be more than a verbal proclamation; it must also be seen in the actions of the church. Newbigin cites the mission of Jesus as the model the church must emulate. It was not only the verbal proclamation of the Good News, but was also the embodiment of that news as well, thus showing that the life of the community to a certain degree already embodies and is the foretaste of the Kingdom of God.[155] The church's mission, simply put, is to continue in the world the ministry of the same divine Spirit who was in Jesus. The presence of Jesus and the Spirit in the world means that the age of the Kingdom of God has dawned,[156] and the church is given certain signs of the Kingdom, such as the powers of healing and blessing, that are recognizable as true signs that Jesus does indeed reign. Mighty works, says Newbigin, are promised to the church as a part of the fulfillment of God's mission on earth, and these signs should be evident in the church in mission. The church is required to go the way of the Master, unmasking and challenging the powers of darkness, as well as bearing the cost of such a confrontation.[157]

The Church as a Witness to the End of History

One aspect of the church's identity that it does not share with other communities of the world is that it is a witness to the end of history. While still engaging the present age, it points definitely to something yet to come. The question is not so much "What is it now?" but "What is it becoming?"[158] "The Church," Newbigin writes, "is not merely a historical reality but also an eschatological one."[159] There can be no missionary encounter with culture, he says, without a recovery of the true apocalyptic, a biblically grounded eschatology.[160]

---

154. Newbigin, *Open Secret*, 28.
155. Newbigin, "A Missionary's Dream," 6.
156. Newbigin, *A Faith*, 86.
157. Newbigin, *Gospel in a Pluralist Society*, 108.
158. Newbigin, *The Household*, 134.
159. Ibid., 135.
160. Newbigin, *A Word*, 77.

Newbigin sees a strong connection between the mission of the church and the eschatological tension that the church experiences. The tension revolves around the fact that the Kingdom of God is both present and is, at the same time, yet to come, meaning that the essence or essential nature of the Kingdom is present while the fullness of the Kingdom is something Christians look for at the consummation of the ages.[161]

The fundamental interconnection between eschatological and missionary elements of the church is clearly seen in Newbigin's doctrine of the Holy Spirit. It is the Spirit who empowers the church to witness, and is the source of the powerful works by which the world is enabled to catch a glimpse of the glory that is yet to be revealed. He is the foretaste of the end and also the One who sends the church forth to the ends of the earth.[162]

Newbigin's eschatological understanding of the church is also Trinitarian:

> God calls the whole created order into being, sustains it in being, and has power to bring it to its proper end. And the coming of Jesus is the revelation of that end within the created order, in him the Creator who is both the beginning and the end was present among men, and by the operation of the Holy Spirit he is still present in the community of believers.[163]

The church has a durable character, moving between promise and fulfillment, both the realization of the new era and, at the same time, the promise of a new age to come. It is an installment of what will come later in its fullness.[164]

The church as a witness to the end of history implies a specific view of history, one that is linear and is leading to an ultimate end.[165] The church bears witness to the real end of history. A history that has no end, Newbigin contends, has no real meaning.[166] Part of the mission of the church is also to 'make history.' The church is that agency through which

---

161. Newbigin, *The Household*, 141.
162. Ibid., 142.
163. Newbigin, *A Faith*, 99.
164. Ibid., 93. Newbigin does not mention who shapes his eschatology. His familiarity with the biblical theology movement suggests that he was influenced to some degree by Oscar Cullmann (with his ideas about the Bible being the record of concrete historical events) and the biblical theology movement.
165. Ibid., 96.
166. Ibid., 95.

God brings history to its goal, and it is the place where the goal of history can be adequately understood.[167] Human history is meaningless if there is no order of being that exists beyond the temporal order. The Christian faith asserts that there is such an order beyond time and history, because the will of God is eternal and God is a being who transcends time.[168]

There are generally two alternatives to the understanding of biblical eschatology: one is to develop utopian ideas where the meaning of history is found in bettering the social order, while the other is to narrow the vision down to individual salvation, where the ultimate "destiny of the individual soul becomes the ultimate goal of the whole story."[169] Christian eschatology transcends the dilemma of the two extremes because it is centered on the resurrection of Jesus Christ. It is through Christ that all things were created and, also through him, all things will be consummated. Were he not the one he could not be the other, reasons Newbigin. The point is that the end of all things is in Christ, not just the destiny of the individual soul. The whole drama of history and of the world consummates in Jesus Christ.[170]

In the era of church, we see the overlap of the ages, the time between the first advent of Christ and his coming again. During this time the church is to be engaged in witnessing to Christ to the ends of the earth. Christ is the end to which everything is pointing and will be consummated in him. He is delayed in coming until this witness of the judgment and salvation of God is carried to the whole world. The true eschatology of the church points to missionary obedience because that is what constitutes the meaning of the time that leads up to the end.[171] The church, therefore, is not an end in itself, nor is it the final goal of history, but has a significant role to play at the end of history. As a part of the church's responsibility in this time of overlapping eras, Newbigin believes, is to foster radical renewal in culture by offering a model for a new understanding of God and reality. Without this radical renewal, he strongly believes, Western culture has no future.[172]

---

167. Newbigin, *Gospel in a Pluralist Society*, 131.
168. Newbigin, *A Faith*, 98.
169. Ibid., 97.
170. Ibid., 98.
171. Newbigin, *The Household*, 135.
172. Newbigin, *Other Side*, 27.

The Unity of the Church

Newbigin sees the unity of the church as a significant testimony to the world about the nature of Christian faith, and even pointing to the essential nature of God. The disunity of the church, to Newbigin, is a contradiction of its essential nature and disqualifies its right to preach the gospel to the nations of the world.[173] The disunity of the church is, he laments, "a public denial of sufficiency of Christ."[174]

Disunity should not be confused with natural diversity that comes from the diversity of nations and races that comprise the church. The church should, of necessity, reflect the variety of the human race.[175] The church must also reflect a rich harmony, becoming what Paul refers to as the manifold wisdom of God.[176]

The Doctrine of Election

Newbigin specifically related the doctrine of election to the fact that God chose a particular community to be the avenue by which God reaches the world.[177] His position on election changed little over his years of ministry, and appears in similar form in a number of his writings. In his book *Sin and Salvation*, written in the 1950s, we read that salvation is offered through the corporate witness of persons chosen by God to be his community.[178] In 1961, he develops this idea even more: God chose a single tribe out of all the tribes of humanity to be his people, his witnesses, and his priests. People become related to the Kingdom by being related to this one nation. Christ accepted as his mission to recall Israel to its true vocation. It was not an election to privilege, Newbigin insists, but an election to responsibility. Each of us hears God's message through the lips of another rather than hearing it as if it came down straight from heaven. In the end, Newbigin believes, the Jews will be saved through the testimony of the Gentiles.[179]

---

173. Newbigin, *A Faith*, 81.
174. Ibid., 82.
175. Ibid.
176. Ibid., 88.
177. Newbigin, *Truth and Authority*, 21–22 and also *Open Secret*, 68.
178. Newbigin, *Sin and Salvation*, 45.
179. Newbigin, *A Faith*, 77–79. Johannes Blauw, in his book titled *The Missionary Nature of the Church* published in 1962 at the request of the International Missionary

Living in Truth and Reality

In *The Gospel in a Pluralist Society* (1989), Newbigin expands on the idea of the salvation of the Jews coming through the Gentiles. He speaks of Paul's 'logic of election' and refers primarily to Paul's Letter to the Romans, chapters 9 through 11. Newbigin addresses the question that emerges from reading Paul's words: What is the meaning of Israel's rejection of the Messiah? Newbigin explains the 'logic of election:'

> Paul's answer is an astonishing one, but it fits exactly what I call the logic of election. God, says Paul, has hardened the hearts of Israel so that the gospel which they reject will—so to say—bounce off the Gentiles. This is exactly what was happening in city after city where Paul was turned out of the synagogues and went to the Gentiles. So the apostasy of Israel has brought salvation to the Gentiles. Does this mean that Israel is lost? No! Impossible! God can never cast off his chosen people. As proof of this he has kept a remnant (as so often in the past) as pledge that Israel is not rejected. The small company of believing Jews is the pledge that Israel is not cast off.[180]

The predominately Gentile church is a part of the fulfillment of God's purposes for the salvation of both the Jews and the rest of the world. The church must never think of its election as election to special privilege, but must be continually reminded that it is elected to missionary responsibility.[181] We can never know why God chose Israel from among all the nations of the world, and we will never fully understand why he has chosen the church to be his witness on earth today,[182] since the source of the election is in the depths of God's gracious will before the foundation of the world.[183]

Council and the World Council of Churches, sought to rediscover the biblical theology that would form the basis for the mission of the church to the world. Blauw believed that Israel's election was for the purpose of God being recognized by the nations. By extension, divine election means that some are called to become the avenue of leading others to Christ. This parallels Newbigin's view.

180. Newbigin, *Gospel in a Pluralist Society*, 83.
181. Newbigin, *The Household*, 132.
182. Newbigin, *Sin and Salvation*, 45, and also *The Open Secret*, 68.
183. Newbigin, *The Household*, 103.

Election and the Confession of Jesus

The Good News is the news of the fact that in Jesus of Nazareth, God seeks to reconcile the world to himself. He is the Chosen One, the elect of God. The election of the church only happens with its incorporation in Christ. "We are not elect," Newbigin insists, "as isolated individuals, but as members in His body."[184] The idea that the gospel is only addressed to individuals and not to societies is a product of post-Enlightenment Western culture. If one looks into the Old Testament one can find no such separation of the individual from the culture of which that person is a part.[185] The mission of the church is the obedient participation in the work of the Holy Spirit whereby the confession that Jesus Christ is Lord becomes the confession of those who become new as a result of that mission.[186]

Newbigin contends that since Christ was a public figure and his message was delivered in the public forum, the gospel is not about the interior life of the soul that is somehow shunted away from public life.[187] Christ challenged the nation with the claim of his Kingship, and it was interpreted, as it should have been, as a challenge to the public life of the nation. It was uncompromising and eventually led to his crucifixion. God the Father, however, raised him from the dead, a public event that Western privatized religion has attempted to change into a purely psychological experience.[188]

The way of Jesus, in the power of his risen life, is neither the way of the solitary spiritual pilgrimage nor a political cause that seeks to create a new social order.[189] The resultant discipleship of those who believe and follow Christ will necessarily be concerned with both the private and public spheres, with the purpose to make visible that ordering of life that has as its fiduciary framework God's revelation in Jesus Christ.[190]

The Gospel as Public Truth

Newbigin's position is quite clear regarding the fact that the gospel is not just for the possession of solitary individuals but is public truth.

---

184. Newbigin, *The Household*, 102.
185. Newbigin, *Gospel in a Pluralist Society*, 199.
186. Newbigin, *Open Secret*, 28.
187. Newbigin, *Other Side*, 32.
188. Ibid., 37–38.
189. Ibid., 37.
190. Ibid.

Christianity is open for public scrutiny and examination.[191] The gospel does not become public truth by propagating a theory, a worldview, or a religion; it becomes public as it is embodied in the church.[192] The story must also be articulated, explicitly stated so that people may truly hear,[193] and it is the role of the Holy Spirit to use the witness of God's people, and bring people world to the point of decision.[194]

Newbigin strongly exhorts the church to fight the tendency to take refuge in a private realm of existence where the focus is on individual salvation and not on public proclamation.[195] The Early Church, he writes, did not regard itself as a society for the promotion of the personal salvation of members. If it had, it would not have suffered but would have enjoyed the protection of the law. It was, because of its public testimony, seen as a threat to the ideology that controlled public life.[196]

The church must have the courage to proclaim the gospel with boldness, in spite of the fact that Western culture believes proper modesty requires one to be agnostic regarding ultimate truth.[197] The church must have the confidence to offer beliefs that can be doubted, and to offer them in humility.[198] The church can expect some kind of public reaction to its message, since the gospel has always been offensive to ordinary common sense. Newbigin articulates how absurd the gospel message must seem to the world:

> ... how utterly absurd and indeed revolting to claim that a Jew from a notoriously troublesome province of the Empire who had been condemned as a blasphemer and executed as a traitor was the Savior of the world! How on earth could anyone believe that?[199]

From the viewpoint of the Roman Empire or modern Western culture, the gospel seems to challenge any sense of reason, so important to both

---

191. Newbigin, *Proper Confidence*, 52.
192. Ibid., 39.
193. Newbigin, "Episcopacy and Authority," 336, and also *A Word*, 155.
194. Newbigin, *Trinitarian Faith*, 45.
195. Newbigin, *Foolishness*, 115; *Honest Religion*, 44–45; *A Word*, 95; and *Trinitarian Faith*, 55.
196. Newbigin, *Other Side*, 33.
197. Newbigin, *The Light*, 115.
198. Newbigin, *Proper Confidence*, 46, 70, and also *Foolishness*, 148.
199. Newbigin, "Context and Conversion," 301.

cultures. In the contemporary sea of relativism, such a claim would, assuredly, be met with much skepticism.[200] Public affirmations of the gospel in the contemporary climate are viewed as 'sectarian' and 'dogmatic,' two words definitely out of vogue in modern Western thought.[201]

CONCLUSION

Newbigin's critique of Western culture appears to be a negative polemic except that he offers one major solution: the radical conversion of the culture. One must ask how he thinks this can come about. His answer is the presence of a community of faith that witnesses to the fact of Christ in the public arena.

Historically, there is another conceivable alternative to what Newbigin posits as his answer to that question, that being a revival, similar to what happened in Britain during the Evangelical Revival through the preaching of John Wesley and George Whitefield. Over a period time Wesley was able to build up an authentic church. The history of missions is full of examples of revivals sweeping over certain geographical areas and, on occasion, whole nations. What Newbigin envisions is not a revival that may influence a nation for a certain era and then fade; he places his hope in the most enduring community of all time, the Christian church. He has a somewhat idealized picture of the church, but remarkably, with the anti-Enlightenment polemics of the post-modern movement, Newbigin's vision for the Christian community of faith may be closer to meeting the demands of the 'age to come' than even he could have envisioned. Rather than trying to be buttressed by evidence demanded by the Enlightenment, the church, Newbigin believes, must be faithful to itself and its Lord. It would then be an authentic Christian community to which people would be drawn.

Can the West be converted? The Enlightenment-influenced mind and the post-modern mind are quick to be skeptical. Perhaps Newbigin is correct in saying that the Enlightenment narrowed the scope of reality, and, in this case, the realm of possibilities. Scientism, at least, believes that truth that is discovered is universal truth, even if that truth does not include any dimension except the natural world. Post-modernism has narrowed reality even more by limiting truth to the confines of a particular community with no possibility of universal application. It does

---

200. Newbigin, *Truth to Tell*, 5.
201. Newbigin, *Proper Confidence*, 50.

not appear, if one is in touch with contemporary Western culture, that the Enlightenment will have the last word. If God is left from the equation in culture, as Newbigin sees it, then post-modernism will also not be the last word. Jesus Christ, the goal of history, *is* the last word, spoken long ago, but, in reality, into the never-ending future. In the end, the 'fact of Christ' will, as Newbigin believes and asserts, prevail.

Newbigin's vision for Europe (and the West) is stated in his book *A Word in Season* as follows:

> When Europe is filled with congregations of believing people who are learning to live by the true story, then Europe will indeed be not just a common market, but a common home.[202]

---

202. Newbigin, *A Word*, 205.

8

Putting Newbigin in Perspective

NEWBIGIN'S CONTRIBUTION

ACCOLADES PRAISING NEWBIGIN'S CONTRIBUTION to the church have already been mentioned. There are, however, some further contributions that become apparent as one does an exposition of his theological and missiological thinking. There are also some challenges to his thinking that need to be addressed. Newbigin is not the first to confront Western culture as a missionary in the Twentieth Century. Francis Schaeffer, for example, began to discern the real issues of Western culture in the middle of the last century. While he believed them to be theological in origin, he saw them manifested in philosophy, art, and literature. Schaeffer's attitude toward culture was somewhat precipitated by Fundamentalism's generally negative attitude toward culture, especially modernism. Coming out of Fundamentalism, it was not unusual that he would be a critic of modern culture; what was unusual was his popular apologetic of the philosophical issues that plague Western culture, which was, for that generation of young evangelicals, quite compelling. Schaeffer's compassion for Western culture in need of salvation was also compelling.

Newbigin, on the other hand, came from within the ranks of the ecumenical movement, a movement generally known to be overly accommodating to culture, especially Western modernist culture. In spite of this, Newbigin mounted a robust polemic against modernism, something that has found favor in the minds of many evangelicals. He also touches on postmodernism as it sought to replace modernism in the latter part of the twentieth century. He shows where Christians can accept some aspects of postmodernism while not aligning itself with other aspects. His relevant critique of Western culture has caused evangelical Christians seriously to

Putting Newbigin in Perspective

consider Newbigin's strategy of confronting Western culture as it would any world culture.

Newbigin's clear theological thinking in the midst of what was a very demanding life of practical ministry is praiseworthy in itself. The fact that he was able to produce compelling books and articles that revealed a deep reflection upon serious philosophical and theological issues facing Western culture is also impressive. The thrust of his thought is, in essence, a serious challenge to Western culture to seek to divert an impending cultural disaster by reconsidering the Biblical worldview, which is, to Newbigin's mind, a superior plausibility structure than the current one. This too is laudable and deserves to be heard and considered. His courage to face forthrightly the epistemological dualism that has subverted Western culture at various points in history and which plagues it at the present time deserves a hearing in the public arena. This was the intent of his focused confrontation with Western culture.

NEWBIGIN'S INNOVATIVE APPROACH TO MISSIONS

Before attempting a final evaluation of Newbigin's thinking, there is need for a general overview and summary of the strengths of Newbigin's mission theology. The most important contribution, which has been stated in various ways throughout this book, is his innovative approach to mission, which is that of applying missiological principles usually thought of as relating only to less developed countries, to modern Western culture. Missions has generally sought to convert persons from a lifestyle of sin and immorality but also to a new worldview that incorporates the teaching and perspective of the Bible. The emphasis in the West has been primarily on the moral aspects of conversion, but Newbigin's emphasis on the conversion on the mind reminds Western people that less has been expected of them than what is expected in non-Western countries. Consequent to his innovative approach, Newbigin delves into a realm of discussion with Western culture's worldview, which entails an encounter with philosophers of modernism that missionaries are not generally accustomed to having to do. Instead of dealing with the superficial or surface level of culture, Newbigin goes for the heart of the issue—Western culture's absorption of the philosophy and principles of modernism, reflected most strikingly in scientism and a dualistic epistemology.

Another strength that Newbigin exhibits is his understanding of the flow of Western culture, especially since the Enlightenment. He has many keen insights into how Western culture deviated from the foundations of culture given to it by Judeo-Christian thinking, most specifically as it was grounded in biblical thought through the influence of Augustine, and the results of that deviation. While many may argue with Newbigin about the details, one cannot but appreciate his attempt to take on the enormous challenge of understanding and assessing Western culture with the honorable motive of seeking to find a solution for its re-conversion and ultimate regeneration.

While there is great need for the academic world to engage in serious discussion about Western culture and produce substantial tools to help Christians positively respond to the crisis of Western culture, one of Newbigin's strengths and certainly one of his gifts to the church is that he has attempted such an intellectual feat primarily as a practitioner and not as an academician. His main experience in academia was in his retirement, but even then his teaching was strongly rooted in his practical experience as a missionary, ecumenical leader, and pastor/teacher. He is an outstanding example to the church that everyone should be engaged in serious intellectual work as a part of the mission of the church. One cannot seek to engage the contemporary world in a mindless fashion, without recognizing the need not only for spiritual depth but also for a mind fully engaged in understanding and appropriately responding to the challenges of culture.

While Newbigin lays much of the blame for Christians retreating from the public square on pietistic Christianity (which is not entirely accurate), he reminds Christians that, for whatever reason, they have generally disengaged from serious public debate. Generally he blames evangelical Christians for being more focused on their own personal salvation and spirituality than in fully engaging culture as a part of their witness.

Newbigin has renewed the discussion of the need for radical conversion, not only the conversion of the heart but also of the mind. At the time of this radical conversion, the allegiance of the person changes to Jesus Christ but there must also be a renewal of the mind to become like the mind of Christ. This means that discipleship and nurturing must not only include spiritual instruction but also instruction on how this faith factors into our understanding of the reality, of God, and the nature of the world. In other words, there is a shift in worldview, from a false and deficient worldview to a true understanding of reality. Newbigin wants Christians to not only grasp truth but also to correctly understand and grasp reality.

Newbigin has reminded us that we need to approach Western culture as a mission field. While the model in his mind may have been similar to what it was in India, where he literally spoke in the public square in his street preaching, that model would not necessarily be appropriate in the West. He does not give us a lot of details on missionary methodology, but he did leave us with his concept of the most effective model for missionary methodology—the church. He describes the manner in which a person in our culture is drawn to Christ by observing the church, which is indwelling the truth of Christ as revealed in the Bible. It is in the indwelling of the story that the church truly acts like a church and then becomes the conduit for God's grace to culture. This process is initiated by the Holy Spirit who leads a person to believe in Christ. The convert then becomes a part of that community which indwells the story and that community nurtures the convert in the story. It is both spiritual and cognitive nurturing, where the convert exchanges the previously unredeemed worldview for a true view of reality, which radically changes the convert's life and thinking.

The vision cast by Newbigin is substantial and timely. While we may argue about some of the details of his thinking we cannot fault him in seeing the need for a truly spiritual and intelligent engagement with Western culture. It is a compelling vision and Newbigin believes it is time to move forward with confidence that Christ and biblical truth have the most substantial and critical answer to Western culture's crisis and, therefore, there is a basis for hope in Western culture's re-conversion.

TOWARDS A CRITICAL EVALUATION

The main question that has been addressed in this book is how Newbigin's theology of mission for the Western world arises from the theological convictions which were formulated in his mind prior to his retirement in 1974 and whether this theology of mission is adequate for the task he sets out to accomplish.

Newbigin uses his theological thought to critique Western culture. First, Western culture is evaluated as to whether it measures up to the criteria of the theology he sees as representing the gist of Christian thought. It does not, in fact, measure up. Second, his theological thought becomes the substance of his theology of mission. His mission is to confront Western culture with these theological tenets in the attempt to replace the prevailing fiduciary framework and plausibility structure, which are causing the demise of Western culture. This would, in essence, restore Christianity to the place of the preferred worldview of Western culture.

The question arises, then, whether his theology of mission, his vision for the conversion of Western culture, is adequate to carry out the task he sets out for the church. While his vision is compelling, there are aspects of his theology of mission that fall short of accomplishing what he desired and need to be addressed. It is important to put Newbigin in perspective.

PUTTING NEWBIGIN IN PERSPECTIVE

One of Newbigin's major contributions to twentieth century missions was, as mentioned earlier, his innovative approach of treating the West as a mission field. Missions has generally sought to convert persons *from* a lifestyle of sin and immorality but also *to* a new worldview that incorporates the teaching and perspective of the Bible, as well as expecting a moral transformation. While the emphasis in the West has generally been on the moral aspects of conversion, Newbigin's emphasis on the conversion of the mind as well reminds Western people that their view of conversion is not fully biblical if it does not substantially change their thinking and subsequently their worldview. Consequently, Newbigin confronts Western culture's prevailing worldview, which entails an encounter with philosophers of modernity, something missionaries, as mentioned earlier, are not generally accustomed to doing. Newbigin goes for the heart of the issue: Western culture's absorption of the philosophy and principles of modernism, reflected most strikingly in scientism and a dualistic epistemology along with the subsequent rejection of the Christian worldview which is the true view of reality.

Many Western Christians point to the loss of spirituality as the main cause for the crisis in the West. This may seem to be true, but Newbigin points to something much deeper and perhaps more profound than that. Western culture has a problem at its fundamental core, a problem with its worldview which colors the rest of culture. Newbigin is bold to call upon the church to try to (re)convert Western culture, recapturing both its heart *and* its mind. He believed that the church, if it would reinsert itself into culture, could pull it off. Newbigin more than likely observed that the church usually sought spiritual renewal without the complementary renewal of the mind. After a time of profound spiritual renewal, Christians would tend to settle back into an over accommodation to culture, which over time would lead to the need for another spiritual renewal.

The question is whether Newbigin might be somewhat overly optimistic about the possibility of the church reconverting the West. The most straightforward answer to that question is that this optimism seems to be unrealistic, especially with the fact that Western culture has rejected (or is in the process of rejecting) Christianity at the present time and there seems to be little substantial evidence to make one believe that Western culture is even remotely interested in seeing Christianity reinstated as the core belief system of culture. Newbigin's vision is for culture to see the wisdom and superior rationality of Biblical truth and how it truly connects humanity with reality. This would lead them to reconsider Christianity or, more specifically, the biblical worldview. It is hard to imagine such a conversion without an extraordinary work of God in the midst of Western culture, which, if and when it occurred, Christians would be wise enough to continue the spiritual renewal to a full renewal of the mind, which would mean replacing culture's plausibility structure and fiduciary framework with a Biblical view. That truly would be a transformation of culture, a reformation badly needed in our day.

Presently, Western culture is not inclined to listen to the Christian witness, but it has not been entirely muted. When Christians insist on articulating their faith as the truth that must be believed to be saved, many in culture would view this as intolerant and irresponsible since an individual's personal spiritual preferences are being challenged and this is considered an infringement upon an individual's personal rights. Rather than be converted, culture may strike back with their own brand of intolerance by attempting to censor Christians or worse, to punish them for their indiscretions. It is possible that suffering may be the way to the fulfillment of Newbigin's dream. He did consider that possibility. This is not entirely outside the realm of possibilities in spite of Western culture's insistence that it espouses religious freedom. However, when a radicalized form of the right of human individual freedom takes precedence, it would seem, all other freedoms are subjected to it in a rather mindless fashion. While human individual freedom is one of the gifts of the Enlightenment, taken in its most radical form, it can become an unreasonable tyrant that can destroy culture by destroying other freedoms and by creating chaos in culture as individual autonomous persons exercise their personal rights with little consideration for others. To witness may be construed to be a form of coercion, as inhibiting the freedom of persons who are not Christian, and therefore viewed as intolerant.

Some may think it may be presumptuous or even unwise to think that the conversion of culture should even be a goal for Christians. The idea does not seem to be seriously considered prior to Constantine but since then there has been some expectation that this can be the goal of Christian witness. Justin Martyr and Tatian, however, in their early apologetic writings in the defense of Christianity, talked about the superiority of Christian philosophy and morality in comparison to the culture of their era. The idea of Christianity seeking to reform culture has some practical value of course and it is not inherently wrong. It is inconceivable, at least from a purely human point of view, given the cultural and religious diversity in the Western world that Christian theological thinking could become the preferred worldview again.

Newbigin sees Augustine's new *arche*[1] as the answer to Western culture's crisis. It must be noted, however, that any worldview accepted as the *arche* of Western culture that does not have its basis in the Bible is not going to be an accurate view of reality, so culture runs the risk of basing its plausibility structure on an inadequate view of reality. If Western culture should recognize this, it may once again consider its options and Christians may be given the opportunity to witness again to the adequacy of Christ and the gospel, but in this case not from a position of power.

No doubt Western culture needs a new *arche* in much the same way it was given to Western culture during Augustine's time. However, Newbigin's dependence upon both Charles Cochrane and Michael Polanyi causes Newbigin not to see that the conversion of culture in Augustine's time was not as pervasive as Cochran, for example, may have understood it to be. There is some question and debate concerning the total effect Augustine has had on Western culture and the church. The dualism that has plagued Western culture may not have completely disappeared from culture at the time of the introduction of the new *arche* by Augustine. It is debatable that even Augustine himself, because of the influence of Neo-Platonism, still held to a form of dualism, believing that the spiritual realm, for example, is superior to the material realm. This led to negative attitudes toward the material world and the human body in the post-

---

1. See chapter 5 for a discussion of the new *arche*.

Augustinian era, with some in the Christian church equating both the material world and the human body with sin or evil.

As mentioned earlier, Newbigin blames some of the reticence of Western Christians to witness publicly on pietistic emphasis upon personal salvation which, once saved and safe, is not concerned with the salvation of cultures. The history of modern missions, however, testifies to the fact that just the opposite is true. Mission history reveals that Pietism played a key role in the beginning of the modern missionary movement and that the center of Pietism, the University of Halle, was also a training institution for missionaries. It was (and is) not only interested in the salvation of souls but also in doing compassionate and social ministry alongside evangelism. It sought to change society as well as individuals.

Newbigin was passionately disposed to the idea of organizational unity of the worldwide of the church. He gives a powerful argument for the need for the church to be unified in his book *The Reunion of the Church: A Defence of the South India Scheme Reunion*. The dream for a world-wide unified church envisioned by John R. Mott, Robert Spear, J. H. Oldham, W. A. Visser 't Hooft, and Newbigin, however, has no real possibility of ever coming about, considering the present ethnic, national, and historical divisions. If a primary prerequisite for Western culture to be converted is the organizational unity of the church, it is not likely to happen. It is hard to conceive that a massive, monolithic organization that has great power and prestige by its size and presence can only have a positive effect on the global mission of the church. It seems that organizational diversity, in the right spirit and with a unifying purpose, might be the better alternative. It might also be the most realistic. Newbigin in his own lifetime saw the ecumenical movement move into very radical social thinking and embrace ideologies that were not compatible with evangelical Christianity. With this as a part of the recent memory of the global church, there is little likelihood that greater organizational unity could bring about a greater good.

THE NEED FOR CONTEXTUALIZATION

Generally, the largest area of concern in a critical analysis of Newbigin's thought is the manner that he has chosen to reach Western culture. His theology of mission fails to go far enough in truly engaging culture. Newbigin does remind the Western church that it can easily become syncretistic, since most Western Christians are not aware of the role and influence of culture on their faith. We are reminded to be aware of the relationship between culture and Christianity and that we need to know our culture with some depth.

From a missiological point of view, however, the failure to utilize appropriate contextualization as a methodology is to ignore the reality of intercultural ministry and the wealth of important insights gained from cultural anthropology. This, I believe, is Newbigin's biggest failure. Newbigin's theological/missiological focus, as profound as it may be in the face of Western culture's acute problem, appears myopic in that he fails to see the validity of anthropological and sociological principles that have benefited missions, both ecumenical and evangelical.

Newbigin positions the church in the midst of culture and beckons it to speak in the public domain but, because of his view of epistemology and contextualization, he offers no substantial method for such a public engagement. The major hurdle standing in the way of an adequate method is his general view of culture, most specifically Western culture. His view of culture tends to be negative, which could indicate that he did not accept the insights of cultural anthropology that would allow him to see cultures in a more positive way.

Anthropology has tended to dominate missions in the last century and this has had both positive and negative results. On the negative side, it tends to reduce missions to a human science, focused almost exclusively on anthropological methodology, often reducing the influence of theology on missions. Missions should be theologically driven, not anthropologically driven. But on the positive side, it does give the missionary valuable insight into the nature and function of culture. Most missionaries remark that an anthropological study of another culture most often gives them keen insights into their own. For Newbigin, his keen insights enabled him to see the weaknesses of Western culture. However, he tends to be too negative toward Western culture. While his hope is to transform culture, he seems to want to accomplish this by being against culture. It is entirely possible that because he was focusing on correcting culture that he did not feel the need to spend a lot of time affirming its positive aspects. There are many cases in which he focuses on one point to the detriment of fully engaging another one. For example, his emphasis upon the conversion of culture dominated his thinking while all the while assuming—and therefore did not spend a lot of time talking about—personal conversion.

Putting Newbigin in Perspective

Contextualization as a term emerged from the ecumenical movement in an attempt to make theological training appropriate to the contexts of the Third World. What has become evident to missionaries and missiologists is that the church, to be truly effective, must be indigenized. It must become, to a certain degree, a church of a particular culture and not be seen as a foreign institution. The presupposition which most missionaries have worked with is that the gospel (and all that is meant by that term) must be appropriately communicated in the forms of a particular culture since there is no supra-cultural language that can be utilized in all contexts. While the truth is objective (it is outside of us and even outside of culture in that it does not ultimately reside within culture) it nevertheless must be understood and communicated within a particular culture.

It is evident that the church has struggled with how the gospel and culture relate to one another. The main concern among missionaries and missiologists is *syncretism*,[2] meaning that, in the process of being assimilated into a culture, ideas that are incompatible with Christianity will become mixed with Christian teaching. The term *contextualization* was developed as a counterpart to *syncretism*.[3] Contextualization "captures in method and perspective the challenge of relating the Gospel to cultures,"[4] but it does not go the extent of inappropriate contextualization or syncretism.

Numerous attempts have been made to define contextualization. Philippine theologian Rodrigo Tano defines contextualization generally as "the process by which the Christian is embodied and translated in a concrete historical situation."[5] He describes the desired outcome of contextualization as being "to make sure that the message and the hearer's response today are equivalent to those in the original situation."[6] Charles Taber defines contextualization as "a process, sometimes intended and sometimes unintended, by which the message which is initially alien takes on a shape more congenial to the total receptor context."[7] However, congeniality does not mean that we try to dispense with the 'offence of the

---

2. The attempt to synchronize incompatible ideas or systems. See Heideman, "Syncretism, Contextualization," 38.

3. Whiteman, "Contextualization," 2.

4. Ibid.

5. Tano, "Toward an Evangelical Asian Theology," 94.

6. Ibid., 96.

7. Taber, "The Limits," 54.

gospel." This is clearly stated in Ross Kinzler's definition of contextualization as "a process by which the Gospel not only takes on the forms and idiosyncrasies of different cultures, but also maintains a critical stance and seeks to transform them."[8]

Contextualization is the natural outcome of the stress upon indigenous principles. The indigenous principles, articulated by Henry Venn and Rufus Anderson in the nineteenth century, are what is known as the 'three selfs,' that is self-governing, self-propagating, and self-supporting.[9] The 'three self' idea means that the church bears the responsibility for growing, supporting, and governing itself. The church also bears the responsibility within particular contexts to articulate the message in an appropriate manner within that cultural context. Newbigin would certainly be aware of the indigenization principle, although his becoming a bishop in the Church of South India may indicate that he did not fully advocate, at least initially, the complete indigenization of the church in India at that particular time. Perhaps he saw it as a temporary arrangement to help the Church in its initial stages since he had such an important role in its creation.

The necessity for contextualization goes much deeper than this; it gets into complex epistemological issues. If contextualization is the attempt to communicate truth to a particular culture in a manner that would allow the hearers to understand the truth as the communicator intended it to be understood, then to a certain degree one must use the epistemology of the culture. A culture creates its own epistemological system that is compatible with its view of reality, which is the cognitive grid that superintends how one perceives and communicates. Language, with all of its concrete, abstract, conceptual, and structural functions, reflects the cultural worldview and the epistemological paradigm. What makes this significant is that all these patterns, structures and systems, are largely unconscious, and becomes, as Michael Polanyi says, a tacit dimension of knowing. He writes:

> In learning to speak, every child accepts a culture constructed on the premises of the traditional interpretation of the universe, rooted in the idiom of the groups to which it was born, and every

---

8. Kinzler, "Mission and Context," 25.
9. Jacobs, "Contextualization," 238.

intellectual effort of the educated mind will be made with this framework of reference.[10]

Newbigin would understand this and may have seen its value in the Indian context, but he does not indicate that he sees the value of contextualization in the Western context. He does, however, recognize that a form of contextualization occurred in the Bible. Contrary to his belief that the questions of culture should not set the agenda for witness, he recognizes that in the book of Acts this is precisely what happened:

> It is a striking fact, moreover, that almost all the proclamations of the gospel which are described in Acts are in response to questions asked by those outside the Church.[11]

Newbigin questions whether the program of contextualization actually solves the problem because it requires at least a provisional acceptance of the thought-world of the culture. There is no logical way, however, to argue *from* the context *to* the gospel, he says.[12] Newbigin's view of contextualization begins with the realization of the need to be sensitive to the needs of people and to understand their situation, but none of these, or even an analysis of the cultural situation based on a principle other than Scripture, should become the starting point for mission. The starting point for mission is God's revelation of himself, to which Scripture is a powerful witness.[13] Again, Newbigin misses the point. If people express a spiritual need or show some intellectual interest in the gospel, this need or interest could become the door to presenting the gospel. He wants to start with the cure before people recognize the fact that they are sick! Obviously Christians do not construct a theology of mission solely on the needs or questions of a particular culture, but certainly a theology of mission would seek to try to respond to need and answer the questions. While all Christian theology may hold to the central or core teachings of the faith, the particular shape or form of that theology may vary from culture to culture since the cultural worldview and the pressing spiritual and intellectual needs help shape that form. Indian theologians have written theology from within the Indian context and the theologies that are

---

10. Polanyi, *Personal Knowledge*, 112.
11. Newbigin, *Gospel in a Pluralist Society*, 116.
12. Newbigin, "Context and Conversion," 302.
13. Newbigin, *Gospel in a Pluralist Society*, 153–54.

produced have the flavor of the context. Certainly the fact that they are written with the Indian context and have some of the characteristics of Indian culture does not invalidate the theology. In fact, it adds to its credibility. It certainly aids in communication.

Newbigin fails to realize that the gospel was appropriately contextualized in Western culture when Augustine gave it the new *arche* or central guiding principle. He was speaking to the need in Western culture for a unifying principle that would help integrate Western culture. His call to repeat this is actually (whether he realized it or not) for another appropriate contextualization of the gospel in the West. What shape or form this would take has not yet been determined. Newbigin did not give a clear or detailed picture of his expectation, but the need is certainly something that must be taken seriously.

It is easier to criticize a culture than it is to find appropriate ways of communicating the truths of the gospel without compromise within that culture. Newbigin is inflexible at this point in relation to Western culture. To confine the approach to Western culture to just 'witness' without any serious attempt at reasonable persuasion is to ignore the valid intellectual aspect of Western persons. Without allowing the culture to set the agenda, it seems reasonable to respond to the needs of a particular culture and particular cultural questions. In Western culture particularly, there are many sincere seekers of truth who would listen to and find satisfactory a reasonable explanation of Christian truth. One need not succumb to Enlightenment epistemology, but it is not possible to write meaningful theology within the Western context without taking this heritage into consideration. The fact that Newbigin is focused on epistemology and not on ancestor worship is itself evidence of the influence of the Enlightenment even on those who speak out against it.

SOURCES OF NEWBIGIN'S DISDAIN FOR CONTEXTUALIZATION

The sources of Newbigin's fear of syncretism are most clearly Karl Barth and Hendrik Kraemer, but also W. A. Visser 't Hooft. In an article about Visser 't Hooft, Newbigin says the following:

> ... he ... saw that this ["foreign missions"] enterprise had been corrupted by the fact that Western churches were hopelessly corrupted by syncretism. They had allowed the Gospel to be con-

fused with European culture, with all kinds of philosophies and with ideologies.[14]

Newbigin's distrust for contextualization is best understood in the context of the ecumenical movement which radicalized the concept by making the political/social context the norm for theology, which to his mind is inappropriate contextualization. The fear of syncretism was no doubt fortified by the change of direction of the ecumenical movement after the International Missionary Council's Strasbourg meeting in 1960, where radically liberal and humanistic theology began to assert itself and did so subsequently through the auspices of the World Council of Churches for the rest of the century. Such inappropriate contextualization meant that theology was reshaped to promote cultural worldviews or ideology rather than Christian theology reshaping culture. Newbigin was continually distressed over what transpired as a result of the Strasbourg meeting. The dream that he shared with the early leaders of the ecumenical movement and the theological work that had been done seemed to be unappreciated and turned on its head. This turn of events caused real disappointment and frustration for Newbigin and it surfaces in his view of epistemology and contextualization. Consequently, it would seem that Newbigin did not see the need to build bridges or any possible connections with culture, at least with Western culture. Any bridge would be, in his mind, an inappropriate accommodation to pagan culture. Interestingly, while in India he preached in the streets, presumably because that was culturally appropriate. Yet he did not do the same in Britain. Further, he spent a lot of time dialoguing and studying with those connected with the Ramakrishna Mission, seemingly without fear of syncretism, yet he did not do a similar thing while in the West. He was contextualizing his methodology both to the Indian and the British contexts.

If one were to ask what missiological approach to Western culture comes out of his theological thought, one would have to say that it is confrontation—the church is to 'encounter' Western culture. The term 'encounter' can mean something benign like meeting someone unexpectedly or it can have a much stronger meaning more like a hostile confrontation. Newbigin was not hostile, but he could confront it.[15] A better way of ex-

---

14. Newbigin, "The Legacy of W. A. Visser 't Hooft," 78.

15. He uses the word 'confront' on page 9 in *Foolishness*. He writes: "From whence comes the voice that can challenge this culture on its own terms, a voice that speaks its

pressing it would be to 'engage' culture, which means to understand it and take it seriously on its own terms. The latter term would allow appropriate contextualization while Newbigin's term does not. Cultures are constantly changing, often from forces within the culture. To confront culture seems to say that it is to be confronted by someone outside culture or worse, from above it! It is possible, however, in the current understanding of the word to think of a friend confronting another out of love. Yet, this is not the impression that one receives from Newbigin's writings. In fact, the Western culture that Newbigin confronts is largely in the past. There is little engagement with contemporary persons who are driving Western culture.

The root of Newbigin's negative view of contextualization, however, appears to be his faulty view of the Enlightenment. Newbigin's major weakness is that he generalizes regarding a vast and complex era in Western history. "Anyone who writes sweepingly of the 'Enlightenment' and 'Post-Enlightenment culture' is liable," observes Vinoth Ramachandra, "to generalizations and one-sided distortions. Newbigin, unfortunately, is no exception."[16] His weakness is compounded by his failure to see that the Enlightenment was more than an epistemological struggle. His strong aversion to the contextualization of the gospel in Western culture is due to the fact that he felt that to contextualize the gospel in an Enlightenment culture was to capitulate to its demands, which he found intolerable. He sees the primary but not the total effect of the Enlightenment on Western culture to be in the area of epistemology. Even his description of the church primarily as a hermeneutical community is a very narrow view of the church. The church has the potential of being a full-blown model of appropriate contextualization. It has the potential of having a holistic impact upon culture, influencing and transforming it in multiple ways that are not possible by focusing almost exclusively on the mind.

Bert Hoedemaker, a Dutch Reformed theologian, disagrees with Newbigin's analysis of the Enlightenment, especially in regards to the comparison (or as Wainwright says, "a polarization") of Christian and modern rationalities. Christian faith has been a part of the problem in that it played a significant part in the development of culture that led to the Enlightenment. Newbigin also underestimates to what extent the

---

own language and yet confronts it with the authentic figure of the crucified . . . Christ so that it is stopped in its tracks and turned back from the way of death?" *Foolishness to the Greeks*, Newbigin (Grand Rapids: Eerdmans, 1986), 9.

16. Ramachandra, *Recovery of Mission*, 156.

Enlightenment had been ally of the Christian faith. Newbigin has tended to focus almost exclusively on the battle for truth when there were other struggles, such as for justice and liberation, which reflect negatively on the history of rationality in the West.[17]

Vinoth Ramachandra believes that Newbigin does not take some major factors that contributed to the rise of secular culture in the West into consideration. The religious wars of earlier centuries were a significant factor for the rise of secular culture in Europe in the seventeenth century. Consequently, Newbigin failed to see that it was more than just epistemology that created the post-Enlightenment culture that exists today.[18] There is more at stake than mere intellectual certitude independent of divine revelation.[19] The core issue, Ramachandra believes, is a question of the divine versus the human in almost every aspect of life. Divine action and intent are seen as antithetical to human freedom. Because of his rather concentrated focus on epistemology, Newbigin could not see that there could be other avenues to reach culture that a contextualized gospel could speak to and gain an important hearing. He failed to see that there needs to be an effective apologetic to contradict the mistaken view that God is antithetical to human freedom. Contextualization is larger than communicating within the fiduciary framework of a given culture. It can mean, for example, modeling community within society in a way that is understood and appreciated by the culture. The emphasis in this community would be the freedom they have in Christ. This would reduce the impact of the confrontational posture that some have attributed to Newbigin's view.

V. Matthew Thomas' dissertation focused on the centrality of Christ in Newbigin's theology and its relevance for inter-religious dialogue.[20] While much of his dissertation is positive toward Newbigin's contribution to mission and theology, he nevertheless criticises Newbigin at certain key points, one of which has to do with the Enlightenment and science. Thomas points to the fact that most of Newbigin's references to the Enlightenment are generally negative. "He does not," notes Thomas, "sufficiently recognise the positive contributions made to Western cul-

---

17. Hoedemaker, *Secularism and Mission*, 42–52, found in Wainwright, *Theological Life*, 385.
18. Ramachandra, *Recovery of Mission*, 159.
19. Ibid., 162.
20. Thomas, "The Centrality of Christ," 3.

ture by Enlightenment philosophy and science."[21] While Newbigin does recognise the positive contributions of the Enlightenment,[22] he believes that it is also responsible for sowing the seeds of its own demise.[23] Thomas acknowledges that Newbigin's critique of the Enlightenment is not entirely negative, and that his criticism is not of science itself, but of modern scientific culture that tends to absolutize science.[24] This is a valid criticism and has been dealt with previously.[25] Newbigin was not focused on the contributions of the Enlightenment, but on the problems it created for Western culture.

To further illustrate Newbigin's misunderstanding of Enlightenment culture that led to his downplaying of contextualization as a methodology for reaching Western culture for Christ, it must be noted that it was not just during the Enlightenment that the Christian worldview was attacked. The Christian worldview was attacked in the early centuries of the existence of the church, and some early apologists utilized cultural ideas and philosophical argument and terminology to explain and defend the Christian faith. Clearly, some degree of contextualization was understood and utilized in these early apologetic works. Vinoth Ramachandra cites Newbigin's mention of Henning Graf Reventlow's work *The Authority of the Bible and the Rise of the Modern World*.[26] Reventlow demonstrates that the humanist tradition of classical Greece and Rome began its attack on the Christian worldview far earlier than the Enlightenment or the rise of modern science. Ramachandra criticizes Newbigin for not picking up on this thesis.[27] Reventlow views do not seem to have changed Newbigin's opinion that the strongest attack on the Christian worldview began with the thought of Descartes and that Christian theologians who responded to this attack sought to counter it by resorting only to reason, revealing that they had accepted the rationalist tradition of the humanists. Newbigin sees this as a capitulation to the humanistic tradi-

---

21. Thomas, "The Centrality of Christ," 194.

22. In a lecture titled "The Gospel as Public Truth" given at Samford University's Beeson Divinity School in Alabama in June of 1997, Newbigin says that the primary benefit Western culture received from the Enlightenment was religious freedom.

23. Newbigin, *Foolishness*, 22ff. Also see, *Gospel in a Pluralist Society*, 187.

24. Thomas, "Centrality of Christ," 208–9.

25. See chapter 5 for this discussion.

26. Newbigin, *Gospel in a Pluralist Society*, 1–2.

27. Ramachandra, *Recovery of Mission*, 164.

tion. Ramachandra, however, believes that if Newbigin had expanded on Reventlow's insights, Newbigin would have had "a more nuanced critique of post-Enlightenment society."[28] Newbigin apparently does not find the Early Church's contextualized response of much value for engaging Western culture. He does not seriously consider the methodology of the second century Greek Apologists who found elements of truth in pagan religions and philosophy and utilized these elements to defend and to propagate the faith. Even Augustine, trained in the classics, utilized his training to articulate the gospel. It is quite possible that there were others who, in fact, did compromise the gospel by allowing culture to dominate their theology but this is certainly not true of all apologists. It does not make sense to reject categorically the thinking of one of the world's major civilizations (the Western world) and reduce engagement to this civilization to mere 'witness.' The Greek apologists saw the need for a greater, more difficult, and more costly engagement. The point is to truly engage culture while at the same time transcending it in order to transform it.

THE SOVEREIGNTY OF GOD AND HUMAN RESPONSIBILITY

Another possible reason for Newbigin's attitude toward contextualization is his theological over-emphasis on the responsibility of God and minimizing the role of the Christian. Newbigin talks about the Holy Spirit working in the heart of persons prior to conversion, an idea evidenced in his discussion of persons who subsequently convert to Christ but testify to the notion that the true God was working in their hearts. A balanced view would admit that persons leading these unconverted persons to Christ play a significant role in cooperation with the Holy Spirit to persuade these persons of the need to believe in Christ. Newbigin minimizes the role of humanity to mere witness rather than that of utilizing a well-informed apologetic, which would require some utilization of the rationality of culture. This further suggests that humans must be willing just to repeat the essential dogma of the Christian faith without any reference to this rationality. This implies that Christians do not have to 'do their homework' in knowing their culture and respecting it to the point of speaking to it in an understandable manner. They merely witness and expect the Holy Spirit to do the rest.

---

28. Ramachandra, *Recovery of Mission*, 164.

Grasping Truth and Reality

At the same time Newbigin insists that the Christian must seek to convince people of the superior rationality of the new plausibility structure offered by Christianity, and also must demonstrate its adequacy.[29] This clearly implies apologetics and careful contextualization, unless witness is purely a monologue without any intention of dialoguing with those who may respond. Newbigin believes that the church has the right to present its worldview alongside other worldviews and the Holy Spirit will convince persons of the superior rationality of the Christian worldview. This does not, however, reflect real engagement with the culture and does not reflect a truly biblical method. It needs to move from witness to the church being 'incarnated' in culture.

Communication theory, espoused by missiologists David Hesselgrave and Charles Kraft, acknowledge the need for the missionary communicator to take responsibility for communication. Their views have been very much a part of missiological thinking for decades. Their theological views causes them to be open to the need for appropriate contextualization, by utilizing communication principles, while Newbigin's theology causes him to see this as an inappropriate accommodation to culture.

Charles Kraft summarizes the goal for communication of the gospel in what he calls the ten principles. The first four clearly place the responsibility on the communicator:

1. The purpose of communication is to bring the receptor (R) to understand a message presented by a communicator in a way that substantially corresponds with the intent of the communicator (C).

2. What is understood is at least as dependent on how R perceives the message, as how C presents it.

3. Communicators present messages via cultural forms (symbols) that stimulate with the receptor's head meanings that each receptor shapes into the message he or she ultimately hears.

4. The communicator, to communicate the message effectively, must be receptor-oriented.[30]

A decision must be made by the communicator as to what cultural forms would best communicate the message. The point that needs to be seen is that the communicator is careful to meet the receptor where that person lives rather than expecting the receptor to have to have to learn the cul-

---

29. Newbigin, *Truth and Authority*, 53–54.
30. Kraft, *Christianity in Culture*, 147–48.

ture or worldview of the communicator to understand. Newbigin asks the unconverted person to listen to a presentation of the worldview of Christianity, be convinced of its superiority, and then choose it. Not only does this appear to be too cerebral but it implies that the Christian does not have to understand the culture of the receptor in any depth because the Holy Spirit will *automatically* make the truth known to the receptor. It releases missionaries from doing their homework.

CONTEXTUALIZATION AND THE SELF-EVIDENCING POWER OF REVELATION

Newbigin does not believe in the necessity of contextualization because of the "self-evidencing power and sublimity of revelation," which he says is due to its "intrinsic grandeur and compelling rightness."[31] There is no need of contextualization if revelation, in and of itself, is so compelling that persons do not need to have it explained. What he is not taking into consideration is the fact that he grew up in a Christian environment where he was enculturated with a particular worldview which would have given him a certain bias that would make such an epiphanal experience as the revelation of God seem to have a 'compelling rightness' to it. Further, revelation is never related to a culture except through persons who, while articulating the gospel, are inspired and guided by the Holy Spirit. The human instrument cannot be ignored in this event, because humans keep their humanity while preaching, and that implies that they will also witness to revelation in a manner generally consistent with their culture. To deny this is not to understand the dynamics of communication. Newbigin attempts to downplay that fact that Western Christians, while not advocating the fiduciary framework or plausibility structure of Western culture, will share the faith in a way distinctively Western. The question is not whether there is contextualization or not; the question is whether contextualization is appropriate or not.

It would seem that a missionary, who deals with cultures and their varying value systems and cultural expectations, would recognize that Western people would not accept such assertions of truth, however compelling they may seem, without some attempt to show their validity. In animistic cultures, for example, there must be the recognition of the power of God over evil spirits, but in Western culture, equally as valid

31. Newbigin, "Revelation," 25.

as animistic culture, people look for a logical reason to believe. Asking Western people to accept his assumptions about God, reality, and the cosmos based on the fact that they seem to have a 'compelling rightness,' may, in fact, not be compelling enough.

The same argument may be used against Newbigin's insistence that one's faith is validated if it puts one in touch with reality. Because of Newbigin's cultural upbringing, his understanding of reality, it could be argued, would have already been shaped by the early Christian influences in his life. Consequently his acceptance of the biblical view of reality would seem compelling to him since it appears to validate a view already formed in his mind. Newbigin does not attempt to address these issues. There must be a significant and detailed attempt on the part of Christians to point out how the biblical view of reality is superior to culture's view. That cannot be done just through witness.

Ultimate reality is a self-revealing God who reveals Himself not in timeless truths or abstract propositional truths *about* God, but through events, and ultimately through Jesus Christ, the incarnate Son of God. God has revealed Himself in history, which is a problem both to Indian mysticism, the Enlightenment, and any form of pietism that would discount God's revelation in actual history. That God has revealed truth through particular historical events is a defining difference, Newbigin contends, between Christian thought and Greek categories, as well as Christian thought and Eastern religions such as Hinduism.[32] While admitting this, he does not explore the implications of this idea. For God to have communicated through history means that God would have communicated through a particular culture. The gospel does not stand apart without being embedded in some culture. It is conceded that God was helping to construct a 'godly' culture for the Hebrews, but they nevertheless shared their culture generally with other nations in their region. That God would utilize culture in itself contradicts Newbigin's insistence upon somehow by-passing Western culture's rationality. Newbigin's view of revelation seems one-sided.

Interestingly, Newbigin does not talk about 'the Word of God' as the substantive words of God given to humanity. Revelation is focused upon God's acts in history that have been recorded in the Scripture, not to the discourses of God to humanity as he works within history. These words

---

32. Newbigin, *Other Side*, 51.

God spoke about himself, his Kingdom, and his purpose are broader than the 'acts' of God to which Newbigin refers, and are more substantive in that they provide explanation of the meaning of these acts.

Contextualization has generally focused on the communication of the substantive aspects of Christianity such as dogma, something which Newbigin avoids since he does not wish to subject Christian dogma to Enlightenment rationality. Although he does not specifically state it, Newbigin is actually advocating a different form of contextualization. He correlates his emphasis upon the acts of God in history with his emphasis upon the church as the hermeneutical community that witnesses to the gospel. This may well be his attempt at a more dynamic form of contextualization, one which focuses more on the living organism of the church living in culture rather than focusing on the contextualization of words.

The above realization nullifies Elaine Graham and Heather Walton's assertion regarding Newbigin's view of revelation. Graham and Walton say that Newbigin believes that values come from an *a priori* reality, given to humanity through revelation. They criticize Newbigin for believing that truth is simply the apprehension of this *a priori* reality, which is authenticated in knowing and not in being. Knowing, for them, is following the "Way," and not to be found within a body of knowledge, something that is a part of the Gnostic tradition.[33] Apparently Graham and Walton have misunderstood Newbigin because nowhere does he ever say that knowing is 'found within a body of knowledge.' Knowing, for Newbigin, is defined primarily, though not entirely, as a personal relationship with a Living God. Good theology, they insist, constantly affirms "a notion of the Divine as fundamentally embodying 'Truth through Being.'"[34] Graham and Walton think that Newbigin's focus on epistemology is, therefore, not in step with emerging theology.[35] His theology is in fact based on truth as given to humanity through God's revelation, ultimately through the Person Jesus Christ.

Graham and Walton are correct, however, to criticize Newbigin for his failure to recognize the ontological aspects of what he is saying. Even though Newbigin emphasizes that truth comes through relationship with God (certainly implying an ontological aspect to this knowing), he

---

33. Graham and Walton, "A Walk on the Wild Side," 5.
34. Ibid., 4.
35. Ibid., 6.

remains focused on epistemology, which seems to imply that he is interested in substantive epistemology actualized in dogma, when in fact his epistemology is rooted in relationship. If Newbigin were to be fully ontological it would be necessary for him to discuss how the being of God is manifested in the beings of his people. This implies a discussion of the topic of God's holiness and how God's holiness becomes an aspect of the Christian's life. He does not pursue this line of thinking, which is unfortunate since it would be a logical conclusion of his thinking and could have led him into a discussion of how God's holiness could be contextualized into contemporary Western society. This should have factored into his thinking about the church. More than a hermeneutical community, the church is to be a sanctified community.

LIMITATIONS TO NEWBIGIN'S EPISTEMOLOGY

Newbigin's epistemology is focused on relational knowing rather than on substantive informational knowing (like facts or dogma or propositional truth). His dogma is presupposed and is verified by a relationship to God. Therefore, is it necessary to believe before knowing, thus making contextualization unnecessary. The question that arises is what does Newbigin think we believe before we know? It is obvious that we must have some understanding preliminary truth on which to have belief. Augustine believed this to be true. Some awareness of facts, dogma, or propositional truth that could have come from witness or story is necessary in order to believe.

Another possible reason for Newbigin's disdain for contextualization is that Newbigin's epistemology is eschatological.[36] The question centers upon the issue of proof and objective truth. At one point Newbigin uses the analogy of a witness in a court as an example of what Christians must do in this present age. The witness cannot be judged to be true until the end of the trial when the judge gives the verdict. The implication is that the testimony of the Christian is provisional until the end when the God validates the testimony through the final verdict (the judgment).[37] To ask for another kind of proof except the testimony of the witness is to 'not understand what is going on.' Foust says that Newbigin is agnostic concerning evidence or empirical demands until everything is validated at the end

---

36. Foust, "Epistemology," 162.
37. Newbigin, *Other Side*, 50.

of time.³⁸ It seems more probable, however, that some empirical evidence would need to be given to corroborate the story of the witness in an effort to establish credibility. This would imply the need for empirical proof to be used by the Christian to corroborate the claims of testimony. Newbigin does not believe this is necessary. However, empirical corroboration is more than provisional truth. Our understanding of it may be provisional but it is still actual truth, valid not only in that it corroborates truth but that it enters into the legitimate desire to validate belief on something that seems reasonable. The desire for some empirical verification is reasonable and no one comes to Christ without some form of evidence to substantiate the value of believing in Christ. His analogy supports an agnosticism that is both detrimental and unnatural to the seeker. Many people come to Christ, for example, based on what they have seen as Christ transforms the lives of other persons. Such empirical evidence is indeed significant and not to be denied. Sometimes, seeing *is* believing! This agnosticism seriously weakens Newbigin's ability to speak to the West and is a possible reason why he was not interested in contextualization. Contextualization would be an apologetic attempt to make a case for the gospel in the present context. If God is self-authenticating (through the work of the Holy Spirit) and full understanding does not come until the end of time, there is no need in Newbigin's mind for contextualization for much the same reasons that he does not embrace apologetics.

CONTEXTUALIZATION AND FIDEISM

Looking at Newbigin's position regarding contextualization from another perspective, one might question whether Newbigin is a *fideist* and if this has anything to do with his attitude toward contextualization. Fideism is essentially a repudiation of rationalism, the assertion that reason cannot prove the truths of religion. Consequently, believers must fall back upon faith alone. John Polkinghorne defines *fideism* as "the bare assertion that something is so as a matter of faith, [thus] needing no element of rational inquiry for its support."³⁹ Utilizing Polkinghorne's definition, Newbigin would be a fideist. This has implications for apologetics and also con-

---

38. Foust, "Epistemology," 162. Newbigin mentions this on occasion. One cannot be absolutely sure (with absolute certainty resting on infallible proofs derived from *reason alone*) that one's faith is not misdirected. The assurance of faith will be *absolutely* verified at the coming of Christ.

39. Polkinghorne, *Reason and Reality*, 50.

textualization. If Newbigin repudiates the rationality of Western culture, then contextualization is not an option, for contextualization requires some use of a culture's rational system to be understood.

However, Newbigin thinks differently. Newbigin defines *fideism* as belief that becomes a sufficient substitute for knowledge.[40] He defends himself against the charge of *fideism* in an article entitled "Certain Faith: What Kind of Certainty?"[41] He gives a three-fold answer to the charge. The first answer is that "the charge appears to rest on the illusion that there is available to us a kind of knowledge which does not rest on faith commitments." For Newbigin, faith is not a substitute for knowledge, but becomes the pathway to knowledge. What Newbigin asserts is that all epistemological systems begin with certain beliefs that are unverifiable, but become the basis from which systems are built. These core beliefs become the way to knowledge. Reason is functional in that it merely works with what is 'given,' and develops the system in a logical, coherent manner. These core beliefs, however, remain uncontested. Newbigin, therefore, does not repudiate reason, but he does recognize its limitations. He recognizes that the basis of sound epistemology is a faith in some uncontested system of belief which determines, to a great degree, a person's epistemology.[42] Consequently, based upon this argument, Newbigin would see no need for contextualization because in the end it does not matter. Persons come to Christ by faith and then begin the process of changing their worldview to fit the Christian worldview. It is both the conversion and transformation (in the sense of re-formation) of the mind. Newbigin does not see the role of contextualization as being necessary to this scenario in the same way that he sees apologetics as unnecessary. He does not see the Christian worldview as in any way connected with culture.

Newbigin's emphasis on faith that precedes knowledge seems fairly straightforward until one asks in what is one supposed to believe before gaining this knowledge. Does this statement mean that one comes to faith in Christ and then begins to assimilate the Christian worldview through the hermeneutical community? Is this initially faith in God or in a set of presuppositions, or both? Who is this Christ? The last question, because of the critical role it plays in conversion, requires a substantive response.

---

40. Newbigin, *Truth to Tell*, 30.
41. Newbigin, "Certain Faith," 348–49.
42. Ibid.

Putting Newbigin in Perspective

Newbigin utilizes the analogy of the scientific community having faith before they are able to do their work and the fact that they approach their work with certain presuppositions that affect their work. The analogy would suggest that what Newbigin means is that before we can know we must accept (by faith) the Christian worldview. Newbigin also says that we must have faith in God, which opens the door to knowing that is essentially personal. It is not clear exactly what he means when he uses the phrase that 'one must believe before one can know.' If one must believe the presuppositions of the Christian worldview, then these presuppositions must be presented in a manner that is understandable within Western culture. If one merely believes in God in a relational manner, it seems that some form of explanation is needed to describe this God in whom one to believe. Actually, the analogy of the scientific community shows some realization on Newbigin's part that a form of contextualization is needed. He pictures the church functioning in a similar way to the scientific community in regard to knowing.

In regards to faith, Newbigin is careful to say that "we are not talking about a kind of 'blind leap of faith,'" but "we are talking of a rational response to a personal calling." This also implies no need for contextualization. It is based on an objective relationship with another Person, not on a cleverly devised contextualized message. It would appear to transcend culture. One might question in what way it is a "rational response." Newbigin seems to be saying that it is an 'intelligent' or 'reasonable' response based on the drawing power of the Person who is calling. However, what is not clear but must certainly be a part of the meaning is that the response must be 'rational' in the sense that the person being called must know something of the Person calling. There must be substantive content that defines the Person as the Son of God, the Savior of humanity, etc. This means that the communication, the plea of God to come to him, must be understandable within a particular culture and usually through the mediation of witness. It is impossible not to do some contextualization as one bears witness about God. The question is not if we will contextualize but if we do so appropriately. A rational response takes place as the response to a reasonably understood call.

Newbigin believes that "the charge [of fideism] implies that the rational arguments of philosophy are more to be relied upon than the testimony of the apostolic witnesses to the events of the Gospel." Newbigin would ask if something would be considered to be true only if it is corroborated by philosophical argument. One must ask Newbigin, in return, what is lost if one's testimony *is*, in fact, corroborated by philosophical argument? Just because one's testimony is corroborated by philosophy or some other form of evidence does not necessarily invalidate the testimony. It does not necessarily mean that philosophical arguments are relied on *more* than testimony; they could, in fact, be complementary. An appropriately contextualized rational argument can be quite compelling depending upon the person who is speaking.

CONTEXTUALIZATION AND APOLOGETICS

Newbigin's reticence toward contextualization has the same basis as his reluctance to utilize apologetic arguments. He fears that by utilizing culture's rationality, one runs the serious risk of compromising the gospel. The reality is, however, that a person cannot fully escape utilizing a culture's rationality (at least in part) if one communicates the gospel in that culture. Newbigin sees contextualization and apologetics as forms of capitulation to the inappropriate demands of Western culture for some form of verification that the message is from God. Newbigin is correct to believe that the generally normal need for verification has taken on gigantic and radical proportions in Western culture, thus making it a barrier to belief. However, few people would make life-changing decisions without some assurance that the choice they are making is valid. That usually requires some form of corroboration or validation by some authority.

God is, of course, the highest authority and if the source of one's beliefs is God, the ultimate source of knowledge, how then, Newbigin asks, could these beliefs be subject to some supposed outside verification, since God being God would be subject to nothing?[43] Newbigin is assuming by this question that outside verification is somehow necessarily held in a superior position to God. Newbigin is also assuming that verification of one's beliefs through careful reasoning or some evidence is intrinsically wrong. If God is the creator of the world and the mind, it seems reasonable that the things of the world and the reasoning capacity of the mind could be used to corroborate the truth of Him who created them without assuming that they have been placed in a superior position. An attempt

---

43. Polkinghorne writes: "If there is a God, who possesses aseity (being-in-itself), then he is self-authenticating; he does not call for evaluation by any other criteria." *Reason and Reality*, Polkinghorne (London: SPCK, 1991), 59.

to corroborate through reasonable means is the correct use the capacity that God has given humans to discern from whom certain assertions come and how they are to be evaluated. Contextualization is an attempt to make culture aware that the call of God is a reasonable consideration for reasonable persons.

Graham and Walton accuse Newbigin of advocating a 'leap of faith' into Christian discipleship, which they define in Gnostic terms, as a people with special knowledge which excludes others who do not have this special knowledge. They accuse Newbigin of representing, "at the very least . . . a vision of a private sectionalized knowledge-elite who cannot dialogue with others."[44] Newbigin responds strongly to the suggestion by Graham and Walton that his position requires a 'leap of faith.' His response is unequivocal: "I have never used and never would use the phrase 'leap of faith.' Christian discipleship is not an irrational leap into the unknown. It is a personal response to a personal call from Him who is the Word made flesh. It is responsible commitment."[45] But he does use the term. He talks about an imaginative leap of faith when he describes the paradigm shift that takes place when new data requires scientists to make such an imaginative leap to a new paradigm. It is, however, not a 'blind' or an irrational leap.[46] The question must be asked how is one to determine, if apologetics and contextualization are dismissed out of hand, whether their response is a "reasonable commitment." Graham and Walton's statement about the inability to dialogue reveals that others note the same tendency in Newbigin toward pronouncement and proclamation but with no intent to dialogue with culture. It is difficult to know what Graham and Walton mean by dialogue, but from an evangelical viewpoint it would mean, at the very least, to be able to listen to another point of view, but also be able to give a reasonable account one's own belief. This implies apologetics and opens the door for a contextualized message that would speak to the dialogue partner. The minds of Western culture would require some explanation as well as witness. There are those who would respond only to witness, but this would not be enough for those who are pursuing truth with their minds as well as their hearts.

---

44. Graham and Walton, "A Walk on the Wild Side," 7.
45. Newbigin, "The Gospel and Our Culture," 3.
46. Newbigin, *Gospel in a Pluralist Society*, 59–60.

Newbigin tries to rule out any evidences whatsoever to be used in support of witness. His reasoning is that the truth needs no corroboration, at least not by arguments from reason dictated by culture. He utilizes philosophers of science, sociologists, and others to substantiate what he is saying. He is, whether he realizes it or not, somewhat accommodating to Western culture that prefers to be persuaded by reasonable argument. He needs to be more accommodating at this point even though Western culture does not limit itself to reasonable argument alone; it can be convinced by a compelling story as well. Both methods of communication have their place.

To press the point further, Newbigin relies on the thinking of American Jesuit historian Michael Buckley for his belief that Christians failed when they used reasoned arguments against the onslaught of Enlightenment rationalism. Buckley, according to Vinoth Ramachandra, believes that religion abandoned what was true to its nature in the face of the humanistic attack and resorted to vindicating itself through philosophy.[47] Christianity, therefore, defended itself with everything except that which was truly Christian. There was no consideration of anything Christological, only the attempt to prove the reasonableness of Christianity through philosophy. Buckley's conclusion is that at that point Christianity surrendered its own competence.[48] Newbigin strongly concurs with this assertion and builds his argument concerning the compromise of the Western church around it. Newbigin is overly dependent on Buckley at this point. To try to prove the reasonableness of Christianity in the context which highly values philosophy and reasoned argument is a good strategy for the church, as long as it did not fall prey to the assumptions of Western philosophy or compromise essential doctrines. It is not necessary for the church to utilize rational argument only, but it seems unwise to rule it out categorically.

CRITERIA FOR JUDGING CHRISTIANITY TO BE TRUE

A part of the consideration of Newbigin's epistemology which affects his views of contextualization and apologetics is his insistence upon no outside standard or criteria to evaluate or validate Christianity. While

---

47. See Buckley's book *At the Origins of Modern Atheism* for a more detailed discussion of this question.

48. Ramachandra, *Recovery of Mission*, 164–65.

this may be valid, it does not mean that there is no way of evaluating its truthfulness. Vinoth Ramachandra cites evangelical philosopher Harold Netlund as one who criticizes Newbigin's view that there is no rational criteria by which one can judge Christianity to be true. More specifically, it is Newbigin's view that since all reason is based upon a prior faith commitment, it is impossible to demonstrate whether the gospel is right or wrong by some supposed neutral norms of rationality. Newbigin, explains Vinoth Ramachandra, believes the starting point of the gospel is the resurrection of Jesus Christ, God's act of new creation, and that there are no philosophical viewpoints or truths superior to this idea, so there is nothing more ultimate or fundamental by which to judge the gospel.[49] Netlund, however, desires to posit an 'objective, non-arbitrary criteria' by which the truth claims of various religious worldviews, including Christianity. He believes Newbigin opens the door to theological *fideism* by rejecting "a rational, context independent adjudication between conflicting cognitive claims."[50]

Netlund sets up ten principles for the evaluation of a worldview, such as non-contradiction, coherence, and internal consistency. Netlund believes these principles to be universally valid but, as Ramachandra points out, certain schools of Hinduism and Buddhism accept these logical rules only to prove their inadequacy in defining the ultimate experience. Ramachandra notes that Netlund's principles are culturally conditioned and not as neutral as he might think.[51] Consequently, Ramachandra ends up defending Newbigin and criticizing Netlund:

> Netlund's confident claim that the ten basic principles he has enunciated are part of the 'stuff of reality' and are 'independent of the neutral states and psychological processes of any human being' is extremely naïve.[52]

Ramachandra believes that there must be a distinction made between the grounds for belief and psychological certainty. While he agrees with Newbigin's position regarding this distinction, he believes that Newbigin fails to put enough emphasis on the role of evidence. Certainty or assurance is given to persons by the Holy Spirit, and this is not a matter of pure

---

49. Ramachandra, *Recovery of Mission*, 168.

50. Ibid. See also Netlund, *Dissonant Voices*, 199. The last phrase is Ramachandra's restatement of Netlund's position.

51. Ibid., 169.

52. Ibid.

logic. It is of equal importance, says Ramachandra, to realize that the Holy Spirit is not a substitute for evidence. "We can," writes Ramachandra, "articulate grounds for belief in God's self-disclosure in Jesus at the same time as we acknowledge our indebtedness to the Holy Spirit's illumination."[53]

This is a valid point, I believe, in view of the previous discussion about Western people needing some evidence that an assertion is true before believing it. It does not have to be either/or; God can use well articulated apologetics as he speaks to the heart of the person and he can make an appropriately contextualized message speak to the mind.

Newbigin's belief that culture's prior faith commitment to something besides Christianity invalidates the use of cultural ideas and its rationality to contextualize does point to the risk of utilizing a culture's rationality. It also fails to consider that missionaries have used concepts and vocabulary of pagan cultures as a means of communicating the gospel and even translating Scripture, which is probably the basic form of contextualization, without compromising the essential teaching of the gospel. It also fails to consider that no human culture is perfectly engineered to be utilized for the sharing the gospel so contextualization, as risky as it may be, is a constant aspect of any indigenous church.

NEWBIGIN'S VIEW OF SCIENCE AS A BARRIER TO CONTEXTUALIZATION

Newbigin desires the conversion of Western culture and, it could be reasoned from his writings, the demise of scientism. Because of his overdependence upon Michael Polanyi, Newbigin strongly reacted to what he perceived to be a threat from science in regard to what society would see as ultimate authority. While science may have overstated its own value and worth in its enthusiasm for progress, it has also recognized its limitations. Newbigin's generalizations about science, its methodologies and intentions, were an over-reaction to the popularity of the sciences in the universities to the detriment of theology (as he perceived it) in the early and middle parts of the twentieth century.

He was especially dogmatic against any thought that scientists approached their work with neutrality. Scientists, however, generally recognize that they approach their work with certain assumptions; it was a part of the tradition that was accumulative and helped to guide scientists in

---

53. Ramachandra, *Recovery of Mission*, 171.

their decisions and evaluation of data. Scientists, in spite of this tradition, try to approach their work with an open mind and as much as possible an unbiased manner so as not to cause them to overlook something new. This seems reasonable, yet Newbigin sees this as somehow a denial of God's existence. They are forced, he thinks, to become methodological atheists. This is not true, of course, for many scientists are Christians and they do not have to set God aside to be scientists. It can be assumed that the vast majority of work scientists do has little to do with God being a part of the equation. However, there are aspects where certain beliefs about the material world held by some Christians may need to be amended if there is absolute evidence that shows them to be in error. This would be an updated version of the question of the earth rotating around the sun.

Knowing is personal and, in the context of Newbigin's view, vertical. It is God revealing himself to us from heaven. He does this by revealing himself to us through historical events. It is personal knowledge because God is revealing himself to persons, yet it is true and factual knowledge. At the same time, Newbigin uses science as an analogy for theological knowledge. There is a scientific tradition of knowing that comes from facts ascertained by previous experiments, found to be true, and passed forward. This knowing is on a horizontal level. New information which would require an imaginative leap would still be on the horizontal level. With Newbigin's definition of truth as being personal and from God, it would seem to exclude scientific discovery from being truth, unless he would admit that there can be truth that comes from God that does not come by special revelation but through scientific discovery. Newbigin (like Barth and Kraemer) has no place for natural theology, but could not the Holy Spirit impress upon the minds of persons that the rational world and the rationality of the scientist could in fact be the result of a rational God who created the world and the scientist with rationality? It would be God using reason and the presence of rationality in the universe to convince the mind of the scientist. There seems to be no place in Newbigin for truth that comes from the cosmos to support the idea of a Creator.

Newbigin's view of science or scientism led him to dismiss what may be one of the most profound ways evangelicals can reach Western culture: through dialogue with science. T. F. Torrance has maintained a critical and positive dialogue with science and scientist/theologian John Polkinghorne is publishing compelling books that deal with ideas and interests that are both theological and scientific. Science and theology are not seen as adversarial. This is, in my estimation, a powerful attempt to contextualize the Christian faith in a positive and meaningful manner. In an animist culture, theological books and discussions will reflect animist issues. In Western culture, theological books would reflect a dialogue with science, or some other area pertinent to the Western context.

NEWBIGIN'S VIEW ON DESCARTES AND LOCKE AS A BARRIER TO CONTEXTUALIZATION

Newbigin's reaction against both Descartes and Locke lead him to a distorted undervaluing of reason, which has affected his epistemology and consequently his views of contextualization and apologetics. Stephen N. Williams believes that Newbigin did not fully understand what Descartes was doing and gave Descartes too much credit for what followed. Williams states that Descartes was seeking, in fact, to champion truth against atheism and professed 'the supreme certitude of faith.' In Descartes' essay on "The Principles of Philosophy," he states that the light of reason "is to be trusted only to the extent that it is compatible with divine revelation." [54] He continues to say that even though reason may not appear to validate what is true, "we must still put our entire faith in divine authority rather than in our own judgment."[55] Williams has pointed out what I believe is a flaw in Newbigin's argumentation in that he tends to choose one aspect of a person's position and focuses upon it until it has a life of its own, detached from its original context. Newbigin also presumes that Descartes and others have a bias *against* faith and *for* reason, and consequently reads these philosophers with that view in mind. It leads to an unbalanced interpretation of their writings.

Vinoth Ramachandra believes that Newbigin makes a mistake in regards to his interpretation of John Locke. Ramachandra says that Newbigin is fond of quoting the phrase "faith is a persuasion of our own minds short of knowledge" (from Locke's *A Third Letter on Toleration*). Newbigin interprets Locke's statement as an example of dualistic epistemology, but the context of Locke's writing is not epistemological, rebuts Ramachandra, but political.[56] Ramachandra interprets Locke's words and intentions in a more positive light:

54. Williams, *Revelation and Reconciliation*, 14.
55. Ibid.
56. Ramachandra, *Recovery of Mission*, 159.

> We know from his other works that Locke did not identify faith with 'subjective opinion' nor confine reason to the objectively demonstrable. He saw faith in divine revelation as apprehending cognitively what reason could not apprehend, and he sought to secure epistemological principles by which religious beliefs could be commanded as rationally unimpeachable.[57]

Stephen Williams concurs with Ramachandra on Newbigin's misunderstanding of Locke but locates the source of Newbigin's error in following Michael Polanyi's lead in believing that Locke's mistake was in elevating demonstrative knowledge at the expense of faith.[58] Williams believes that the theological use of Michael Polanyi's thought led to an indictment not of Descartes but of Locke.[59] According to Williams, Locke, through all his writings, sought ways to set up a relationship of knowledge and faith.[60] Williams explains:

> Locke seeks to give religious belief a status that permits it to apprehend cognitively what reason cannot apprehend, to do so on unimpeachably rational grounds and to apply this permission to the most important issue going, namely religion.[61]

What Locke is doing is connecting faith with propositions 'above reason' (as distinguished from those 'according to reason'), and therefore cannot be attained by rational deduction.[62]

Newbigin's misinterpretation of the thinking of both Descartes and Locke cause him to distrust the use of reason in coming to faith. It led to downplay the possibility that God could use apologetic argument and appropriate contextualization of Christian faith to lead people to Christ. It led to an over-emphasis on the work of God in the lives of people while minimizing the Christian's responsibility to fully engage culture. It led to a fear of syncretism that caused Newbigin not to be able to press two very powerful methodologies, apologetics and contextualization, into service for converting Western culture.

---

57. Ramachandra, *Recovery of Mission*, 159.
58. Williams, *Revelation and Reconciliation*, 25.
59. Ibid., 23.
60. Ibid., 27.
61. Ibid., 43.
62. Ibid., 33.

UTILIZING CONTEXTUALIZATION FOR REACHING WESTERN CULTURE

It is difficult to see how one is to engage culture (or even 'confront' it) without communicating with it in some significant manner. All cultures have negative and positive, or good and bad aspects if one views them theologically. Western culture would not be an exception to this. It is necessary to challenge Newbigin's mostly negative position by stating that a more positive approach is not only possible but necessary. Writers of the volume *Christian Mission in Western Society*,[63] for example, are proponents of an 'authentic inculturation [contextualization] of the gospel' within Western culture, seeing Western culture in the same manner that missionaries would view other cultures, therefore desiring to communicate within and dealing with specific issues that are a part of that particular culture. This is what missionaries do, and a missionary engagement of Western culture must include 'inculturation.' The thesis of the book is that "all contributors, to some extent, reflect a positive desire to inculturate the gospel authentically and open up a productive dialogue between mission theology and Western societies."[64] The writers are oriented around the following theme: "What mission might look like when aspects of that culture are appreciated and valued."[65] This approach would certainly provide a basis for positive communication of the gospel in a culture already suspicious of the Christian faith. Graeme Smith's view of The Gospel and Our Culture movement is that it is hostile toward Western culture and holds that the gospel cannot be inculturated within Western culture.[66] If Christians perceive the movement in this manner, certainly non-Christians would see it the same way.

There have always been missionaries who have denigrated local cultures because of the assumption that a particular culture is totally pagan. There have also been those missionaries who have made every effort to appreciate cultures other than their own and have encouraged converts to appreciate their own culture, with the realization that certain aspects of culture will need transformation. For example, one motto floating around among Western missionaries in Asia in the 1980s said that it was the de-

---

63. Simon Barrow and Graeme Smith, eds.
64. Wooten, "Foreword," 9.
65. Graeme Smith, "Introduction," 12.
66. Ibid., 22.

sire of missionaries to create a church which was 'fully Asian and fully Christian.' There was recognition that not everything Asian was contrary to the gospel and that Christianity there would take on an Asian flavor. It appears that when Newbigin turns his attention toward the West, this cultural appreciation is either absent or subdued.

Newbigin's approach of mere witness to the gospel seems rather simplistic, which does not take seriously the complexity of the culture. Simon Barrow makes this point quite succinctly:

> For these reasons, many would suggest, it can no longer be said straightforwardly (if it ever could) that the 'missionary task' with regard to the Bible is 'just to proclaim it'—as if its contents stood uncomplicatedly apart from the cultures in which they are transmitted and read. What Western Christians are confronted with instead is the theological task of discerning and performing the purposes of God amid the varied narratives of a visual, interactive, multiscriptural, intertextual society.[67]

This is a more positive and productive approach to Western culture.

Another alternative to the general way of doing contextualization that may well be an acceptable alternative to the traditional manner of doing contextualization is Paul Hiebert's idea of critical contextualization. Paul Hiebert's article on "Critical Contextualization"[68] discusses the implications of culture in relation to contextualization. Another critical factor which enters into this discussion is what Harvie Conn calls the emergence of Consciousness Two—the move of Western culture away from positivist science to post-modern science, and the awareness of global cultures, with the concomitant awareness of cultural relativism. In colonial times, Western culture and especially West science were seen as universally valid and a part of the (necessary) civilizing aspect of culture, but a new awareness and a new appreciation for the diverse cultures of the world led to a different situation in missions. It has had both a positive and negative effect on contextualization. In an attempt to make Christianity not seem foreign, there have been some attempts to contextualize the gospel inappropriately. This is what Newbigin believes is happening in Western culture. The process of contextualization is, of course, riddled with many dangers.

67. Barrow, "Afterword," 243.
68. See Hiebert, "Critical Contextualization," 104–12. It is also a chapter in Hiebert's book, *Anthropological Reflections*, 75–92.

Hiebert's critical contextualization moves the discussion one step beyond its traditional limits and allow for a truly appropriate form of contextualization in Western culture. Unlike Newbigin, Hiebert believes it is good for the church in each culture to develop its own indigenous form of Christianity in an appropriate manner, but as a global church we cannot be satisfied with just that. There is great benefit to being mutually interdependent with the global church, especially in the areas of biblical and theological studies. In relation to culture, the discussion turns to "metacultural grids" where we can compare and translate between various items in various cultures. The idea of 'complementarity' emerges, where each culture is seen to be a map or blueprint of that particular culture, but will have areas of overlap and be complementary to other cultures. In order to have a more adequate view of reality, we need to see it from diverse viewpoints and from the variety of perspectives. This would also ensure that the gospel is not captured by any particular culture and that would safeguard biblical truths.

Hiebert advocates "critical realism" as a new perspective that is emerging in the area of epistemology. In attempting to overcome the objectivism of positivistic science (discredited by Michael Polanyi in his book *Personal Knowledge*) and subjectivism, critical realism affirms both the objective and subjective nature of knowledge. This is close to what Newbigin advocated and could prove to be very helpful in the missionary endeavor to reach Western culture.

Hiebert sees the use of theories as a positive contribution to the discussion of contextualization. Theories, like maps, are complementary and therefore one map does not cancel another out, but may contribute information that can be utilized by another map and also in the development of a metatheoretical model. Metatheoretical models can be developed to compare the various maps and help to translate meaning from one map to another or one culture to another.[69]

Hiebert articulates the steps to critical contextualization with the first step being the exegesis of the culture, which means the uncritical gathering of information about the beliefs and customs of the people. The purpose of step one is to understand. The second step is the exegesis of Scripture and construction of the hermeneutical bridge. Hiebert has an excellent description of this step:

---

69. Hiebert, "Critical Contextualization," 109.

> The leader must also have a metacultural framework that enables him or her to translate the biblical message into the cognitive, affective, and evaluative dimensions of another as culture. This step is crucial, for if the people do not clearly grasp the biblical message originally intended, they will have a distorted view of the gospel. This is where the pastor or missionary, along with theology, anthropology, and linguistics, has the most to offer in an understanding of biblical truth and in making it known in other cultures. While the people must be involved in the study of Scripture, so that they grow in their own abilities to discern truth, the leader must have the metacultural grids that enable him or her to move between cultures. Without this, biblical meanings will often be forced to fit the local cultural categories. The result is the distortion of the message.[70]

The last element in this process of critical communication is to have a critical response to the data. It means to evaluate the culture in light of biblical understandings. From this critical evaluation one can embrace, reject, modify, substitute, or create new symbols depending on the result of the evaluation and the needs that come forward.[71] The model of critical contextualization, I believe, is a positive alternative to Newbigin's reticence to utilize cultural tools to communicate and explain the gospel.

Hiebert's model reinforces a number of truths about the relationship between Christianity and culture that missiologists have discovered: One, effective communication of the gospel involves a clear understanding of culture and the dynamics of culture in communication. Two, effective communication of the gospel cannot be accomplished without an understanding of cultural forms and patterns, which carry meaning in culture. Three, we must communicate universal and eternal truths in particular and temporal language forms. Four, culture has always played a significant role in the receiving of revelation (in oral and written form) and in communication of the gospel. So, we can say that culture has played a role in God's self-disclosure in human history. Five, that there has always been and continues to be a mutual relationship between the gospel and culture, which has a mutual effect. The gospel is affected by culture in the areas of language (forms and symbols of concepts) and methods of communication (the methods used to convey and relay messages in culture). The gospel affects culture when it confronts evil in culture. The gospel plants

---

70. Hiebert, "Critical Contextualization, 109–10.
71. Ibid., 110.

biblical ideas, concepts, and morality in a culture and can cause cultural transformation (on various scales of magnitude). The gospel and culture are always in creative tension. The gospel must not be captured by culture even though culture seeks to incorporate everything into its system.

This view of the relationship between the gospel and culture is a standard belief in contemporary missions. It is difficult to understand why Newbigin would not see them as applicable to Western culture.

BEYOND NEWBIGIN

Newbigin has made a substantial contribution in reminding Christians of the need to recognize that conversion is more than a subjective, spiritual experience; it is also a change of mind. This means that to be fully Christian, Christians must come to the point of intellectual apprehension of the Christian worldview. However, he did not go far enough in explaining the breadth of his vision or how it would be accomplished, at least in sufficient detail. With this in mind, it is necessary to move beyond Newbigin, perhaps jumping forward not only from what he said, but what he implied.

What is needed is a more holistic and more comprehensive methodology for reaching Western culture. It should be multifaceted. Far from dismissing revival and personal spiritual experience, which Newbigin tends to do, it is necessary for Western culture to experience serious spiritual rebirth, something that would bring new life to a dying culture. What needs to be envisioned is not just an emotional renewal but a true transformation of the spirit of Westerners that would bring about a cultural reformation that would radically change the heart and inclinations of culture. There needs to be emphasis upon spiritual growth and maturity, combining an emphasis on sanctification with one on conversion. God has elected persons and nations to be the avenue of winning others. In every instance of such election, the one characteristic that was required of those chosen was that they be holy. God wants to be represented by a holy people, because they would truly represent his nature and that of itself would be one of the ways God would reach the West. The revival envisioned must, of course, start with the church. T. F. Torrance, while discussing the role of a realist evangelical theology, points to renewal as a starting point:

Putting Newbigin in Perspective

> Hence, a realist evangelical theology which in responsible commitment to the nature of God's self-revelation is church-oriented, must seek to engage the church in repentant rethinking of all its interpretation, preaching, and teaching, although the onto-relational character of theology implies that this cannot really be done without a radical renewal of the whole interpersonal life and mission of the church.[72]

A radical renewal of the church is the place to begin when seeking to revive culture.

This brings to mind the great Korean Revival of 1905 that began when missionaries banded together for prayer and confession. It had such a profound affect upon Korean Christian workers that they emulated the missionaries and revival broke out in the Korean church which has lasted for a hundred years. Korea's traditional anti-foreign sentiments, its desire to remain isolated from the rest of the world, and the dominance of Buddhism made it the least likely place for such a revival. Yet, evangelical Christianity continues to grow in number and strength and has the potential of reshaping South Korea's traditional worldview.[73]

Os Guinness is positive about the possibilities that modern culture affords the church. He says that "there are further aspects of modernization that represent extraordinary opportunities for mission."[74] Modern culture seeks to be an open culture and that very openness means that it cannot be a totally closed to ideologies or religions that may desire to express themselves.[75] Guinness believes that modernity offers a special challenge to revival, especially with its overly individualized form of faith and the belief that revival would come primarily through the effort of Christians, rather than dependence upon God. He is optimistic about God's ability to bring about revival. He says that "while many Christians no longer have a practical expectation of revival, those who count on God's sovereignty over modernity have every reason to look to God for revival again."[76]

---

72. Torrance, *Reality and Evangelical Theology*, 47.

73. Having served as a missionary in Korea for seven years between from 1977–1986, I saw firsthand the continuing effects of the great revival of the early twentieth century both on the church and on the nation.

74. Guinness, "Mission modernity," 331.

75. Ibid., 332.

76. Ibid., 331.

Newbigin does not seem to consider the role of corporate and concerted prayer on behalf of Western culture as a part of its conversion. Western culture must recognize its sin and rebellion against God and seek forgiveness. That must take place before any thought of exchanging one fiduciary framework for another can be contemplated. Corporate prayers of faith to God would be countercultural in the face of Western culture's belief system. Os Guinness sees prayer and fasting as a direct challenge to modernity. Prayer and fasting "is an emphatic repudiation of modern technique and an open acknowledgement that when we wrestle with modernity, we do not wrestle with flesh and blood."[77] He sees them as "singularly appropriate for unmasking modernity" because the spiritual purpose of prayer and fasting directly challenges the lie of modernity.[78]

It is not enough to talk to God; the church must learn how to speak to culture. Newbigin's reticence to recognize the value of appropriately contextualized apologetics leaves the church with no opportunity to truly dialogue with culture. It is necessary for the church to seek aggressively to explain to Western culture exactly what it is all about in a way that is compelling and allows people to see that it is a true and relevant alternative to the present fiduciary framework of culture. It must seek to persuade in ways that truly meet the minds and hearts of persons in Western culture, laying out what it truly means to be a Christian in the present world context, especially in relation to the other truth claims. Os Guinness believes that now is the time for persuasive apologetics. In fact, he believes "evangelicals are growing persuasionless at a time of extraordinary apologetic opportunity."[79] With culture in deep disarray, there are "too few evangelicals with the convictions, courage, compassion, and imagination to exploit the vacuum."[80]

T. F. Torrance is more desirous of engaging culture rather than confronting it. He believes that theology should develop appropriate modes of conceptuality. He writes:

> ... theological science can and should play a basic role in clarifying the nature of its onto-relational subject matter and the distinctive kind of order which in embodies. And it can lead the way forward

---

77. Guinness, "Mission modernity," 347.
78. Ibid.
79. Ibid., 346.
80. Ibid.

by penetrating into the intelligible structure of these relations and developing the appropriate modes of conceptuality through which they can be brought to expression and thereby allowed to exert their creative power upon the whole range of human life and thought. Far from schematizing Christian theology into the patterns of the prevailing culture, this should have the opposite effect of transforming the very foundations of culture.[81]

This I believe is the appropriate approach to find ways to communicate with culture without compromising the gospel and is a much more reasonable approach to Western culture.

What must be attempted is to boldly rearrange culture's synthesis. Bert Hoedemaker speaks to the normal way in which religion and rationality in human societies seek a synthesis. Religion and rationality always function as a mixture, with each held in tension from the other. The function of faith is to help build bridges from one to the other. But when modernity came, rationality turned on religion and formed a new synthesis where rationality is first, followed by religion, and then by faith. What is needed is a new synthesis, where religion is once again given a place in the mixture and is not dominated by rationalism.[82]

The church, however, is more than a didactic, hermeneutical, or apologetic community. If it is truly a discipling community, then it will nurture the spiritual the life of the community. If it is truly to engage the world, then it must be seen as a truly contextualized compassionate community that welcomes those whose lives have been significantly affected by sin and will be a therapeutic community to those who suffer. It must be much more than a community that shares a different worldview than Western culture; it must be far more holistic than that. Since much of Jesus Christ's ministry on earth involved the healing of diseases, it can be deduced that he did not have a condescending view of the material world, but saw the healing of the body as an integral part of his work on earth. We can do no better.

Those who have been chosen by God to be the means of reaching others are also called to be holy, to truly represent God's nature and purpose in the world. As one reads the Bible, it becomes clear that one of the things that defines God's people is that they accept the requirement of a radical lifestyle that would positively reflect who God is. Rather than

81. Torrance, *Reality and Evangelical Theology*, 47.
82. Hoedemaker, "Mission Beyond Modernity," 212–33.

a return to legalism, the concern of the church is how it can best represent, best please, and best communicate God to the Western world. This topic is not a popular one in the present church primarily because it has accepted Western culture's belief in the absolute autonomy of individual personal rights, which makes even the discussion of a life-style that might in some manner infringe on their perceived right to manage their own lives without any consideration of the life of the community a threat to their freedom. What is being suggested is that the main concern be how to reflect truly God in the Western world, which would require Christians to subordinate their personal freedom under the priority of pleasing God. Guinness says that modernity requires truth be practiced and that only in the practice of truth will the gospel seem plausible to modern culture.[83]

In a culture that is becoming more visual, Newbigin's epistemological emphasis seems rather one-sided and monochromatic. There has been, as Guinness suggests, "the shift from word to image, action to spectacle, exposition to entertainment, truth to feeling, conviction to sentiment, and authoritative utterance to discussion and sharing."[84] Even though this may represent a shift in the wrong direction, it nevertheless must be addressed or we will discover that we are only speaking to ourselves. It is possible that we already are!

The Christian worldview could be communicated in the arts. God is able to reach Western culture through the medium of art in a way perhaps just as compelling as through words alone. Christian faith is holistic, having emotive and aesthetic aspects that may be more appealing and compelling than a sermon. Just how Christians will use art to reach Western culture remains to be seen.

Newbigin strongly supported the idea that the work for social justice was salvation in action. He also recognized that personal righteousness and justice are not often integrated. Since Christians highly value human life because it is the creation of God, it only seems natural that Christians would be engaged in the pursuit of social justice. The fact that in history Christians have often shown-up on the wrong side of the issue, it would be a powerful witness if the church would come out as strongly and with as much passion as the anti-slavery advocates of the eighteenth and nineteenth century.

---

83. Guinness, "Mission modernity," 345.
84. Ibid., 336.

John Stott sees the role of the church as a model to the larger human community in the way that human rights and justice should be experienced. He writes:

> The Church should be the one community in the world in which human dignity and equality are invariable recognised, and people's responsibility for one another is accepted; in which the rights of others are sought and never violated, while our own are often renounced; in which there is no partiality, favouritism or discrimination; in which the poor and the weak are defended, and human beings as God made them and meant them to be.[85]

Beyond what goes on inside the community of faith, the church must press for the same considerations regarding human value and human rights in Western society, especially for the disenfranchised.

WEAKNESSES IN NEWBIGIN'S THEOLOGY OF MISSION

It is important, at his point, to try to summarize what I believe are Newbigin's main weaknesses since we have addressed his strengths at great length already.

While Newbigin appears to desire to transform culture, which is certainly the priority of his mind, his criticism of Western culture seems to be predominately negative, so much so that he would appear to be against culture. There does not seem to be any points of connection nor any possible way to build bridges to Western culture.

It is obvious that he has been strongly influenced by Karl Barth at this point except for one important aspect, that being that for a radical conversion culture to happen the church must use persuasion in the public square. Instead of an existential crisis moment where God reveals himself in a substantial way primarily through the proclamation of the Word, the church must seek to persuade culture of the superiority of the Biblical view of reality. How can this be done if there are no points of real contact with the rationality of culture? Newbigin talks about it being necessary to speak from within the rationality of a culture, but when it comes to Western culture, he seems to leave little room for a Christian to engage it.

In regards to the public square, the place of cultural engagement where Newbigin believes Christians have left, it is somewhat difficult to discern in his writings just what re-engaging culture in the public square

---

85. Stott, *Decisive Issues*, 161.

entails. There are Christian voices being raised in every aspect and arena of Western culture. While the majority of Christians do not feel competent to speak in the public square, there are those who do and who do challenge the drift of culture at the present time. If he means for Christians to prepare themselves in areas that would give them leadership or at least a greater voice in society, then his point would be valid. He does lament that average Christians, also the key to the re-conversion of the West, are failing to witness to their faith on a daily basis. The context of the West is different than India where religion by and large is still in vogue. If the failure in the West is due to fear or to the lack of passion to share the gospel, then it is unlikely that the West will be converted. That Christians have entirely left the public square is a generalization that has too many exceptions to be a valid criticism.

It would appear that the best avenue for convincing modern culture would be to engage in a conversation with science. Yet, in spite of his understanding of the difference between science and scientism, he seems intently focused upon this negative radicalized form of science which seems at least in his mind to dominate Western culture. It is obvious that he is fully aware of the necessity of scientific methodology of not seeking a supernatural explanation for phenomena n the physical world, but he is correct to criticize scientists who use this narrow, pragmatic methodology as ultimate criteria for dismissing the supernatural and God from the any discussion of cause.

Newbigin explains the role of culture in understanding truth but his explanation can lead to misunderstandings. There is ultimate or absolute truth about and from God that is objective (it does not originate within us or culture), but this truth is not accessible to us except through the medium of culture. We cannot understand nor communicate truth without the need to use some facet of culture. This is what complicates the work of missionaries. In Newbigin's explanation of this fact, he is often misunderstood to be saying that this truth that can only be known through culture is limited to culture. He is attempting to contrast this with truth that has been revealed by a living God in real history. It is not a static truth (or eternal truth as the Greek would have understood it) unconnected to a real God and real history. God has, from the very beginning of his conversation with humans, revealed himself to us through some aspect of culture, primarily language. In a sense all of us indwell a cultural rationality that desires to set the parameters of our thinking and confine us to that particular cultural view. It is a miracle that ultimate truth can be and is communicated through cultural languages. God has incarnated his words and his Word in particular cultures and still managed to communicate truth about himself within these cultures.

As has been stated before, Newbigin does not give enough attention to the positive results of the Enlightenment, not because he does not recognize them but because of his focus on the negative results that are having a serious effect on contemporary culture. Again, he assumes certain things that he does not articulate and this can cause misunderstanding. Could some of the positive outcomes of the Enlightenment be a good place for Christians to build bridges with culture as a part of the ongoing discussion of a positive and necessary theology of mission to Western culture? This seems like a viable option but this was not Newbigin's focus.

Newbigin reacted strongly against Western individualism to such an extent, it appears, that he placed an inordinate amount of emphasis on cultural conversion while saying little about personal conversion. His rationale was most likely that Christians are over-emphasizing the individual aspect so he would turn his attention to corporate conversion. There is a larger concern in his thinking for unity and community. He has a strong aversion to the idea of autonomous man and to the Western preoccupation with individual human rights. He was also a firm believer in the ideology of the worldwide, organizational unity of the church, emphasizing the corporate community versus the individual.

Mission, of course, is about reaching individuals as much as cultures and, while this has been the preoccupation of Western missions, it need not be replaced with an equally faulty idea of purely corporate conversion. He does not do that. A detailed study of his view of conversion will indicate that he did see the value of individual conversions, but was quick to remind us that that person must be immediately incorporated in a community of faith that indwells the story.

It is difficult to separate Newbigin from the charge of being a fideist. His lack of emphasis on apologetics and the need to engage persons in culture in serious dialogue with certain evidences to support our argument is, in the context of Western culture, a failure to appreciate or take Western culture seriously. Persuading in the context of Western culture would include rational argument and/or the need for some corroborating evidence to validate a truth claim. Otherwise, how can we be sure of the source such truth claims? It is reasonable to want to be convinced before making a decision to commit one's life to an assertion of truth. What it takes to be convinced in the West may be different than what it takes it India. The truth does not always appear to be self-authenticating as Newbigin believes and needs, at times, some further explanation and even collaboration.

CONCLUSION

It would be difficult to concur with Geoffrey Wainwright's designation of Newbigin as a Father of the Church even though he was a 'Bishop-theologian.'[86] The reason for this is that while his theology is compelling, it does not have the depth to merit such a distinction as a Church Father. While he does appeal to many facets of the global church, he is not recognized as a leader by many outside the ecumenical movement.

Newbigin could easily be placed along side such great twentieth century missionary statesmen as J. H. Oldham and Willem Visser 't Hooft, who were active in global Christian affairs and whose thinking continue to influence the present generation of missionaries and missiologists. He had all the qualifications of a missionary statesman of extraordinary ability. Perhaps more than any other missionary statesmen of recent history, he was capable of down-to-earth street preaching and, within hours, was able to sit down with the greatest theologians of the twentieth century and carry on theological conversation. His work was incredibly local and international at the same time. He saw with unusual clarity the forces at work in Western culture and he proposed a bold and somewhat audacious plan for its recovery. He was fully engaged in every aspect of ecclesiastic life, from pastoring and administration to theological debate and international missionary conferences. His consistency of thought, boldness of vision, and persistence in ministry contribute to his positive influence on the church around the world. His passion has instilled confidence in another generation of those who seek the realization of God's purposes in this world. His personal life was exemplary and above reproach, filled with devotion to God and complete dedication to the calling God placed on his life.

The question always arises as to whether Newbigin's vision for Western culture is feasible. He would answer that it is both feasible and necessary because he believed that all other plausibility systems and fidu-

---

86. Wainwright, *Theological Life*, v.

ciary frameworks would eventually fail. Western culture, if it truly wanted to connect with reality, would acknowledge the superior rationality of Christianity. Such optimism does not merely reflect his temperament, but also reflects his confidence in God and the power of the gospel to convert a civilization as formidable as the West.

Bibliography

SELECTED WRITINGS OF LESSLIE NEWBIGIN

Newbigin, Lesslie. "Address on the Main Theme, 'Jesus Saviour of the World.'" Given at the Synod Assembly of January 1972. *South India Churchman*, February 1972, 5-8.

———."All in one Place or all of One Sort: On Unity and Diversity in the Church." In *Creation, Christ and Culture: A Festschrift in Honour of Professor Thomas F. Torrance*, edited by R. W. A. McKinney, 288-306. Edinburgh: T & T Clark, 1976.

———. "Authority: to Whom Shall We Go?" Sermon preached on the text John 6:66-71 at St. Mary's, the University Church at Cambridge on 6 May 1979, under the general theme of "Voices of Authority." No pages. Accessed on January 15, 2008. Online: http://www.newbigin.net/assets/pdf/79atws.pdf.

———. "Beyond the Familiar Myths." *The Gospel and Our Culture Newsletter*. Spring 1989, 1:1-2.

———. "The Bible: Good News for Secularised People." Keynote Address during the Europe/Middle East Regional Conference in Eisenbach, Germany in April 1991.

———. "The Bible and Our contemporary Mission." *Clergy Review* 69, no.1 (1984): 9-17.

———. "Bible Study on Romans 8." Bible study given at the Conference on 'Church in the Inner City' in Birmingham, England in September 1976.

———. "A British and European Perspective." In *Entering the Kingdom: A Fresh Look at Conversion*, edited by Monica Hill, 57-68. MARC Europe: British Church Growth Association, 1973, 1978. Also published by the Billy Graham Evangelistic Association and MARC Europe, 1989.

———. "Can a Modern Society be Christian?" Second Annual Gospel and Culture Lecture, London: Kings College, November 1995.

———. "Can I Be Christian?"—VII. *Spectator*, May 1938, 800.

———. "Can the Churches give a Common Message to the World?" *Theology Today* 9 (January 1953): 512-28.

———. "Can the West be Converted?" *IBMR* 11 (January 1987): 2-7.

———. "The Centrality of Christ." *Fraternal*, 1976, 177:20-28.

———. "The Centrality of Jesus for History." In *Incarnation and Myth: The Debate Continued*, edited by Michael Goulder, 197-210. London: SCM, 1979.

———. "Certain Faith: What Kind of Certainty?" *Tyndale Bulletin* 44, no. 2 (1993): 339-50.

———. "Christ and the Cultures." *Scottish Journal of Theology* 31, No. 1 (1978): 1-22.

———. "Christ and the World of Religions." *Churchman*, 1983, 97:16-30.

———. "The Christian Faith and the World of Religions." In *Keeping the Faith: Essays to Mark the Centenary of Lux Mundi*, edited by Geoffrey Wainwright, 310-40. London: SPCK, 1989.

Bibliography

———. "Christian Faith in a Secularised World." Unpublished manuscript written ca. 1989.

———. *Christian Freedom in the Modern World.* London: SCM, 1937.

———. "Christianity and Culture." (April 1990). Accessed on January 17, 2008. Online: http://www.newbigin.net/assets/pdf/90cc.pdf. No pages.

———. "A Christian Vedanta?" In *The Gospel and Our Culture Newsletter* (Spring 1992) 12:1–2.

———. *Christian Witness in a Plural Society.* London: The British Council of Churches, 1977.

———. "The Church: Catholic, Reformed, and Evangelical." In *The Episcopalian*, May 1964, 12–15, 48.

———. "Come Holy Spirit: Renew the Whole Creation." In *Selly Oak Colleges Occasional Paper* No. 6. Birmingham, UK, 1990.

———. "Comments on 'The Church, the Churches and the World Council of Churches.'" *Ecumenical Review* 3 (1951): 252–54.

———. "Common Witness and Unity." *IRM* 69 (1980): 158–60.

———. "Confessing Christ in a Multi-religion Society." In *Scottish Bulletin of Evangelical Theology* 12 (Autumn 1994): 125–36.

———. "Context and Conversion." *IRM* 68 (1979): 301–12.

———. "Conversion." In *A Concise Dictionary of Christian World Mission*, edited by Stephen Neill, et al., 147–48. Nashville and New York: Abingdon, 1971.

———. "Conversion." *The Guardian Madras*, December 29, 1954, 409.

———. "Conversion." *Religion and Society* 13, no. 4 (1966): 30–42.

———. "Cross-currents in Ecumenical and Evangelical Understandings of Mission." *IBMR* 6 (October 1982): 146–51.

———. "Culture, Rationality and the Unity of the Human Race." In *The Gospel and Our Culture Newsletter.* (Autumn 1989) 3:1–2.

———. "Culture and Theology." *The Blackwell Encyclopedia of Modern Christian Thought.* Edited by Alister E. McGrath, 98–100. Cambridge, MA: Blackwell Publishers, 1993.

———. "A Decent Debate about Doctrine: Faith, Doubt and Certainty." GEAR (Group for Evangelism and Renewal): United Reformed Church, 1993.

———. "The Dialogue of Gospel and Culture: Reflection on the Conference on World Mission and Evangelism, Salvador, Radia, Brazil." *IBMR* 21 (April 97): 50–51.

———. "Does What Happened Matter?" *The Australian Christian* 25 (March 1998): 308.

———. "Ecumenical Amnesia." *IBMR* 18 (January 1994): 2–5.

———. "The End of History." *The Gospel and Our Culture Newsletter.* (Summer 1992) 13:1–2.

———. "The Enduring Validity of Cross-cultural Mission." *IBMR* 12 (April 1988): 50–53.

———. "Episcopacy and Authority." *Churchman* 104, no. 4 (1990): 335–339.

———. "The Episcopacy and the Quest for Unity." Notes of a discussion at the Annual Conference of CCLEPE and Ecumenical Officers at Swanwick, September 1978.

———. Lamin Sanneh and Jenny Taylor. *Faith and Power: Christianity and Islam in 'Secular' Britain.* London: SPCK, 1998.

———. *A Faith for This One World?* London: SCM, 1961.

———. "A Fellowship of Churches." *Ecumenical Review* 37, no. 2 (1985): 175–81.

———. *The Finality of Christ.* Richmond, VA: John Knox, 1969.

———. *Foolishness to the Greeks: The Gospel and Western Culture.* Grand Rapids: Eerdmans, 1986.

Bibliography

———. "Foreword." In *Everyman Revived: The Common Sense of Michael Polanyi.* Revised edition by Drusilla Scott, iv–v. Grand Rapids: Eerdmans, 1995.

———. "Foreword." In *Roland Allen: Pioneer, Priest, and Prophet.* Hubert J. B. Allen, xiii–xv. Grand Rapids: Eerdmans, 1995.

———. "Foreword." In *Missionary Methods: St. Paul's or Ours Roland Allen.* Hubert J. B. Allen, i–iii. Grand Rapids: Eerdmans, 1962.

———. "Foreword." In *Enlightenment and Alienation.* Colin Gunton, vi–vii. Basingstoke, Hanks, UK: Marshall Morgan and Scott, 1985.

———. "Foreword." In *The Theology of Christian Mission,* edited by Gerald H. Anderson, xi–xiii. Nashville: Abingdon, 1961.

———. *The Good Shepherd: Meditations on Christian Ministry in Today's World.* London: Mowbray, 1977.

———. "The Gospel and Culture." Manuscript of an address given at a conference organised by Danish Missions Council and the Danish Churches Ecumenical Council in Denmark on 3 November 1995. No pages. Accessed on January 5, 2008. Online: http://Newbigin.net/assets/pdf/95gc.pdf.

———. "The Gospel and Modern Western Culture." An address given to the Swedish Missions Council, 1993.

———. "The Gospel and our Culture." Address given at the NMC/CFWM World Mission Conference, "Doing God's will in our Plural Society." December 12–15, 1989. Published in 1990 by London: Catholic Missionary Education Centre. *Mission Today Pamphlet no. 47.*

———. "The Gospel and Our Culture: A Response to Elaine Graham and Heather Walton." In *Modern Churchman* 34, no. 2 (1992): 1–10.

———. "The Gospel as Public Truth." In *The Gospel and Our Culture Newsletter,* Spring 1991, 9:1–2.

———. "The Gospel as Public Truth." Lecture given at Samford University's Beeson Divinity School, Birmingham, Alabama, June 1997.

———. "The Gospel as Public Truth." Editorial in *Touchstone: A Journal of Ecumenical Orthodoxy* 5 (Summer 1992): 1–2.

———. "The Gospel in a Culture of False Gods." 1998. Interview by Andrew Walker of Lesslie Newbigin, extracted from Andrew Walker's book *Different Gospels: Christian Orthodoxy and Modern Theologies.* Hodder and Stoughton, 1988. No pages. Accessed on January 5, 2008. Online: http://www.shipoffools.com/Cargo/Features98/Newbigin/NewbiginInterview.html.

———. *The Gospel in a Pluralist Society.* London: SPCK, 1989.

———. "The Gospel in Today's Global City." Birmingham, UK: *Selly Oak Occasional Colleges Paper* No. 16.

———. *The Holy spirit and the Church.* Madras: Christian Literature Society, 1972.

———. *Honest Religion for Secular Man.* Philadelphia: Westminster Press/London: SCM Press, 1966.

———. *The Household of God: Lectures on the Future of the Church.* London: SCM PRESS, LTD, 1957.

———. "I Believe." In *I Believe,* edited by M. A. Thomas, 73–88. Madras: SCM, 1946 (Address given at the Regional Leaders' Conference in Madras in December, 1945).

———. "I Believe in Christ." In *I Believe,* edited by M. A. Thomas, 101–14. Madras: SCM, 1946 (Address given at the Regional Leaders' Conference in Madras in December, 1945).

Bibliography

———. "I Believe in God." *I Believe*, edited by M. A. Thomas, 89–100. Madras: SCM, 1946. (Address given at the Regional Leaders' Conference in Madras in December, 1945)

———. "Integration—Some Personal Reflections." *International Review of Missions* 70 (1981): 247–55.

———. "Introduction." Introduction to a series of articles in "The Church of England Newspaper" on The Gospel and Our Culture Conference at Swanwick in 1992 on the theme "The Gospel as Public Truth," published in London: CEN Books, 1992:1–3.

———. "Jesus Christ." In *A Concise Dictionary of Christian World Mission*, edited by Stephen Neill, et al., 307–9. Nashville and New York: Abingdon, 1971.

———. "Jesus, Saviour of the World." *South India Churchman*, February1972, 5–8.

———. *Journey into Joy* Grand Rapids: Eerdmans, 1972.

———. "The Kingdom of God and our Hopes for the Future." *The Kingdom of God and Human Society*. R. S. Barbour, ed. Edinburgh: T. & T. Clark, 1993:1–12.

———. "The Legacy of W. A. Visser 't Hooft." *IBMR* 16 (April 1992): 78–80, 82.

———. *The Light has Come: An Exposition of the Fourth Gospel*. Grand Rapids: Eerdmans, 1982.

———. "Light of the Risen Lord." *Leading Light*, 1994, no. 3:10.

———. *Mission and the Crisis of Western Culture: Recent Studies by Lesslie Newbigin*. (Handsel Booklet) Edinburgh: Handsel, 1989.

———. "Mission and Missions." *Christianity Today*. Vol. 4 No. 22:94.

———. "A Missionary's Dream." *Ecumenical Review* 43 (January 1991): 4–10.

———. *Mission in Christ's Way: Bible Studies*. Geneva: WCC Publications, 1987.

———. "Mission in a Pluralist Society." Mimeograph copy 1990:1–32. Subsequently published as chapter 14 (158–76) in *A Word in Season*.

———. "Mission in the 1980s." *Occasional Bulletin of Missionary Research*. Vol. 4 No. 4:154–55.

———. "Mission in the 1990s: Two Views." (Part I. Anna Maria Aagard and Part II. Lesslie Newbigin). *International Bulletin of Missionary Research* 13 (July 1989): 98–102.

———. "Missions." Unpublished manuscript written ca. 1991. No pages Accessed January 15, 2008 Online: http://Newbigin.net/assets/pdf/95gc.pdf.

———. "Mission to Modern Western Culture." *The San Antonio Report: Your Will be Done: Mission in Christ's Way*. Geneva: World Council of Churches, 1990:62–166 Excerpt from evening address given to the Commission on Mission and World Evangelism, San Antonio, 1989).

———. "Modernity in Context." In *Modern, Postmodern, and Christian*. John Reid and David Pullinger, 1–12. Lausanne Occasional Paper no. 27, Lausanne Committee. Carberry, The Handsel, 1996.

———. "Muslims, Christians and Public Doctrine." *The Gospel and Our Culture Newsletter*. (Summer 1990) 6:1–2.

———. "The Nature of the Christian Hope." *Ecumenical Review*, 1952, 4:282–84.

———. "New Birth into a Living Hope." Address on the text 1 Peter 1:3 given in 28 August 1995 at the European Area Council of the World Alliance of Reformed Churches, meeting at Pollock Halls, Edinburgh, Scotland from 28 August to 3 September 1995 on the theme "Hope and Renewal Times of Change."

———. "One Body, One Gospel, One World." *Ecumenical Review*, January 1959, 11:143–56.

———. "On the Gospel as Public Truth: Response to the Colloquium." Response to the colloquium in Leeds, England in August 1996.

Bibliography

———. *The Open Secret: an Introduction to the Theology of Mission.* Grand Rapids: Eerdmans, 1978, revised edition, 1995.
———. *The Other Side of 1984: Questions for the Churches.* Geneva: WCC, 1983.
———. "The Other Side of 1990." Presentation at Clare College, Cambridge University. No date given but likely 1989.
———. "The Other Side of 1990." In *Into the 1990s: The Church in the 1990s*, edited by Nicholas Sagavsky, 4–8. Nottingham: Grove Books Limited, 1990.
———. "Our Missionary Responsibility in the Crisis of Western Culture." Address to German missionary administrators in May, 1988 (12 mimeographed pages).
———. "The Pattern of Partnership." In *A Decisive Hour for the Christian Mission*. Norman Goodall, et al., 34–45. London: SCM Press, 1960.
———. "The Place of Christianity in Religious Education." Paper presented in March 1989 in relation to the passage into law of the Education Reform Act (1988). No pages. Accessed on January 17, 2008. Online: http://Newbigin.net/assets/pdf89pcre.pdf.
———. "Pluralism and the Church." Address at the second of two regional conferences jointly sponsored by The Gospel and Our Culture movement and the British and Foreign Bible Society, on the theme "Freedom and Truth in a Pluralist Society," April 10–12, 1991 at the Swanwick Conference Centre.
———. "Preface." In *Towards the Twenty-first Century in Christian Mission*, edited by J. M. Phillips and R. T. Coote, 1–6. Grand Rapids: Eerdmans, 1994.
———. "The Present and Coming Christ." *Ecumenical Review.* (January 1954) 6:118–22.
———. *Proper Confidence: Faith, Doubt, and Certainty in Christian Discipleship.* Grand Rapids: Eerdmans, 1995.
———. "Recent Thinking on Christian Beliefs: viii. Mission and Missions." *Expository Times* 88, no. 9 (June 1977): 260–64.
———. Rejoinder to "Mission and Unity in the Missionary Ecclesiology of Max Warren." Ossi Haaramaki. *IRM* 72:271–72.
———. *The Relevance of Trinitarian Doctrine for Today's Mission.* WCC—CWME: Edinburgh House, 1967.
———. "Religion, Science, and Truth in the School Curriculum." *Theology* 91 (1988): 187–91.
———. "Religious Pluralism: A Missiological Approach" *Studia Missionalia* 42:227–44.
———. "Religious Pluralism and the Uniqueness of Jesus Christ." *IBMR* 13 (April 1989): 50–54.
———. "Reply to Konrad Raiser." *IBMR* 18 (April 1994): 51–52.
———. "Response to David Stowe." *IBMR* 12 (October 1988): 151–53.
———. "Response to Hoedemaker." Response to an essay by Hoedemaker titled "Enlightenment Eclipse and the Problem of Western Christianity: Towards a Discussion with Lesslie Newbigin," written in preparation for a conference in the Netherlands (1990).
———. "A Response." Response to the lead article "The Word of God?" by Rev John Coventry, SJ, *The Gospel and Our Culture Newsletter*, Summer 1991, 10:2–3.
———. *The Reunion of the Church: A Defence of the South India Scheme.* London: SCM, 1948.
———. "Revelation." Theology paper presented at Westminster College, Cambridge, 1936.
———. Review of *The Communication of the Gospel* by David Read. *IRM* 41:526–28.
———. Review of *The Myth of Christian Uniqueness*, edited by John Hick and Paul Knitter. *International Bulletin of Missionary Research* 13 (April 1989): 50–52.

Bibliography

———. Review of "No Other Gospel: Christianity Among the World Religions" by Carl E. Braaten. *First Things*, no. 24 (June/July 1992): 56–58.

———. Review of *Sharing a Vision* by Archbishop George Carey. (London: Darton Longman & Todd, 1993) in *Theology*. 97, no. 776 (March-April 1994): 132–33.

———. "Salvation." In *A Concise Dictionary of Christian World Mission*, edited by Stephen Neill, et al., 537–38. Nashville and New York: Abingdon, 1971.

———. "The Secular-Apostolic Dilemma." In *Not Without a Compass: Jesuit Education Association Seminar on the Christian Education in India Today*, edited by T. Mathias, et al., 61–71. New Delhi: Jesuit Educational Association of India, 1972.

———. *Signs of God Amid the Rubble: The Purposes of God in Human History*, edited by Geoffrey Wainwright. Grand Rapids: Eerdmans, 2003.

———. *Sin and Salvation*. London: SCM, 1956.

———. "Some Thoughts on Britain From Abroad." *The Christian News-Letter*. Supplement, 12 October 1947, No. 298:8–11.

———. *A South India Diary*. London: SCM, 1951.

———. "Speaking the Truth to Caesar." *Ecumenical Review* 43 (July 1990): 372–75.

———. "The Student Volunteer Missionary Union." In *The Christian Faith To-Day*, 95–104. London: SCM, 1933.

———. "The Summons to Christian Mission Today." *IRM* 48:177–89.

———. Thanksgiving Sermon. Preached at the Service for the 50th Anniversary of the Tambaram Conference of the International Missionary Council *IRM* 77:151–53.

———. "Theism and Atheism in Theology." *The Gospel and Our Culture Newsletter*, Winter 1991, 8:1–2.

———. "Theological Education in World Perspective." In *Ministers for the 1980s*, edited by Jock Stein, 63–75. Edinburgh: Handsel, 1979.

———. "The Threat and the Promise." *The Gospel and Our Culture Newsletter*, August 1990, 7:1–2.

———. *Trinitarian Doctrine and Today's Mission*. Edinburgh, Scotland: Edinburgh House Press, 1963. Also, Mackays of Chatham PLC, Kent, England: Paternoster, 1998.

———. *Trinitarian Faith and Today's Mission*. Richmond, VA: John Knox, 1964.

———. "Trinitarianism." In *A Concise Dictionary of Christian World Mission* edited by Stephen Neill, et al., 607. Nashville and New York: Abingdon, 1971.

———. "The Trinity as Public Truth." In *The Trinity in a Pluralistic Age: Theological Essays on Culture and Religion*, edited by Kevin Vanhoozer, 1–8. Grand Rapids: Eerdmans, 1997.

———. *Truth to Tell: The Gospel as Public Truth* Grand Rapids: Eerdmans, 1991.

———. *Truth and Authority in Modernity*. Valley Forge, PA: Trinity International Press, 1996.

———. *The Unfinished Agenda*. Grand Rapids: Eerdmans, 1985. Updated version published in 1993 with a "Postscript: 1982–92."

———. "Way out West: The Gospel in a Post-Enlightenment World." *Touchstone: A Journal of Ecumenical Orthodoxy* 5 (Summer 1992): 22–24.

———. "The Welfare State: A Christian Perspective." *Theology* 88 (May 1985): 173–82.

———. "What Is a 'Local Church Truly United?'" *Ecumenical Review* 29 (April 1977): 115–28.

———. "What is Culture?" Address prepared for the first regional conference jointly sponsored by The Gospel and Our Culture Network and the British and Foreign Bible Society on the theme "Mission to Our Culture in the Light of Scripture and the

Bibliography

Christian Tradition," held at Hoddesdon, Hertfordshire, England on October 15–17, 1990.

———. "What is the Ecumenical Agenda?" Response to a request from Thaddeus Horgan, Managing Editor of "Ecumenical Trends," asking Newbigin, as a part of a group of thirty persons, to write a four hundred word essay on the same theme for possible publication, 1986.

———. "What Kind of Britain?" Manuscript circulated among friends, of an address delivered in London on August 1994.

———. "Whose Justice?" *Ecumenical Review* 44 (July 1992): 308–11.

———. *A Word in Season: Perspectives on Christian World Missions*. Grand Rapids: Eerdmans/ Edinburgh: St. Andrew Press, 1994.

OTHER SOURCES

The American Heritage Dictionary. Boston: Houghton Mifflin (Second College Edition), 1985.

Anderson, Gerald, ed. *The Theology of the Christian Mission*. Nashville: Abingdon, 1961.

Arendt, Hannah. *The Human Condition*. Chicago: The University of Chicago Press, 1958.

Augustine. *On the Freedom of Choice of the Will*. Translated by Thomas Williams. Indianapolis: Hackett, 1993.

Barclay, Oliver R. *What ever Happened to the Jesus Lane Lot?* Leicester, England: Inter-Varsity, 1977.

Barrow, Simon. "Afterword." *Christian Mission in Western Society*. Simon Barrow and Graeme Smith, eds. London: Churches Together in Britain and Ireland, 2001:235–58.

———, and Graeme Smith, eds. *Christian Mission in Western Society*. London: Churches Together in Britain and Ireland, 2001.

Barth, Karl. *Church Dogmatics*. Volume 1/1 Edinburgh: T & T Clark, 1957.

———. *Church Dogmatics*. Volume 3/2 Edinburgh: T & T Clark, 1960.

———. *Church Dogmatics*. Volume 4/1 Edinburgh: T & T Clark 1956.

———. "The Community for the World." *Church Dogmatics*. Volume 4/3 Edinburgh: T & T Clark, 1962:762–95.

———. *Evangelical Theology: An Introduction*. Grand Rapids: Eerdmans, 1963.

———. *The Humanity of God*. Atlanta, GA: John Knox, 1961.

Bassham, Rodger C. *Mission Theology*. Pasadena, CA: William Carey Library, 1979.

Bavinck, J. H. *An Introduction to the Science of Missions*. Translated by David H. Freeman. Phillipsburg, NJ: Presbyterian and Reformed, 1960.

Beardsley, Monroe C., ed. *The European Philosophers from Descartes to Neitzsche*. New York: Random House, 1960, 1988, 1992. Modern Library Edition.

Beeby, H. Dan. "He Swung the Lamp of Resurrection." Address given at Lesslie Newbigin's funeral on 7 February 1998. No pages. Accessed on January 17, 2008. Online: http://www.shipoffools.com/Cargo/Features98/Newbigin/NewbiginBeeby.html.

———. "Lesslie Newbigin: biography" No pages. Accessed on January 17, 2008. Online: http://www.gospel-culture.org.uk/newbio.htm

———. "Lesslie Newbigin Remembered." *IMNR* 22 (April 1998): 52.

———. "My Pilgrimage in Mission." *IBMR* 17 (January 1993): 2–26.

———. "The Reformed Tradition and the Heritage of Lesslie Newbigin: Resources for mission in modern/postmodern culture." A one-sheet summary of resources and insights received from Dr Beeby on April 28, 2000.

Bibliography

———. "A White Man's Burden, 1994." *IBMR* 18 (January 1994): 6–8.

Berger, Peter L. *A Rumor of Angels: Modern Society and the Rediscovery of the Supernatural.* Garden City, NY: Anchor Books, Doubleday and Company, 1970.

———. *The Heretical Imperative: Contemporary Possibilities of Religious Affirmation.* Garden City, NY: Anchor Press/Doubleday, 1979.

———. Brigette, and Hansfried Kellner. *The Homeless Mind: Modernization and Consciousness.* Mississauga, Ontario, Canada: Random House of Canada, 1974.

Berkhof, Hendrikus. *Christ: The Meaning of History.* Translated by Lambertus Buurman. Grand Rapids: Baker, 1979.

Bevans, Stephen. *John Oman and His Doctrine of God.* Cambridge, UK: Cambridge University Press, 1992.

Bewkes, Eugene G., et al. *The Western Heritage of Faith and Reason.* New York: Harper & Row, 1963.

Blauw, Johannes. *The Missionary Nature of the Church: A Survey of the Biblical Theology of Mission.* New York: McGraw-Hill Book, 1962.

Bloom, Allan David. *The Closing of the American Mind.* New York: Simon and Schuster, 1987.

Bolich, Gregory. *Karl Barth and Evangelicalism.* Downers Grove, IL: InterVarsity, 1980.

Bosch, David J. *Transforming Mission: Paradigm Shifts in Theology of Mission.* Maryknoll, NY: Orbis, 1991.

———. *Witness to the World: The Christian Mission in Theological Perspective.* Atlanta: John Knox, l980.

Bowden, John. *Karl Barth.* London: SCM, 1971.

Brickley, Michael J., S J. *At the Origins of Modern Atheism.* New Haven, CT: Yale University Press, 1987.

Briggs, John A.Y. "Jerusalem Conference (1928)." In *Evangelical Dictionary of World Missions*, edited by Scott Moreau, 516.

Brinton, Colin. *The Shaping of Modern Thought.* Englewood Cliffs, NJ: Prentice-Hall, 1963.

Brown, Colin. *Philosophy and the Christian Faith.* Downers Grove, IL: InterVarsity, 1975.

Brunner, Emil *The Mediator: A Study of the Central Doctrine of the Christian Faith.* Translated by Olive Wyon. London: Lutterworth, seventh impression, 1952.

Buckley, Michael J., S.J., *At the Origins of Modern Atheism.* New Haven, CT: Yale University Press, 1987.

Butterfield, Herbert. *The Origins of Modern Science.* New York: The Free Press, 1957.

Buber, Martin. *Eclipse of God.* New York: Harper & Row, 1952.

———. *I and Thou.* Translated by Walter Kaufman. New York: Charles Scribner's Sons, 1970.

Cairns, David. *David Cairns: an Autobiography.* London: SCM, 1950.

Calvin, John. *Institutes of the Christian Religion.* Translated by Henry Beveridge. 2 volumes. Grand Rapids: Eerdmans, 1981.

Church of England Newspaper, "Lesslie Newbigin Dies after a Short Illness." February 6, 1998, 5.

Clements, Keith. *Faith on the Frontier: A Life of J. H. Oldham.* Edinburgh and Geneva, 1999.

Clouser, Ray A. *The Myth of Religious Neutrality: An Essay on the Hidden Role of Religious Belief in Theories.* Notre Dame: University of Notre Dame, 1991.

Bibliography

Cochrane, Charles. *Christianity and Classical Culture: A Study of Thought and Action from Augustine to Augustus.* London: Oxford University Press, 1944.

Conway, Martin. "Profile: Lesslie Newbigin's Faith Pilgrimage." *Epworth Review* 21, No. 3 (September 1994): 27–36.

Copleston, F. C. *Aquinas.* Harmondsworth, Middlesex, England: Penguin, 1955 (1986 printing).

Crane, Brinton. *The Shaping of Modern Thought.* Englewood Cliffs, NJ: Prentice-Hall, 1963.

Crocker, Lester G., ed. *The Age of Enlightenment.* New York: Walker and Company, 1969.

Dawson, Christopher. *Religion and the Rise of Western Culture.* London: Sheed & Ward, 1950.

Denney, James. "St. Paul's Epistle to the Romans." In *The Expositor's Greek Testament* Vol. II. W. Robertson Nicoll, ed., 555–725. Grand Rapids: Eerdmans, reprinted, September 1976.

Descartes, René. *Discourses and Meditations.* Translated, with an introduction, by Laurence J. Lafleur. Indianapolis: Bobbs-Merrill Educational Publishing, 1960.

Dewey, Margaret. "The Gospel and Western Culture." A pamphlet in the Thinking Missions (53 January 1987) series published by The Society for the Propagation of the Gospel, Oxford: Bocando Press Limited, 1987.

Dooyeweerd, Herman. *In the Twilight of Western Thought.* Nutley, NJ: The Craig Press, 1980.

Drescher, Hans-Georg. *Ernst Troeltsch: His Life and Work.* Minneapolis: Fortress, 1993.

Eliot, T. S. *Christianity and Culture: The Idea of a Christian Society and Notes Toward the Reformation of Culture.* New York: Harcourt, Brace and World, 1940/1949.

Feynman, R. P. *The Character of Physical Law.* Cambridge, Massachusetts: MIT Press, 1965.

Foust, Thomas F., et al. *A Scandalous Prophet: The Way of Mission after Newbigin.* Grand Rapids: Eerdmans, 2002.

Foust, Thomas F. "Epistemology." In *A Scandalous Prophet: The Way of Mission after Newbigin.* Thomas F. Foust, et al., 153–62. Grand Rapids: Eerdmans, 2002.

Frank, Philipp. *Philosophy of Science: The Link between Science and Philosophy.* Englewood Cliffs, NJ: Prentice-Hall, 1957 (friend and successor of Einstein at University of Prague).

Frei, Hans W. *The Identity of Jesus Christ: The Hermeneutical Bases of Dogmatic Theology.* Philadelphia: Fortress, 1975.

———. *The Eclipse of Biblical Narrative: A Study in Eighteen and Nineteenth Century Hermeneutics.* New Haven: Yale University Press, 1984.

Friedman, Maurice. *Encounter on the Narrow Ridge: A Life of Martin Buber.* New York: Paragon House, 1991.

Fuller, Steve. *Philosophy of Science and its Discontents.* New York: The Guilford Press, 1993.

———. *Thomas Kuhn: A Philosophical History of our Times.* Chicago: The University of Chicago Press, 2000.

Gairdner, W. H. T. *Echoes from Edinburgh, 1910: An Account and Interpretation of the World Missionary Conference.* New York: Layman's Missionary Movement, no date indicated.

Gay, Peter. *The Enlightenment: An Interpretation: The Rise of Modern Paganism.* New York: W.W. Norton and Company, 1966.

Bibliography

Gilson, Etienne. *The Unity of Philosophical Experience*. New York: Charles Scribner's Sons, 1937.

Glasser, Arthur F. "Conciliar Perspectives: The Road to Reconceptualization." In *Contemporary Theologies of Mission*, edited by Arthur F. Glasser and Donald A. McGavran, 82-99. Grand Rapids: Baker, 1983.

Glasser, Arthur, and Donald A. McGavran, eds. *Contemporary Theologies of Mission*. Grand Rapids: Baker, 1983.

Goheen, Michael W. "As the Father Has Sent Me, I Am Sending You." In *J. E. Lesslie Newbigin's Missionary Ecclesiology*. Zoetermeer: Uitgeverij Boekencentrum, 2000.

———. "Gospel and Cultures: Newbigin's Missionary Contribution." Paper presented at the Cultures and Christianity A. D. 2000 International Symposium of the Association for Reformational Philosophy, 21-25 August, 2000, Hoeven, Netherlands.

———. "The Missionary Calling of Believers in the World: Lesslie Newbigin's Contribution." In *A Scandalous Prophet: The Way of Mission after Newbigin*. Thomas F. Foust, et al., 37-54. Grand Rapids: Eerdmans, 2002.

Graham, Elaine and Heather Walton. "A Walk on the Wild Side: A Critique of the Gospel and Our Culture." *Modern Churchman* 33, no. 1 (1991): 1-7.

Green, Colin J. D. "Trinitarian Tradition and the Cultural Collapse of Late Modernity." In *A Scandalous Prophet: The Way of Mission after Newbigin*. Thomas F. Foust, et al., 65-72. Grand Rapids: Eerdmans, 2002.

Greene, Colin J. D. "Lesslie Newbigin—A Bible Society Perspective." *TransMission*. Special Edition, 1998:14-15.

Guinness, Os. "Mission modernity: seven checkpoints on mission in the modern world." In *Faith and Modernity*, edited by Philip Sampson, 322-352. Oxford: Regnum Books International, 1994.

Gunton, Colin E. *Christ and Creation*. Carlisle: Paternoster, 1992.

———. "Knowledge and Culture: Towards an Epistemology of the Concrete." In *The Gospel and Contemporary Culture*, edited by Hugh Montefiore, 84-102. London: Mowbray, 1992.

Guthrie, S. C., Jr. "Oscar Cullman." In *A Handbook of Christian Theologians*, edited by Dean G. Peerman and Martin E. Marty, 338-54. New York: New America Library (a Meridian Book), 1965.

Guy, Robert Calvin. "Theological Foundations." In *Church Growth and Christian Mission*, edited by Donald M. McGavran, 40-56. New York: Harper and Row, 1965.

Haaramaki, Ossi. "Mission and Unity in the Missionary Ecclesiology of Max Warren." *IRM* 72 (1983): 267-72.

Hackett, Stuart C. *Oriental Philosophy*. Madison, WI: The University of Wisconsin Press, 1979.

Halton, Gerald. *Science and Anti-Science*. Cambridge, MA: Harvard University Press, 1957.

Hasel, Gerhard. *Old Testament Theology: Basic Issues in the Current Debate*. Grand Rapids: Eerdmans, 1972.

Hazard, Paul. *The European Mind: 1680-1715*. Cleveland, OH: Meridian Books/The Word Publishing Company, 1963. (Originally published in French in 1935)

Heibert, Paul G. *Anthropological Reflections in Missiological Issues*. Grand Rapids: Baker, 1994.

———. "Critical Contextualization," *IBMR* 2 (July 1987): 104-12.

Bibliography

———. "Critical Issues in the Social Sciences and their Implications for Mission Studies." *Missiology* 24, no, 1 (January 1996): 65–82.

———. "Epistemological Foundations for Science and Religion." In *Anthropological Reflections in Missiological Issues*, 19–34. Grand Rapids: Baker, 1994.

Heideman, Eugene S. "Syncretism, Contextualization, Orthodoxy, and Heresy." *Missiology: An International Review* 25, no.1 (January 1997): 37–49.

Heim, David. *Christian Century* 104, no. 28 (7 October 1987): 864–65.

Heinrich VII, Prinz Reuss. "Christian Politics." *Theology* 89 (1986): 41–42.

Helm, Paul, ed. *Objective Knowledge: A Christian Engagement*. Leicester: InterVarsity, 1987.

Hepburn, R. W. "Positivism" In *A Dictionary of Christian Theology*, edited by Alan Richardson, 260–61. Philadelphia: The Westminster Press, 1969.

Heron, Alasdair I. C. *A Century of Protestant Theology*. Philadelphia: Westminster, 1980.

Hesselgrave, David. *Communicating Christ Cross Culturally*. Grand Rapids, MI: Zondervan, 1978.

Hick, John and Paul Knitter, eds. *The Myth of Christian Uniqueness*. Maryknoll, NY: Orbis, 1997.

Hoedemaker, Bert. "Mission Beyond Modernity: A Global Perspective." In *Christian Mission in Western Society*, edited by Simon Barrow and Graeme Smith, 212–33. London: Churches Together in Britain and Ireland, 2001.

———. "Rival Conceptions of Global Christianity: Mission and Modernity, Then and Now." In *A Scandalous Prophet: The Way of Mission after Newbigin*. Thomas F. Foust, et al., 13–22. Grand Rapids: Eerdmans, 2002.

———. *Secularism and Mission: A Theological Essay*. Harrisburg, PA: Trinity Press International, 1998.

Hoekendijk, J. C. *The Church Inside Out*, edited by L. A. Hoedemaker and Pieter Tijmes. Translated by Isaac C. Rottenberg. Philadelphia: Westminster, 1964.

Hopkins, C. Harold. *John R. Mott 1865–1955: A Biography*. Grand Rapids: Eerdmans, 1979.

Howard, David M. *Student Power in World Evangelism*. Downers Grove, IL: InterVarsity, 1970.

Hunsberger, George R. *Bearing the Witness of the Spirit*. Grand Rapids: Eerdmans, 1998.

———. "Conversion and Community: Revisiting the Lesslie Newbigin-M. M. Thomas Debate." *IBMR* 22 (July 1998): 112–17.

———. "The Newbigin Gauntlet: Developing a Domestic Missiology for North America." *Missiology: An International Review* 19 (October): 391–408.

———. "Renewing Faith during the Postmodern Transition." *TransMission*. Special Edition, 1998:10–13.

Hunsberger, George R. and Craig Van Gelder, eds. *The Church Between Gospel and Culture: The Emerging Mission in North America*. Grand Rapids: Eerdmans, 1996.

Jackson, Eleanor "A Tribute to Bishop Lesslie Newbigin." Anglican Communion News Service, No. 1514, issued on 18 February 1998.

Jacobs, David R. "Contextualization in Mission." In *Toward the 21st Century in Christian Mission*, edited by James M. Phillips and Robert T. Coote, 235–44. Grand Rapids: Eerdmans, 1993.

Jaki, Stanley L. *Means to Message: A Treatise on Truth*. Grand Rapids: Eerdmans, 1999.

James, William. *The Will to Believe*. New York: Longmans, Green and Company, 1912.

Bibliography

Jerusalem Meeting I. M. C. 1928. New York and London: International Missionary Council, 1928.

Kaiser, Christopher. *Creation and the History of Science*. London: Marshall Pickering, 1991.

Kant, Immanuel. *Critique of Pure Reason*. Translated by J. M. D. Meiklejohn. London: J. M. Dent and sons, 1934 (last printing in 1988).

———. "The Postulates of Practical Reason." *Critique of Practical Reason*. (1788) Translated by T. K. Abbot. London: Longmans, Green. 6th edition, 1909, with revisions by the editor. In *The European Philosophers: From Descartes to Nietzsche*, edited by Monroe C. Beardsley. 476–83. New York: The Modern Library, 1960, 1988, 1992 Modern Library Edition.

Kinzler, Ross. "Mission and Context: The Current Debate about Contextualization." *Evangelical Missions Quarterly*, January 1978, no.1:23–29.

Kirk, J. Andrew. Notes from an interview with him on January 19, 1999.

———. "Mission to the West: On the Calling of the Church in a Postmodern Age." In *A Scandalous Prophet: The Way of Mission after Newbigin*. Thomas F. Foust, et al., eds. 115–27. Grand Rapids: Eerdmans, 2002.

———. *Theology and the Third World Church*. Downers Grove, IL: Inter-Varsity, 1983.

Knitter, Paul F. *No Other Name?* Maryknoll, NY: Orbis, 1985.

Kraemer, Hendrik. *The Christian Message in a Non-Christian World*. London: Edinburgh House Press, 1938.

Kraft, Charles H. *Christianity in Culture*. Maryknoll, NY: Orbis Books, 1979.

Kuhn, Thomas. *The Structure of Scientific Revolution*. Chicago: The University of Chicago Press, 1962.

Küng, Hans. *Theology for the Third Millennium*. Translated by Peter Heinegg. New York: Anchor Books, Doubleday, 1988.

Kuyper, Abraham. *Principles of Sacred Theology*. Translated by J. Hendrik De Vries. Grand Rapids: Eerdmans, 1954.

Ladd, George Eldon. *A Theology of the New Testament*. Grand Rapids: Eerdmans, 1974.

Lehmann-Habeck, Martin. "What We have Seen and Heard: Confessions and Resistance Today." *IRM* 73 (1984): 397–404.

"Lesslie Newbigin, 1909–1998." *IBMR* 22 (April 1998): cover.

Levenson, Jon D. "The Bible: Unexamined Commitments of Criticism." *First Things*, February 1993, 24–33.

Lindbeck, George A. *The Nature of Doctrine*. Philadelphia: Westminster, 1984.

———. Review of *The Gospel in a Pluralist Society* by Lesslie Newbigin. *IBMR* 14 (October 1990): 182.

Lonergan, Bernard. *Method in Theology*. Toronto: The University of Toronto, 1971.

Lundy, Mary Ann. "Tribute to Bishop Lesslie Newbigin." A press release from the World Council of Churches on 2 February 1998.

Mackintosh, H. R. *The Christian Apprehension of God*. New York: Harper and Brothers 1925.

———. *The Originality of Christian Message*. New York: Charles Scribner's Sons, 1920.

———. *Types of Modern Theology: Schleiermacher to Barth*. London: Nisbet and Co. Ltd., 1937.

MacIntyre, Alasdair. *Whose Justice, What Rationality?* London: Gerald Duckworth & Company, 1988.

Manheim, Werner. *Martin Buber*. New York: Twayne Publishers, 1974.

Bibliography

Markus, R. A. "Augustine" In *A Critical History of Western Philosophy*, edited by D. J. O'Conner, 79–97. London: Collier-Macmillan, 1964.

Mayer, Frederick. *A History of Ancient and Medieval Philosophy*. New York American Book Company, 1950.

McCoy, Charles S. *When Gods Change: Hope for Theology*. Nashville: Abingdon, 1980.

McCaughey, J. Davis. *Christian Obedience in the University: Studies in the life of the Student Christian Movement of Great Britain and Ireland: 1930–50*. London: SCM, 1958.

McGavran, Donald M., ed. *Church Growth and Christian Mission*. New York: Harper and Row, 1965.

McGrath, Alister E. *The Genesis of Doctrine: A Study in the Foundations of Doctrinal Criticism*. Oxford: Basil Blackwell, 1990.

———. *T. F. Torrance: An Intellectual Biography*. Edinburgh: T & T Clark, 1997.

McGuire, J. E. "Scientific Change: Perspectives and Proposals." In *Introduction to Philosophy of Science*, by Merrilee H. Salmons et al., 132–78. Englewood Cliffs, NJ: Prentice Hall, 1992.

McKinney, Richard W. A. *Creation, Christ, and Culture: A Festschrift in Honour of Professor Thomas F. Torrance*. Edinburgh T & T Clark, 1976.

Montefiore, Hugh, ed. *The Gospel and Contemporary Culture*. London: Mowbray, 1992.

Moreau, A. Scott, general editor. *Evangelical Dictionary of World Missions*. Grand Rapids: Baker, 2000.

Morrison, John D. "Heidegger, Correspondence Truth and the Realist Theology of Thomas Forsyth Torrance." *The Evangelical Quarterly* 69, no. 2. (1997): 139–55.

Mullins, Phil. "Michael Polanyi and J. H. Oldham: In Praise of Friendship." *Appraisal* 1, no. 4 (October 1977): 179–89.

Mullins, Phil. "Michael Polanyi." (11/03/1891—2/02/1976) This article was originally found online at: ~http://www.voyager.co.nz/~dozer/polanyi.html but is no longer available. Similar articles by the same author can be found at the Polanyi Society website online at: http://www.missouriwestern.edu/orgs/polanyi/.

Mullins, Phil. "The Papers and Michael Polanyi's Career." This article was originally found online at: ~http://www.mwsc.edu/edu/~polanyi/guide/3pprs.html but is no longer available. Similar articles by the same author can be found at the Polanyi Society website online at: http://www.missouriwestern.edu/orgs/polyanyi/.

Murphy, Nancey. *Anglo-American Postmodernity: Philosophical Perspectives on Science, Religion and Ethics*. Boulder, CO: Westview Press, a Division of Harper Collins, 1997.

Murray, Douglas. Review of *The Other Side of 1984* in *Scottish Journal of Theology* 39, no. 3 (1986): 402–4.

Neely, Alan. "Missiology." In *Evangelical Dictionary of World Missions*, edited by A. Scott Moreau et al., 633–35. Grand Rapids: Baker, 2000.

Neill, Stephen, et al., eds. *A Concise Dictionary of Christian World Mission*. Nashville and New York: Abingdon, 1971.

Neill, Stephen. *The Unfinished Task*. London: Edinburgh House Press, 1957.

Netlund, Harold. *Dissonant Voices: Religious Pluralism and the Question of Truth*. Grand Rapids: Eerdmans, 1992.

Netlund, Harold A. *Encountering Religious Pluralism: The Challenge to Christian Faith and Mission*. Downers Grove, IL: InterVarsity, 2001.

Niebuhr, H. Richard. *Christ and Culture*. New York: Harper and Row, 1951 (1st Harper Colophon edition 1975).

Bibliography

Niebuhr, Reinhold. *The Nature and Destiny of Man: A Christian Interpretation*. London: Nisbet and Company, Vol. 1: *Human Nature*, 1941; Vol. 2: *Human Destiny*, 1943.

Niles, D. T. *Who is this Jesus?* Nashville: Abingdon Press, 1968 ("The Finality of Jesus Christ," 87–107).

O'Conner, D. J., ed. *A Critical History of Western Philosophy*. London: Collier-Macmillan Limited, 1964.

The Obituary of The Right Reverend Lesslie Newbigin. *The Times* (London). 31 January 1998, 25.

Oden, Thomas C. "So What Happens After Modernity? A Postmodern Agenda For Evangelical Theology?" In *The Challenge of Postmodernism: An Evangelical Engagement*, by David Dockery, 392–406. Grand Rapids: Baker, 1995.

Oman, John. *Grace and Personality*. (Third Edition, Revised) Cambridge: at the College Press, 1925.

———. *Honest Religion*. Cambridge: Cambridge University Press, 1941.

———. *The Natural and the Supernatural*. Cambridge: at the University Press, 1931.

Osborn, Lawrence. Review of *Proper Confidence*, by Lesslie Newbigin. *Theology* 99 (March-April 1996): 142–43.

Ostathios, Metropolitan Geevarghese. "More Cross-Currents in Mission." *IBMR* 7 (1983): 175–76.

Panikkar, Raymundo. *Unknown Christ of Hinduism*. London, 1964.

Pannenberg, Wolfhart. "Christianity and the West: Ambiguous Past, Uncertain Future." *First Things*, December 1994, 18–23.

———. *Christianity in a Secularized World*. New York: Crossroad, 1989.

———. "How to Think About Secularism." *First Things*, June/July 1996, 27–32.

———. *Theology and the Philosophy of Religion*. London: Darton, Longman & Todd, 1976.

Pannenberg, Wolfhart, ed. *Revelation as History*. London: Collier-Macmillan, 1968.

Phillips, James M. and Robert T. Coote, eds. *Toward the 21st Century in Christian Mission*. Grand Rapids: Eerdmans, 1993.

Polanyi, Michael. *Knowing and Being*. Edited with an introduction by Marjorie Greene. Chicago: University of Chicago Press, 1969.

———. *Personal Knowledge: Towards a Post-Critical Philosophy*. Chicago: The University of Chicago Press, 1958, 1962, 1974.

———. *Science, Faith, and Society*. Chicago: The University of Chicago Press, 1964.

———. *The Tacit Dimension*. Garden City, NY: Anchor Books, Doubleday and Company, 1966, 1967.

Polkinghorne, John. *The God of Hope and the End of the World*. New Haven, CT: Yale University Press, 2002.

———. *Quantum Theory: A Very Short Introduction*. Oxford: Oxford University Press, 2002.

———. *Reason and Reality: The Relationship between Science and Theology*. London: SPCK, 1991.

"A Presbyterian Bishop in India." *The Best of Bishop Lesslie Newbigin*. A special booklet of some of Newbigin's articles published by *International Bulletin of Missionary Research*. New haven CT: OMSC, 1998.

Puddefoot, John. *Michael Polanyi (1891–1976)*. The article was originally found online at: http://www.users.dircon.co.uk/~pudepied/MP.htm but is not longer available. Similar articles can be found online at the Polanyi Society website at: http://www.missouriwestern.edu/orgs/polanyi/.

Bibliography

Rae, Murray, et al., eds. *Science and Theology: Questions at the Interface.* Grand Rapids, MI: William B. Eerdmans Publishing Company, 1994.

Raiser, Konrad. *Ecumenism in Transition: A Paradigm Shift in the Ecumenical Movement.* Geneva: WCC, 1991.

Raiser, Konrad. "Is Ecumenical Apologetics Sufficient? A Response to Lesslie Newbigin's 'Ecumenical Amnesia.'" *IBMR* 18 (April 1994): 50–51.

Ramachandra, Vinoth. *The Recovery of Mission: Beyond the Pluralist Paradigm.* Carlisle, Cumbria: Paternoster, 1996.

———. Review of *A Word in Season*, by Lesslie Newbigin. *Themelios* 22 (April 1997): 68–69.

Reid, John, and David Pullinger. *Modern, Postmodern and Christian.* Lausanne Occasional Paper No. 27, Lausanne Committee. Carberry: Handsel, 1996. Newbigin authored Chapter 1, "Modernity in Context," 1–12.

Richardson, Alan. *Christian Apologetics.* London: SCM, 1947.

Robinson, John. *Honest To God.* London: SCM, 1963.

Robinson, Martin. *To Win the West.* Crowborough: Monarch, 1996.

Russell, Bertrand. *The Scientific Outlook.* London: George Allen & Unwin, 1931.

Russell-Jones, Iwan. "The Greater Blessing." No pages. Accessed January 17, 2008. Online: http://www/newbigin.net/assests/pdf/lngb_r.pdf.

Salmon, Merrilee H., et al. *Introduction to Philosophy of Science.* Englewood Cliffs, NJ: Prentice Hall, 1992.

Sampson, Philip, et al., eds. *Faith and Modernity.* Oxford: Regnum Books International, 1994.

Scherer, James A. "Mission Theology." In *Toward the 21st Century in Christian Mission*, edited by James M. Phillips and Robert T. Coote, 193–202. Grand Rapids: Eerdmans, 1993.

Schmidlin, Joseph. *Katholische Missionslehre.* Münster, 1923

Scott, Drusilla. *Everyman Revived: The Common Sense of Michael Polanyi.* Revised edition. Grand Rapids: Eerdmans, 1995.

Scott, Waldron. *Karl Barth's Theology of Mission.* Downers Grove, IL: InterVarsity, 1978.

Second Assembly of the World Council of Churches. *The Christian Hope and the Task of the Church.* New York: Harper & Brothers, 1954.

Shenk, Wilbert R. "Encounters with 'Culture' Christianity." *IBMR* 18, no. 1 (January 1994): 8–10, 12–13.

———. "Lesslie Newbigin's Contribution to Mission Theology." *IBMR* 24 (April 2000): 59–63. Also published in *The Bible in TransMission.* Special Edition, 1998:3–6.

Smith, Graeme "Introduction." *Christian Mission in Western Society*, edited by Simon Barrow and Graeme Smith, 11–28. London: Churches Together in Britain and Ireland, 2001.

Speer, Robert E. *The Finality of Jesus Christ.* New York: Fleming H. Revell, 1933.

Stafford, Tim. "God's Missionary to Us, Part I." *Christianity Today*, December 2, 1996, 24–33.

Stockwell, Eugene L. Review of *A Word in Season*, by Lesslie Newbigin. *IBMR* 19 (July 1995): 128–29.

Stone, Ronald H. *Reinhold Niebuhr: Prophet to Politicians.* Nashville: Abingdon, 1972

Stowe, David. "Modernization and Resistance: Theological Implications for Mission." *IBMR* 12 (October 1988): 146–51.

Stromberg, Jean. "Christian Witness in a Pluralistic World: Report on Mission/Dialogue Consultation." *IRM* 76, no. 307 (July 1988): 412–36.

Stott, John. *Decisive Issues Facing Christians Today.* Grand Rapids: Baker, 1984 and 1990.

Bibliography

Taber, Charles. "The Limits of Indigenization in Theology." *Missiology* 6, no.1 (January 1978): 53-79.

Tano, Rodrigo D. "Toward an Evangelical Asian Theology." In *The Bible and Theology in Asian Contexts*, edited by Bong Ring Ro and Ruth Eshenaur, 93-118. Taichung, Taiwan: Asia Theological Association, 1984.

Tatlow, Tissington. *The Story of the Student Christian Movement of Great Britain and Ireland*. London: Student Christian Movement Press, 1933.

Temple, William. *Christian Faith and Life*. London: SCM, 1931.

———. *Faith and Modern Thought*. London: Macmillan and Company, 1913.

———. *The Universality of Christ*. London: SCM, 1921.

Thomas, M. M. "Mission and Modern Culture." Review of *The Other Side of 1984*, by Lesslie Newbigin. *Ecumenical Review* 36, no. 3 (July 1984): 316-22.

Thomas, V. Matthew. "The Centrality of Christ and Intra-religions Dialogue in the Theology of Lesslie Newbigin." PhD diss. presented to the Faculty of Theology of the Toronto School of Theology, 1996.

Thorogood, Bernard G. "Apostolic Faith: An Appreciation of Lesslie Newbigin, born 8 December 1909." *IRM* 79, no. 313 (January 1990): 66-85.

Thorson, Walter R. "Scientific Objectivity and the Listening Attitude." In *Objective Knowledge: A Christian Engagement*, edited by Paul Helm, 59-75. Leicester: InterVarsity, 1987.

Torrance, T. F., ed. *Belief in Science and in the Christian Life: The Relevance of Michael Polanyi's Thought for Christian Faith and Life*. Edinburgh: Handsel, 1980.

Torrance, Thomas F. "The Church in the New Era of Scientific and Cosmological Change." In *Theology in Reconciliation*, 267-93. London: Geoffrey Chapman, 1975.

———. *Divine and Contingent Order*. Oxford: Oxford University Press, 1981.

———. *The Framework of Belief*. Colorado Springs, Colorado: Helmers & Howard, 1989.

———. *The Christian Frame of Mind*. Colorado Springs, Colorado: Helmers & Howard, 1989.

———. "The Legacy of Karl Barth." *Scottish Journal of Theology* 39, no. 3 (1986): 289-308.

———. *Reality and Scientific Theology*. Edinburgh: Scottish Academic Press, 1989.

———. *Reality and Evangelical Theology*. Downers Grove, Illinois: InterVarsity, 1999.

———. *Theology in Reconciliation*. London: Geoffrey Chapman, 1975.

———. *Theological Science*. London: Oxford University Press, 1969.

———. *Transformation and Convergence in the Frame of Knowledge*. Grand Rapids: Eerdmans, 1985.

———. *The Trinitarian Faith: The Evangelical Theology of the Ancient Catholic Church*. Edinburgh: T. & T. Clark, 1988.

Tracy, David. *Plurality and Ambiguity: Hermeneutics, Religion, Hope*. San Francisco: Harper & Row, Publishers, 1987.

Turner, Harold. "Lesslie Newbigin—A New Zealand Perspective." *TransMission*. Special Edition, 1998:7-8

Van Engen, Charles. *Mission on the Way: Issues in Mission Theology*. Grand Rapids: Baker, 1996.

———. "Theology of Missions" In *Evangelical Dictionary of World Missions*. A. Scott Moreau, general editor, 949-51. Grand Rapids: Baker, 2000.

Van Gelder, Craig. "Postmodernism and Evangelicals: A Unique Missiological Challenge." *Missiology* 30, no. 4 (October 2002): 491-504.

Bibliography

van Huyssteen, Wentzel. *Theology and the Justification of Faith: Constructing Theories in Systematic Theology*. Grand Rapids: Eerdmans, 1989.

Vicedom, Georg. *The Mission of God*. Saint Louis: Concordia, 1957.

Visser 't Hooft, W. A. *No Other Name*. London: SCM, 1963.

Wainwright, Geoffrey. *Lesslie Newbigin: A Theological Life*. New York: Oxford University Press, 2000.

Walker, Andrew. "Remembering Lesslie." No pages. Accessed on January 19, 2008. Online: http://www.ship-of-fools.com/Cargo/Features98/Newbigin/NewbiginWalker.html

Walsh, Martin J. *A History of Philosophy*. London: Geoffrey Chapman, 1985.

Warneck, Gustav. *Evangelische Missionslehre*. Gotha, 1897.

West, Charles. "Gospel for American Culture: Variations on a Theme by Newbigin." *Missiology* 19, no. 4:431–41.

———. "Mission to the West: A Dialogue with Stowe and Newbigin." *IBMR* 12 (October 1988): 153–56.

———. Review of *Proper Confidence*, by Lesslie Newbigin. *IBMR* 19 (October 1995): 180–81.

———. Review of *The Relevance of Trinitarian Doctrine for Today's Mission*, by Lesslie Newbigin. *IRM* 3 (April 1964): 245–46.

Whitehead, Alfred North. *Science and the Modern World*. New York: Macmillan, 1925 (Lowell Lectures, 1925).

Whiteman, Darrell L. "Contextualization: The Theory, the Gap, the Challenge." *IBMR* 21 (January 1997): 2–7.

Wiles, Maurice. "Comment on Lesslie Newbigin's Essay." In *Incarnation and Myth: The Debate Continued*. Michael Goulder, ed. London: SCM, 1979:211–13.

Williams, Stephen N. *Revelation and Reconciliation: A View on Modernity*. Cambridge: Cambridge University Press, 1995.

———. "Theologians in Pursuit of the Enlightenment." *Theology* 89, no. 7 (September 1986): 368–74.

Wolfe David L. *Epistemology: The Justification of Belief*. Downers Grove, Illinois: InterVarsity, 1982.

Wooten, Jane. "Foreword." *Christian Mission in Western Society*, edited by Simon Barrow and Graeme Smith, 9. London: Churches Together in Britain and Ireland, 2001.

Yates, Timothy. *Christian Mission in the Twentieth Century*. Cambridge: Cambridge University Press, 1994 (Biographical sketch of Newbigin on pages 237–44).

Yannoulatos, Bishop Anastasios, et al. "In Tribute to Bishop Lesslie Newbigin." *IRM* 79:86–101.

www.ingramcontent.com/pod-product-compliance
Lightning Source LLC
Chambersburg PA
CBHW071235230426
43668CB00011B/1440